SLC

Local, characterful guides to Britain's special places

Simon Richmond

EDITION 1

Bradt Guides Ltd, UK
The Globe Pequot Press Inc, USA

COVID-19

Please note that work on this book was completed during the Covid-19 pandemic. Because of the impact of the crisis on tourism, some businesses or services listed in the text may no longer operate. We will post any information we have about these on ⊘ bradtguides.com/updates. And we'd of course be grateful for any updates you can send us during your own travels, which we will add to that page for the benefit of future travellers.

Reprinted September 2023   First edition published May 2022
Bradt Guides Ltd
31a High Street, Chesham, Buckinghamshire, HP5 1BW, England
www.bradtguides.com
Print edition published in the USA by The Globe Pequot Press Inc,
PO Box 480, Guilford, Connecticut 06437-0480

Text copyright © 2022 Simon Richmond
Maps copyright © 2022 Bradt Guides Ltd; includes map data © OpenStreetMap contributors
Photographs copyright © 2022 Individual photographers (see below)
Project Managers: Emma Gibbs & Anna Moores
Cover research: Ian Spick

ISBN: 9781784778279

British Library Cataloguing in Publication Data
A catalogue record for this book is available from the British Library

Photographs © individual photographers credited beside images & also those picture libraries credited as follows: Alamy.com (A); Shutterstock.com (S); Superstock.com (SS); Tunbridge Wells Commons Conservators (TWCC)

Front cover The White Cliffs (Tomasz Galaz/S)
Back cover View towards Rochester (Valery Egorov/S)
Title page Dover Castle (English Heritage)

Maps David McCutcheon FBCart.S
Typeset by Pepi Bluck, Perfect Picture
Production managed by Zenith Media; printed in the UK
Digital conversion by www.dataworks.co.in

AUTHOR

Simon Richmond (⊘ simonrichmond.com) is an award-winning travel writer and photographer. In a journalism career spanning 30 years, he's written and researched over 150 guidebooks and non-fiction titles. An apostle for the Slow Travel ethos, his most memorable travel experiences have included overland trips from the UK to Hong Kong via the Baltic States and the 'Stans; from Istanbul  to Kathmandu via Iran, Pakistan and India; across Russia, several times, by the Trans-Siberian Railway; and from Perth to Sydney on the Indian Pacific train. He's also hiked across the Malaysian rainforest, England's Lake District and the Japanese Alps. Check out some of Simon's photographs and Kent discoveries at 🖸 @slowtravelkent and see some of his sketches at 📘 urbansketchersfolkestone.

AUTHOR'S STORY

I first realised how special Kent's countryside and coast were on weekend hiking adventures and seaside breaks from London, where I lived in the 1990s. Wanderlust then took me overseas for the next two decades. When I returned to the UK in 2012, I was determined to live beside the sea, in a community that embraced the creative arts. Whitstable, Margate and Ramsgate were all contenders, but it was a visit to Folkestone in October 2014 to check out its arts triennial that sealed the deal. I was instantly smitten with the resurgent resort's edgy, thought-provoking public artworks, lush coastal park and colourful Creative Quarter. Within two weeks I'd bought a flat there.

Making Folkestone my home remains one of the best decisions of my life. It put me in the ideal place to research and write *Slow Travel Kent*, a project I proposed to Bradt back in 2015. It took a pandemic for our schedules to align! In researching this guidebook I've returned to favourite locations such as Canterbury, Dungeness and Sissinghurst, digging deeper into what makes them so special. I've travelled to remoter parts of Kent, like the isles of Grain and Sheppey, quirky locations with unique charms. I defy anyone not to feel their spirits lifted while hiking stretches of its stunning coast, gazing across the Channel, or taking in the idyllic views from atop the North Downs. From its storied historical landmarks to the delicious variety of its produce and gorgeous gardens, Kent has so much to offer. It's found a special place in my heart and I hope, as you use this guidebook to make your own Slow way around Kent, that it work its charms on you, too.

ACKNOWLEDGEMENTS

It is never easy writing a first edition of a guidebook and it has been even more of a challenge to do so throughout the lockdowns caused by the Covid-19 pandemic. Under such circumstances, I salute the team at Bradt for their patience and support during the longer-than-expected process of getting *Slow Travel Kent* across the finishing line. Editors Anna Moores and Emma Gibbs were instrumental in helping shape, polish and fact-check my initial draft.

For specific assistance with research, my thanks go out to Jonathan Buckingham-Dudley and Hannah Kelly at Port Lympne Reserve; Mary Hayward and Rebecca Ibbotson at the National Trust; Troy Scott-Smith and Joanna Simmonds at Sissinghurst; staff at the Kent Wildlife Trust; Princess Olga Romanoff and Alexandra Mathew at Provender House; Lynnette Crisp at Chatham Historic Dockyard Trust; Nathan Crouch at Canterbury Cathedral; Sara Whines at English Heritage; Len Howell at Dover Castle; and Charlotte Allen at Elmley National Nature Reserve.

A major *merci* to Donna Jones for leading the way on transitioning to living in Kent a decade ago and for the insights and knowledge she provided on her slice of the Weald. I would also like to thank the many people who have made me feel so welcome in Folkestone and who continue to bring creativity, companionship and fun into my life there. Most importantly, I am so very grateful for the kindness, love and support of my partner Steve Boyd. Thank you for providing the gentle encouragement and extra enthusiasm needed when this project felt its most overwhelming and for accompanying me on my endless Kent explorations. I'm so looking forward to us building a life together in the Kent countryside and chortling together in our very own Kentish garden for many years to come – the adventures have only just begun!

CONTENTS

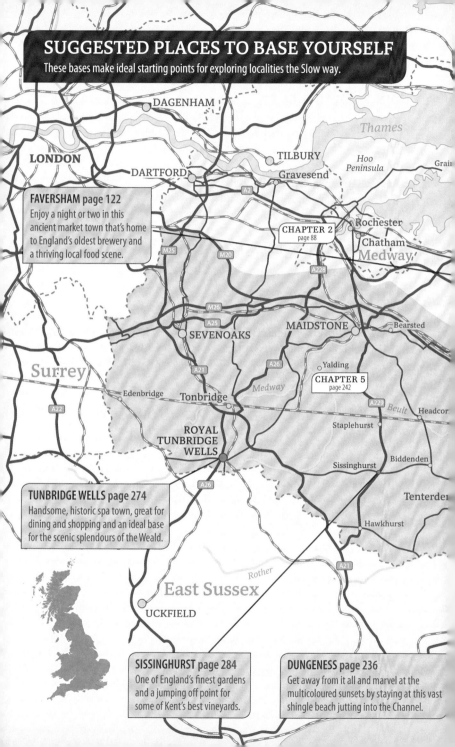

SUGGESTED PLACES TO BASE YOURSELF

These bases make ideal starting points for exploring localities the Slow way.

FAVERSHAM page 122
Enjoy a night or two in this ancient market town that's home to England's oldest brewery and a thriving local food scene.

CHAPTER 2 page 88

CHAPTER 5 page 242

TUNBRIDGE WELLS page 274
Handsome, historic spa town, great for dining and shopping and an ideal base for the scenic splendours of the Weald.

SISSINGHURST page 284
One of England's finest gardens and a jumping off point for some of Kent's best vineyards.

DUNGENESS page 236
Get away from it all and marvel at the multicoloured sunsets by staying at this vast shingle beach jutting into the Channel.

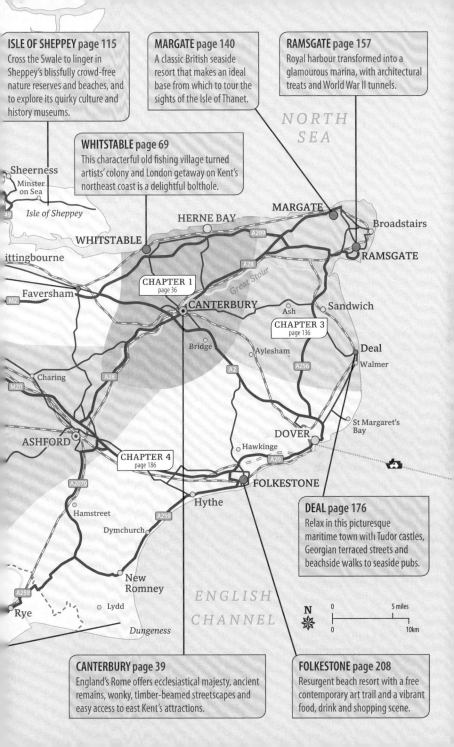

ISLE OF SHEPPEY page 115
Cross the Swale to linger in Sheppey's blissfully crowd-free nature reserves and beaches, and to explore its quirky culture and history museums.

MARGATE page 140
A classic British seaside resort that makes an ideal base from which to tour the sights of the Isle of Thanet.

RAMSGATE page 157
Royal harbour transformed into a glamourous marina, with architectural treats and World War II tunnels.

NORTH SEA

WHITSTABLE page 69
This characterful old fishing village turned artists' colony and London getaway on Kent's northeast coast is a delightful bolthole.

Sheerness
Minster on Sea
Isle of Sheppey
49

ittingbourne

Faversham
M2

Charing
A28
M20

ASHFORD

A2070

Hamstreet

Dymchurch

A259

New Romney

A259
Rye

Lydd

Dungeness

HERNE BAY

WHITSTABLE

CHAPTER 1
page 36

CANTERBURY

Bridge

A2

A299

A28
Great Stour

Ash

CHAPTER 3
page 136

Aylesham

A256

MARGATE

Broadstairs

RAMSGATE

Sandwich

Deal
Walmer

St Margaret's Bay

DOVER

Hawkinge
A20

CHAPTER 4
page 186

Hythe

FOLKESTONE

DEAL page 176
Relax in this picturesque maritime town with Tudor castles, Georgian terraced streets and beachside walks to seaside pubs.

ENGLISH CHANNEL

N

0	5 miles
0	10km

CANTERBURY page 39
England's Rome offers ecclesiastical majesty, ancient remains, wonky, timber-beamed streetscapes and easy access to east Kent's attractions.

FOLKESTONE page 208
Resurgent beach resort with a free contemporary art trail and a vibrant food, drink and shopping scene.

GOING SLOW IN
KENT

Kent is a county for all seasons. In spring, lie on a picnic blanket beneath frothy clouds of cherry and apple blossoms in the orchards of the Brogdale National Fruit Collection, near Faversham. In the heat of July, ride on the small-scale Romney, Hythe and Dymchurch Railway to the otherworldly shingle beach at Dungeness, where you can lunch on seafood fresh off local boats. Or catch the coastal breeze during a hike across the chalk wild flower meadows atop Dover's White Cliffs, followed by a cream tea at the South Foreland Lighthouse. In autumn, along the forest paths of Bedgebury National Pinetum or in the grounds of Scotney Castle, be dazzled by burgundy, rust and gold-leaved trees. And in December, listen to (or even join in) carol singing in the awesome World Heritage site that is Canterbury Cathedral.

Kent is tailor-made for Slow Travel moments like these. Yes, you can zip through parts of the county on motorways and high-speed rails but riding the slow trains and navigating the B-roads remains the best way to appreciate Kent's superbly varied landscapes, wildlife, history and culture. Ancient footpaths, droveways and country lanes meander across two Areas of Outstanding Natural Beauty (AONB) – the North Downs and the Kent Weald. These rural byways offer no end of leisurely ambles or bicycle rides between picturesque villages like Elham, Eynsford, Chiddingstone and Wye, places that turn the clock back centuries with their Kentish ragstone and half-timbered buildings, churchyards of ancient lichen-covered gravestones, and cosy tea houses and wooden-beamed pubs. They are the epitome of bucolic, romantic England.

Just 21 miles from France at the narrowest point of the Strait of Dover, Kent has been Britain's doorway to continental Europe for millennia.

1 The village of Eynsford. **2** Scotney Castle. ▶

THE SLOW MINDSET

Hilary Bradt, Founder, Bradt Travel Guides

> **We shall not cease from exploration**
> **And the end of all our exploring**
> **Will be to arrive where we started**
> **And know the place for the first time.**
> T S Eliot, 'Little Gidding', *Four Quartets*

This series evolved, slowly, from a Bradt editorial meeting when we started to explore ideas for guides to our favourite part of the world – Great Britain. We wanted to get away from the usual 'top sights' formula and encourage our authors to bring out the nuances and local differences that make up a sense of place – such things as food, building styles, nature, geology or local people and what makes them tick. Our aim was to create a series that celebrates the present, focusing on sustainable tourism, rather than taking a nostalgic wallow in the past.

So without our realising it at the time, we had defined 'Slow Travel', or at least our concept of it. For the beauty of the Slow Movement is that there is no fixed definition; we adapt the philosophy to fit our individual needs and aspirations. Thus Carl Honoré, author of *In Praise of Slow*, writes: 'The Slow Movement is a cultural revolution against the notion that faster is always better. It's not about doing everything at a snail's pace, it's about seeking to do everything at the right speed. Savouring the hours and minutes rather than just counting them. Doing everything as well as possible, instead of as fast as possible. It's about quality over quantity in everything from work to food to parenting.' And travel.

So take time to explore. Don't rush it, get to know an area – and the people who live there – and you'll be as delighted as the authors by what you find.

From the landing of Romans in 55BC to the opening of the Channel Tunnel nearly 2,000 years later, Kent has been central to English history. Via the Cinque Ports of Dover, New Romney, Sandwich and Hythe, the county was enriched economically by trade and culturally through the welcoming of refugees like the Huguenots. The county's abundant stock of castles and manor houses, including Knole, Hever and Chartwell, have been homes to British royalty, American tycoons and eminent politicians. Its museums and galleries are storehouses of treasures and curiosities, while its landscapes and communities have inspired artists and writers and continue to do so in regenerated resorts such as Folkestone and Margate, both riding a wave of 21st-century creativity and enterprise.

Kent's many nature reserves and gorgeous gardens are sanctuaries of calm and serenity. There are more species of orchids here than in any other county, as well as rare butterflies and introduced animals like Exmoor ponies and European bison, used to keep the land open to a wider biodiversity. In lesser-visited locations, such as the Isle of Grain, the Isle of Sheppey and Romney Marsh, it's hard to believe you are within an hour or two of London. Take your travels slowly through Kent and you'll be amazed how much there is to discover, enjoy and savour.

KENT LANDSCAPES

Lapped by the English Channel to the south, the North Sea to the east and the Thames Estuary to the north, Kent covers 1,442 square miles at the most southeast edge of England. It has a diverse landscape of ridges and valleys created by bands of soft clay, porous chalk and various forms of sandstone formed during the Cretaceous period which ended some 60 million years ago. The hard sandstone forms striking outcrops in the Weald, such as the High Rocks National Monument near Tunbridge Wells, while the chalk is most dramatically exposed along the coast with the vertiginous white cliffs of Thanet and around Dover.

Fields and woodlands form a rich patchwork across Kent's two AONBs – the 340 square mile **Kent Downs** (⊘ kentdowns.org.uk), spanning from the eastern edge of Greater London to the coast at Folkestone and Dover, and the **High Weald** (⊘ highweald.org), the Kent slice of which falls between Hever in the west and Tenterden in the east. The AONBs are storehouses of biodiversity, as are Kent's special and rare habitats such as the vegetated shingle of Dungeness and the London

UNESCO SITES IN KENT

Kent already has one UNESCO World Heritage Site – the Canterbury religious triumvirate of the cathedral, St Augustine's Abbey and St Martin's Church. In 2021 work began to secure the county a second UNESCO designation: either for the Kent Downs AONB to become a Global Geopark, or for the Strait of Dover to be declared a Biosphere Reserve or World Heritage Site. Running until 2023, this cross-Channel effort is being spearheaded in Kent by the Kent Downs AONB. A network of local ambassadors is being established, with the aim of encouraging more sustainable tourism experiences across Kent, and a series of new sculptures have been added along the North Downs between Canterbury and Dover.

clay marshlands of the Hoo Peninsula and the Isle of Sheppey. Over 20,000 species have been recorded in the county – nearly 30 per cent of all UK species – including over 3,400 rare and threatened species, such as late spider orchids and five out of the seven rarest bumblebees in the UK. Of particular note are chalky grasslands – Kent is one of the few places in the world that has this type of habitat, where as many as 50 different species of plants can grow per square yard. With careful land management, including grazing by cattle, competitive species can be kept under control, allowing more delicate herbs and orchids to flourish.

Three major rivers run through Kent: the Darent, a chalk stream that flows between Westerham and Dartford Marshes in West Kent; the Medway, which divides east and west Kent and is tidal in its upper reaches as it empties into the Thames Estuary; and the Stour (also known as the Great Stour), which makes its way from the Kent Downs to Pegwell Bay via Canterbury and Sandwich.

GARDENS

Kent's gardens are among England's finest. They include horticultural blockbusters such as **Sissinghurst** (page 285), **Hever Castle** (page 262), **Penshurst Place** (page 266) and **Chartwell** (page 251) that combine both serene landscapes with historic houses. To learn more about Kent's historic gardens, a good place to start is the **Kent Gardens Trust** (⊘ kentgardenstrust.org.uk). Among their publications are books on the Kent commissions of the celebrated 18th-century English landscape gardeners Lancelot 'Capability' Brown, who redesigned the grounds at **Leeds Castle** (page 297) and **Chilham Castle** (page 86), and Humphry Repton, who worked at **Cobham Hall** (page 97) and **Bayham Abbey** (page 281).

Enter your planned trip dates to Kent at the website of the **National Gardens Scheme** (⊘ ngs.org.uk) to discover scores more gardens, big and small, that are open to the public. These horticultural sanctuaries are a wonderful way to experience unique approaches to garden design and to meet with the local owners. The scheme also raises money for health and nursing charities through its admission fees and the garden owners' provision of teas and cakes.

---

1 Doddington Place. **2** Water Lane. ▶

KENT'S TOP FIVE LESSER-KNOWN GARDENS

Beyond the famous names, some of my favourite Kent gardens are the less well-known ones:

Doddington Place (page 132) A renovated Edwardian rock garden, 150-year-old Wellingtonias underplanted with snowdrops and dreamy cloud pruning of giant yew bushes.

Godinton House & Gardens (page 299) A mass of daffodils in spring, delphiniums in June and dahlias in autumn; a short drive away from Ashford.

Pines Garden (page 200) A statue of Winston Churchill overlooks this St Margaret's Bay haven which also includes a small lake and poetry path.

Prospect Cottage (page 237) A remarkable garden coaxed from the unpromising shingle beaches facing Dungeness nuclear power station, with sculptures made from driftwood, stones, old tools and found objects.

Restoration House (page 108) An extraordinary set of historic gardens hidden away in the heart of Rochester and only open between June and September.

KENT WILDLIFE

Among the thousands of rare species found in Kent, there are significant populations of some of the UK's most threatened wildlife, including turtle doves, nightingales, Adonis blue butterflies, and shrill carder bees.

For over 60 years, the **Kent Wildlife Trust** (⏀ kentwildlifetrust.org. uk) has been saving and protecting the county's woods, meadows, lakes, moorland and coastline. It directly manages over 69 nature reserves, covering some 9,330 acres, ranging from the Iron Age hillfort Bigbury Camp, west of Canterbury, to the Romney Marsh Visitor Centre and Nature Reserve. It also maintains a further 68,000 acres on behalf of Kent local authorities and has a wide range of projects on the go that always need volunteer help. Check its website for courses and study days at its three visitors centres – in Romney Marsh (page 231), Sevenoaks (page 255) and Tyland Barn (Chatham Rd, Sandling ME14 3BD; closed at the time of research) near Maidstone. Topics covered range from Kent's geology to identifying birds of prey and nature-friendly gardening. Other Kent organisations running wildlife and nature-related courses and events include the **North East Kent Marine Protected Area** (⏀ thanetcoast.org.uk) and the **Medway Valley Countryside Partnership** (⏀ medwayvalley.org).

Birdwatchers are well served in Kent. The **RSPB** (⌂ rspb.org.uk) manages six reserves – Blean Woods (page 69), Capel Fleet (page 121), Cliffe Pools (page 99), Dungeness (page 236), Northward Hill (page 101) and Tudeley Woods (page 269) – where you can spot a wide range of birdlife, from woodpeckers and nightingales to peregrine falcons and various species of owl. Among the other wildlife that you may, with some patience and a good eye, be able to spot around the county are: fallow and sika deer in the grounds of Knole (page 255); tiny scorpions – a colony of over 10,000 of them live in the dock wall of Blue Town at Sheerness (page 118); adders – the only venomous snake in the UK, found living mostly in the High Weald, the Greensand Ridge and the coastal habitats of north Kent; and seals – in Pegwell Bay (page 165) and around the coast of Thanet, as well as on the Goodwin Sands.

Kent also offers guaranteed wildlife experiences at animal parks such as **Wildwood** (page 77) and **Howletts** (page 79) near Canterbury and **Port Lympne Reserve** (page 228) near Hythe. For more of a farmyard experience there is also **Kent Life** (⌂ kentlife.org.uk), a farm park near Maidstone, and the **Rare Breeds Centre** (⌂ rarebreeds.org.uk), a working 100-acre farm at Woodchurch between Ashford and Tenterden that is home to many rare and native breeds of farm livestock, including pigs, sheep, horses, chickens and cows.

KENT ARCHITECTURE

Much can be learnt about Kent's history and society from its architectural landmarks, which range from the Medway Megaliths, Neolithic stone burial chambers built some 5,000 years ago, to the 20th-century Denge Sound Mirrors near Dungeness. Magnificent Dover Castle spans pretty much every historical epoch, with the hilltop fortress containing the remains of a Roman lighthouse, a Saxon-era church and an underground tunnel network used as recently as during the Cold War, as well as its early medieval central keep.

Roman occupation of Britain, which lasted nearly 500 years, has left an enduring architectural mark on Kent. Most notable is Richborough Roman Fort and Amphitheatre (page 174), the remains of what once was the official gateway to Roman Britannia. For more on Roman Kent, see the box on page 170.

The imprint of the Normans, from the 11th century onwards, is easiest seen in ecclesiastical locations like Rochester Cathedral, while medieval Kent is well represented in old market towns and villages like Faversham and Chiddingstone and the wooden-framed architecture of the Cinque Ports. Timber is also the basis of Kent's many Wealden Hall houses, the grandest of which is Penshurst Place, built in 1341 – its soaring, chestnut-beamed hall has been unaltered for nearly 700 years.

In comparison, the Tudor castles at Deal and Walmer have been much altered since their original constructions as sea-facing forts to protect against foreign invasion. Deal also sports wonderful examples of human-scale Georgian architecture in its conservation zone, though easily Kent's most impressive set of Georgian buildings are those at the Historic Dockyard Chatham. Tunbridge Wells's Pantiles are another gem from that age, but the spa town also has many handsome buildings from Victorian times when the celebrated architect Decimus Burton was hired to create a new look for it. Burton also laid out the fashionable sections of West Folkestone. The 19th century was the boom time for construction across Kent of one of its most iconic types of vernacular architecture: the oast house (see box, page 268).

Standout works of contemporary architecture in Kent include the **Turner Contemporary** gallery in Margate, the world's first multi-storey skate park **F51** in Folkestone, and Ashford's high-tech **Curious Brewery**, which has been nicknamed the 'cathedral of brewing'. More notable buildings from the last few decades make up the architectural trail **CHALKUP21** (see box, page 196), including the visitor centre at **Samphire Hoe**, the manmade stretch of coastline near Dover, constructed from the spill from the Channel Tunnel excavations.

SACRED KENT

Among the most beautiful and historical works of architecture in Kent are its churches. While it may not be the largest or most magnificent of the nation's cathedrals, Canterbury stands supreme as the mother church of the Anglican communion. It was from here that St Augustine began spreading Christianity to the pagan Anglo-Saxons in 597. That fact, and the martyrdom in the cathedral of Archbishop Thomas Becket in 1170, has made Canterbury a sacred place of pilgrimage for over a thousand years. Equally venerable is Rochester Cathedral, established in 604. It too became a pilgrimage centre in the 13th century when William of Perth, a pious Scot, was murdered in Rochester on his way to the Holy Land.

The Reformation saw the great monasteries of Kent disbanded and destroyed. The atmospheric ruins of **St Augustine's Abbey** (page 50) and **Bayham Abbey** (page 281) are worth visiting for their history and ongoing spiritual atmosphere. **The Friars** at Aylesford (page 296) and **Minster Abbey** (page 166), two of Kent's medieval centres of worship, were revived in the 20th century and both now offer the opportunity to go on spiritual retreats.

There are hundreds more churches scattered across Kent, from lonely chapels to grand Victorian edifices. Whether you are spiritually inclined or not, many are worth visiting for the craftsmanship they display, the artworks they contain and the insight they provide into the communities that built and continue to maintain them. For more Kent churches that deserve attention, consult the listings of the **Churches Conservation Trust** (⊘ visitchurches.org.uk). The Trust also manage St James' in Cooling (page 101) and St Mary the Virgin in Fordwich (page 78) where it's possible to camp overnight; for more information and to make a booking go to ⊘ champing.co.uk.

Christianity is not the only religion to have left its sacred mark on Kent. Jewry Lane in Canterbury hints to Judaism's ancient roots in the city. Canterbury's old synagogue is now a music hall for The King's School while in Margate the old shul is in the process of being turned into a multicultural centre by the **Cliftonville Cultural Space** (⊘ cliftonvilleculturalspace. com). Very occasionally open for services or special visits are the historic synagogues in **Ramsgate** (see box, page 160) and **Chatham** (page 110). To dig deeper into Kent's Jewish history, a fine source of information is the **National Anglo-Jewish Heritage Trails** (⊘ jtrails.org.uk) which, in addition to Canterbury and Ramsgate, also has information about past Jewish life and landmarks in Dover and Sheerness.

Adding some Indian subcontinental spice to Kent's sacred spaces is Gravesend's **Guru Nanak Darbar Gurdwara** (page 96), the largest Sikh complex in Europe. The building is remarkable both as a beautiful piece of architecture and as a living and welcoming spiritual community.

PILGRIMAGES IN KENT

Pilgrimages are the original form of Slow travel and Kent has been a prime destination for these on-foot journeys with a spiritual dimension ever since St Augustine arrived to convert the pagan Anglo-Saxons in the 6th century AD. Pilgrimages to Canterbury peaked between the murder of Archbishop Thomas Becket in 1170 and the Dissolution of the Monasteries in the 16th century.

The routes through the English countryside these medieval pilgrims were following far predate Christianity's foothold in Britain. Tracks along the South and North Downs, linking Avebury and Stonehenge with the narrowest part of the English Channel, existed in the Stone Age. Romans troops would also have marched these old ways before constructing Watling Street and other metalled tracks in the first century AD.

Depending on their departure point, pilgrims would have used a variety of routes to reach Canterbury. Those heading to Becket's shrine from continental Europe would have followed some, or all of the **Via Francigena** (see box, page 49), a 1,000-mile route connecting Rome to Canterbury, via Dover and the North Downs Way. The **British Pilgrimage Trust** (⊘ britishpilgrimage.org) have resurrected what they call the **Old Way**, a 250-mile, three-week walk from Southampton to Canterbury as featured on a 14th-century Gough Map (⊘ goughmap.org) of Britain.

TOP FIVE CHURCHES

The following are among my favourite churches in Kent, picked for their beautiful artworks and architecture as much as for their historical associations.

All Saints' Church Tudeley (page 269). The only church in the world where all the stained-glass windows are designed by Marc Chagall.

Shrine of St Augustine & National Pugin Centre Ramsgate (page 161). Neo-Gothic beauty designed by Victorian architect Augustus Pugin and his sons. Pugin is buried here and there's also a relic of St Augustine.

St Mary's Church Speldhurst (page 278). Beautifully detailed stained-glass windows designed by key members of the Pre-Raphaelite movement, including William Morris and Edward Burne-Jones.

St Nicholas Barfrestone (page 205). This tiny rural church is adorned with some of the finest Norman stone carvings in Britain.

St Thomas Becket Fairfield (page 232). Marooned in Romney Marsh, this incredibly photogenic 13th-century church has often been used as a filming location.

The '**Pilgrim's Way**', however, as outlined at ⌀ pilgrimswaycanterbury. org and in books such as Cicerones' *Walking the Pilgrims' Way*, is very much a 20th-century invention, based partly on conjecture, partly on romance. This 153-mile route connects Winchester Cathedral to Canterbury Cathedral, the initial 34 miles following St Swithuns Way to Farnham in Surrey, and the remaining 119 miles largely the same as the North Downs Way National Trail (⌀ nationaltrail.co.uk/en_GB/trails/ north-downs-way/trail-information).

There are also a couple of other contemporary pilgrimage routes entirely within Kent. The **Royal Saxon Way** (⌀ geopaethas.com/a-long-walk), a 36-mile route between Folkestone and Minster, starts and finishes at churches that hold relics of the early English saints Eanswythe and Mildreth, while **The Augustine Camino** (⌀ augustinecamino. co.uk) is a creation of Ramsgate-based walking couple Andrew and Paula Kelly. This 70-mile route starts at Rochester Cathedral and makes its way, in seven stages via Aylesford Priory and Canterbury Cathedral, to the Shrine of St Augustine in Ramsgate.

A TASTE OF KENT

Kent's reputation for supplying some of England's most delicious food and drink is well deserved. You can dine on everything from freshly shucked oysters and cracking fish and chips to the farm-to-table degustation menus at Michelin-starred restaurants and gastropubs. Hardly a week goes by without some tempting new culinary venture being launched, with specific foodie hotspots being Margate, Faversham, Deal, Folkestone, Tunbridge Wells and Whitstable.

The county has been a centre of horticultural excellence for centuries. Legend has it that it was Henry VIII who first branded the county the 'Garden of England', after so enjoying a bowl of Kentish cherries. It was under the same monarch that large-scale growing of fruit in Kent began after Richard Harris, Henry's fruiterer, established England's first fruit collection on 105 acres at Teynham, a village between Sittingbourne and Faversham. Today Kent continues to be home to the National Fruit Collection at Brogdale (page 128).

Kent is also home to 15 traditional fruit orchards managed by local communities – **Kent Orchards** (⌀ kentorchards.org.uk) has details on them all. Visiting these orchards is a wonderful opportunity to learn about Kent's agricultural heritage, as well as to taste fruits fresh from the trees. There are many other community growing projects across the country to discover, such as Margate's **Windmill Community Gardens** (⌂ windmillcommunitygardens.org), Folkestone's **Locavore Growing Project** (⌂ locavoregrowingproject.org), the **Abbey Physic Community Garden** in Faversham (page 125) and **Deal Hop Farm** (⌂ dealhopfarm.org.uk).

Foods that are Kent specialities include the super-sweet **gypsy tart**, a shortcrust pastry pie with a caramel-like filling made from evaporated milk and brown sugar; **Canterbury apple tart** with a filling of grated apples and lemon, topped with apple slices; **Kentish rarebit**, a toasted sandwich of cheese and apple slices popularised by the fruit pickers in Kent's orchards; and **cobnuts**, a local type of hazelnut, harvested while green in mid-August and with brown shells and husks by mid-October.

A comprehensive resource on food, drink and craft businesses in Kent is **Produced in Kent** (⌂ producedinkent.co.uk). One of their projects is **Kent Food Trails** (⌂ kentfoodtrails.co.uk) from which you can download guides to the county's cherry and apple orchards and berry farms, vineyards, ciders and juices, hops and beer, cheeses and dairy produce, and craft distilleries.

TOP FIVE RESTAURANTS

The best places to eat in Kent are no secret and you will need to make advance reservations for my top five picks. If they are booked up, there's no shortage of excellent alternative options.

Angela's Margate (page 146). MSC-certified seafood cooked simply but to perfection. Their sister operation Dory's is also excellent.

Fordwich Arms Fordwich (page 79). Picturesque pub beside the Stour with a gourmet menu that showcases the cream of Kent and UK produce.

The Goods Shed Canterbury (page 66). The super-fresh and hyper-local ingredients for their dishes come directly from the suppliers in the adjoining food market.

The Small Holding Kilndown (page 284). A symphony of small courses, painstakingly crafted from the produce grown in their adjoining market garden.

The Sportsman Seasalter (page 74). The nearby beaches and fields provide ingredients and inspiration for the multi-course banquets served in this peerless seaside pub.

BEER & CIDER

The ancient crafts of beer and cider making are alive and well in Kent. The common hop *Humulus lupulus* (meaning 'wolf of the woods' in Latin) was imported from Belgium and first planted in Kent sometime in the 16th century. In his *Tour of the Whole Island of Great Britain*, published in 1724, Daniel Defoe described east Kent as the 'mother of all hop grounds'. Kent's chalky soils are particularly suited to growing hops and hop gardens, as they were known, were a feature of every parish of the county by the middle of 19th century.

Although not grown on the same scale now, hops and beer making remains integral to Kent's agricultural heritage and landscape. There are over 40 breweries in the county, ranging from Britain's oldest, **Shepherd Neame** (page 123), based in Faversham since 1573, and **Curious Brewery** (page 298) in Ashford, established as a micro-brewery in 2011 but now so successful it has a huge, state-of-the-art facility with taproom and restaurant, to small-scale operations like **Breakwater Brewery** in Dover (page 198) and Tenterden's **Old Dairy Brewery** (page 292).

Apples have been grown in Kent since Roman times, and 12th-century maps show that St Augustine's Abbey in Canterbury had a monastic orchard with apple and pear trees, from which ciders would have been made. In recent years there has been a revival of craft cider making in Kent with producers including **Kentish Pip** in Bekesbourne (page 80), **Biddenden** (page 288) and the **Kent Cider Company** (⌁ kentcider.co.uk) who set up their stall every Saturday at Faversham Market and at the Rochester Farmer's Market on the third Sunday of the month.

Micropubs – compact free houses that keep things real by serving a curated list of cask ales and ciders and little else – are a Kent speciality. One of the originators of the concept, **The Butcher's Arms** (⌁ micropub.co.uk), is in the east Kent village of Herne. It's based in what used to be a butcher's shop and one of its founding principles is to help promote conversation between customers. Needless to say, micropubs are a perfect way to connect with locals. You'll find a comprehensive list at ⌁ micropubassociation.co.uk and the Kent Rail Ale Trail (⌁ kentrailaletrail.co.uk) has a downloadable guide to 37 of the county's micropubs that can be accessed within an easy walk of a train station.

The Kent branch of CAMRA, the Campaign for Real Ale ($\oslash$ kentcamra. org.uk), is a super resource for searching out characterful Kent pubs and keeping up to date on events. Look out for the **Kent Green Hop Beer Fortnight** ($\oslash$ kentgreenhopbeer.com), held over the last week of September and first week of October when local brewers release beers made from just-harvested hops.

WINE

It has been nearly 2,000 years since the Romans are thought to have brought grape vines to the British Isles. The Domesday Book of 1086 recorded three vineyards in Kent – today there over 50 and the county is one of the leading producers in England's booming wine scene.

Kent's combination of free-draining chalky soil and a mild climate with sufficient sunlight and cooling coastal breezes means its 'terroir' is particularly suited to the production of sparkling wines – so much so that the Champagne house Taittinger has invested in a 69-acre plot of land on a former apple farm near Chilham to plant Chardonnay, Pinot Noir and Pinot Meunier grapes to produce English bubbly. This French-British venture, titled Domaine Evremond, planted its first vines in 2017 and so it will be a few more years before their wines debut on the market. In the meantime, they are collaborating with six other major local wineries (Balfour, Biddenden, Chapel Down, Gusbourne, Simpsons and Squerryes) to promote Kent-produced wines through **Wine Garden of England** ($\oslash$ winegardenofengland.co.uk).

There are many other excellent smaller vineyards to search out on your travels around Kent, with many of them offering guided tours and tutored tastings. These including **Chartham Vineyard** (page 85) near Canterbury and **Westwell** ($\oslash$ westwellwines.com) near Ashford, both of which are aiming to be more sustainable in their production of wine; **Mount Vineyard** (page 249) in Shoreham; **Elham Valley Vineyard** near Elham; **Mereworth Wines** ($\oslash$ mereworth. co.uk), seven miles northeast of Tonbridge; and **Terlingham Vineyard** ($\oslash$ terlinghamvineyard.co.uk) on the North Downs hills above Folkestone, run by a South African winemaking family. For a comprehensive list of the county's vineyards see $\oslash$ kentvineyards.com.

◀ **1** Bore Place. **2** Chapel Down Vineyard, Tenterden. **3** A Shepherd Neame brewery tour. **4** Preparing oysters, Whitstable.

Cycle The Vineyards (℘ 07913 701162 ⊘ cyclethevineyards.com) offer guided cycling tours of some of Kent's top vineyards, including Chapel Down, Squerryes and Gusbourne, that last between one and three days.

FARMERS' & ARTISAN FOOD MARKETS

Should you wish to take home some of Kent's local produce, there is no shortage of farmers' markets and specialist food markets and delis scattered around the county. **Kent Farmers' Markets** (⊘ kfma.org.uk) lists details of scores of regular fresh-produce markets.

Recommended farm shops and delis include **Canterbury's Goods Shed** (see box, page 66), **Macknade** in Faversham (page 127), with branches also in Ashford and Tunbridge Wells, **The Cheese Room** in Rochester (page 110), **Quex Barn** at Birchington-on-Sea (page 152), **Gibsons Farm Shop** in Wingham (page 176) and **Country Fayre** in Folkestone (page 220).

FORAGING

A superb Kent Slow Travel experience is to keep your eyes peeled for wild edibles, be it mushrooms and wild garlic in the county's forests and woods, blackberries and other berries on the hedgerows, or shellfish along the coast. However, foraging for food is not something to be undertaken lightly: there are plenty of poisonous plants and fungi to be wary of and it's important not to break any laws by trespassing on private property. For example, to collect seaweed from the shore and seabed in England, it is necessary to obtain permission from the relevant landowner, which in most cases is the Crown Estate or local authorities. With all this in mind, the best plan of action is to sign up for a guided foraging walk or course with a trained expert. Reputable courses are offered by Brogdale National Fruit Collection near Faversham (page 128), Chartham-based Miles Irving, author of *The Forager Handbook* (page 85), Bore Place (page 265) and The Wild Kitchen in Deal (page 180).

As well as foraging skills, Michael White (⊘ ruralcourses.co.uk) can teach you food smoking and curing, sausage and cider making, beekeeping and hedgerow winemaking from a base near Sissinghurst. Jack Raven Bushcraft (℘ 07553 763397 ⊘ jackravenbushcraft.co.uk) near Ashford also offer a one-day foraging course, alongside other bushcraft and craft courses.

CREATIVE KENT

Kent's beautiful landscapes have long inspired artists. J M W Turner was captivated by the skies and maritime scenes around Margate. Samuel Palmer, a key member of the Victorian Romanticism movement, settled in Shoreham where he made art from the scenery of the Darent Valley and North Downs. And in Cranbrook a 'colony' of artists coalesced around painters Frederick Daniel Hardy and Thomas Webster, who favoured scenes from everyday life in the Weald.

Charles Dickens had a lifelong association with and love of Kent. Rochester, Maidstone and Cobham are among the local backdrops to his novels, albeit thinly disguised as, respectively, Cloisterham, Muggleton and Dingley Dell. Other famous writers with Kent links include Christopher Marlowe, born and schooled in Canterbury; Jane Austen, whose father's family hailed from Tonbridge and whose brother Edward lived at Goodnestone Park and Godmersham Park; Ian Fleming, who lived at St Margaret's Bay and set several of his James Bond books in Kent locations; Vita Sackville-West, who wrote some of her novels and all of her gardening columns at Sissinghurst; H G Wells, who lived for 13 years in Sandgate (and where there's an annual writing competition in his name ⏚ hgwellscompetition.com); and H E Bates,

KENT IN CONTEMPORARY WRITING

One of the best ways to get under the skin of Kent is to read about it in novels and non-fiction books that conjure up a sense of the place. Award-winning author David Mitchell studied English in Canterbury and uses his knowledge of Kent locations such as Gravesend in his novels *The Bone Clocks and Utopia Avenue*. Richard Osman's entertaining and mega-selling *Thursday Murder Club* mysteries are set in a fictional retirement community in Kent, as well as other real locations such as Folkestone. The Booker Prize-winning novel *Last Orders* by Graham Swift, made into a film by the director Fred Schepisi, is about a road trip from London, via Rochester, Chatham and Canterbury, to Margate.

Few writers have captured the wild beauty of Dungeness as well as Derek Jarman does in his memoirs *Modern Nature* and *Smiling in Slow Motion*. *On the Marshes* by Carol Donaldson is a blend of memoir and evocative travelogue, with an environmental focus, that follows the writer in her journey across north Kent from Gravesend to Whitstable. The coastal communities of north Kent are also part of the focus in *Estuary* by Rachel Lichtenstein, a travelogue about the Thames Estuary.

SIMON RICHMOND

SIMON RICHMOND

SIMON RICHMOND

whose *Darling Buds of May* and subsequent Larkin family novels eulogised rural Kent of the 1950s.

Kent continues to be a powerful draw for a contemporary generation of creatives, with extra incentives being cheaper rents than London and a slew of prestigious festivals. Leading the way has been Whitstable, where the **Whitstable Biennale** (⟨ whitstablebiennale.com), held every two years since 2002, promotes emerging artists in film, performance and sound. Margate's art scene has been running hot ever since the opening of the Turner Contemporary in 2011 (see box, page 142). Meanwhile, **Dover Arts Development** (⟨ dadonline.uk) is behind many great projects in and around Dover, while in Romney Marsh it's the **IMOS Foundation** (⟨ imosfoundation.org), and in Rochester and Chatham **Nucleus Arts** (⟨ nucleusarts.com) that are the catalysts for local creative endeavours. **Creative Folkestone** (⟨ creativefolkestone.org.uk) has, arguably, had the biggest impact on the arts in Kent with its ambitious public art triennial, sponsorship of the town's Creative Quarter and the annual book festival.

Among other Kent arts and literary festivals to keep tabs of on your calendar are the **Canterbury Festival** (⟨ canterburyfestival.co.uk) in October; **Chiddingstone Literary Festival** (⟨ chiddingstonecastle.org. uk/literary_festival) at the end of April, early May; **Sevenoaks Literary Festival** (⟨ sevlitfest.com) at the end of September; and the **Wealden Literary Festival** (⟨ wealdenliteraryfestival.co.uk) at the end of June.

CRAFT COURSES

A wonderful way to connect creatively with Kent and its cultural traditions is to take a craft course. Some of the best are held at **Brogdale Collections** in Faversham (page 128) and include classes in basket weaving, bee keeping, cider and hedgerow wine making. At **Sandwich Medieval Centre** (page 169) you can sign up to learn blacksmithing, wheat weaving, calligraphy, illuminating manuscripts, and bread baking and mead making using centuries-old methods.

Aylesford School of Ceramics (⟨ school.aylesfordpottery.co.uk) will teach you how to throw pots and make other fired-clay objects at its studios within the grounds of The Friars (page 296). Other pottery

◀ **1** Hever Festival. **2** Margate's Antony Gormley sculpture with the Turner Contemporary behind. **3** *Holiday Homes* artwork, Folkestone. **4** Colourful beach huts, Lower Leas Coastal Park.

courses are offered by **The Ceramics Studio** (⊘ theceramicsstudio.co.uk) near Tunbridge Wells and **Carol Foster Ceramics** (⊘ carolfosterceramics. co.uk) in Whitstable.

Kent Downs (⊘ kentdowns.org.uk/findyourspace-artsandcraft) lists several other arts and craft courses and experiences, including spinning and dyeing wool with **Spinning Earth Wool** (⊘ spinningearthwool. co.uk) in Wye; and working with stained glass by **Creative Retreats** (⊘ creativeretreatsandholidays.co.uk) in Chilham.

ACTIVE KENT

Kent's beautiful countryside of woodlands, hills, valleys and waterways, plus over 350 miles of coastline, makes the county a choice location for a wide range of outdoor activities. The go-to site for all things active in Kent is **Explore Kent** (⊘ explorekent.org) which offers comprehensive information on beaches, canoeing, cycling, horseriding, outdoor gyms, parks, open spaces, running and walking. **Everyday Active Kent** (⊘ everydayactivekent.org.uk) is another good touchpoint for activities across the county.

CYCLING

Kent offers a superb diversity for cycle touring – from flat, family-friendly and traffic-free coastal routes to muscle-challenging climbs up to the North Downs and across the undulating Kentish Weald.

Each of the five chapters lists the best cycle routes in the area covered and places that you can hire bicycles locally. **Sustrans** (⊘ sustrans.org. uk) publish the *Kent Cycle Map*, covering the National Cycle Network routes and other routes in the county.

Spokes (⊘ spokeseastkent.org.uk) campaigns for cycling to be a major part of a sustainable transport policy for east Kent. They usually organise a group guided ride on the last Sunday of the month – see the website for details and for tons of useful information on cycling in the county, including a journey planner. For more links to cycling clubs and groups across Kent see ⊘ cyclinguk.org/cycle/cycling-kent.

WALKING

Kent is superb walking country, with over a dozen long-distance, named routes plus scores of day hiking options along some 4,200 miles of countryside and coastal paths. There are 12 walks, detailed with route maps, in this guide and information on several others.

If you'd like to join other walkers, look into the regular guided walks offered by **Kent Ramblers** (∂ kentramblers.org.uk). Their website has lots of suggestions for walks across the county and they also publish three excellent guidebooks: *Three River Valley Walks in West Kent*, covering the Darent, Eden and Medway paths; The *Tunbridge Wells Circular Walk*; and a *Guide to the Kent Coast Path*, covering a 66-mile section of the England Coast Path from Camber in East Sussex to Ramsgate.

Also check **Dover Walkers Are Welcome** (∂ doverwalkersarewelcome. org.uk), **Elham Valley Walkers** (∂ elhamvalleywalkers.co.uk) who organise the annual Elham Valley Walking Festival, and **Walk Kent** (∂ walkkent.co.uk) which includes the family-focused walking groups Woodland Wanders and Little Wanders. The **White Cliffs Walking Festival** (∂ whitecliffswalkingfestival.org.uk) is held over six days in August with a packed itinerary of walks in and around Folkestone, Dover, Deal and Sandwich. An inspirational resource with a focus mainly on west Kent is **Kent Walks Near London** (∂ kentwalksnearlondon.com). This passion project of journalist and musician Adam McCulloch has detailed instructions for 27 walks, all within easy day-trip reach of the capital.

LONG-DISTANCE WALKS

The following are the major multi-day hiking routes through Kent. Also see the previous section on Pilgrimages in Kent (page 17) for details on the various pilgrimage routes.

Darent Valley Path 19 miles. Start: Chipstead. Finish: Dartford. Follows the Darent from its source in the Greensand Hills near Sevenoaks until it connects with the Thames Estuary.
Eden Valley Walk 15 miles. Start: Cernes Farm, just west of Edenbridge where the path leaves the Vanguard Way. End: Tonbridge. Shadows the Eden and Medway rivers through the High Weald.
Elham Valley Way 22½ miles. Start: Hythe. Finish: Canterbury. Traces the beautiful Elham River valley through the North Downs AONB. For more information see ∂ elham.co.uk or download the detailed PDF from Explore Kent.
England Coast Path 91 miles. Start: Camber, East Sussex. Finish: Whitstable, Kent. Hugging the coast from the sand dunes of Camber around to the oyster stalls of Whitstable. The next 26-mile stretch of the path – from Whitstable to Ridham Docks in Iwade – has been agreed and is set to be opened during 2022. For route descriptions see ∂ nationaltrail.co.uk and ∂ explorekent.org.

Greensand Way 108 miles. Start: Haslemere, Surrey. Finish: Hamstreet, Kent. Named after the sandstone ridge which crosses Hampshire, Surrey and Kent. The Kent section starts just south of Westerham at Goodley Stock; download the detailed PDF from Explore Kent.

High Weald Landscape Trail 90 miles. Start: Horsham, West Sussex. Finish: Rye, East Sussex. The Kent section of this Wealden walk starts in Groombridge and exits the county just south of Wittersham. For more detailed route maps see ✍ highweald.org.

Medway Valley Walk 28 miles. Start: Tonbridge. Finish: Rochester. Follows the Medway River. Covered in detail in the Kent Rambler's *Three River Valley Walks* guidebook (page 29).

Miners Way 27 miles. Start & Finish: Sholden. Circular walking and cycling route through the East Kent countryside linking villages and sites that are connected to this area's industrial and mining heritage. The White Cliffs Countryside Partnership (✍ whitecliffscountryside.org. uk) publish a guidebook to the trail.

North Downs Way 156 miles. Start: Farnham, Surrey. Finish: Dover, Kent. Runs along the chalk ridge of the North Downs, crossing the county boundary into Kent near Cuxton. There's also a loop in the trail that you can follow around Canterbury. For more information see ✍ nationaltrail.co.uk/en_GB/trails/north-downs-way. Detailed PDFs of the trail can be downloaded from Explore Kent.

Royal Military Canal Path 28 miles. Start: Seabrook Kent. Finish: Cliff End, East Sussex. Shadows the early 19th-century canal built as a defence against invasion by the French. The initial 4.3-mile section from Seabrook to West Hythe has been improved to create a route that can also be followed by cyclists and wheelchair users, as well as those on horseback.

Saxon Shore Way 153 miles. Start: Gravesend, Kent. Finish: Hastings, East Sussex. This route follows the shoreline of Kent as it would have been familiar to Romans in 300AD – which means that in several places it goes far inland.

Stour Valley Walk 58 miles. Start: Lenham. Finish: Shellness Point. Follows the Stour River from its source in springs near the village of Lenham, northwest of Ashford, to its outflow into Pegwell Bay near Sandwich.

Tunbridge Wells Circular Walk 27½ miles. Start/Finish: Tunbridge Wells. Experience some of the most beautiful scenery of the Weald, taking in key sights such as Tudeley Church and Groombridge Place and Gardens. The Kent Ramblers publish a guide to the walk and others in the area. Explore Kent also has downloadable pamphlets to the route on its website, as well as four shorter circular trails starting and finishing in Tunbridge Wells.

Vanguard Way 66 miles. Start: Croydon, Greater London. Finish: Newhaven, East Sussex. The Kent section of this route passes nearby Westerham and Edenbridge where it intersects with the Eden Valley Walk (page 29). For full details see ✍ vanguardway.org.uk.

Wealdway 82 miles. Start: Gravesend, Kent. Finish: Eastbourne, East Sussex. This north–south cross-country route takes in sections of the North Downs, South Downs and the Weald, passing through Tonbridge and Tunbridge Wells along the way.

TOP FIVE BEACHES

The following are my personal picks of the best beaches in Kent. For more places to spread your towel and break out the suntan lotion, the Beach Guide (⏚ thebeachguide.co.uk) lists another 50 more Kent beaches.

Greatstone Beach (page 233) Two miles of golden sands, safe swimming and sand dunes that are a Site of Specific Scientific Interest, supporting many rare plant species. Reachable by the cute Romney, Hythe and Dymchurch Railway.

Botany Bay (page 145) Fossick for fossils around the rock pools, chalk cliffs and stacks on this sandy beach between Broadstairs and Margate.

Whitstable West Beach (page 71) A mile of shingle split into cosy sections by wooden groynes, running from the town's harbour to neighbouring Seasalter. Great for sunsets.

Viking Bay (page 154) Broadstairs' prime crescent of sand, with all the facilities of the town immediately to hand, plus a sheltered spot to learn to surf.

Lower Leas Coastal Park (page 212) Folkestone's shingle Mermaid Beach is good for swimming, with cafés nearby and a half-mile of beach huts that are also an artwork.

WATER-BASED ACTIVITIES

Fordwich-based **Canoe Wild** (page 79) can take you paddling in canoes, kayaks and paddleboards along the Great Stour between Canterbury and Grove Ferry. Offering a similar service along the Royal Military Canal is **Seapoint Canoe Centre** (page 221), while **Bewl Water** (page 282), on the border of Kent and Sussex, is a popular destination for a wide variety of watersports, including sailing, canoeing and paddleboarding.

Thanet is the place to head to learn to surf or stand-up paddleboard (SUP) in the sea, with courses offered by **Kent Surf School** in Broadstairs and **Joss Bay Surf School** in Joss Bay (both page 155). Ramsgate is one of the UK's top kitesurfing destinations, hosting the British Freestyle Kitesurfing championships in August. The town's Royal Harbour is also a good place to organise boat trips, as is Dover Marina, home to **Dover Sea Safari** (⏚ doverseasafari.co.uk). Their main boat trips include views of the White Cliffs from out in the Channel, and sailing to the seal colonies in Pegwell Bay and to Goodwin Sands. There are boat tours from both Whitstable (see box, page 72) and Queenborough (page 117) harbours to view the rusting remains of the World War II defensive Maunsell sea forts.

HOW THIS BOOK IS ARRANGED

I've broken down coverage of Kent into five broadly geographical chapters, starting with Canterbury and surrounds. This chapter also includes the coastal towns of Whitstable and Herne Bay, as well as surrounding nature areas and villages such as Blean Woods, Fordwich and Bridge. Chapter 2 covers north Kent, which is broadly anywhere above the M2 and all sights of interest between Gravesend and Faversham; a few places that are along the North Downs are also covered here. Chapter 3 takes in the resort towns of Margate, Broadstairs and Ramsgate, as well as essentially the easternmost parts of Kent including Sandwich, Deal and Walmer. Chapter 4 is southeastern Kent from Dover through to the Romney Marshes and Dungeness, and Chapter 5 is west Kent, the Kentish Weald and sections of the Kent Downs as far east as Wye near Ashford.

MAPS

The double-page map at the front of this book shows which area falls within each chapter. Each of the five chapters also begins with a map featuring numbered stopping points that correspond to numbered headings in the text. The ♀ symbol on these maps indicates that there is a walk in that area. Featured walks are also given simple sketch maps.

LISTINGS

Accommodation recommendations have their own chapter, starting on page 306. The main chapters also contain reviews of my favourite places to eat, drink and shop – as with the sights listed, this is a selective list with all the places chosen because they offer something unique and special. I've provided a telephone number and a website or other online information source where available and when it's useful. Postcodes are also provided for all rural and off-the-beaten-track destinations. Opening hours have also been included, but do check directly before you visit as these may be subject to change.

I've not listed admission fees for attractions as these often change, too, and are subject to various concessions depending on age, whether travelling in a family group, etc. Again, always check directly with an attraction beforehand to avoid any unpleasant shocks. If a description does not say admission is free, you should expect to be charged.

ADDITIONAL INFORMATION

Visit Kent (⊘ visitkent.co.uk) is the umbrella site for promoting the county. Local tourist information centres and other useful sources of online information are listed at the beginning of each chapter.

Kent Life (⊘ kentlifemagazine.co.uk) is a monthly glossy magazine with a variety of interesting features on Kent attractions, events, new openings, etc. Published bi-monthly and with a more youthful and cultural edge on Kent is **Cene Magazine** (⊘ cenemagazine.co.uk).

Isle (⊘ islemagazine.co.uk) is a glossy biannual magazine with general features and listings, available free from visitor information centres, hotels, restaurants and other outlets across Thanet.

With a more hyper-local focus are the **Broadstairs Beacon**, **Deal Despatch**, **Folkestone Foghorn**, **Margate Mercury**, **Ramsgate Recorder** and **Whitstable Whistler**, all magazines published by ⊘ brightsidepublishing.com – they are all free and available from tourist-related and hospitality businesses in their respective towns.

Tune into **BBC Radio Kent** ⊘ bbc.co.uk/sounds/play/live:bbc_radio_ kent for traffic news as well as local-interest stories and interviews.

GETTING THERE & AROUND

Kent has a decent network of bus and trains routes and with some careful planning and patience it's possible to reach – within reasonably close walking range – many of places listed in this guide by public transport. If you're not up for long walks, then for the most rural locations a car will certainly be handy.

National Express (⊘ nationalexpress.com) runs coaches to about 20 Kent locations, mostly in the east of the county, from London's Victoria Coach Station. These include Canterbury, Dover, Folkestone, Margate, Ramsgate and Whitstable. For **drivers**, the fastest roads into the county are the A2/M2, M20 and M26, all of which branch off from the M25.

Southeastern (⊘ southeasternrailway.co.uk) is Kent's main train company. Their high-speed services from London St Pancras run along three routes: to Ebbsfleet (near Gravesend), Ashford, and onwards to Folkestone and Dover; the same stations to Ashford and then via Canterbury West to Ramsgate and Margate; and along the north Kent coast to Gravesend, Rochester, Faversham, Whitstable, Herne Bay, Margate, Broadstairs and Ramsgate.

Trains operated by **Southern** (⏀ southernrailway.com) serve a handful of Kent stations from London, including Gravesend, Strood, Rochester, Chatham, Eynsford, Sevenoaks, Edenbridge, Penshurst, Tonbridge and Appledore.

PUBLIC TRANSPORT

The best way to plan a Slow travel route around Kent is to use **Kent Connected** (⏀ kentconnected.org), an online service providing comparisons for travel by different methods – public transport, car, cycling or walking – between any two points in the county.

Depending on your Kent itinerary there are a couple of travel passes that can work out to be good value. The **Kent Rover** covers three consecutive days of unlimited off-peak travel (after 10.00 on weekdays, any time on weekends) on Southeastern trains across most of Kent for £45 per adult (with up to four children at £5 each).

The main bus companies covering Kent are **Arriva** (⏀ arrivabus. co.uk) in the west and **Stagecoach** (⏀ stagecoachbus.com) in the east. To connect between the two sides of the county you'll likely have to transit via the main cities and towns, such as Ashford, Canterbury and Maidstone. All bus companies operating in Kent offer the **Discovery ticket** – valid for a day it offers unlimited travel across the county and costs £9 for an adult, £7.20 for a child and £17.50 for a family of up to five people.

FEEDBACK REQUEST

At Bradt Guides we're aware that guidebooks start to go out of date on the day they're published – and that you, our readers, are out there in the field doing research of your own. You'll find out before us when a fine new family-run hotel opens or a favourite restaurant changes hands and goes downhill. So why not tell us about your experiences? Contact us on ⏀ 01753 893444 or ✉ info@bradtguides.com. We will forward emails to the author who may post updates on the Bradt website at ⏀ bradtguides.com/updates. Alternatively, you can add a review of the book to Amazon, or share your adventures with us on social media.

🅕 BradtGuides 🅘 BradtGuides & @slowtravelkent
🅣 BradtGuides

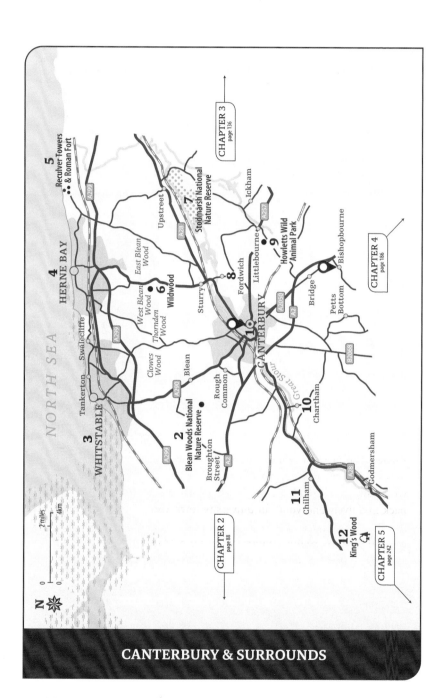

CANTERBURY & SURROUNDS

1
CANTERBURY & SURROUNDS

Nestled near the North Downs and bisected by the River Stour, Canterbury is a city with a great many tales to tell. The 250ft tower of the cathedral, the mother church of the Church of England, can be spied for miles around, over the treeline, rooftops and the city's partially intact Norman castle wall. This stone beacon has been guiding pilgrims and visitors to 'Britain's Rome' for centuries.

The gargoyles, statues and figures in stained glass that adorn the cathedral are silent witnesses to key moments in English history, not least the murder of Thomas Becket here in 1170. This superb example of ecclesiastical architecture, together with the atmospheric ruins of St Augustine's Abbey and venerable St Martin's Church, comprise a single UNESCO World Heritage Site.

Within the city walls, there are fascinating smaller museums and lovely gardens to relax in. There are punt trips down the Stour (also known as the Great Stour) which ripples gently along languid, tree-shaded channels. Or you can wander narrow, traffic-free streets, lined with wonky wood-beam medieval houses, where you may feel like you've slipped through a crack in time. Turn a corner and you're right back in a lively and youthful university town with all the essentials of modern urban life, including a vibrant food and drink scene.

Amid the lush, rolling countryside around Canterbury nestle bucolic villages, such as Fordwich and Chilham, and nature reserves like Blean Woods and Stodmarsh – all ideal for exploring on foot. Also within the city's administrative boundaries are the coastal towns of Whitstable, known for its oysters, working harbour and arty 'Islington-on-Sea' vibe, and Herne Bay, a classic British seaside resort within walking distance of the dramatic Roman-era site of Reculver where the ruined towers of a medieval church rise up from the headland. For a combination of city, countryside and coast, this part of Kent is hard to beat.

GETTING THERE & AROUND

Public transport to Canterbury is excellent. There are six Park and Ride car parks on the city's edge, from where you can walk or catch buses to the centre.

TRAINS

This is a superb area of Kent to explore by train. Canterbury has two train stations: **Canterbury West**, a few minutes' walk north of Westgate, is connected by high-speed trains with London St Pancras (51 minutes); and **Canterbury East**, just south of the city walls by Dane John Gardens, that has services to London Victoria (just under 2 hours). Ashford, Margate, Ramsgate, Dover, Faversham and Rochester are all easy to get to by train from Canterbury, as are the villages of Chartham, Chilham, Fordwich and Bekesbourne. Whitstable and Herne Bay are also served by direct trains from London St Pancras and London Victoria.

BUSES

Canterbury's bus station is at the end of St George's Street, next to the Whitefriars shopping centre. For timetables to surrounding towns and villages check with Stagecoach ⊘ stagecoachbus.com.

CYCLING

Canterbury is made for cycling, with many traffic-free routes. As well as the Crab and Winkle Way (see box, page 67) to Whitstable, there's the Great Stour Way following National Cycle Route 18 eastwards towards Ashford via Chartham and Wye (page 245). This route forms part of the 47-mile Pilgrims Cycle Trail from Rochester to Canterbury; for more information see ⊘ explorekent.org/activities/pilgrims-cycle-trail.

Kent Cycle Hire (⊘ 01227 388058 ⊘ www.kentcyclehire.com) has hubs in Canterbury, Whitstable and Herne Bay, allowing you to pick up a bike from one location and drop it off another.

---

i **TOURIST INFORMATION**

Canterbury The Beaney House of Art & Knowledge, 8 High St ⊘ 01227 862162
⊘ canterbury.co.uk ⏱ 10.00–17.00 Mon–Sat, 11.00–16.00 Sun.

1 CANTERBURY

🏠 **7 Longport** (page 307), **Canterbury Cathedral Lodge** (page 306), **The Corner House Canterbury** (page 307), **The Falstaff** (page 306), **House of Agnes** (page 306)

The Cantiaci, an Iron Age Celtic tribe, had long lived on this stretch of the Stour River when the Romans began their conquest of England in AD43. The Romans named their hillfort Durovernum Cantiacorum, making it a hub on Watling Street, the paved road connecting the ports of Durbis (Dover), Rutupiae (Richborough), Requlbium (Reculver) and Portus Lemanis (Port Lympne) to London and beyond.

Nearly 300 years of Roman rule saw Canterbury develop into a well-ordered town with a forum, temple, theatre and public bath. However, all of this swiftly fell into ruin after the Roman withdrawal from Britain around AD410. In the next century Canterbury was settled by pagan Anglo-Saxons, who were well established by the time Augustine showed up in 597 with a team of monks on a papal mission to reintroduce Christianity to England. Bertha, the Frankish wife of local Saxon ruler Ethelbert, was a Christian so the king was open to conversion and in 601, Augustine baptised him. Ethelbert subsequently granted Augustine permission to build a monastery and church, on the site of an old Roman basilica, which would eventually become Canterbury Cathedral.

The assassination of Archbishop Thomas Becket in 1170 (see box, page 46), transformed the cathedral into one of the most important pilgrimage shrines of medieval Europe. Canterbury prospered, then suffered after Henry VIII ordered the destruction of Becket's shrine in 1538 during the Dissolution of the Monasteries. The cult of Becket may have been squashed, but the cathedral remained and refashioned itself as the mother church of the Church of England. In 1685, some 200,000 French Protestants fled to England to escape persecution in Catholic France. Many settled in Canterbury and introduced silk weaving to the city – an industry that thrived until the early 19th century.

By this time all but one of the Norman gates in the city walls had been destroyed to facilitate road traffic. In 1830 Canterbury also gained southern England's first passenger railway, connecting it to Whitstable on the coast. During World War II the city endured 135 air raids in which bombs destroyed over a thousand buildings, a third of the medieval centre. Amazingly, the cathedral survived largely unscathed.

In the 1950s, rebuilding of Canterbury began and has continued in the subsequent decades with the addition, outside the old city walls, of the University of Kent at Canterbury and Christ Church College.

Since 1988 the cathedral, the ruins of St Augustine's Abbey and ancient St Martin's Church have been inscribed as one World Heritage site. According to UNESCO, together these three sites 'reflect milestones in the history of Christianity in Britain'. All three can be visited in a day and are within easy walking distance of each other. Most visitors will be enthralled by these religious monuments but you don't have to look too hard to also find examples of poor or negligent city planning that sit uncomfortably with Canterbury's medieval core. The closure of department stores Debenhams and Nasons on and just off the High Street has left some of the heritage

"The city's time-worn city centre remains enchanting, especially if you approach it one step at a time."

buildings in the city centre in a perilous position. A report, *Canterbury Take Care!*, published in 2021 by SAVE Britain's Heritage, warns that the situation is approaching a 'national emergency'. While this may be overstating the level of crisis, the tension between preservation and modernisation is very real. How Canterbury tackles these challenges, as it continues to attract ever growing numbers of tourists and students, will shape the city in the years to come. In the meantime, the city's intimate, time-worn city centre remains enchanting, especially if you approach it, as have legions of pilgrims down the years, one step at a time. The town's three universities attract staff and students from around the world, making Canterbury one of the most cosmopolitan places in Kent.

CANTERBURY CATHEDRAL

✆ 01227 762862 ⚲ canterbury-cathedral.org ⏰ 10.00–16.00 Mon–Sat, 12.30–16.00 Sun
Originally named Christ Church and part of a monastic community, England's first cathedral has been a sacred place of Christian worship for over 1,400 years. It was on the pilgrimage route to Rome soon after its foundation in the early 7th century by St Augustine, the Benedictine monk tasked with reintroducing Christianity to Britain. Much of the

CANTERBURY CATHEDRAL: **1** Christ Church Gate. **2** View towards the cathedral. **3** A scene from the medieval Miracle Windows that surround the site of Becket's shrine. **4** The Great Cloister. **5** The Crypt – one of the oldest parts of the cathedral. **6** Exploring the Quire. ▶

main building was reconstructed between 1070 and 1077 during the time of Norman Archbishop Lanfranc, replacing the earlier Saxon church destroyed by fire.

Following the grisly murder in 1170 that made a saint of Archbishop Thomas Becket, pilgrims from across Europe began to flock to Canterbury. Becket's shrine was destroyed during the Reformation, but that loss doesn't diminish the cathedral's grand architecture and other important tombs, including those of Edward the Black Prince, Henry IV and his wife Joan of Navarre. The cathedral is the seat of the Anglican leader, the Archbishop of Canterbury, and the site of his investiture.

Although described as 'England in Stone', the building is mainly constructed from hard-wearing Caen stone – a creamy beige-coloured limestone imported from Normandy. Added to and adapted down the centuries, repairs and maintenance are an ongoing process – there are 25 stonemasons on staff for this very purpose, plus a team of conservators for the 12,900ft^2 of stained glass, some of it dating back to medieval times.

The **Canterbury Journey**, a £30 million schedule of improvements and renovations to the cathedral, began in 2016 with key elements completed in 2021. The west end of the Nave and Christ Church Gate now gleam after major repairs and facelifts. The western precincts have been relandscaped, the old uneven cobbles replaced with smooth stone paving. There's a new visitor centre, including a free viewing gallery, exhibition area and community studio. Inside the cathedral, there are also two new exhibitions of treasures from the church's extensive collection.

Tickets for entry are purchased from the **visitor centre**, accessed from Buttermarket, next to the Christ Church Gate. Check the website before your visit as public openings times can change at short notice owing to various church events; also see the website for times of daily church services which anyone is free to attend.

To do the cathedral and its grounds justice, reckon on spending at least two hours here. **Guided tours** (£5 in addition to the admission charge) are highly recommended and can be booked in advance via ✉ visits@canterbury-cathedral.org.

Christ Church Gate

The magnificent twin-towered **Christ Church Gate** is the main entrance to the church precincts, its gatehouse providing a stone frame for the cathedral's pair of west end towers and central Bell Harry Tower.

The elaborately detailed gate itself is best admired as you approach along narrow Mercery Lane towards Buttermarket. With Burgate to the right and Sun Street to the left, this is one of finest confluences of medieval streets in England, an architectural ensemble that would have been familiar to Chaucer and his contemporaries.

Originally constructed in the early 16th century, the gate is elaborately carved and decorated with a band of heraldic symbols and Tudor coats of arms immediately above the arched doorway. Over this is a bronze sculpture of Christ, created in 1990 by the German artist Klaus Ringwald and replacing the original that was destroyed in 1643. Above, to the right of the statue, look out for the coat of arms of the Wills family (of Wills tobacco). Dame Janet Stancomb-Wills and her sister funded the reconstruction of the gate's twin towers in 1937 – the originals had been torn down over a century earlier.

"Originally constructed in the early 16th century, the gate is elaborately carved and decorated with a band of heraldic symbols."

Today, a World War I memorial stands at the centre of cobbled **Buttermarket**, which takes its name from a dairy market that was once held here. However, back in the 17th century the location was known as the Bull Stake, as cattle were chained up here and baited by dogs (the adrenalin would make their meat more tender), before being slaughtered in nearby Butchery Lane.

The South West Porch

Before entering the cathedral through the **South West Porch**, take note of the much bigger **processional entrance** around the corner. This gives direct access to the central corridor of the Nave and is only opened for key services and occasions, such as the enthronement of the archbishop. In niches above and around both doors are 55 stone statues of people connected with Canterbury and the cathedral. The first six figures, including St Augustine, were erected in 1864; the most recent additions (from 2015) are of Queen Elizabeth II and the Duke of Edinburgh.

The South West Porch was completed in 1415 and is thought to celebrate Henry V's victory at the Battle of Agincourt. As you pass under it, look up to see the 29 bosses (heraldic shields) of influential families who fought beside the king and were associated with the construction of the porch.

The Nave

Completed in 1405 in the style known as Perpendicular Gothic, the **Nave** is the cathedral's awe-inspiring public gathering space. Built on Norman foundations, the 216ft-long hall has a vaulted ceiling, held aloft by ranks of slender 78ft-tall pillars, and is thought to have been designed by master stonemason Henry Yevele.

Much damage was done to the cathedral by Puritans during the English Civil War, including the destruction of many of the Nave's original stained-glass windows, as well as the marble **font** dating from 1639. Fortunately, the remaining pieces of the wonderfully decorative font were saved and in 1663 it was returned, refurbished, to the north end of the Nave.

A large carved stone screen splits off the Nave's east end from the Quire (or Choir) and the rest of the cathedral, areas reserved during pre-Reformation times for monks and the clergy. Known as the **Pulpitum**, the screen dates to around 1450 and displays six statues believed to be (from left to right) Henry V, Richard II, Ethelbert, Edward the Confessor, Henry IV and Henry VI.

As you approach the Pulpitum, be sure to look up at the dazzling, kaleidoscopic fan vault ceiling in the cathedral's central tower. Known as **Bell Harry,** this 250ft structure was completed at the end of the 15th century to replace an earlier Norman steeple.

South West Transept

Before moving down into the crypt, pause to admire the various elements of the **South West Transept,** including the coloured light flooding through the Great South Window, the cathedral's largest expanse of stained glass. On the transept's east side is the Warriors' Chapel, commonly known as the **Buffs' Chapel** because of its historical links to the Royal East Kent Regiment, nicknamed the Buffs. Hung with regimental flags, its central Purbeck marble tomb is that of the wealthy and powerful Lady Margaret Holland (1385–1439), who commissioned the chapel as it is seen today and who died just 11 days after its completion. She lies between her successive husbands, both of whom had died much earlier and whose remains were moved from elsewhere in the cathedral to be entombed beside her. To accommodate Lady Margaret's tomb, the 1228 grave of Archbishop Stephen Langton was shifted to the back of the chapel – the foot of his tomb juts out the chapel's external wall.

The Crypt

Europe's largest Romanesque crypt is one of the few places where you can get a sense of how the cathedral looked back in Norman times. Compared to the majestic, lofty halls above, it's an intimate, dimly lit space with stout columns, the capitals of which are decorated with strikingly unchristian images of animals, birds and fantastic monsters.

The gloom at the crypt's west end makes it ideal to display some of the cathedral's most precious and delicate possessions. In what is known as the **Treasury**, an exhibition tells the building's history through specific objects, including the Black Prince's 'achievements' – the 14th-century armorial jupon (tabard), helmet, gauntlets and sword scabbard that originally lay on top of his tomb in the Trinity Chapel.

The Black Prince's name is also attached to the Chantry in the crypt's South East Transept. This chapel was built in 1363 in thanksgiving for the prince's marriage to his cousin Joan, the 'Fair Maid of Kent'. Since 1880 it has been called the **Huguenot Chapel,** which acknowledges the many protestant refugees from northern Europe

"The form of a human body is made from 210 medieval iron nails, recovered after the refurbishment of part of the cathedral's roof."

who settled in Canterbury from the 16th century onwards; they and their descendants came to worship at the cathedral. Services in French are still held every Sunday at 15.00 in this chapel.

For the first 50 years after his assassination, until the construction of the grand shrine in Trinity Chapel, Becket's tomb was housed in the eastern end of the crypt. Dangling on an almost 5ft steel thread from the stone ceiling vault here is *Transport*, a work of art by Antony Gormley. The life-sized form of a human body is made from 210 medieval iron nails, recovered after the refurbishment of part of the cathedral's roof.

North West Transept & The Martyrdom

Stairs connect the crypt with the **North West Transept**, the scene of the most shocking murder in all of English ecclesiastical history. Pursued by four of Henry II's knights, 52-year-old Thomas Becket had fled here on 29 December 1170. According to the eyewitness testament of the monk Edward Grim, the archbishop held tight to one of the cathedral's pillars to prevent his assailants from seizing him. One of the knights drew his sword, slicing off the crown of Becket's head, after which two

A SHRINE TO A TURBULENT PRIEST

Picture the scene. It's Christmas 1170 at Bures Castle in Normandy. Henry II is livid to learn that the Archbishop of Canterbury Thomas Becket has excommunicated several bishops, including the Archbishop of York, who are supporters of the king. He cries out his infamous line asking who will rid him of Becket – or something along those lines – in French, his native language. This prompts four knights to immediately ride for England, their self-appointed mission to change the archbishop's mind on the excommunications or, failing that, to extradite him to Normandy – a plan that goes spectacularly wrong.

Henry II and Becket had not always been at daggers drawn. The pair were partying buddies for years when Becket was Royal Chancellor – which is why the king appointed his not especially pious pal as archbishop in 1162, trusting Becket to protect the Crown's interests against those of the equally powerful church. However, much to Henry's surprise and displeasure, Becket took his new role far more seriously than expected, throwing off his former worldly trappings, embracing asceticism and defending the rights of the church over those of the monarch. The rift between the king and his chief cleric was so severe that for nearly two years Becket sought refuge in France. Pope Alexander III eventually brokered a truce that enabled Becket's return to Canterbury in 1170, but the archbishop was still in no mood for compromise with Henry – thus sealing his fate.

Far from helping Henry in his quest for absolute authority, Becket's assassination turned public opinion in favour the church. Immediately after his murder in the cathedral (page 45), the canny monks collected Becket's blood and diluted it with water to

more knights joined in the slaughter with the fourth keeping the monks at bay. Grim himself nearly lost his arm in the melee. When the killing was done, the floor was awash with Becket's blood and brains.

The murder site, known as **The Martyrdom,** is marked by a carved paving stone, an altar and *Swords Point*, a dramatically lit wall sculpture designed by architect and sculptor Giles Blomfield in 1986 that has two metal swords and their shadows forming the four blades that ended Becket's life. A plaque also records the historic visit in 1982 by Pope John Paul II, who prayed here together with Archbishop Robert Runcie.

Don't overlook other nearby features of this corner of the cathedral, in particular the fine tracery vaulting of the **Dean's Chapel** and the entrance to the upper level of the **Water Tower** which houses a new exhibition devoted to the collection of silver and other precious religious items. An open doorway in the exhibition hall allows a glimpse into the Harry Potter-esque **Howley-Harrison Library**.

be distributed in vials as a cure-all to the sick. Pieces of his skull were also saved as relics. Soon, miracles were being reported and pilgrims from across Europe made their way to worship at the tomb of the martyr. Pope Alexander II canonised Becket in 1173; a year later a penitent Henry II, barefoot and dressed in sackcloth, walked from Canterbury's St Dunstan's Church (page 59) to pray for forgiveness at the cathedral, giving the royal seal of approval to the cult of Becket.

In 1220, Becket's remains were transferred from the cathedral's crypt to the newly built Trinity Chapel where they were encased in a golden casket, encrusted with precious jewels. This glittering shrine – one of the religious wonders of medieval Europe – was destroyed in 1538 by order of Henry VIII. Becket's reputation as a defender of Catholic power was an anathema to a king.

The Becket **Story** (⊘ thebecketstory.org. uk) is a superb online resource launched in 2020 to coincide with the 850th anniversary of the archbishop's death. It includes recreated images of his jewel-encrusted shrine, as well as other items such as the golden reliquary that contained a piece of Becket's skull, hacked off during his murder. You can also learn more about Becket's life and times, and about many aspects of medieval pilgrimages.

The battle of wills between king and priest also inspired stage and film dramas. T S Eliot wrote the verse play *Murder in the Cathedral* for the 1935 Canterbury Festival and it was performed in the cathedral's Chapter House. In 1959, Jean Anouilh weighed in with *Becket or the Honour of God*, which was adapted into the 1964 film *Becket* starring Richard Burton as Becket and Peter O'Toole as Henry.

The Quire & South East Transept

From the North West Transept, mount the steps to the entrance through the Pulpitum leading to the **Quire**, noting the stone chair where a monastic bouncer once denied entry to all except monks and other religious notables. At the cathedral's heart, the Quire was built between 1175 and 1184 and is an early example of Gothic church architecture. Its focus is the **St Augustine's Chair,** carved from Purbeck marble and possibly dating to the 13th century – it is here, on the high altar, that the archbishops of Canterbury are enthroned.

In the South East Transept are the four **Bossanyi Windows**, beautiful stained-glass creations commissioned in the 1950s from the Hungarian artist Ervin Bossanyi, which replaced 12th-century windows blown out during World War II. Look for the small padlock on the lower left window: the keyhole is in the shape of a swastika, a reference to the family members Bossanyi lost during the Holocaust.

Trinity Chapel & the Corona

A single burning candle, resting on flagstones worn down by centuries of kneeling pilgrims, marks the spot in **Trinity Chapel** where Thomas Becket's venerable shrine stood between 1220 and 1538. In a piece of religious theatre, the canon would have raised a wooden canopy via a rope pulley to reveal the golden, jewel-studded tomb beneath to the awe-struck visitors. None of this remains, but you can admire the artistry of 13th-century floor mosaic and 36 roundels that are collectively known as the **Opus Alexandrinum**.

"The canon would have raised a wooden canopy via a rope pulley to reveal the golden, jewel-studded tomb beneath."

The chapel houses Canterbury's only tomb of a monarch. Lying side by side are Henry IV and his second wife Joan of Navarre; alabaster figures of the couple adorn the top of the tomb, their heads resting on red-painted pillows. On the other side of the chapel is the tomb of Edward of Woodstock, aka the Black Prince. Only 45 when he died in 1376, Edward was heir to the throne and one of the greatest warriors of medieval England – copies of his 'achievements' (page 45), are displayed above the tomb.

Trinity Chapel is connected to the **Corona**, the most eastern part of the cathedral. This circular chapel was created specifically for the relic that contained a saved piece of Becket's skull, and which was destroyed during the reign of Henry VIII. Today the chapel is dedicated to saints and martyrs of recent times, including Dr Martin Luther King Jr.

The Water Tower & Healing Garden

An exit from the northside of the crypt connects to the base of the **Water Tower**, built in the 1160s as part of an ingenious system to bring spring water to the cathedral from over a mile away. The Norman arches and pillars are neatly carved with some historical graffiti.

Nearby, the wonderfully tranquil **Healing Garden** was planted in the 2000s around the ruins of what was once the monk's dormitory. The beds around ruined columns contain herbs that were used by the monks for healing purposes.

The Great Cloister & Chapter House

Another contemplative place is the **Great Cloister**, a square, covered walk around a central green space used by the monks for work and meditation. The cloister's handsome vaulted roof is punctuated with painted bosses; look for the one that depicts an elderly man, thought to be Henry Yevele, the 14th-century master stonemason who masterminded the rebuilding of parts of the cathedral.

Accessed off the east corridor of the Cloister is the **Chapter House**, the largest such hall of its type in England. The monks once assembled here to discuss daily activities, a meeting that always began with a reading of a chapter from the Book of Benedictine. Look up to admire its beautifully detailed oak ceiling, and the stained-glass east and west windows, depicting important people associated with the cathedral from King Ethelbert and Queen Bertha to Queen Victoria, the reigning monarch at the time of the creation of these windows in 1896.

VIA FRANCIGENA & THE NORTH DOWNS WAY ART TRAIL

Imagine walking from Canterbury, following a route that ends up – three countries later – in Rome. Such is the ambitious undertaking of the **Via Francigena** (⊘ viefrancigene. org), a spiritual and historical pilgrim route based on the one followed by Sigeric, the Archbishop of Canterbury, in 990. Should you not have time for the full 1,367 miles, try tackling the Kent section which runs for 19½ miles from Canterbury to Dover via the North Downs Way National Trail and can be covered in around seven to eight hours. Along this section of the route it's possible to engage with three new artworks, unveiled at the end of 2021 and early 2022, that are part of the North Downs Way Art Trail. Each artwork doubles as a bench, allowing walkers a moment to rest, reflect and more fully appreciate the surroundings.

At Barham Downs, eight miles southeast of Canterbury, Polysemic's *Sedile Francigena* is designed to be a map 1/1,000,000th the length of the Via Francigena trail, with 1/500th of its elevation. At the village of Woolage, a further mile southeast, is *After the Black Gold* by the architectural practice CHANNEL. It comprises a green oak shelter with two lean-to slate roof pitches oriented towards the old Snowdown colliery and the village houses originally built for the miners. The third artwork, *Monumenta Romana* by Charles Holland Architects, is on the Waldershare Estate, seven miles north of Dover. It is inspired by the Palladian-style Belvedere, an 18th-century folly that can also be seen in the grounds of the surrounding estate.

Having reached the coast, you can return to Canterbury by taking the train from Dover Priory, or from the intervening stations along the route, to Canterbury East station. A sign board outside St Augustine's Abbey provides more information on the Via Francigena.

Kent War Memorial Garden & Quenin Gate

Much of the cathedral's 23 acres of grounds is off limits to the public. But there are public gardens and the ruins of the old monastery around the south and east side of the cathedral, where you'll also encounter the **Canterbury War Horse**. This impressive 20ft-tall sculpture, made from wood and rope, was created by the staff and students of Canterbury School of Visual Arts in 2018 to mark the centenary of the end of World War I.

On the far east side of the precincts is the **Kent War Memorial Garden**. Once a bowling green, this walled garden – created to honour those who perished in World War I – is sandwiched between the original monastery walls and the old Roman city walls. Its mixed borders bloom with a glorious range of scented flowers through the seasons, including roses and a centuries-old wisteria. The garden can also be accessed through the **Quenin Gate**, a pedestrian route through the city walls dating back to 1448 and named after a much earlier Roman gate, long since blocked up.

The Saxon queen Bertha is believed to have used the Quenin Gate (aka the Queen's Gate) to leave the city on her daily walks to St Martin's; to reach the next part of the World Heritage site, exit the gate and cross the ring road to Lady Wootton's Green to find a **statue of Bertha** being welcomed to Canterbury by King Ethelbert.

ST AUGUSTINE'S ABBEY

Longport ✆ 01227 767345 ✆ Apr–Sep 10.00–18.00 daily, Oct 10.00–17.00 daily, Nov–Mar 10.00–16.00 Sat & Sun; English Heritage

The bustle of contemporary Canterbury evaporates in the verdant and atmospheric grounds of this ruined abbey. Augustine began building a monastery soon after his arrival in Canterbury in 597 and was buried here in 604, by which time his mission to reintroduce Christianity to England had firmly taken root. Soon he was revered as a saint, from which comes the abbey's name.

The abbey was pretty much rebuilt under Norman rule and then vastly expanded up until the Dissolution of the Monasteries in 1538. Thereafter, parts of it were turned into a royal palace and gardens, but it mainly fell into ruin and remained that way until the mid 19th century when the MP Alexander James Beresford Hope began to raise money to preserve what was left of the site. He founded a missionary college here in 1848, the buildings of which today form part of Kings School and are accessed through **Fyndon's Gate** at the head of Lady Wootton's Green. The twin-towered stone gate is named after Abbot Fyndon, who had it rebuilt in the early 14th century as the main entrance to the abbey.

The modern entrance to the site is now from nearby Longport. You'll first pass through a well-presented exhibition on the abbey's history, architecture and the routines of medieval monastic life. Emerging from here, you then follow a route around the ghostly stone foundations of a complex that once was rivalled Canterbury Cathedral. Reading the interpretive boards and listening to the downloadable audio app all help provide a vivid sense of the abbey in its heyday. Note the covered area protecting the remains of tombs of Augustine and other early archbishops. In the site's northeast corner, look out for the Anglo-Saxon-era St Pancras Church which has flat Roman bricks in its ruined walls. The wooded Campanile Mound, in the southeast corner where a 15th-century bell tower once stood, provides the best view across the site back towards the cathedral.

ST MARTIN'S CHURCH
North Holmes Rd 🕿 01227 768072 🔗 martinpaul.org 🕘 09.00 Sun & noon Thu for services

The final third of Canterbury's World Heritage Site is the most senior in terms of age. Considered to be the oldest parish church in England still in regular use, St Martin's traces its history back to the late 6th century and possibly even earlier. The building, which has sections that include Roman brickwork, was given by King Ethelbert to his Christian wife Bertha, for use as her private chapel. It was here that Augustine baptised Ethelbert around 610. Surrounding the church is a pleasant hillside graveyard in which are buried local notables including the artists Thomas Sydney Cooper (page 54) and Mary Tourtel, who drew the original Rupert the Bear cartoon strips. The graveyard's back terrace provides a panoramic view of the city.

CANTERBURY ROMAN MUSEUM
Butchery Ln 🕿 01227 785575 🔗 canterburymuseums.co.uk/romanmuseum 🕘 10.00–17.00 daily

A visit to this underground museum will give you a vivid sense of the ancient Roman town on which modern Canterbury rests. In 1886, workmen digging a drainage system uncovered a floor mosaic, 8ft beneath street

level and thought to date back to AD300. In the aftermath of World War II bombings, further excavations of the site around Longmarket revealed more geometric and floral paving and the remains of a well-to-do Roman town house, warmed by a hypocaust (an underfloor heating system). Left in situ, these discoveries are the centrepiece of Canterbury Roman Museum which displays many other archaeological finds from this and other sites around the city, including a wonderful collection of Roman glass and pottery. The reconstruction of a Roman marketplace includes ancient pieces of Roman leather in the sandal stall. Most intriguing are the remains of two military swords found in an unusual double grave. Swords were valuable weapons not commonly buried along with their owners. The intact male skeletons indicate that neither person had fallen in battle and might quite possibly have been poisoned or died of other unnatural causes – all clues suggesting a Roman chapter to Canterbury's murder mystery tales.

ALONG THE HIGH STREET

The narrow, cobbled medieval streets of Butchery Lane and Longmarket branch into broad High Street. Running on a northwest–southeast axis between St George' Gate and Westgate, this pedestrian thoroughfare is Canterbury's commercial spine, lined mainly with shops, restaurants and cafés. Distinctly contemporary at its southern end, where you'll find the **Whitefriars shopping centre** and other modern buildings, it offers up a more diverse historical character the closer you get to Westgate.

A personal favourite among Canterbury's superb stock of heritage architecture, is **The Beaney House of Art & Knowledge** (18 High St ✆ 01227 862162 ⊘ canterburymuseums.co.uk/the-beaney ⊙ museum & gallery 10.00–17.00 Tue–Sat, 11.00–16.00 Sun). This combined museum, art gallery, library and tourist information centre is named after the building's Victorian benefactor, Dr James George Beaney. Hailing from humble beginnings, Beaney made his fortune in Australia and left money in his will for an 'institute for working men' to be built in his birthplace of Canterbury. This gorgeous building, with its elaborate façade of mock Tudor brickwork and terracotta, opened in 1898. The sensitively executed modern extension to the rear contains the library, visitor information centre and temporary exhibition spaces.

◀ **1** Punting along the River Stour through Westgate Gardens. **2** St Augustine's Abbey.

The Beaney's eclectic exhibits range from a fascinating display of ethnographic treasures gathered from around the globe by Kent explorers and collectors to Bagpuss, Nogin the Nog and the Clangers, all creations of local children's programme makers Peter Firmin and Oliver Postgate. Its art collection is epoch and genre spanning: the elegantly posed Van Dyck portrait of Kent landowner Sir Basil Dixwell, resplendent in expensively dyed black silk robes, hangs beside the Edwardian-era *The Little Girl at the Door* by Harriet Halhed and much more modern works by the likes of David Hockney and John Bratby.

Downstairs in the Garden Room is The Beaney's prized collection of works by Canterbury artist Thomas Sidney Cooper (1803–1902), notable for his accomplished oils of landscapes and livestock. Look out for Cooper's final, unfinished canvas – a vivid scene of sheep in a wintery field – painted when he was 99.

At the junction with Best Lane, the 6½ft-tall bronze of **Geoffrey Chaucer** is a joint work unveiled in 2016. Sam Holland designed the statue of the medieval writer dressed as a Canterbury pilgrim, while Lynn O'Dowd created the plinth in the shape of a horse hoof decorated with bas-reliefs inspired by *The Canterbury Tales*. Chaucer's work was

TWO CANTERBURY TALES

Written between 1387 and Geoffrey Chaucer's death in 1400, *The Canterbury Tales* is a collection of yarns wrapped up in a story about a diverse group of pilgrims making their way from a London tavern to the cathedral city. To pass the time on the journey, each pilgrim recites a tale. Written mainly in verse, Chaucer was inspired by popular folk stories and legends of the time. A classic of early English literature, the book is particularly notable for its multidimensional depiction of 14th-century society, from the noble knight to the humble miller and oft-married Wife of Bath.

Michael Powell's 1944 film *A Canterbury Tale* takes its opening narration and scene of medieval pilgrims direct from *The Canterbury Tales'* General Prologue. Moments later, however, it deftly segues into a World War II propaganda story, focusing on a British soldier, a US soldier and a land girl thrown together in the Kent countryside. The three strangers solve a local mystery, before making their way to bomb-damaged Canterbury where each find their own small blessings. Powell, the film's director, grew up in Bekesbourne, just outside of Canterbury and attended the city's King's School. The locations he chose, including the villages of Chilham (page 85) and Fordwich (page 78) conjure an idyllic picture of England, designed to boost the spirits of war time audiences.

one of the first printed books in England, a fact referenced by the printer's blocks spelling out the author's name atop the plinth. Despite being the most famous of many writers associated with Canterbury, the characters in his tales only reached as far as the village of Harbledown on their pilgrimage to the city, and whether Chaucer himself was ever here is also unconfirmed.

Diagonally opposite the Chaucer statue, the **Eastbridge Hospital** (5 High St, ✆ 01227 471688 ⌂ eastbridgehospital.org.uk) dates back to the 12th century and was founded as a place of hospitality for those on pilgrimage to Canterbury. Its full name is the Hospital of St Thomas the Martyr, Eastbridge – but it was not really a hospital in the way the word is understood today as a place solely for the care of the sick. Today, parts of the building are an almshouse and off limits to the public. Among the historic sections that are open to public view are the Gothic undercroft where pilgrims used to sleep, the refectory where they dined, and the chapel where they prayed, with its soaring oak-beamed ceiling that's a marvel of 13th-century woodwork.

"These tranquil gardens, which border a channel of the Stour River, have recently been replanted to better reflect their medieval origins."

Next to the Eastbridge Hospital is the entrance to the **Fransciscan Gardens** (⌂ franciscangardens.org.uk ⌚ 10.00–17.00 Tue–Sun) on the grounds of England's first Franciscan Friary, built in 1267, during the lifetime of St Francis of Assisi. The only friary building to remain is the small **Greyfriars Chapel**, thought to have originally served as a guesthouse. One room of the building was used as a prison cell in the 19th century. These tranquil, hidden-away gardens, which border a channel of the Stour River, have recently been replanted to better reflect their medieval origins. They now include a meadow of grasses and wild flowers, a cutting garden packed with seasonal herbs, vegetables and flowers, and many newly planted fruit trees and willows. Quietly overseeing it all is a small statue of St Francis, rescued from the river in 2020.

On the northwest side of the King's Bridge over the Stour, is the **Old Weavers' House** (1–3 St Peter's St ⌂ weaversrestaurant.co.uk) one of Canterbury's most photographed buildings. The half-timbered structure, with foundations dating back to the 12th century, has long connections, as its name indicates, to the weaving industry. Some of the Walloon and

Huguenot refugees who settled in Canterbury in the 16th century are thought to have set up their looms here, producing cloth for the next 200 years. In addition, between 1899 and 1914, the building housed a weaving school to train women in the skill. Today the mainly Tudor-era interior is taken up by a restaurant which has an outdoor section overlooking the river and from which you can board the rowboat tours offered by Canterbury Historic River Tours (page 65).

THE KING'S MILE

Rather than a single street, the **King's Mile** (⌂ thekingsmile.org.uk) covers a series of contiguous and neighbouring streets east of the High Street and north of the cathedral. It's a picturesque district; at its heart is Palace Street, which is dotted with a good range of independent shops, cafés, bars and restaurants.

On the corner of Palace Street and King Street stands **Crooked House**, a comically wonky, early 17th-century half-timbered building, home now to the charity Catching Lives, second-hand bookshop. Alterations to an internal chimney are believed to have originally caused the structure to slip sideways and it's thought that the house inspired a description of a lop-sided property in Dickens' *David Copperfield* (the quote is inscribed across the building's façade). Although it looks like it could topple over any second, the building has long since been stabilised internally by a steel frame.

Opposite, at the bottom of The Borough, is a stone gate opening into the section of the cathedral precincts occupied by **The King's School**. England's oldest public school dates back to the cathedral's foundation and has had Royal Charter since 1541. The playwright Christopher 'Kit' Marlow was a student here, along with William Harvey, who discovered the circulation of blood, and the distinguished Tudor gardener John Tradescant. More recent 'Old King's Scholars' include the actor Orlando Bloom and author Michael Morpurgo. Girls were first admitted to the school in the early 1970s.

King's campus is spread over several buildings within and outside the old city walls. Within the King's Mile district, at 33–34 King Street, is the entrance to the school's music recital hall which occupies the

1 Old Weavers' House. **2** World War I memorial, Buttermarket. **3** Crooked House. **4** The Beaney House of Art & Knowledge. **5** The Goods Shed. **6** Butchery Lane. ▶

GORDON BELL/S

DMITRY NAUMOV/S

ANDREW FLETCHER/S

THE BEANEY/CANTERBURY MUSEUMS & GALLERIES

LOIS GOBE/S

Old Synagogue. This Jewish house of prayer, dating to 1848, has a distinctive Egyptian Revival style of architecture with a pair of 30ft-tall pillars flanking the doorway. Regular services ceased to be held here in 1911, but the record of Jews living in the Canterbury goes back to at least the 12th century when the city was home to major Jewish financiers of the day and their families. Another clue to this long-since vanished community is **Jewry Lane**, west of High Street.

WESTGATE & WESTGATE GARDENS

1 Pound Ln ✐ 01227 808755 ⊗ onepoundlane.co.uk ◷ museum noon–15.45 Sun–Fri

An excellent elevated view over Canterbury can be had from the battlements atop the 60ft-tall towers of **Westgate**. The sole intact survivor of the city's original seven gates, Westgate is also the largest medieval gate in England, built around 1380 as an extra defence for the city during the Hundred Years' War. Originally approached over a drawbridge, the gate and the connecting 19th-century buildings of 1 Pound Lane later did service as a gaol and police station. The history of the complex is explained in a small museum within the gate, which is accessed through The Pound Kitchen & Bar which now occupies the old police buildings. A fun way to experience the gate is to sign up to play one of the three **Escape Room** games here – full details are on the website.

The drawbridge across the Stour was replaced by a Kentish ragstone bridge in the 16th century and the wall between Westgate and the castle was demolished in 1647 during the English Civil War. Along this stretch of the Stour now runs **Westgate Gardens**, one of the prettiest of Canterbury's public parks. Before entering the gardens, peer from Westgate bridge over into the reed-filled stream to see if you can make out the 2008 artwork *Alluvia*. Created by Jason de Caires Taylor, the sculpture is of two female forms, cast in cement and recycled glass resin, that appear to be swimming along the riverbed.

Inside the gardens is the handsome **Tower House**, built around 1850 and incorporating a 14th-century bastion from the old city walls. The property, which can be hired for private events, was bequeathed to the city council in 1936, along with its surrounding gardens, to be enjoyed by the public. The garden's most extraordinary feature is a ridiculously chubby Oriental plane tree that is believed to be over 200 years old. A fine walk and cycle route runs through the gardens and along the Stour to the village of Chartham, three miles southwest.

ST DUNSTAN'S CHURCH

80 London Rd 🖉 01227 786109 ⟜ dunstanmildredpeter.org.uk ⊘ 09.30–16.30 daily

Walk five minutes from Westgate to the corner of London Road and St Dunstan's Street to find this modest-looking church named after a 10th-century Archbishop of Canterbury. Its most famous feature – the remains of Sir Thomas More's head – lies buried in a lead casket in an underground vault.

More was Lord High Chancellor to Henry VIII when he enraged the king by refusing to recognise the annulment of his marriage to Catherine of Aragon and his self-appointment as the head of the Church of England. More paid the price with his life and was executed on 6 July 1535. His head was mounted on a pike on London Bridge, but rescued by his beloved daughter Margaret, who had married Canterbury-based William Roper. It

"Its most famous feature – the remains of Sir Thomas More's head – lies buried in a lead casket in an underground vault."

was Margaret who had her father's remains interred in the Roper Vault at St Dunstan's; she and her descendants are also buried there. Beautiful stained-glass windows in the church's Roper Chapel include portraits of More, who was canonised in 1935, as well as members of his family and those involved in this episode of high Tudor drama.

It was from St Dunstan's that Henry II commenced his barefoot walk to Canterbury Cathedral on 12 July 1174, the first stage of his public penance for the murder of Thomas Becket (see box, page 46). This made the church an important calling point on the journeys of subsequent medieval pilgrims to the cathedral.

On your way to the church, take note of the **Roper Gate** on the north side of St Dunstan's Street. This fine example of decorative Tudor brickwork was once the entrance to the long-since demolished 16th-century Place House, home to William and Margaret Roper.

CANTERBURY CASTLE & DANE JOHN GARDENS

The Norman-era ruins of a **castle keep**, at the junction of the ring road and Wincheap, and close to Canterbury East train station, is the most prominent landmark of the city walls. The castle grounds, accessed off Gas Street, have been closed since 2017 because of falling masonry from the ruined structure; the city council plan repairs and it is hoped the site will reopen in the future.

Canterbury to Fordwich loop

✿ OS Explorer map 150; start: Canterbury West Station, Station Rd West, CT2 8AN ♀ TR145583; 6½ miles; easy

T his circular walk takes around 2½ hours at a steady pace, allowing time to see some of Canterbury's sights or linger over lunch at the **Fordwich Arms** (page 79), should you wish to make a day of it. The route is mostly along gravelled or paved roads. In winter, there can be some muddy patches along the Stour Valley, particularly in the woods near Fordwich.

1 With your back to the **station**, cross Station Road West (B2248) and enter Kirby's Lane immediately on the right. At the fork, go left, then right to continue along Orient Place to North Lane. Turn left, and then right on to The Causeway to cross a channel of the Great Stour River. After the second bridge, turn right and follow Pound Lane until you reach **Westgate**. Turn left on to St Peter's Street which merges into High Street.

2 Pause at **King's Bridge**; punts and sightseeing boats glide down this narrow channel of the Stour with the half-timbered **Old Weavers' House** on one side and **Eastbridge Hospital** on the other. Continue down High Street, past the handsome exterior of **The Beaney House of Art & Knowledge**, and turn left at Guildhall Street. At the four-way junction continue straight ahead along Palace Street, at the end of which is the **Crooked House**, one of Canterbury's most photographed buildings. Turn right on to Borough Street and follow the road round until you reach Broad Street; here, turn right and proceed to the junction with Military Road. Turn left, cross the road and continue to pedestrian St Thomas Place – turn right on to this street; after a short while, it connects to North Holmes Road which runs uphill past Canterbury Christ Church University campus.

3 When you reach the graveyard surrounding **St Martin's Church**, turn sharply left and climb uphill along St Martin's Avenue; the road will become a footpath that you'll follow to the junction with King's Park. Detour a short way to the left to view the remains of **St Augustine's Conduit House**, the 12th-century waterworks that supplied nearby St Augustine's Abbey. Turn right along King's Park, joining the footpath that leads out on to Chaucer Road; here, turn right again and walk to the crest of the hill, past the housing development on the former Howe army barracks. At the top of the hill, take the second of the two paths that veer left to follow a broad gravelled track across open ground. Walk straight on, crossing two cattle grids. Enjoy the sweeping views here across the countryside, speckled with bright yellow gorse between January and June.

4 Pass under power lines; where the gravel path veers left, **take the grass footpath on the right**, going downhill through a wooded area and across a couple of tiny footbridges.

Keep going until you reach the edge of **Canterbury Golf Club**. Cross the fairway, aiming for the signed footpath on the far side. Follow this path through the wood, over another footbridge to the edge of a crop field. A path cuts directly across the field; turn right at the end and follow the edge of the field out towards a stile which leads to a small lane past a row of cottages. At the junction you'll emerge on to King Street with **The George and Dragon** pub opposite.

5 You are now on the edge of tiny **Fordwich**, a charming village to explore (page 78) which includes the outstanding gourmet food pub the Fordwich Arms. For the return leg to Canterbury, you will be initially following part of the Stour Valley Path and National Cycle Network 1 – a signpost shows the way through the wooden gate next to The George and Dragon's car park. Note that the gravel path, which meanders through the meadow beside the Stour, can get flooded as this is the tidal limit of the Stour. The path eventually crosses a bridge, going into a sheltered area of mixed woodland. Continue walking along this easy-to-follow path for about ten more minutes.

6 The path forks shortly after a small fishing lake known as **Reed Pond** – stay on the right, following this route until you emerge on to Brymore Road with the Northgate Ward Community Centre on your left. Turn left, passing the community centre and walk along Military Road, past **All Saints Church**, turning to the left when you reach the city council offices. Continue across Chaucer Road to pedestrian Falala Way, then turn right at the junction with Craddock Drive. Follow the footpath off Craddock Drive, over Military Road and then alongside Tourtel Road to emerge near the Northgate roundabout.

7 Cross **Northgate** and walk through the car park towards Sainsbury's. Walk around the supermarket building to the car park's far left and join the footpath, following the Great Stour River back into the centre of Canterbury. Continue beside the river to St Radigunds Street. Turn right here and cross the road and a small footbridge over a branch of the river to enter pretty **Abbots Mill Gardens** – a water mill stood here for 800 years until it was destroyed by fire in 1933. A little of the mill's metalwork remains as a feature of the garden, part of which is planted with a community apple orchard.

8 Turn left out of the garden and follow the river around the back of the **Marlowe Theatre** to The Friars. The large face mask sculpture here is *Bulkhead* by Rick Kirby; it's made from scrap metal salvaged from ships around the Kent coast; Kirby was inspired by a line from Christopher Marlowe's *Doctor Faustus* about Helen of Troy being 'the face that launch'd a thousand ships'. Follow The Friars right past the theatre to High Street, then turn right. You are now on St Peter's Street: continue straight ahead, through Westgate and along St Dunstan's Street, back to the junction with Station Road West where a right turn will bring you back to the train station. ▶

Canterbury to Fordwich loop

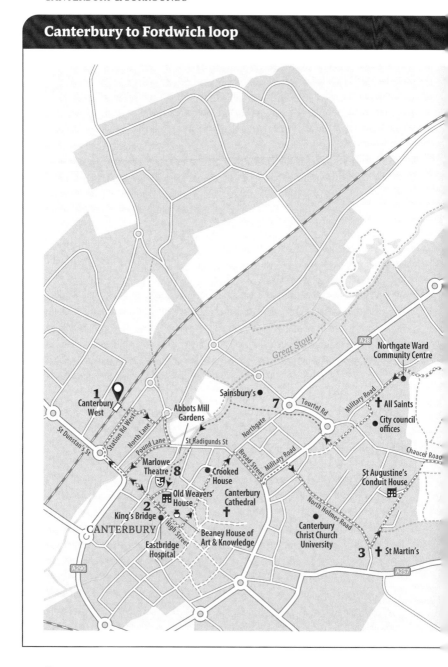

Great Stour

A28

Northgate Ward
Community Centre

Sainsbury's

1
Canterbury
West

7 Tourtel Rd

Military Road

✝ All Saints

St Dunstan's St

Station Rd West

North Lane

Pound Lane

Abbots Mill
Gardens

St Radigunds St

Northgate

City council
offices

Chaucer Road

Marlowe
Theatre

8

Crooked
House

Broad Street

Military Road

St Augustine's
Conduit House

Old Weavers'
House

Canterbury
Cathedral
✝

2
King's Bridge

High Street

North Holmes Road

CANTERBURY

Eastbridge
Hospital

Beaney House of
Art & Knowledge

Canterbury
Christ Church
University

Canterbury
Christ Church
University

3 ✝ St Martin's

A290

A257

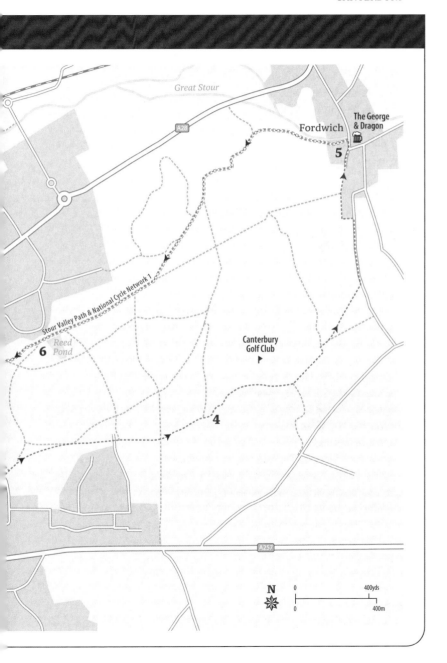

Great Stour

A28

Fordwich

The George
& Dragon

5

Stour Valley Path & National Cycle Network 1

Reed
Pond

6

Canterbury
Golf Club

4

A257

N

0		400yds
0		400m

The first Norman castle, built soon after 1066, was located in nearby **Dane John Gardens** which are bordered by the best-preserved stretch of the city walls; you can walk along the ramparts here to St George's Street. Dane John is a corruption of the Norman word *donjon* meaning a castle mound. However, the green hill (and viewpoint) that is the most prominent feature of the gardens dates back even further to AD1, when it was created as a Roman burial mound. The surrounding attractive gardens, laid out in the 18th century, also feature a Victorian bandstand, an avenue of 200-year-old lime trees and a modern fountain.

ENTERTAINMENT

The city's main annual event is the **Canterbury Festival** (✆ 01227 452853 ⊘ canterburyfestival.co.uk), which usually runs from mid-October to early November. Held in one form or another since the 1920s, this arts and culture festival covers it all, from classical music to themed walks around the city and surrounds. Venues include the cathedral, and cabaret and live music shows in the Spiegeltent, a temporary venue erected off Kingsmead Road near Sainsbury's.

Curzon Canterbury Westgate Hall Rd ✆ 03333 210104 ⊘ curzoncinemas.com. This cinema's three auditoriums have comfy seats in which to recline and watch mostly indie films and live screenings of plays, operas and other cultural events. There's also a lobby café-bar that's a pleasant hang-out in its own right. In 2022 another three-screen branch of the Curzon opened at the new commercial and retail development The Riverside (⊘ canterburyriverside.co.uk) on the River Stour.

Gulbenkian University of Kent ✆ 01227 769075 ⊘ thegulbenkian.co.uk. For over 50 years the University of Kent's arts centre has staged live theatre, cinema and other events.

Malthouse Theatre Malthouse Rd, off St Stephen's Rd ✆ 01227 287234 ⊘ malthousetheatre.co.uk. The King's School's state-of-the-art theatre, in the converted red-brick Victorian malthouse. Used mainly for student productions, it's a compact venue that's a useful addition to Canterbury's range of performance spaces.

Marlowe Theatre The Friars ✆ 01227 787787 ⊘ marlowetheatre.com. Taking its name from the Canterbury-born, 16th-century playwright Christopher (Kit) Marlowe, this contemporary venue borders the Stour. The theatre also manages and stages events at the **Marlowe Kit**, a 13th-century building on Stour Street that was once an almshouse for impoverished priests (hence it's also known as the Poor Priests Hospital).

TOURS

Three companies offer regularly scheduled and private punting or rowboat tours along the Stour. A couple more can expertly guide you on foot around the medieval heart of town.

Canterbury Guided Tours 📞 01227 459779 🌐 canterburyguidedtours.com. Founded back in 1948, all the guides for this reputable company have top level Blue and Green Badge accreditation. Their flagship tour (£10) departs from the Buttermarket at 11.00 daily year-round, with an additional 14.00 tour April to October. They last 90 minutes and gain you access to usually off-limits parts of the city such as The King's School.

Canterbury Historic River Tours 📞 01227 379600 🌐 canterburyrivertours.co.uk. Join informative day or evening rowboat tours that push off from the landing next to the Old Weavers' House, beside the central King's Bridge. The minimum fee is £40 for two people, plus £15 per additional adult. During October they also offer a 'chilling tales' themed tour.

Canterbury Punting Co Water Ln 📞 01227 464797 🌐 canterburypunting.co.uk. Young gents in natty waistcoats and straw boaters, with a good line in historical patter, are the 'chauffeurs' of these river tours in wooden punts. You can just show up and join a shared tour from £12 per person or book a private tour from £100 for a minimum of six people. Tours depart from the company's Mooring Café.

The Canterbury Tours 📞 0845 5190267 🌐 thecanterburytours.com. Tour guide and ghost hunter John Hippisley will take you on a journey into Canterbury's dark side on his 90-minute haunted-theme walks. He also offers a two-hour itinerary that reveals some of the city's hidden history. Rates start from £10 per person booked online.

Westgate Punts 📞 07494 170640 🌐 canterburypunts.uk. Make an advance booking or just show up at the moorings beside the Westgate bridge to join these punted tours of the Stour which last between 35 minutes and an hour depending on the route taken. The longer ones will get you out of the city into the countryside, where you may be lucky enough to see cormorants fishing for river eels.

FOOD & DRINK

Canterbury is an old hand at providing hospitality to visitors and you're bound to find somewhere that suits whatever you fancy – be it quaint tea room, real ale pub, ethnic or fine dining. Also look out on weekends for the street food market **City Feast** (🌐 cityfeast.co.uk) – during its 2021 season it was located along the Stour River next to the Marlowe Theatre.

Café des Amis 2 Westgate Grv 📞 01227 464390 🌐 cafédez.com 🕐 noon–22.00. A reliable fixture of the city's restaurant scene since 1988, this French-sounding place in an Olde English building actually serves tasty and good-value Mexican food. There's plenty on the menu to choose from, including fat burritos, sizzling fajitas and many vegan and gluten-free menu options.

The Corner House 1 Dover St 📞 01227 780793 🌐 cornerhouserestaurants.co.uk 🕐 noon–14.30 & 17.30–21.00 Mon–Sat, noon–15.00 & 18.00–20.30 Sun. A 16th-century

THE GOODS SHED

Station Rd West ℘ 01227 459153 (restaurant) ⟁ thegoodsshed.co.uk ☉ market: 09.00–17.00 Tue–Sat, 10.00–16.00 Sun; restaurant: noon–15.00 Tue–Sun, 18.00–21.00 Fri & Sat

Conclusive proof that Kent really *is* the garden of England, The Goods Shed has been showcasing the county's best food and drink from independent suppliers since 2002. The converted Victorian brick good shed next to Canterbury West train station is home to a farmers' market, gourmet food hall, restaurant, café-deli, and a cocktail bar with food counter. The nose-to-tail butchers sources meat from small-scale farms within a 20-mile radius of Canterbury, while fish and seafood is delivered straight from the fishing boats in Broadstairs daily. You'll also find an excellent range of fruit and vegetables grown across Kent, a delectable array of artisan cheeses, locally baked sourdough breads and craft ales from Docker, and wines from boutique vineyards and winemakers. The stalls provide ingredients used in the restaurant's dishes, such as wild bass with crab and tarragon broth, and duck liver parfait with pickled rhubarb. It's all delicious, but my favourite section is the bar **Wild Goose** (⟁ wildgoosefood.com), which serves inspired and inventive seasonal cocktails and tapas-style small plates of food.

coach house with wood-beamed ceilings is the atmospheric setting for this restaurant run by award-winning chef Matt Sworder. The menu is classy, solid gastropub food, big on local produce such as seafood from Broadstairs and duck and venison from the Stour Valley. They also have four rooms (but note there will be traffic noise from the city ring road outside).
The Foundry Brew Pub 77 Stour St ℘ 01227 455899 ⟁ thefoundrycanterbury.co.uk ☉ noon–midnight Mon–Sat, noon–18.00 Sun. At this award-winning craft brewery, distillery, bar and restaurant, you can enjoy some 16 unfiltered and unpasteurised lagers and ciders, all made on-site. The food menu mixes English pub classics such as fish and chips with American brewpub grub like nachos, burgers and beer-braised barbecue pork ribs. Located just off the High Street, it occupies a former Victorian industrial foundry where cast metal items such as lamp posts were made and exported around the world.
Garage Coffee 17 Sun St ⟁ garageroasted.co.uk ☉ 09.00–17.00 Mon–Sat, 10.00–16.00 Sun. Flagship store of the roaster whose flavoursome artisan coffees you'll find in good cafés across the region. Their signature 'Maypole' is a creamy blend of Mexican and Columbian beans with overtones of chocolate, fig and hazelnuts.
Kitch 4 St Peter's St ℘ 01227 504983 ⟁ kitchcafe.co.uk ☉ 09.00–17.00 daily. This cosy little café, with outdoor seating right on High Street, specialises in fresh homemade food made with seasonal ingredients, including free-range meat and eggs from local farms. There's a tempting range of breakfast/brunch options as well as plenty of dishes that are gluten-free or vegan. Also recommended for their wide range of coffee, tea and other drinks.

Moat Tea Rooms 67 Burgate ✆ 01227 784514 ⌂ moattearooms.co.uk ⊙ 9.00–17.00 Mon–Sat, 10.00–17.00 Sun. If this tea room's handsome 16th-century building doesn't stop you in your tracks then the freshly baked cakes displayed temptingly in the window are sure to. There are some 40 loose-leaf teas and infusions on offer and a decent range of coffee options. Their courtyard garden, accessed through the neighbouring shop, is like a secret oasis in the heart of Canterbury.

The Parrot 1–9 Church Ln, St Radigunds ✆ 01227 454170 ⌂ parrotcanterbury.co.uk ⊙ noon–23.00 Mon–Sat, noon–22.30 Sun. It may not be Canterbury's oldest continually run pub (that honour goes to the 15th-century King's Head on Wincheap), but The Parrot does occupy a building that dates back to 1370. Medieval beams, old oak floors and brick fireplaces make this an atmospheric place for a pint from Faversham-based brewery Shepherd Neame. The food menu has plenty of pub grub classics and there's also a courtyard beer garden.

Veg Box Café 17B Burgate ✆ 01227 456654 ⌂ thevegboxcafe.co.uk ⊙ 09.00–17.00 Sun–Wed, 09.00–22.00 Thu–Sat. From homemade granola and a full vegan breakfast to mango rainbow rolls and a creamy coconut Sri Lankan curry for dinner, this veggie café delivers wholesome, organic meals throughout the day. The salads are particularly appealing and include a range of fermented toppings. Outdoor tables facing Burgate are sheltered by a stone arcade.

SHOPPING

With its pedestrian High Street, good range of independent retailers and conveniently central Whitefriars shopping centre, Canterbury is a very pleasant place to indulge in some retail therapy.

CRAB & WINKLE WAY

Taking its name from the nickname given to the Victorian-era railway that once linked Canterbury to Whitstable, the eight-mile Crab & Winkle Way (⌂ crabandwinkle.org) is a cycle and walking route between the cathedral city and the coast. Following about 20% of the old railway line, which operated between 1830 and 1953, the way forms part of Route 1 (Inverness to Dover) of the National Cycle Network. It's mostly traffic free and passes through Blean Woods as well as the University of Kent campus. The pedal uphill out of Canterbury is the steepest section and there are more undulations around the middle stretch – catch your breath and rest at Winding Pond, dug out in 1829 to store the water needed for the steam engines that used to pull the carriages along the line. If you don't have your own wheels, bicycles can be hired in both Canterbury and Whitstable and full details of the route, including a downloadable map, can be found on the website.

The Chaucer Bookshop 6 Beer Cart Ln ⌂ chaucer-bookshop.co.uk ☺ 10.00–16.00 Mon–Sat. If you're looking for an antiquarian and second-hand bookshop in Canterbury (and there are plenty of them, including a decent Oxfam one on High Street), then this is the pick of the crop. Spread over two floors in an 18th-century building, their titles are neatly arranged by category. There's also an excellent range of vintage maps and prints, as well modern cards and wrapping paper.

Lilford Gallery 3 Palace St ⌂ lilfordgallery.com ☺ 10.00–17.00 Mon–Sat, 11.00–16.00 Sun. Specialising in original contemporary works of art, including many that take local locations as a theme, this is one of the city's standout galleries and well worth a browse. Alongside works by superstar creatives such as Tracy Emin, Damien Hurst and Sir Antony Gormley, look out for the layered, Canterbury streetscapes of Anna Allworthy.

Madame Oiseau 8 Borough ⌂ madame-oiseau.com ☺ 10.30–16.00 Tue–Sat. It's a family affair at this divine chocolate shop run by self-taught chocolatière, Sandrine May. Everything is handmade in small batches with the finest quality ingredients from the dark orangettes and milk chocolate rubber ducks to bars and slabs studded with candied ginger, dried fruit and nuts.

Platform 27 St Dunstan's St ⌂ platform-shop.co.uk ☺ 10.00–17.30 Wed–Sat, 11.00–16.00 Sun. Located beside the level crossing to Canterbury West train station, Platform specialises in 'uncommon goods' – by which they mean a tightly edited range of contemporary art, prints, textiles and homewares. Kent-based talents represented include Jim Moir (aka comedian Vic Reeves).

Rock Paper Scissors 22–24 Stour St ⌂ rockpaperscissors.co.uk ☺ 10.00–17.30 Mon–Sat, 10.30–16.30 Sun. Good things can come out of a pandemic. Screen-printer Liz Wellstead and her cousin and business partner Charlie Wilkie launched this gallery-like gift shop in 2020, and its selection of cool, creative homewares, jewellery, beauty products, artworks and more is inspired. You are guaranteed to find something unique and special, from Dawn Cole's cyanotype print kits to the matchbox collages of Andrew Malone.

NORTH & EAST OF CANTERBURY

🏠 **The Duke William** (page 307) ⛺ **Glamping at Preston Court** (page 307), **Nethergong Camping** (page 307)

A swathe of woodland, ideal for walks, occupies the high ground to the north and east of Canterbury. Emerging from the trees and descending to the coast, you'll encounter the seaside resort towns of Whitstable and Herne Bay. Further east along the coast stands the sentinel Reculver Towers and remains of a Roman fort, while inland are a couple more fine locations in which to encounter wildlife.

2 BLEAN WOODS NATIONAL NATURE RESERVE

Rough Common Rd, Rough Common CT2 9DD 🖉 01227 464898 🖉 rspb.org.uk

Canterbury is blessed with having these woods, a haven of biodiversity and Site of Special Scientific Interest, practically on its doorstep. Covering 11 square miles, this nature reserve is a series of adjacent ancient woodlands north of Canterbury including Thornden Wood, East and West Blean Woods and Clowes Wood. From the old English word *blean*, meaning 'rough ground', the wood is managed by a partnership of various bodies including the RSPB, Kent Wildlife Trust and the Woodland Trust. It's a rich woodland habitat including oak, beech, conifers, hornbeam and sweet chestnut. In late spring, swathes of bluebells carpet the forest floor. A haven for endangered woodland birds, such as nightingales, woodpeckers and nightjars, the woods are also the breeding ground for the largest UK population of the rare heath fritillary – a butterfly you are most likely to see fluttering through the foliage in June and July.

Since 2022 there has been much excitement in West Blean and Thornden Woods, where four European bison have been introduced alongside three Exmoor ponies in a large fenced-off section of the forest. Free roaming elsewhere in the woods are four longhorn cattle and four Iron Age pigs. All are part of the Wilder Blean rewilding project (page 77). There are excellent walking trails across the reserve, including the Big Blean Walk, a 25-mile waymarked route that draws a circle route through the woods between Stelling in the west and Hicks Forstal in the east. In Thornden Woods you'll also find the Blean Wildart Trail, a one-mile easy-to-follow loop that takes you past wood-carved artworks, a tunnel woven from willow and many informational sign boards about the rich variety of surrounding trees.

3 WHITSTABLE

🏠 **The Front Rooms** (page 307), **Hotel Continental** (page 306)

Long popular with the 'DFL' (down from London) set, Whitstable's shabby chic appeal lies in that it has never severed ties with its fishing and boatbuilding roots. The colourful sail craft spread across the town's shingle beaches and bobbing in its working harbour easily outnumber the trendy design shops and artisan cafés. Urban hipsters may now prefer Margate and Folkestone, but there's still plenty in Whitstable's favour as a cool weekend getaway, not least its laid-back vibe, gourmet food scene and superb opportunities for coastal walking.

And there are oysters, which Whitstable fisherfolk have been harvesting from the Thames Estuary since Roman times. In the mid 19th century the town supplied London with an incredible 700 million bivalves a year. Sadly, the local oyster fields were devastated by an imported parasite in 1921, and now native oysters (*Ostrea edulis*) are a rarity. Instead, it's mainly cultivated European or rock oysters (*Crassostrea gigas*) which are served up in Whitstable's seafood shacks and restaurants; these are also the ones you can safely eat year-round, rather than only in months with an 'r' in them.

If you are an oyster fan, then bookmark the end of August in your diary for the **Oyster Festival** (⊘ whitstableoysterfestival.co.uk). The town's other big event is the visual arts **biennale** (⊘ whitstablebiennale.com), with a focus on young and emerging artists and experimental works.

Town centre & west to Seasalter

To find out more about the town's history of oyster fishing and shipbuilding, start by paying a visit to the interesting **Whitstable Museum** (Foresters' Hall, 5A Oxford St ⊘ 01227 264742 ⊘ whitstablemuseum.org). Also on display here is the Invicta steam locomotive built by George and Robert Stevenson for the 19th-century railway that connected Whitstable to Canterbury; and an exhibit on Peter Cushing, the Hammer horror actor, who also played Dr Who and who was a town resident for 35 years until his death in 1994.

From the museum, head straight to the seafront, where the shingle beach, stabilised by a toothcomb of timber groynes, is fringed with clumps of green sea cabbage, pink and white valerian and yellow ragwort. Walking west you'll pass the Old Neptune pub (page 73), charming sea-facing cottages, a caravan park and a row of rustic, multicoloured beach huts. Keep going for another couple of miles to arrive at the village of Seasalter, location of The Sportsman, one of Kent's top restaurants (page 74). There are glorious views on this walk towards the Isle of Sheppey and the light is amazing towards sunset.

Returning to Whitstable's town centre, it's always worth swinging by the **Horsebridge Arts Centre** (11 Horsebridge Rd ⊘ 01227 281174 ⊘ thehorsebridge.org.uk) to see what exhibition they have on.

◀ **1** Reculver Towers. **2** Stodmarsh National Nature Reserve. **3** Blean Woods.
4 Wheelers Oyster Bar, Whitstable.

BOAT TRIPS FROM WHITSTABLE

Whitstable harbour is the starting point for boat tours out into the Thames Estuary to view up close the rusting remains of the World War II defensive Red Sands Sea Fort as well as the Kentish Flats Offshore Wind Farm. Part of a network of Maunsell Forts, named after their designer Nigel Maunsell, the Red Sands Fort, comprised of five gun towers, a searchlight tower and a central control tower, was built in 1942 to protect London from airstrikes and sea raids. In the 1960s they were taken over by pirate radio stations but more recently they have been the focus of a preservation effort; see ⊘ project-redsand.com for more details.

The most elegant vessel on which to approach these otherworldly structures is the *Greta* (⊘ 07711 657919 ⊘ greta1892.co.uk), an 80ft sailing barge built in 1892; winds permitting, *Greta*'s sails will be raised for part of what can be up to a six-hour round trip, starting from £54 per person. Shorter tours on motor-powered boats, for around £40, are offered by **Oyster Coast Watersports** (⊘ 01227 806108 ⊘ oystercoastwatersports.co.uk) and also by **Whitstable Boat Trips** (⊘ 07383 441811 ⊘ whitstableboattrips.co.uk). These operators also run jaunts to a sandbar at the Swale River's mouth where sightings of seals are pretty much guaranteed.

Harbour to Tankerton

Whitstable's working harbour is a hive of activity with fishing tugs and sail boats coming and going, a fish and seafood market and a lively **harbour market** (⊘ harbourmarketwhitstable.co.uk) of craft stalls and food and drink outlets. Keeping it real is the harbour's gravel processing plant; outside its gates is *Gamecock*, a 1906 vessel that is one of the few remaining oyster smacks built in Whitstable, and which is in the process of being restored.

Continuing eastwards along the coast, past a row of almshouses, is Tower Hill and the gatehouse to **Whitstable Castle** (⊘ 01227 281726 ⊘ whitstablecastle.co.uk). Never a fortress, this castellated mansion was built in the 1790s as a private home and was previously known as Tankerton Towers. Today it's the focal point for a delightful public park packed with flower beds, shady trees, a bowling green and kids' play area. It's also one of the nicest spots in town for tea (page 74).

Past the castle grounds, you can either stick to the high ground of Tankerton's grassy clifftop or descend to the beachside promenade, which is lined with painted wooden chalets.. Low tide will reveal the Street, a sandbank that runs at right angles to the shingle beach for about half a mile.

¶¶ FOOD & DRINK

You've not really had the full Whitstable experience until you've slurped a freshly shucked oyster beside its shingle beaches or working harbour. The largest purveyor of them is the **Whitstable Oyster Fisheries Company** (⌔ whitstable.rocks) set up by an Act of Parliament in 1793. It has its hand in several local operations, including the **Royal Native Oysters Stores** and the **Lobster Shack** beach bar. If oysters are not to your taste, fear not, as there are plenty of alternative options.

Blueprint Coffee 4 Oxford St, Whitstable ⌚ 09.00–15.00 Mon, Wed & Thu, 09.00–16.00 Fri & Sat, 10.00–16.00 Sun. Nirvana for artisan coffee lovers, the skilled baristas at this minimalist café and bookshop make wonderful espressos, flat whites and drip-filter coffees. Their regularly changing choice of beans come with tasting notes. While you wait for your brew, browse their neatly displayed and curated selection of books and coffee-connected goodies.

The Cheese Box 60 Harbour St ⌔ thecheesebox.co.uk ⌚ 10.00–15.00 Mon, 10.00–16.00 Wed & Thu, 10.00–17.00 Fri & Sat, 11.00–16.00 Sun. Since 2008 this shop has been specialising in the very best selection of British cheeses. Whatever your taste in cheeses – be it soft, hard, blue, washed rind or those made with sheep or goats' milk – you are sure to find it here. There's also a small bar where you can enjoy tapas plates of cheese served with wine.

JoJo's 2 Herne Bay Rd, Tankerton ⌕ 01227 274591 ⌔ jojosrestaurant.co.uk ⌚ noon–16.30 Thu–Sat, 18.00–22.30 Wed–Sat, noon–17.00 Sun. Overlooking the beach at Tankerton, JoJo's is a stylish little treasure specialising in Mediterranean meze dishes mostly made with local ingredients – even some grown in their own garden. The interior has a touch of Ibiza glamour to it. They are also open for lunch on Wednesdays during school holidays.

The Old Neptune Marine Tce, Whitstable ⌕ 01227 272262 ⌔ thepubonthebeach.co.uk ⌚ 11.30–20.30 Mon–Sat, noon–20.30 Sun. There's been a pub right next to the shingle beach since the early 19th century, and 'The Neppy', as it is affectionately known to its regulars, is the current incarnation. It's the best spot to enjoy a drink while watching the sunset and they also serve decent pub grub.

Pearson's Arms Horsebridge Rd, Whitstable ⌕ 01277 773133 ⌔ pearsonsarmswhitstable. co.uk ⌚ noon–23.00 Mon–Thu, noon–21.00 Fri & Sat, noon–18.00 Sun. Climb the stairs at this seaside pub to find a relaxed bistro with a solid and unpretentious menu of local seafood, meat and vegetable dishes. If you're not so hungry – or want to try a cross section of their menu – their small plates are the way to go and include mouth-watering options such as salt and pepper squid with soy ponzu sauce – delicious with their perfectly crispy triple-cooked chips.

Samphire 4 High St, Whitstable ⌕ 01227 770075 ⌔ samphirewhitstable.co.uk ⌚ 08.00–21.30 Sun–Thu, 08.00–22.00 Fri & Sat. It's all good at this Kentish bistro, whether you're here for a breakfast of fluffy pancakes topped with crispy bacon, a supper of their fish pie or a rump of Romney Marsh lamb served with wild garlic and local asparagus.

The Sportsman Faversham Rd, Seasalter CT5 4BP ℘ 01227 273370 ⬦ thesportsmanseasalter. co.uk ⏱ noon–20.30 Mon–Sat. Bookings are essential for this lonely seaside pub, around four miles west of Whitstable, which looks an unlikely candidate for one of the most feted restaurants in Kent. All doubts evaporate once the dishes from chef-patron Stephen Harris' multi-course taster menu start to arrive at the table. Ingredients are seasonal and hyper local – some sourced from the pub's own polytunnel and kitchen garden.

Tower Hill Tea Gardens Tower Hill, Whitstable ⏱ 10.00–16.00 daily. An adorable wooden shack with a thatched roof (including two thatched birds!) serves up teas, coffees, cakes and sandwiches to be enjoyed in a verdant, flower-filled garden with breezy coastal views. On a sunny day, it's a little piece of heaven.

Wheelers Oyster Bar 8 High St, Whitstable ℘ 01227 273311 ⬦ wheelersoysterbar.com ⏱ 10.00–16.00 Mon & Tue, 10.00–17.00 Thu–Sun. Founded in 1865 by the wonderfully named Richard Leggy Wheeler, this pink-painted beauty is one of the best restaurants in town for a seafood feast, which might include crab cakes, monkfish marinated in buttermilk and honey, or lobster lasagne. If you don't want to eat in, pre-order a gourmet picnic box or see what takes your fancy at their shopfront raw bar.

🛍 SHOPPING

A **farmers' market** (⬦ whitstablefarmersmarket.com) is held at the Old Coal Yard, Belmont Road, opposite the Labour Club, every second and fourth Saturday of the month between 09.00 and 13.00 – pick up organic produce and deli delights from the likes of the Cheesemakers of Canterbury.

There's a fine selection of independent shops and galleries to browse along High Street, which merges into Harbour Street. Swing by **Frank** (65 Harbour St ⬦ frankworks.eu ⏱ 10.30–17.00 Mon, Wed–Fri, 10.30–17.30 Sat, 11.00–17.00 Sun) for its always interesting selection of contemporary works by crafters, artists and printmakers, many from north Kent.

Lovers of vintage and retro clothing, furniture and homewares will also have a field day in Whitstable, with **Valentines** (21 Oxford St ⬦ valentines-vintage.com ⏱ 10.00–17.30 Sat, 11.00–16.00 Sun) always offering eye-catching and affordable pieces.

4 HERNE BAY

In many respects Herne Bay conforms to the classic blueprint of a British seaside town. The beach, like that at Whitstable five miles west, is shingle divided by groynes. Along the attractive promenade is a pier, an Art Deco bandstand, sunken gardens, then something unique: a

Portland stone **clock tower**, the gift of a wealthy Victorian widow Anne Thwaytes. The 82ft timepiece, opened in a grand ceremony in 1837 that included a military band, circus acts and fireworks, is a cherished local landmark and adds a note of architectural gravitas to a seafront peppered with amusement arcades and fish and chip shops.

Fairground attractions, food and drinks stalls and a local crafts market occupy the cheerfully painted stub of what was once the UK's second-longest **pier** (⌀ hernebaypier.co.uk). Since 1980, when much of the degraded boardwalk was demolished, the pier head has been stranded some 3,700ft out to sea, framed on the horizon by a wind farm and the darker forms of the World War II Maunsell Forts (page 72). The best view of the disintegrating pier head and back towards land can be had from the end of **Neptune's Arm**, a concrete breakwater built just east of the pier in the 1990s to protect the town from sea flooding.

Herne Bay's more historic houses are clustered towards its eastern end where grassy Beacon Hill is the location for the handsome Edwardian entertainment venue **The King's Hall** (⌀ thekingshall.com). Wander back into the town centre along Charles Street, aiming for the **Seaside Museum** (12 William St ✆ 01227 367 368 ⌀ theseasidemuseumhernebay. org ☉ 11.00–14.00 Thu & Sat) which has a small but interesting collection of local exhibits and artefacts.

While not as fashionably arty as Whitstable, Herne Bay is not without its creative corners. Art galleries are dotted around town, the best of them being the blue-painted **She Rose** (165 Mortimer St ⌀ jooakley. co.uk ☉ 10.00–16.00 Thu–Sat), the studio space of painter and linocut print artist Jo Oakley. Jo occasionally holds linocutting classes here as well as other events. Also search out **Beach Creative** (Beach St ✆ 0300 1111913 ⌀ beachcreative.org ☉ 10.00–16.00 Tue–Sun), a community gallery focusing on local artists in a building that includes a café and the tourist office.

¶¶ FOOD & DRINK

A Casa Mia 60 High St ✆ 01227 372947 ⌀ acasamia.co.uk ☉ 17.00–23.00 Mon–Thu, noon–15.30 & 17.00–23.30 Fri & Sat, noon–22.00 Sun. The pizzas at chef Gennaro Esposito's restaurant meet the exacting standards of the pizza grading authorities in his hometown of Naples. These delicious rounds of pliable dough, topped with the finest quality ingredients, including homemade pork sausage or beef and chicken meatballs, emerge with perfectly charred crusts from the restaurant's wood-fired beehive oven.

Bay Leaf Coffee House 133 Mortimer St 🕾 01227 370461 🕘 09.00–16.00 Mon–Sat, 10.00–16.00 Sun. This dog-friendly café specialises in Sri Lankan food, including curries and hoppers – bowl-shaped pancakes made from fermented rice flour and coconut milk. The coffee is by local roasters Garage coffee and the teas from Margate-based Chai Wallah. They also have some amazing cakes, including a divine vegan chocolate cake.

Four Fathoms, High St 🕾 01227 364411 🖉 ourfathoms.co.uk 🕘 16.00–23.00 Thu & Fri, noon–23.00 Sat & Sun. Part of the Shepherd Neame stable of pubs, this classy boozer, a block back from the promenade, is highly rated for its modern British food menu. The choice of ingredients is inspired, from Kentish pork cheeks in their version of osso buco to pulled barbecued jackfruit for a vegan burger.

Wallflower Café 116 High St 🕾 01227 740392 🖉 vegan-café.co.uk 🕘 09.00–17.00 Tue– Sat. Tucked away at the rear of its High Street location, with windows facing on to a car park, Wallflower is worth searching out for its creative and nutritious vegan food which includes non-meat versions of burgers, sausage rolls and fish-finger sandwiches. Try the smoky beans on toast with feta or a daily special such as the bang bang broccoli wrap.

5 RECULVER TOWERS & ROMAN FORT

Reculver Ln, Reculver CT6 6SS; free entry; English Heritage

Easily visible from Herne Bay, three miles to the west, the majestic ruins of the medieval Church of St Mary and the Roman fort Regulbium cut a dramatic dash atop the grassy banks of an eroded promontory. From around AD200 to 400, the Roman fort protected the mouth of the long-since silted up Wantsum Channel which once separated the Isle of Thanet from the rest of Kent.

Half of the land occupied by the fort has long since been washed away, with just the scant ruins of the east wall and a small guard chamber remaining. In the 7th century the monastery of St Mary's was founded here and King Eadbehrt II of Kent was buried here in the 760s. Although the church thrived for centuries, it could not withstand the forces of nature chipping away at the coastline. Much of the complex was torn down in 1805 to build another church on safer ground further inland, with the twin 12th-century towers spared because of their usefulness as a navigational aid.

A great way to get here is to walk or cycle from Herne Bay along the **Oyster Bay Trail**, a coastal route that runs for just under seven miles from Swalecliffe through to **Reculver Country Park**, which protects this important location for bird and insect life. The park's main car park and its visitor centre, which includes a decent **café** (🖉 hathats.co.uk

☺ Apr–Oct 08.00–19.00 daily; Nov–Mar 09.00–16.00 Mon–Fri, 08.00–17.00 Sat & Sun), are just below the site ruins. It's the ideal spot to rest and gaze out to the shallow waters of the estuary where Barnes Wallis and his team tested prototypes of the 'bouncing bombs' used in the dam buster raids on Germany during World War II.

6 WILDWOOD

Wealden Forest Park, Canterbury Rd, Herne Common CT6 7LQ ✆ 01227 712111
⌂ wildwoodtrust.org ☺ 10.00–17.00 daily

Unlike other Kent wildlife parks where the big game and primates of Africa are the star attractions, at Wildwood the focus is on native species. Run by conservation charity the Wildwood Trust, there is everything from large European brown bears to badgers and adders. Conservation and education are at the heart of what Wildwood does and among their programmes are ones to help save the endangered species such as the Eurasian beaver, water vole, hazel dormouse and red squirrel, as well as using wild horses and even bison (see box, below) to help restore Kent's nature reserves. There's a good café and a kids' play area on the 40-acre site.

BISON IN KENT: THE WILDER BLEAN PROJECT

Some 6,000 years after their ancestors died out in the UK, European bison are being introduced into Kent's West Blean and Thornden Woods as part of Wilder Blean, a project managed jointly by the Wildwood Trust and Kent Wildlife Trust (KWT) that aims to reverse rapid species loss in the woodlands. Thanks to a £1 million grant from People's Postcode Lottery, four bison – one male and three females – have been freely roaming across a 500-acre fenced section of the woods, away from public footpaths, since spring 2022. The bison are part of a controlled trial to see if Europe's largest land animal can help in the natural management of the woodlands, leading to increased biodiversity. Alongside the bison, small numbers of other grazing animals - longhorn cattle, Iron Age pigs and Exmoor ponies – have also been released in the woods. Each will interact with the woodland in different and hopefully beneficial ways. Referred to as 'ecosystem engineers', the bison munch their way through brambles, create dust baths and eat bark, eventually killing trees, thus naturally clearing and opening up the wood for others species to have a chance to thrive. KWT are already offering expert-led wildlife 'safaris' in the woods to explain more about this exciting rewilding project. In the meantime, if you want to be sure of sighting bison, of which there are only about 2,500 globally, a pair of captive-bred animals, Haydes and Orsk, are part of the collection at Wildwood.

7 STODMARSH NATIONAL NATURE RESERVE

10 Stour Valley Cl, Upstreet CT3 4DB ✆ 0845 600 3078 ♦ gov.uk; free entry

Midway between Canterbury and Margate on the Great Stour River is this nature reserve, owned by Natural England. It measures only one square mile, but protects the largest reedbed in southeast England. It's a habitat that is favoured by birds such as the marsh harrier and

"The reserve is also a sanctuary for migrating birds such as swallows and house martins in the summer and starlings in the winter."

the rare bittern that fishes for roach, rudd and eels between the reeds. When they feel threatened, the bittern tilt their long, pointed beaks into the air and sway to blend in with the reeds. The reserve is also a sanctuary for migrating birds such as swallows and house martins in the summer and starlings in the winter; sometimes thousands of birds can be seen here as they stop overnight before continuing their journey in the morning. Along the designated nature trails are five hides from which to observe birds.

It's not just about birdlife here, however. Stodmarsh also harbours other rare species of wildlife including the shining ramshorn snail and water voles, although you're unlikely to spot either of these small creatures during any walks here. The nearest train station is Sturry, five miles southwest, from which it's around an hour's walk via Fordwich. Refreshments can be had at the ivy-covered **Grove Ferry Inn** (Grove Ferry Rd, Upstreet CT3 4BP ✆ 01227 860302 ♦ groveferryinn.co.uk), a pleasant pub with a terrace and beer garden right next to the Stour River.

8 FORDWICH

This pretty village is just under three miles northeast of Canterbury; the closest train station is Sturry, a ten-minute walk north across the Stour. The Romans built their road to Reculver across the river here and in 1184 King Henry II granted Fordwich a Merchant Guild Charter; it remains a limb of the cinque port of Sandwich, which is the reason this tiny place can claim to be 'Britain's smallest town'. In the Middle Ages, before the upper reaches of the Stour had silted up and were still navigable, the Caen stone used to build Canterbury Cathedral was offloaded in Fordwich, the closest point that boats could reach the city.

Everything in Fordwich is less than a few minutes' walk from each other. The decommissioned **St Mary's Church**, parts of which date back to the late 11th century, is the central landmark; if it's open, step inside to admire the 17th-century pew boxes and wall paintings, as well as the mysterious Fordwich Stone. This 5½ft-long oolitic limestone block is carved with a pattern of Norman arches holding up what looks like a scalloped tile roof. Legend has it that it once housed relics of St Augustine. Over the centuries, the stone has shuttled back and forth between here and Canterbury Cathedral, returning to rest in Fordwich in 1877. It's possible to 'camp' overnight inside St Mary's, booking via ⊘ champing.co.uk.

Fordwich's adorable miniature **Town Hall**, built in 1544, is only accessible on Sundays between May and September (⊙ 13.30 to 16.00) but you can always stand outside admiring its herringbone brickwork, blackened timber beams and stone undercroft.

The best way to experience the languid waterways of the Stour around Fordwich is to contact locally based **Canoe Wild** (⊘ 07947 835688 ⊘ canoewild.co.uk). They rent out canoes, kayaks and paddleboards, or you can join one of their guided paddle tours, or take private or group lessons.

ᵗ⌶ FOOD & DRINK

Fordwich Arms King St, CT2 0DB ⊘ 01227 710444 ⊘ fordwicharms.co.uk ⊙ pub noon–23.00 Tue–Sat, noon–18.00 Sun; restaurant noon–14.30 & 18.00–21.00 Tue–Sat, noon–16.00 Sun. Treat yourself to a top-notch gourmet meal in this handsome 1930s oak-panelled dining room and bar. Rising culinary star chef-patron Daniel Smith creates seasonal menus that draw on the best Kentish ingredients, sourced direct from local farms and producers.

9 HOWLETTS WILD ANIMAL PARK & SURROUNDS

Bekesbourne Ln, Bekesbourne, Littlebourne CT4 5EL ⊘ 01227 721286 ⊘ aspinallfoundation.org/howletts ⊙ Mar–Oct 09.30–18.00 daily; Nov–Feb 09.30–17.00 daily; last entry 90 mins before closing

The Aspinall family have run this 90-acre park, three miles south of Canterbury, since 1957. Today it's part of a conservation charity which is also responsible for Port Lympne near Hythe (page 228) and which has done sterling work in helping to save and breed rare and critically endangered species such as western lowland gorilla, black rhino and clouded leopard. The Aspinall Foundation has committed to rewilding the park's entire herd of 13 African elephants and at the time of research was raising the funds to undertake this ambitious project. There are a lot more animals that will remain part of the Howletts menagerie, although don't come expecting guaranteed sightings – the animals are allowed to roam freely in spacious enclosures that include appropriate foliage and shelter. Chances are high, though, that you will encounter some of the many primates – Howletts has more of them than any other wildlife park in the UK. It's also possible to have your own experience of swinging through the trees on the Treetops Challenge high-ropes course, while back at ground level there's a woodland walk past life-sized recreations of Ice Age animals including a woolly mammoth and sabre-toothed smilodon.

"Don't come expecting guaranteed sightings – the animals roam freely in spacious enclosures."

Next to Howletts is **Woolton Farm** (CT4 5EA ✆ 01227 250151 ⌂ wooltonfarm.co.uk ⏲ 10.00–18.00 Thu–Sat, 10.00–16.00 Sun), an award-winning producer of wines and ciders. The heart of the farm is its vast thatched-roof **barn**, a building dating back to the 14th century, in which you can sample Woolton's various tipples. There are always five or more of its delicious Kentish Pip Ciders on tap and they also serve teas, coffee, cakes, bakes and other light snacks. In a fruit garden behind the barn are eight bell tents that can be rented for basic overnight accommodation (you'll need to bring your own linens); the farm also has three self-catering properties.

SOUTH & WEST OF CANTERBURY

⌂ **Beechborough** (page 307), **The Pig – at Bridge Place** (page 306)

There are several charming villages south and west of Canterbury, along the course of the Stour River and close by the uplands of the North Downs, the pick of which is Chilham which is at the crossroads of the Pilgrims and the North Downs ways. En route there from the cathedral city you might also want to linger in Chartham which has several attractions that will appeal to lovers of good food and wine.

South of Canterbury, there are fine walks around the tiny village of Bishopbourne, which for a small place it has several claims to fame. Joseph Conrad, the author of *Heart of Darkness* and *The Secret Agent*,

---

1 Chilham Castle. **2** Chartham Vineyard. ▶

Bishopbourne, Bridge & Petts Bottom walk

✿ OS Explorer map 150; start: Mermaid Inn, The Street, Bishopsbourne CT4 5HX
♥ TR190524; 4½ miles; easy

- -

This circular walk follows a short section of the Elham Valley Way as it shadows the Nailbourne, a tributary of the Stour; it takes around two hours. Foodies will want to make a whole day out by combining the walk with a meal at one of three high-quality restaurants along the route. It begins at the attractive village of Bishopbourne, little more than a couple of streets, which is so named because the Archbishop of Canterbury owned the land around here from 11th century.

1 From the Mermaid Inn (✆ 01227 830581 ⏁ mermaidinnbishopsbourne.co.uk ⊙ noon–21.00 Mon–Wed, noon–22.00 Thu, noon–23.00 Fri & Sat, noon–19.00 Sun), an attractive red-brick pub with a beer garden, walk north down The Street towards the junction with Frog Lane (to the right) and Crows Camp Road (to the left). Along the way, note the pretty cottages, including Ivy Cottage, home to the novelist and botanical writer Jocelyn Brook, and the Arts and Crafts village hall, named Conrad Hall after Joseph Conrad.

2 Immediately to the right of 13th-century St Mary's Church (CT4 5JB ⏁ barhamdownschurches. org.uk/bishopsbourne.htm ⊙ 10.00–16.00 Thu–Sun) is the gateway to Oswalds, the modest villa in which Joseph Conrad spent the final five years of his life. Inside St Mary's, note the west window with stained glass by Burne-Jones and William Morris, while in the graveyard the grave of Revd Joseph Bancroft Reade lies close to the church's north wall. Head to the east side of the graveyard and go through a gate into the parkland of Bourne House.

3 Keep going until you reach **Bourne House**. Built in 1701, this is considered the finest Queen Anne building in Kent. You'll get superb views of its red-brick façade as you follow the footpath, which runs beside the Nailbourne that flows through the lake in front of the house. Out of sight, behind the house, a tunnel was dug for the old Elham Valley railway line so that the views from Bourne would not be disrupted. During World War II a rail-mounted howitzer was hidden away in the tunnel, ready to be rolled out if need to fight the enemy. After admiring Bourne House, continue north along Bourne Park Road. On the right you'll pass the turn off for a footpath that is a slightly shorter route to the junction with Bridge Hill.

4 A few hundred yards further on the left, a driveway off Bourne Park Road leads to **The Pig – at Bridge Place** (Bourne Park Rd, Bridge, CT4 5BH ✆ 01227 830208 ⏁ thepighotel.com ⊙ noon–14.30 & 18.30–21.30 daily). Dating to around 1638, Bridge Place has had a colourful history, including a stint as a live music venue and nightclub in the 1960s and 70s that hosted such rock legends as the Kinks, Pink Floyd and Led Zepellin. The Pig hotel group

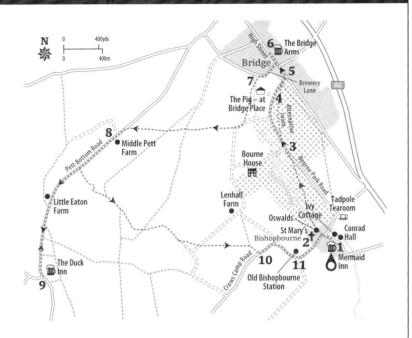

have transformed the house, playing up its heritage and boho rock 'n' roll elements, and adding on an excellent restaurant and a superb walled kitchen garden that is a joy to admire and open to non-guests.

5 At the junction of Bourne Park Road and **Bridge Hill**, turn left and walk along High Street and into the village, past St Peter's Church.

6 Further along the High Street are several pubs, the best of which for food is **The Bridge Arms** (53 High St, CT4 5LA 𝒥 01227 286534 ⊘ bridgearms.co.uk ⊙ noon–22.00 Tue–Sun). This 16th-century coaching inn has had new life breathed into it by Daniel and Natasha Smith, the young team who have also transformed the Fordwich Arms in Fordwich (page 79) into such a gourmet success. From the Bridge Arms, backtrack along High Street and then turn right into Brewery Lane, following it around into Mill Lane.

7 Shortly after the corner, a **footpath** on the left, leads across fields that run alongside the boundary of The Pig – at Bridge Place. Where the footpath joins a farm track, turn right and keep going in the same direction along the footpath, with a hedge to your left. The track goes uphill and across a bridge that spanned the old Elham Valley railway route, which closed in 1947. ▶

Bishopbourne, Bridge & Petts Bottom walk continued ...

Keep on in a straight direction across the fields until the path emerges on Pett Bottom Road beside Middle Pett Farm.

8 At the **farm** turn left and walk for a mile down Pett Bottom Road to the **The Duck Inn** (Petts Bottom, CT4 5PB ✆ 01227 830354 ⌂ theduckpettbottom.com ⏲ noon–22.30 Wed–Sat, noon–16.00 Sun). This isolated gastropub, which gets a name check in Ian Fleming's *You Only Live Twice*, just happened to be a favourite country pub of Bond's creator. A blue plaque outside the pub makes the bold claim that Fleming wrote *You Only Live Twice* while staying here – an unlikely fiction, even for the hard-drinking author. The Duck Inn is also notable for having a wishing well and a pair of stocks outside its front door.

9 From **The Duck Inn**, retrace your steps back along Pett Bottom Road, passing Little Eaton Farm, to find the **footpath** on the right that cuts through the fields. Take this path and keep going, with the hedge to your left, then head through a gap in the hedges and over an open field towards a small wood. The path follows the edge of the wood. After about 400yds, turn sharply left, away from the wood, and cross the field, aiming for a track going into the woodland ahead. Head into the woods and then out again, following the footpath with a field to your left and the woods to your right.

10 When you reach a much larger field, fork left across it, aiming towards the chimneys of the Crows Camp property; the buildings of Lenhall Farm should also be visible to your left. Where the footpath joins **Crows Camp Road**, turn left and follow the road back into Bishopsbourne.

11 As you cross the bridge, look down to the left to see the old **Bishopsbourne train station**; even though it's now a private residence the platform and signals have been retained. A footpath on the right cuts across the field to join up with Park Lane; follow this back to the Mermaid Inn. Alternatively, for another food option, stick to Crows Camp Road and head past the church and along Frog Lane to the junction with Bourne Park Road. Opposite is the entrance to the commercial compound where you'll find the convivial **Tadpole Tearoom** (Frog Ln, CT4 5HR ✆ 01227 830178 ⌂ tadpoletearoom.com ⏲ 08.30–17.00 Tue–Sun) serving a good range of light meals and caffeinated drinks.

lived in the village from 1919 until his death in 1924, as did the Revd Joseph Bancroft Reade, who was the rector of Bishopsbourne's St Mary's church from 1863 to 1870. A scientific man of the cloth, he was the first Englishman to photograph the moon and was a supporter of Darwin's theory of evolution at a time when many in the clergy denounced it.

10 CHARTHAM

The pretty village of Chartham has its own train station, but there's a lovely 4-mile walk here from Canterbury. The walk shadows the Great Stour, a river that has provided the water power for village mills for centuries – from a corn mill in 11th century to a textile mill in the 14th century and finally an 18th-century paper mill that was in operation until 1955. The paper mill still produces tracing paper, but Chartham today is becoming better known as a destination for sourcing good food and wine.

Wild foods expert Miles Irving, author of the acclaimed *Forager Handbook*, is based in Chartham and runs regular, day-long **foraging courses** (Unit 1, Deanery Farm Oast, Bolts Hill, CT4 7LD ✆ 01227 732334 ⌂ worldwild.org.uk), during which participants are taught to find, identify, gather and prepare seasonal wild plants and foods from the surrounding area.

Flying the flag for vegetable diversity, **The Wonky Parsnip** (Horton Farm, Cockering Rd, CT4 7LG ✆ 07876 251376 ⌂ thewonkyparsnip. com) grows over 150 different varieties of produce on two acres, from edible flowers to pumpkins and Mexican tomatillos. At various times of year you can drop by this compact farm to pick your own produce or have a meal at a pop-up supper club. The team also occasionally offer food and wine tours of the farm and surrounds.

The history of winemaking around the village goes back to the 11th century when monks grew vines here. Part of Burnt House Farm, **Chartham Vineyard** (Station Rd, CT4 7HU ⌂ charthamvineyard. co.uk ◷ 10.30–17.00 Sat) only planted their vines in 2013 but they are already producing award-winning wines and are working towards being accredited under the Sustainable Wines of Great Britain scheme; visit their vineyard shop where there are free tastings and an art gallery.

11 CHILHAM & SURROUNDS

Six and a half miles southwest of Canterbury, Chilham is the epitome of an old English village, complete with a castle, ancient church and a square surrounded by 15th- and 16th-century wood-beamed buildings. Mentioned in the Domesday Book, there's been a fortress in Chilham, on the hill overlooking the River Stour, since 709. Human settlement goes back even further as attested by **Julliberrie's Grave**, an earthen long barrow above the east bank of the river, likely built some 6,000 years ago. It's hard to get excited about this Iron Age mound,

which is barely a bump on the landscape, but the **castle** (CT4 8DB
🖉 01227 733100 🖉 chilham-castle.co.uk) is another matter. The fine
brick manor house was built in 1616 by Sir Dudley Digges, whose family
had close links with William Shakespeare. Behind it stands a stone keep,
all that remains of the original Norman-era construction. This private
estate occasionally opens its gardens to the public and runs house tours
and other events, including outdoor performances of Shakespeare's plays.
The 25 acres of gardens are superb, with three long terraces providing
panoramic views over the castle's park and surrounding woodlands. The
topiary and Irish yew trees are particularly dramatic, looking like giant
green chess pieces. At the time of research, the castle was up for sale, so
check ahead to see whether gardens are open before heading here.

At the opposite end of Chilham's central square stands the handsome
church of **St Mary's** (CT4 8BY 🖉 friendsofstmaryschilham.org) which
dates back to the 12th century. Local lore has it that the remains of
Thomas Becket are buried in its graveyard. The shrine of St Augustine
also spent a few years in the church following the Dissolution of the
Monasteries, before it vanished from the pages of history. Ponder
these legends while enjoying a pint at the **White Horse Inn** (CT4 8BY
🕘 11.00–22.00 daily), a historic pub right on the village square.

Two and a half miles south of Chilham is another stately home –
Godmersham House. Jane Austen's brother Edward inherited this
estate to which the novelist was a frequent visitor; Godmersham is said
to have inspired *Mansfield Park*. The house, which is part of the design
on the £10 note featuring Austen, is closed to the public but you can
view it in the distance from surrounding walking trails and there is
a small **heritage centre** (The Granary, Godmersham Park, CT4 7DT
🖉 godmershamheritage.webs.com 🕘 Apr–Oct 09.00–noon Mon) on
the old estate road, next to St Lawrence Church.

12 KING'S WOOD

Covering about two square miles between Chilham and the neighbouring
villages of Challock and Boughton Lees is **King's Wood**, one of Kent's
largest ancient woodlands. Once used for hunting by royalty, this is now
a working woodland, managed by the Forestry Commission, and an
important habitat for wildlife such as the nightjar, a rare nocturnal bird.
The woods are a wonderful place to go walking, especially so in late spring
when bluebells form a bluey-purple carpet amid the oak, lime, beech

and conifers. The **Friends of King's Wood** (⌂ friendsofkingswood. org) have a series of walking routes which you can download from their website. The **Kentish Stour Countryside Partnership** also have a sculpture trail (⌂ kentishstour.org.uk/major-projects/stour-valley-creative/forest-studio) that you can follow through the wood from the main car park on White Hill.

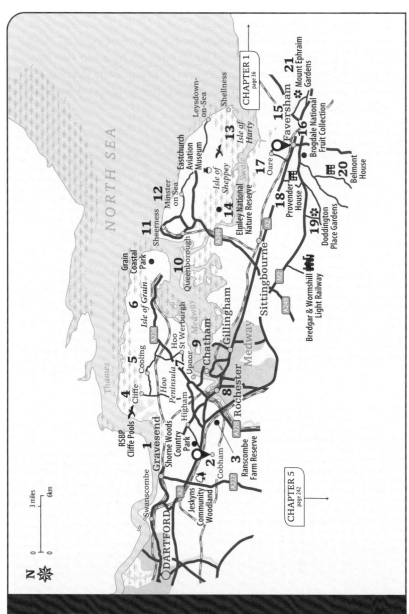

NORTH KENT: GRAVESEND TO FAVERSHAM

Map labels:

N

3 miles
6km
0
0

NORTH SEA

Thames

Isle of Grain

Medway

Swale

Isle of Sheppey

Isle of Harty

Shellness

Leysdown-on-Sea

Eastchurch Aviation Museum

Minster on Sea

Sheerness

Queenborough

Grain Coastal Park

Hoo Peninsula

Hoo St Werburgh

Upnor

Cooling

Cliffe

RSPB Cliffe Pools

Gravesend

Swanscombe

Shorne Woods Country Park

Higham

Cobham

Ranscombe Farm Reserve

Jeskyns Community Woodland

DARTFORD

Rochester

Chatham

Gillingham

Medway

Sittingbourne

Elmley National Nature Reserve

Faversham

Oare

Brogdale National Fruit Collection

Mount Ephraim Gardens

Belmont House

Provender House

Doddington Place Gardens

Bredgar & Wormshill Light Railway

A2

A249

A228

A228

A227

M2

A249

CHAPTER 1
page 36

CHAPTER 5
page 242

1 2 3 4 5 6 7 8 9 10 11 12 13 14 15 16 17 18 19 20 21

2

NORTH KENT: GRAVESEND TO FAVERSHAM

The motorways and high-speed train lines that slice through north Kent tempt many to breeze through with barely a backwards glance: this often-maligned quarter of the county is noticeably more urban and industrial around the Medway. But slow your pace and you'll soon notice the mud flats and salt marshes of the river estuaries, the beaches along the coast and the ancient woodlands and farmlands of the North Downs. Many north Kent towns have millennia-long histories and royal associations. There's a legacy of strategic military defences, including Norman and medieval castles, Napoleonic forts and historic naval dockyards.

The Thames Estuary and two of the county's major rivers – the Medway and the Swale – are the region's defining geographical features. On the Medway is the ancient cathedral city of Rochester, originally a settlement along Watling Street, the old Roman road that is now buried beneath the tarmac of the A2 and M2. Nearby is the historic port of Gravesend, the naval dockyards of Chatham

"Slow your pace and you'll soon notice the mud flats and salt marshes of the river estuaries."

founded by Henry VIII, and the marshlands of the Hoo Peninsula, a place teeming with birdlife: all these places will be familiar to fans of Charles Dickens, who found inspiration for his literary works in their distinctive landscapes and landmarks. While much of the Kent Downs is covered in Kent Weald & Downs (page 241) the village of Cobham is most easily accessed from either Gravesend or Rochester, so is included here.

East of the Medway towns is the Swale, a region named after the saltwater channel that separates the Isle of Sheppey from mainland Kent. Remote and blessed with sublime landscapes, Sheppey is a regional highlight, particularly if you're into quirky, historical locations and birdlife. On the south side to the Swale, nestled inland along a meandering creek, Faversham is a gorgeous medieval town which nurtures a thriving food and drink scene, anchored by one the UK's oldest breweries. It is an ideal base for surrounding sights such as the former Gunpowder Works at Oare, now a country park; the orchards of Brogdale National Fruit Collection; and the blissful gardens of Belmont House, Doddington Place and Mt Ephraim.

GETTING THERE & AROUND

TRAINS

This region is a good one to explore by train and has benefitted greatly from the development of the Eurostar high-speed rail network and associated tracks. Fast trains from London St Pancras provide direct connections to the area's main towns including Gravesend (22 minutes), Rochester (37 minutes), Chatham (40 minutes), and Faversham (1 hour 6 minutes). Trains from London on the slower Thameslink line (⊘ thameslinkrailway.com) head out to Rainham via Gravesend, Rochester and Chatham. The closest train station for Cobham is Sole Street, while Ranscombe Farm Reserve is walkable from Cuxton station. To reach the Isle of Sheppey you'll need to change trains at Sittingbourne, a total journey time of around 1 hour 30 minutes from London to Sheerness.

BUSES

Buses cover the more rural locations in north Kent. Services around the region are provided by Arriva (⊘ arrivabus.co.uk), who also run the Fastrack (⊘ go-fastrack.co.uk) service that connects Gravesend with Ebbsfleet International train station; and Nu-Venture (⊘ nu-venture. co.uk). Stagecoach (⊘ stagecoachbus.com) has services between Faversham and Canterbury. Chalkwell (⊘ 01795 423932 ⊘ chalkwell. co.uk) run services to and around the Isle of Sheppey.

CYCLING

Route 1 of the National Cycling Network (NCN) connects Gravesend, Rochester, Chatham and Faversham. The **Heron Trail**, a 15½-mile circular route through the Hoo Peninsula, is also a national route (NCN 179), while the **Pilgrims Trail** (NCN route 17) links Rochester to Canterbury. There are also a couple of cycle routes on the Isle of Sheppey: the 6.3-mile **Sheerness Way** and the eight-mile, mainly traffic-free **Isle of Harty Trail** – details for both can be found at ⊘ explorekent.org.

1 GRAVESEND

First recorded as Gravesham in the 11th-century Doomsday Book, the port of Gravesend, around 20 miles east of central London, is where ships entering the Thames take on a river pilot for the journey upstream. It is this strategic location on the capital's principal river that has shaped the town's fortunes. Among the historical personalities connected to Gravesend are the Native American chief's daughter Pocahontas, the Victorian army officer Major-General Charles George Gordon, and Charles Dickens, who spent his final years living in the nearby village of Higham. In more recent times, the town was a disembarkation point for the Windrush generation of immigrants from the Caribbean. Today it is home to a 15,000-strong community of Sikhs from India's Punjab state who have built an impressive temple, providing Gravesend with some welcome cultural diversity.

About a ten-minute walk north of Gravesend train station, squashed between the modern St George's shopping centre and the Thames riverbank, is **St George's Church** (Church St *◊* stgeorgesgravesend. org). In the graveyard, atop a plinth, stands an open-armed statue of **Pocahontas**, a 1958 copy of the one created by William Ordway Partridge in 1907 for Jamestown, Virginia, USA. The statue, a memorial tablet and stained-glass windows within the church are all in remembrance of the Native American woman who died and was buried here in 1617. Also inside the church is a memorial tablet to General Gordon (famous for being assassinated in Khartoum), who lived in Gravesend between 1865 and 1871 and is fondly remembered for carrying out many charitable works for the poor during that time.

From St George's churchyard, you can cut through Jury Street to the cobbled High Street, the spine of Gravesend's Heritage Quarter.

THE DEATH OF POCAHONTAS

You may know of plucky Pocahontas through the Disney animated film, but her true story is a tragic tale of the impact of British colonialism on Native Americans. Born in 1595, Pocahontas, meaning 'playful little girl', was the daughter of chief Powhattan. As a teenager she famously pleaded for the life of Captain John Smith, the leader of the Jamestown colony who, legend has it, she fell in love with. Taken as a hostage by later English settlers to the colony, Pocahontas converted to Christianity, changed her name to Rebecca and married another settler, John Rolfe, with whom she had a child, Thomas.

In 1616 the Rolfe family sailed for England where Pocahontas attended the court of James I and became a celebrity in London society. She was also briefly reunited with John Smith who had left Jamestown in 1609 badly wounded, and whom Pocahontas had previously believed was dead. However, while in London, Pocahontas's health declined, and she became gravely ill. On the Rolfes' return to the American colony in March 1617, their voyage had barely begun when their ship was forced to pull into Gravesend to offload the dying woman. Pocahontas was buried in the chancel of St George's Church, a place reserved for the most notable people of the parish. The exact location of her grave is unknown as the original church burnt down in 1727 and was replaced with the current building in 1733.

Here, admire the classical stone façade of the **Old Town Hall** (⌂ oldtownhallgravesend.co.uk) added to the mid-18th-century building in the 1830s. Pass between the fluted columns and along a covered passage to the courtyard in front of the Borough Market. Turn around and look up before entering the market to view a colourful **mosaic** of Gravesend's crest, created in 1991 on the back wall of the Town Hall. Featuring a giant blue porcupine at the helm of a green row boat, the crest is believed to have been the inspiration for the 'pea-green boat' in Edward Lear's famous rhyme *The Owl and the Pussycat*; Lear's father lived in Gravesend and the 19th-century artist and man of letters often visited.

Stretching between Queen and High streets, **Borough Market** (⌂ gravesendboroughmarket.co.uk ☉ 09.00–17.00 Tue–Thu, 09.00–21.00 Fri & Sat, 10.00–16.00 Sun) is one of Kent's oldest markets with a charter dating back to the 13th century. Presided over by a statue of Queen Victoria, the covered market hall is best visited for its variety of food stalls and its regular specialist markets, including ones for vintage items, LP records and crafts. There's also a tourist information stall here (see box, page 91), well stocked with leaflets and history books.

A short walk down to the riverside West Street will take you to the historic pub The Three Daws (page 96) and **Gravesend Pier,** built in 1834 and the oldest cast-iron pier in the world. The pier is the starting point for the 140-mile Saxon Shore Way (page 30). Take a moment before walking out on to the stubby gantry to admire the outdoor gallery of reproductions of paintings and sketches by local artist **Gerald Vaughan** along the riverbank, which vividly illustrate what this section of the Thames looked like in the 1960s. Angled off the end of the pier is a modern pontoon from which you can catch the **passenger ferry** (⌀ jetstreamtours.com; ⊙ 06.00–19.00 Mon–Sat, every half hour) that takes just five minutes to cross the river to the docks at Tilbury; locals have been making this cross-Thames voyage for at least the last 500 years.

The pontoon also provides a prime view towards the red-painted lightship **LV21** (⌀ lv21.co.uk) moored at St Andrews Quay. Launched in 1963, Light Vessel 21 is a floating lighthouse that saw most of her service off the Kent coast. Decommissioned in 2008, the ship is now a floating art and performance space. She's docked opposite Elizabeth Gardens where there is a statue to the heroic **Squadron Leader Mahinder Singh Pujji DFC**, one of the first Sikh pilots to volunteer for the RAF in World War II, who spent his retirement years in Gravesend.

Continuing along Royal Pier Road, you'll pass **St Andrew's,** consecrated in 1871 and now used as an arts centre. Next door, the **Mission House** was used by General Gordon as a reading room to teach poor children. Further along, the lawn in front of the Clarendon Royal Hotel has the remains of one of the artillery blockhouses built during the reign of Henry VIII. At the entrance to Royal Terrace Pier, turn right up Harmer Street and then left on to The Terrace to reach the entrance to the **Riverside Leisure Area**. In this park you'll find Gravesend's oldest building: **Milton Chantry** (Fort Gardens, Commercial Pl ⊙ May–Sep noon–17.00 Sat & Sun; English Heritage), the remains of a leper hospital dating back to 1322. In its 700 years the chantry has served as a Tudor-era chapel, a pub and a barracks for the adjacent **New Tavern Fort**. Originally built in the 18th century, the fort was extensively remodelled while under the command of General Gordon in the 1870s. A statue of Gordon, unveiled in 1893, stands in the adjacent formal gardens which include a duck pond.

A short walk north of Fort Gardens over the railway line brings you to the grand archway though which is the main entrance to the

Cobham: parks, woods & nature reserves

❀ OS Explorer map 163; start: Shorne Woods Country Park, Brewers Rd, Shorne DA12 3HX
📍 TQ684700; 6½ miles; easy

If you've ever wondered what Kent's countryside may have looked like in prehistoric times then the National Trust-managed section of Cobham Wood will give you something of an idea. This ancient wood pasture is a Site of Special Scientific Interest (SSSI). This circular walk also takes in three more parks and woodland reserves, offering up a superb range of natural landscapes, some of it within the Kent Downs AONB, as well as the charming village of Cobham with a history stretching back to the 12th century. There's paid parking at Shorne Woods (⊘ kent.gov.uk/leisure-and-community/kent-country-parks/shorne-woods-country-park) or you can arrive here by the Nu-Venture bus services 416 or 417; the nearest station is Sole Street, just under one mile southwest of Cobham.

1 From the car park beside the visitor centre at Shorne Woods Country Park, walk back to Brewers Road and cross into coppiced Brewers Wood, following the marked Darnley Trail route to emerge on Park Pale Road, where you should turn left and walk along the road that's signed towards Cobham Golf Course.

2 Cross over the A2 using Park Pale Bridge and then follow the road under the Channel Tunnel rail link and look for the footpath on the left. Head along the Darnley Trail with the train line to your left, turning right when you reach open fields; continue with the woodlands on your right and fields on your left.

3 At the gate for the entrance into the National Trust-managed Cobham Wood, ignore the track to the right and go straight ahead, following the path that heads initially slightly uphill and then more steeply towards the crest of hill.

4 When you reach the footpath crossroads, turn right to follow the main route of this walk into Cobham Wood. For a longer walk, turn left to explore the trails of Ranscombe Farm Reserve (page 98), one of the UK's most important sites to spot rare wild flowers.

5 The broad path leads directly to the impressive Darnley Mausoleum and then continues in a more or less straight line to Lodge Lane. Along the way you are likely to encounter the shaggy highland cattle whose grazing helps naturally control the bramble, thistles and bracken that sprout in these woods of ferns, ancient oak, chestnut and ash trees.

6 From South Lodge Barn at the southern corner of the National Trust property, follow Lodge Lane to the Cobham War Memorial at the junction of Halfpence Lane. A driveway off to the right leads to Cobham Hall, now a private school and only open to the public on specific days. Cross the road and walk down The Street.

7 After about a quarter of a mile you'll reach the 13th-century church dedicated to St Mary Magdalene, housing one of the finest collections of medieval brasses in England. Opposite the church is the half-timbered Leather Bottle Inn, an atmospheric pub with connections to Charles Dickens. Continue walking along The Street.

8 At Owletts, a National Trust property that was once home to the architect Sir Herbert Baker, turn right and follow the footpath that leads into Jeskyns Community Woodland (⌖ forestryengland. uk/jeskyns). Created in 2006, this 360-acre of woodland has six trails and a fruit orchard. Jeskyns' is a habitat for threatened bird species including yellowhammers and corn buntings. Continue along the footpath to the brow of the hill.

9 A few steps off the footpath is Hollybush Corner, which provides a panoramic view over the park, framed through a towering pair of abstract figures carved from single pieces of timber. Retrace your steps back to the Darnley Trail footpath which heads downhill before entering a more shaded and often muddy section between two privately owned woods. The route emerges from the woods at the railway and the A2.

10 Cross Thong Lane Bridge over the motorway and pass the entrance to the Inn on the Lake to re-enter Shorne Woods Country Park. The Darnley Trail climbs uphill and switches back on itself.

11 When you meet a junction of various trails through the park, pick up the Heritage Trail (marked in brown) and follow it back to the visitor centre (⊘ 10.00–17.00 Mon–Fri, 09.00–17.00 Sat & Sun) which has a café.

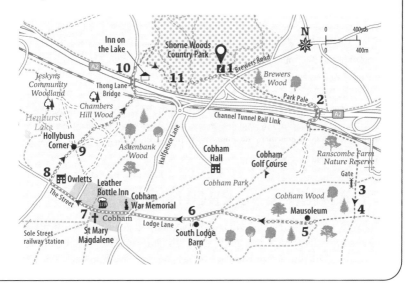

Guru Nanak Darbar Gurdwara (Khalsa Ave ✆ 01474 350611 ⌂ gurunanakdarbar.org ⊙ 04.00–19.00 daily). Opened in 2010 and named after the founder of Sikhism, this marble and granite clad temple is the largest such complex in Europe. Inlaid with mosaics and carvings on the exterior, the interior is dazzling, with chandeliers hanging over a grand staircase and beautifully detailed domes here and in its main prayer hall. As is the Sikh tradition, all are welcome to enter, provided they adhere to rules including removal of shoes and covering the head with a piece of cloth. The dining hall and kitchen, a feature of all gurdwaras, provides free meals to all comers.

🍴 FOOD & DRINK

Marie's Tea Room 17 High St ✆ 01474 335149 ⌂ mariestearoom.co.uk ⊙ 10.00–16.00 Tue–Sun. Sample Marie's own unique and delicious blends of loose-leaf teas – such as the smoky apple-and-vanilla-flavoured Campfire at Jamestown – at this cute café next to the old Town Hall. Afterwards, go next door to their emporium to buy teas to take home as well as their own brands of coffee, drinking chocolate, and chocolate bars.

Pad Thai Live Borough Market ⌂ padthailive.com ⊙ 10.30–16.30 Tue–Thu, 10.30–20.30 Fri & Sat, 10.30–15.30 Sun. At the Queen Street end of the market hall, this award-winning Thai street food operation is the real deal. Thai cooks dish up authentically spicy and piquant dishes, including their signature pad thai noodles, from a bright yellow-and-pink-painted open kitchen.

Reliance Fish Restaurant 4 Queen St ✆ 01474 533593 ⌂ reliancefishrestaurant.com ⊙ 11.00–20.00 Mon–Thu, 11.00–21.00 Fri, 10.30–21.00 Sat, 13.30–19.00 Sun. This family-run operation is the go-to place in Gravesend for fish and chips. You can eat inside the smartly tiled shop, which celebrated its centenary in 2020.

The Three Daws Town Pier ✆ 01474 566869 ⌂ threedaws.co.uk ⊙ noon–23.00 daily. This riverside inn with a deck overlooking the Town Pier oozes salty maritime atmosphere. It first gained its licence in 1565, but its history as a hostelry for the denizens of Gravesend's docklands goes back perhaps a century earlier. Their menu is a notch up from standard pub grub, with a focus on Kentish ingredients.

2 COBHAM & SURROUNDS

Beloved by Dickens, the village of Cobham, five miles southeast of Gravesend, dates back at least to the 12th century. Two days before his death in 1870, the author rode in his carriage from his home at Gads Hill Place to the park surrounding Cobham Hall, where he took his last walk.

The ancestral home of the Earls of Darnley since the early 18th century and a private girls' school since 1962, **Cobham Hall** (Brewers Rd, DA12 3BL ✐ 01474 823371 ♗ cobhamhall.com) is about a 30-minute walk east of the village. It's a mainly Tudor-period building and only open for visitors during the school's summer holiday – check their website for details.

Adjacent to the hall is **Cobham Woods** (South Lodge Barn, Lodge Ln, DA12 3BS ✐ 01732 810378; National Trust). Once part of the original Cobham estate, these are among England's last remaining ancient wood pastures. In the woods, walk up William's Hill to view up close the extraordinary **Darnley Mausoleum**. Constructed in 1786 by George Dance the Younger to a classically inspired design by the architect James Wyatt, the Portland stone building with a pyramid roof and a dry moat cost the equivalent of £1 million in today's money. It's decorated outside with symbols of death, but no-one was ever laid to rest here as the mausoleum was never consecrated. By the early 2000s the mausoleum was in a sorry state, a victim for decades of neglect and vandalism. It has since been restored and is usually open for tours on the first Sunday of the month between April and September.

The third earl, who commissioned the mausoleum, is buried back in Cobham village at historic **St Mary Magdalene Church** (The Street, DA12 3DB ✐ 01474 813495 ♗ cobham-luddesdowne.org). The oldest part of this church, dating back to 1220, is its chancel, in the floor of which are embedded 15 medieval brasses, believed to be the world's finest such collection. They include an image of John de Cobham,

THE ASHES

For cricket fans, Cobham Hall is sacred ground as this is the original home of the Ashes, a terracotta urn believed to contain the burnt remains of a cricket ball. The urn (or maybe another one made from silver) was first presented to Ivo Bligh, 8th Earl of Darnley and captain of the England cricket team, during a victorious tour of Australia in 1883. Bligh and his team had pledged to regain honour for England after being trounced by Australia the previous year at London's Oval cricket ground – a defeat that had prompted a mock obituary of English cricket's death in *The Sporting Times*. After the earl died in 1927, the urn was passed on to the Marylebone Cricket Club (MCC) where it has since become the symbolic trophy that England and Australia compete for during their annual Test series. Replicas of the urn are held aloft by the victorious team.

the 3rd Baron Cobham who built Cooling Castle (page 101) and who died in 1408. Also in the chancel is the impressive marble and alabaster table tomb of George Brooke, the 9th Baron Cobham, and his wife Anne Bray, dated 1561. For permission to take rubbings of the brasses, contact the church.

Before leaving the village, swing by **Owletts** (The Street, DA12 3AP ✆ 01732 810378 ☉ Apr–Sep 10.00–16.00 Sun; National Trust). Originally built in 1683, this symmetrical red-brick house is where the architect Sir Herbert Baker (1862–1946) was born, grew up and lived later in his life. The gardens, parts of which were designed by Gertrude Jekyll, are a pleasant spot for a picnic. Inside you can view furniture that Baker had specially commissioned and his delicate watercolour 'diary' of his overseas travels: he is most famous for his building designs in South Africa and India.

⑪ FOOD & DRINK

Leather Bottle Inn 54–56 The Street, DA12 3BZ ✆ 01474 814327 ⌂ theleatherbottle. pub ☉ noon–23.00 Mon–Sat, noon–21.00 Sun. Dickens often stayed in rooms 2 and 6 at this atmospheric inn, his visits here informing scenes from *Pickwick Papers*. With its walls plastered with Dickens-related art and memorabilia, plus pleasant gardens and a traditional pub food menu, it remains an excellent reason for lingering in Cobham today.

3 RANSCOMBE FARM RESERVE

A228 Sundridge Hill, Cuxton ME2 1LA ✆ 01634 245413 ⌂ plantlife.org.uk/ranscombe

For centuries wild flower collectors have been drawn to the woods and farmlands around Cuxton, nine miles southeast of Gravesend. Rare species such as meadow clary, hairy mallow, rough poppy and corncockle are now protected here within the 620-acre

"This landscape combines an arable farm with nature reserve areas of ancient woodland and species-rich chalk grassland."

Ranscombe Farm Reserve. This landscape, which has largely been unaltered since the 18th century, combines an arable farm with a nature reserve that includes large areas of ancient woodland and smaller areas of species-rich chalk grassland. As well as beautiful wild flowers, the reserve's ten miles of footpaths provide a chance to encounter rare insects, such as grizzled skipper butterflies and various species of bumblebee. The fallow deer originally came from the old deer park at Cobham Hall, and you may also see skylarks and buzzards. In April the woods are carpeted with bluebells, while in May you can hunt out the deep purple and white lady orchid and the greenish-yellow man orchid. The reserve is one mile north of Cuxton railway station and buses from Chatham and Rochester stop nearby.

HOO PENINSULA

⚲ **Eternal Lake Nature Reserve** (page 308)

Bordered by the Thames and the Medway, the fertile salt marshes and high chalk bluff of the Hoo Peninsula have been settled and farmed for many centuries. Despite its proximity to London and the main north Kent towns, the peninsula is one of the least visited parts of the county. The Hoo (which possibly comes from a Saxon word meaning 'spur of land') inspired the 'dark flat wilderness, intersected with dykes and mounds and gates' that's the backdrop for the opening scenes of Dickens' *Great Expectations*. But far from being funerial and depressing, this is an alluring landscape of ancient castles, important bird reserves and a breezy community-created seaside park covering an old military fort. The people who live here also have fascinating stories to tell, which you can listen to in the online project **Histories of the Hoo Peninsula** (⌂ hoo-peninsula.com).

4 AROUND CLIFFE

Clay and chalk used to be dug out of the marshy ground to make Portland cement on the peninsula's west coast, near the village of Cliffe. When the quarries were abandoned in the late 20th century, they began filling up with ground water, transforming an unsightly industrial area into a haven for birdlife, in particular waders and wildfowl. **RSPB Cliffe Pools** (Salt Ln, ME3 7SX ✆ 01634 222480 ⌂ rspb.org.uk; free entry) is a 570-acre patchwork of saline lagoons, fresh pools, grassland, scrub and saltmarsh. Tread its well-signposted, muddy gravel paths to spot species including avocet, lapwing, little egret and dabbling ducks such as teal, mallards and pintails. Or come to relish the wide open spaces and big skies on this stretch of the Thames Estuary.

Nearby is the 60-acre, privately owned **Eternal Lake Nature Reserve** (Buckland Lake Reserve, Salt Ln, ME3 7RT ✆ 01634 963 718 ⌂ eternallake.org) which offers viewing opportunities for a similar range

of birdlife. There's accommodation (page 308) here as well as a great little café (page 103). The reserve also hosts a range of activities and spiritual events including yoga and tai-chi classes and gong sound baths.

5 COOLING

From Cliffe, head two miles inland to the high ground around the tiny village of Cooling, home to **Cooling Castle**, built by the Cobham family in the 1380s. The twin turrets of the stone gatehouse are as much as you will see of this ruined fortress as it now a private estate owned by the musician Jules Holland. The graveyard of the village's **St James' Church** (30 Main Rd, ME3 8DQ ⊘ coolingchurch.org.uk ⊙ 10.00–16.00 daily) inspired the scene at the start of *Great Expectations* where Pip encounters the escaped convict Magwich. Here are what have become known as 'Pip's Graves' – the gravestones of 13 babies that Dickens describes in the novel as 'little stone lozenges each about a foot and a half long'.

A five-minute drive, or 20-minute walk, east of Cooling is **RSPB Northward Hill** (ME3 8DS ⊘ 01634 222480 ⊘ rspb.org.uk; free entry). Part of a working farm set on a ridge overlooking the peninsula's northern marshes, the reserve is home to the UK's largest heronry with over 150 pairs. There are also breeding pairs of little egrets here. Of the three colour-coded trails, Yellow is the shortest at three quarters of a mile and provides sweeping views across the marshes from the Ernie Helmsley viewpoint. The two-mile Green route runs past the Sweeney viewpoint and Gordon's hide to a viewpoint overlooking the heronry; and the 2.3-mile Red trail covers the bluebell woodland and cherry orchard where you may encounter nightingales, marsh harriers and, in spring, lapwings who come here to breed.

6 ISLE OF GRAIN

East of Cooling, a lonely road snakes out to the easternmost end of the peninsula. The Isle of Grain, which as its name implies was once separated from the Hoo by the now silted-up Yantlet and Colemouth creeks, is dominated by the National Grid's liquid natural gas importation facility and the cranes of Thamesport. These behemoth industrial structures have an otherworldly allure (an episode of *Dr Who* was once filmed out here) but press on to reach the village of

◄ **1** Isle of Grain. **2** Darnley Mausoleum, Cobham. **3** Upnor village. **4** RSPB Cliffe Pools.

St James at the end of the road. There's a church here that dates back to at least Norman times, but it's the community-run **Grain Coastal Park** (ME3 0BS ⌂ friendsofgraincoastalpark.co.uk) that's the main draw. Coastal paths offer expansive views across to Essex and the Isle of Sheppey. Walk alongside cockleshell and sandy beaches towards a causeway that runs to the **Grain Tower**, a gun tower built in the mid 19th century to protect the mouth of the Medway from foreign attack. The park, which also includes wild flower meadows and maze-like tracks through a largely grassed over Victorian fort, is an wonderful spot for a picnic.

7 UPNOR & SURROUNDS

The picturesque village of Upnor, on the River Medway at the southwest end of the Hoo Peninsula, is like a stage set. A narrow cobbled high street, bookended by two pubs, leads downhill to the river from a car park past weatherboarded 17th- and 18th-century homes to the gatehouse of **Upnor Castle** (Upnor Rd, ME2 4XG ☎ 01634 718742 ⊙ 10.00–16.00 Tue–Sun; English Heritage). Commissioned in 1559 by Elizabeth I to defend Chatham dockyard from attack, the stone castle juts into the Medway with its arrow-shaped Water Bastion. In June 1667, the fortress failed to prevent the Dutch navy destroying several Royal Navy ships anchored at Chatham and stealing the flagship *Royal Charles*.

At the top of High Street, turn left to follow the Saxon Way footpath towards the Hoo Marina – along the way you'll pass the **London Stones**, which marked the boundary for fishing rights for the capital, and the restored figurehead for the HMS *Arethusa*, an 1849 warship that was the last British vessel to go into battle under sail, during the Crimean War. The yachts, houseboats and other maritime craft at **Hoo Marina** float alongside an estate of prefabricated homes, built on the site of a former brickworks.

Look for the 127ft spire of **Hoo St Werburgh's Church** (Church St, ME3 9AL ⌂ hoochurch.org.uk) in the village of Hoo St Werburgh and walk in that direction from the marina. Named after a Saxon princess, there's been a church here since at least the 11th century, and its lofty wood-beamed nave and chancel and fine stained-glass windows are well worth a look. Royal coats of arms for Elizabeth I and James I are mounted on the wall either side of the main north entrance. The round walk here from Upnor will take you around two hours.

¶ FOOD & DRINK

Pureplanet Café Eternal Lake Nature Reserve, Salt Ln, Cliffe ME3 7RT ⊘ eternallake.org
⊙ 08.30–17.30 daily. One of the best places to dine on the Hoo Peninsula, with an outdoor
deck overlooking the reserve's spring-fed chalk lake. They serve dishes made with organic
vegetables, along with vegan and gluten-free menu options.

Tudor Rose 29 High St, Upper Upnor ME2 4XG ℘ 01634 714175 ⊘ tudorroseupnor.co.uk
⊙ noon–22.00 daily. Next to the entrance to Upnor Castle, this Shepherd Neame pub offers
a cosy saloon bar and enclosed beer garden. It's a good choice for vegetarians as they have a
dedicated plant-based menu with many options.

MEDWAY TOWNS

Going from east to west, Strood, Rochester, Chatham, Gillingham and
Rainham make up the sprawling conurbation of the Medway towns.
Plenty of much-needed urban improvement and regeneration projects
are either underway or being touted for Medway. The most interesting
and historic places to visit are in Rochester and Chatham, where the
locals are known respectively as 'proudies' and 'rowdies' – which neatly
sums up the social dichotomy between these adjacent riverside towns.

8 ROCHESTER

🏠 **North Downs Barn** (page 307)

> A brilliant morning shines on the old city. Its antiquities and ruins are
> surpassingly beautiful, with the lusty ivy gleaming in the sun and the
> rich trees waving in the balmy air.
> Charles Dickens, *The Mystery of Edwin Drood*

Rochester's 'antiquities and ruins' – which include England's second-
oldest cathedral, the remains of a Norman-era castle and city walls, and
a wealth of heritage architecture spanning the 15th to 19th centuries
– continue to make it one of the most visually attractive and historically
fascinating towns in Kent. It is an ancient settlement, pre-dating the
arrival of the Romans who built the first bridge across the Medway and
fortified the town.

The town's connections to Charles Dickens are heavily mined, with
café and shop names such as 'Copperfields' and plaques on buildings
which had walk-on parts in his novels and short stories. Twice a year
(usually in June and December) Dickens enthusiasts join costumed

actors and musicians in a festival celebrating the writer's life and works – see ⊘ rochesterdickensfestival.org.uk for details.

Rochester is compact and easy to explore on foot – you'll need a full day to do all its sights justice and to soak up its unique atmosphere. Everything you'll want to see or do is on or close by High Street, which is a block west of the train station on Corporation Street (the A2).

The town's spiritual heart is its venerable **cathedral** (⊘ 01634 843366 ⊘ rochestercathedral.org ⊙ 10.00–16.00 Mon–Sat, 13.00–15.00 Sun), located just off High Street. Consecrated in 1130 in the presence of Henry I, the Norman Romanesque building replaced a much smaller Anglo-Saxon church established here in 604, thus making Rochester the second-oldest cathedral in the country. Since the mid 13th century it has been a place of pilgrimage, associated with the martyr William of Perth, the patron saint of adopted children. In 1201, the pious Scot was murdered a short way outside of Rochester. After various miracles were associated with his corpse, he was proclaimed a saint in 1256 and a shrine was built to him in the cathedral.

The building has undergone many alterations and additions over the centuries, but you get the strongest impression of its antiquity at the magnificent **West Door** on Boley Hill. This yellow Caen stone portal, carved with images of Christ, angels and other symbolic representations, was described by Dickens as 'like looking down the throat of time.'

Stout stone columns line either side of the nave and are linked by arches decorated with a jagged rick-rack pattern. Ahead, the Quire is screened off by the Pearson Pulpitum, a 1904 Weldon stone screen with eight statues of figures connected to the cathedral's history including St Andrew and Justus, the first Bishop of Rochester. Moving through to the Quire, check the northeast wall for a surprisingly vivid fragment of a 13th-century painting of the Wheel of Fortune. Compare this to the 2004 fresco of Jesus's baptism by Russian iconographer Sergei Fyodorov in the North Transept. The Sanctuary, to the rear of the cathedral, was remodelled by architect George Gilbert Scott in the 1870s and features a zodiac circle design on its tiled floor. Take a breather in the Cloister Garth, a courtyard garden bordered by ruins of the priory that was once attached to the cathedral, then descend into the Crypt where there is an exhibition on the cathedral's history and a pleasant café. The cathedral is often used to display contemporary artworks, too – check their website to see what might be currently on exhibition.

Squaring up to the ecclesiastical majesty of the cathedral are the commanding ruins of Norman **Rochester Castle** (Castle Hill ✆ 01634 335882 ☉ castle keep 10.00–17.00 Tue–Sun; English Heritage), a symbol of royal secular power. Within the old bailey – now a public park – is England's tallest castle keep, 125ft of Kentish ragstone and Caen stone from Normandy, built around 1127. The keep's southeast turret is circular, unlike the other square turrets, because it had to be rebuilt after King John's successful siege of the castle in 1215. Much more damage was done to the fortress during the siege of 1264 – the castle never recovered and in the second half of the 16th century stones from it were used to build Upnor Castle. The wooden floors and ceilings of the keep are long gone, leaving a ghostly stone shell in which you can make out the doors, windows and fireplaces of the formerly grand interior. Intact stairwells provide access to the battlements at the top of the keep for a bird's-eye views over Rochester.

Along High Street

Rochester's bunting-strung High Street is jam-packed with historic and architecturally notable buildings. The following description, which starts from the Medway bridge end of the street, covers the most prominent of them. The handsome 1909 **Halpern Conservancy Board Building** is at number 15. From here, the Medway Conservancy Board controlled river traffic around Rochester up until 1969. Today the building houses Café Nucleus (page 109) and **The Halpern Pop**, a small gallery run by the arts charity Nucleus Arts. Also look for the repurposed red telephone box outside which is a mini gallery for local print artists.

At number 17, the **Guildhall**, built in 1687 and now a museum (✆ 01634 332900 ☉ 10.00–17.00 Tue–Sun), is topped by a splendid weathervane in the shape of an 18th-century warship. The impressively decorated court hall, once used by the city council, was the gift of the magnificently named Sir Cloudesley Shovell, MP for Rochester between 1695 and 1707, whose portrait hangs in the hall alongside those of other grandees and worthies. The museum is packed with interesting items and displays including a section about the castle siege of 1215, and a new permanent exhibition about Dickens. Not to be missed is the three-level reconstruction of a hulk – decommissioned ships used in the late 18th and early 19th century as floating gaols for convicts and prisoners of the Napoleonic wars. In desperately grim conditions, some prisoners created delicate decorative items from scraps of straw, bone and human hair – examples of such jewel boxes and model ships are on display. The Guildhall's colonnade was once a marketplace.

With a giant clock protruding from its elegant façade, it's easy to spot the **Old Corn Exchange** (⌂ therochestercornexchange.co.uk) near the corner with Northgate. This 1706 building, which has also served as a butchers' market, a courtroom and a cinema, is now used for weddings and other events.

At number 95 is a modern building housing the **Medway Visitor Information Centre** and the **Rochester Art Gallery and Craft Case** on the ground floor and the **Huguenot Museum** (✆ 01634 789 347 ⌂ huguenotmuseum.org ⊙ closed temporarily at time of research) on the first floor. The displays here detail the contributions made to Britain's economy and culture by these religious refugees from 17th-century Europe, and include oil paintings, silver and pieces of silk from the collection of **La Providence** (⌂ frenchhospital.org.uk). This charity, which has supported the Huguenot community since 1718, runs the almshouses on Theobold's Square just off High Street.

Next to the visitor centre is the **Six Poor Travellers' House** (97 High St ✆ 01634 842194 ⌂ richardwatts.org.uk/poor-travellers ⊙ Mar–Oct 11.00–13.00 & 14.00–16.00 Wed–Sun). Step inside to learn the history of this compact Tudor-era property which for nearly 400 years offered one night's free lodging, supper and a fourpence allowance to poor travellers passing through Rochester. The charity that manages the house is named after the eminent Richard Watts who left the property in his will for this purpose. Watts, an MP for Rochester, died in 1579 and is buried in the cathedral. Dickens visited in 1854 and wrote his Christmas story *The Seven Poor Travellers*, based on his impressions of the house and its occupants – one room in the house is devoted to this episode, while others are set up as they would have been for the travellers. There's also a tranquil courtyard garden brimming with flowers and herbs.

The last major stop on this wander down High Street is handsome **Eastgate House** (✆ 01634 332700 ⊙ 10.00–17.00 Wed–Sun), a three-storey late Elizabethan house that belonged to Sir Peter Buck, a senior officer at the Royal Tudor Dockyard. Many of the house's original

1 View over the Medway towards Chatham's Historic Dockyard. **2** Chatham's Victorian Ropery. **3** Rochester High Street. **4** Rochester Castle. **5** HMS *Gannet*, Chatham. ▶

features and decorations have been carefully restored, including its oak wall panelling and moulded ceilings. In the public garden next to Eastgate House is a charming **Swiss wooden chalet** that Dickens once used as his writing retreat at his Gad's Hill home – he was working on *The Mystery of Edwin Drood* in the chalet the day before he died.

Restoration House
17–19 Crow Ln ✆ 01634 848520 ♐ restorationhouse.co.uk ⊙ Jun–Sep 10.00–17.00 Thu & Fri
A short walk up along Crow Lane from High Street towards the shady park **The Vines** will bring you to Restoration House. For much of the year this handsome property is closed and all you'll be able to do is admire its Mannerist brick façade and fancy ironwork gate. Visit during its summer opening days, however, and you are in for a special treat that includes access to a superbly restored and decorated interior and a stunning set of gardens hidden away in the heart of Rochester.

Believed to be the model for 'Satis House', the home of the reclusive Miss Haversham in Dickens' *Great Expectations*, Restoration House gets its name from when Charles II stayed for a night in 1660, on the eve of his restoration to the monarchy. With sections dating back to

THE EMPTY CHAIR POETRY TRAIL

Rochester has more sites associated with Charles Dickens per square mile than any other place in the UK. The **Empty Chair Poetry Trail** (♐ wordsmithery.info/chair) was created to mark the 150th anniversary of Dickens' death in 1870. Ten poets wrote new poems inspired by the author which have been printed on boards and placed outside locations with links to Dickens' life, **Gad's Hill Place** (Gravesend Rd, Higham ME3 7PA ♐ gadshillplace.co.uk) which was the author's home for the last 15 years of his life. Now part of a girls' school, the house can be visited on a handful of weekends each year, between April and October. The witty verse here, *The Clash of the Titans* by the late Rosemary McLeish, recalls the time when Hans Christian Andersen came to stay with Dickens – a visit that didn't go well!

The Rochester poems are beside the Guildhall, the Swiss Chalet behind Eastgate House, The Vines park and the Catalpa tree outside the cathedral's West Door. From 1817 to 1822, Dickens' father, a clerk in the Navy Pay Office, was stationed at the dockyards in Chatham, so you'll also find a poem there and ones at Chatham Library and Waterstones on Chatham's High Street, too. The final two poems are at the Parish Hall in Chalk (Dickens spent his honeymoon at this village, 2½ miles southeast of Gravesend) and at St James' church in Cooling (page 101). The trail's website gives full details of where to find the poems.

the mid 15th century, the property is the result of the 17th-century amalgamation of two separate houses with much of its current garden belonging to an earlier Tudor-era hall, long since demolished.

Antique dealer Robert Tucker and his partner Jonathan Wilmot bought the property in 1994 when it was in a sorry state (it had previously been owned by the entertainer Rod Hull, who had gone bankrupt). Their remarkable restoration of the property included painstaking dry scraping of wall paint to reach the 17th-century colours and detail. Fine oil portraits, several landscapes by Gainsborough and an Aubusson tapestry hang beside works by contemporary painters, piles of books and finds from Rochester's flea markets. It's a glorious jumble that's both respectful of the house's rich history and a reflection of the owners' eclectic tastes.

Samuel Pepys wrote in his diaries that he kissed a 'pretty young woman' in the cherry garden here in 1667. The cherry trees have long gone and in their place is a gorgeous double walled garden, interlinked by a formal pond, and including topiary yew hedges, a Victorian greenhouse, wild flower meadow, vegetable plot and an ornate box parterre which replicates the design of the house's front Jacobean door. The discovery of a Tudor wall running alongside the neighbouring property led Tucker and Wilmot to buy that plot. It has since been transformed into a dramatic multilevel 17th-century-style Italian garden with fountains, a gazebo and statues. Seating is scattered around the gardens on which to enjoy refreshments from the house's tea shop, with the proceeds going to a local hospice.

TOURS

City of Rochester Society 95 High St ⌀ city-of-rochester.org.uk ⊙ Apr–Oct 14.15 Wed, Sat, Sun & bank hols. Local guides from the society lead free walking tours of the town's sights, covering Rochester's history from the Romans to the present day. Tours depart from in front of the Medway Visitors Centre.

⊺⊦ FOOD & DRINK

Café Nucleus Halpern Conservancy Board Building, 15a High St ✆ 01634 406971 ⌀ cafenucleus.co.uk/rochester ⊙ 09.30–17.00 Mon–Thu, 09.30–22.00 Fri & Sat, 10.00–17.00 Sun. This award-winning café and restaurant adds a colourful burst of new life to one of High Street's grandest buildings. Local ingredients are championed on their menus which cover brunch dishes, fancy afternoon teas and blow-out banquets in the maximalist decorated boardroom upstairs. There's also a bar, a small art gallery and a Mediterranean-themed garden which is perfect for a coffee break.

The Cheese Room Botanicals 60 High St ✆ 01634 845270 ⬧ thecheeseroomrochester.co.uk ⏱ 10.00–22.00 Tue & Wed, 10.00–23.00 Thu & Fri, 09.00–23.00 Sat, 09.00–17.00 Sun. In a wonky-beamed heritage building next to Northgate, or at outdoor tables with a view on to the cathedral and castle, tuck into superior cheese toasties and other items off the cheesy-themed menu. The botanical side of the equation comes from their offering of more than 70 gins, with flavour profiles ranging from fruity to herbaceous. They also have a nearby **deli and café** (74 High St ⏱ 09.30–15.00 daily) for take-aways or quick bites.

Deaf Cat Coffee 83 High St ⬧ thedeafcat.com ⏱ 09.00–17.00 Mon–Sat, 10.00–17.00 Sun. Serving their own blends of coffee and 16 different types of tea, this indie café gets its name from Bob, Dickens' favourite cat, who happened to be deaf. The café has striking wall art and a collection of coffee pots from around the world.

CHATHAM INTRA
HIGH STREET HERITAGE ACTION ZONE

Referred to on old maps as 'Chatham Intra' or 'Chatham Without', the stretch of High Street between Rochester's Star Hill and Chatham's Sun Pier as it shadows the U-bend in the River Medway has long had an unsavoury reputation. Back in the 19th century, when there were no less than 30 pubs along the street, it was lamented as 'the wickedest place on earth'.

A measure of decorum was bestowed on the street when the **Chatham Memorial Synagogue** (366 High St ⬧ chathamshul.org.uk) was built in 1869. The Baroque-style building replaced an earlier complex of wooden cottages and was built as a memorial to Captain Lazarus Simon Magnus who served three terms as Mayor of Queenborough on the Isle of Sheppey and who died tragically from a self-administered overdose of chloroform at the age of 39. The building is rarely open to the public, but you can take an online tour of the synagogue via its website.

In 2021, Medway council was awarded £1.6 million in government funding to help revitalise the Chatham Intra area. Among the projects sponsored so far is an interactive **poetry walk** (⬧ allysinyard.co.uk/medwayintrapoetrywalk) with QR codes at points along the street that activate the compositions. One of the QR codes is at **INTRA** (337–341 High St ✆ 01634 753299 ⬧ intraarts.org), a community arts venue which has interesting exhibitions in its window gallery. Also check out what is happening at **Sun Pier House** (Sun Pier ✆ 01634 401549 ⬧ sunpierhouse.co.uk) which has a gallery, artists' studios, a café and some very cool street art on its car park walls. A car boot fair with a focus on art, craft, vintage and handmade items is held in the car park on the first Saturday of the month.

The George Vaults 35 High St ✆ 01634 817165 ⚹ georgevaults.com ⏲ 09.00–23.00 Sun–Wed, 09.00–24.00 Thu–Sat. Hidden beneath this contemporary brasserie and wine bar is a 14th-century vaulted crypt that was discovered in 2002 when the building was being renovated. There's a large courtyard area and they offer everything from a full English breakfast to late-night cocktails.

🛍 SHOPPING

A good **farmers' market** is held on the third Sunday of the month from 09.00 until 13.00 in the Blue Boar Lane car park, just off High Street.

Baggins Book Bazaar 19 High St ✆ 01634 811651 ⚹ bagginsbooks.co.uk ⏲ 10.00– 17.45 Thu–Mon. Bibliophiles will feel as if they've died and gone to heaven on entering Baggins, England's largest second-hand bookshop. Across several levels and stretching for an entire street block, there are tomes on every subject you could imagine.
Fieldstaff Antiques 93 High St ✆ 01634 846144 ⚹ fieldstaffantiques.com ⏲ 10.00– 17.00 Mon–Sat, 10.00–16.00 Sun. Among the many antique and curio shops along the High Street, this one has perhaps the widest and most appealingly displayed selection.
Store 104 104 High St ⚹ store104.co.uk ⏲ 10.00–17.00 daily. A curated selection of books sit alongside arts and crafts by local artists and yarns for knitting in this quirky family-run store that's put the old Leonard's department store to good use. Tucked away in the back of the shop is the Art-Deco gentleman's club-like Victoria café.

9 CHATHAM

🏠 **Ship & Trades** (page 307)

Chatham and Rochester couldn't be closer neighbours, the one town shading into the other around the U-bend of the Medway, but the difference between the two is stark. Chatham's working-class, maritime roots have long placed it at the opposite end of the social spectrum from genteel Rochester. However, the town has a proud naval tradition and is looking to refashion itself into more of a leisure destination, particularly around its historic docks.

When they were at their most extensive – in the early 20th century, when submarines were being built and serviced here – two thirds of the dockyards were in neighbouring Gillingham. Much of this site has since been redeveloped by **Chatham Maritime Trust** (⚹ cmtrust.co.uk) into housing, retail and the campuses of three universities. The Trust run an annual food and drink festival and offer watersports activities in the former dock basins. If you're visiting the dockyard, come prepared as you'll be spending the better part of a day walking long distances, often outdoors, to fully explore this 80-acre site, which includes superb exhibitions and the chance to climb aboard a masted Victorian sloop, a World War II destroyer and a submarine that ran missions during the Cold War. Among the other sights around Chatham, the main one is the remains of **Fort Amherst**, now an extensive park, which can easily be visited on a walk between the dockyards and bus and train stations.

The Historic Dockyard Chatham

Entrance off Main Gate Rd, ME4 4TY ✆ 01634 823800 ⌂ thedockyard.co.uk ⊙ Feb–Mar & Nov 10.00–16.00 daily; Apr–Oct 10.00–17.00 daily

In 1550 a royal decree proclaimed that 'all the Kinges shippes should be harborowed in Jillyngham Water – saving only those that be at Portsmouth'. From this time, and for over 400 years, the economic and social life of Chatham and the adjacent communities along this sheltered stretch of the Medway revolved around the Royal Dockyard. At its height in the 18th century, the dockyard employed more than 10,000 people and covered 400 acres. Over 500 ships and submarines for the Royal Navy were built here. When it closed in 1984, the dockyard's 18th-century core was transferred to a charity which now runs the **Historic Dockyard Chatham**, an outstanding tourist attraction that celebrates the 'Age of Sail' when Britain's maritime power was supreme.

The dockyard may look familiar. That's because its Georgian and Victorian buildings and cobbled lanes are often used for filming period films and TV shows; one of the most popular **tours** is the one themed around locations used in the BBC drama *Call the Midwife*.

Immediately to the right of the main entrance, the interactive and multimedia Command of the Oceans galleries provide a crash course on the history of the site, how it operated at its peak and its significance in terms of providing the nautical means for Britain to secure a global empire. Lord Nelson's flagship HMS *Victory* was built here between 1759 and 1765 and one of the galleries' star exhibits is a 19½ft scale model of the *Victory* built for the 1941 film *That Hamilton Woman*.

Before heading out to explore the dockyard, do not miss the fascinating exhibit on the gunship HMS *Namur*, launched in 1756 and in service until 1833. This second-rate ship of the line was broken up soon after, and 168 pieces of its timber frame were carefully stored beneath the floorboards of the dockyard's wheelwright's shop. Seemingly forgotten, they were rediscovered in 1995 during a renovation of the site. Why exactly they were buried here in this way remains a tantalising mystery, the answer to which may be explained by the *Namur's* distinguished service in naval battles around the world.

On entry to the dockyard it's a good idea to book ahead for the fascinating 30 minute tours of the **Victorian Ropery** (included with your ticket) to which you'd be wise to head next as it is at the far end of the site. All kinds of rope, from three-strand, flexible hawser to the hefty nine-strand cables to which anchors were attached, were made in this extraordinary quarter-mile-long brick building – its length enabled the laying of single 1,000ft pieces of rope. **Master Ropemakers** (⊘ master-ropemakers.co.uk) still make rope here and there are demonstrations of the 1811 machinery in action from Monday to Friday at 12.15.

Three historic vessels, each examples of the types of craft built, repaired and refitted at the dockyard, can be boarded: the elegant, masted 1878 HMS *Gannet* which was powered by a steam engine as well as sails; the 1944 HMS *Cavalier*, once the navy's fastest destroyer and active until 1972; and HMS *Ocelot*, a 1962 submarine that is huge fun to clamber through and makes you marvel at how a crew of 68 men spent months cooped up in such claustrophobic conditions.

You can breathe easier inside the cathedral-like space of **No 3 Covered Slip**. When completed in 1838 this was the largest wide-span timber building in Europe. Also known as the Big Space, the slip is the now used to display wide range of massive objects and craft including the largest collection of lifeboats in the UK, a 1944 midget submarine and a pointy Polaris A3 ballistic missile. Climb up to the mezzanine level to truly appreciate the slip's size and the artistry of its construction.

"Meticulously detailed model ships from a collection of over 3,000 are among the treasures on permanent display."

Meticulously detailed model ships from a collection of over 3,000 are among the treasures on permanent display in the galleries of **No 1 Smithery**. Also here are some wonderful oil paintings capturing naval scenes as varied as the joyous *Queen Victoria's Diamond Jubilee Review at Spithead* in 1897 by Charles Dixon and the dramatic *Shipwreck with a Paddle Tug Towing a Lifeboat in a Gale* by Richard Henry Nibbs. Joseph Farington's bird's eye view of the dockyard provides an insight into how Chatham looked at the end of the 18th century.

There are a couple of cafés in the dockyard, as well as **Nelson's Brewery** (⌆ nelsonbrewery.co.uk) where you can enjoy freshly made pints of craft ale. However, my tip is to pack a picnic and enjoy it in the lovely walled gardens hidden behind the 1704 **Commissioner's House**, the oldest intact naval building in the UK.

Other sights

A ten-minute walk north of the historic dockyard is **Copper Rivet Distillery** (Leviathan Wy ⌀ 01634 931122 ⌆ copperrivetdistillery.com), based in the Victorian Pump House Number 5. When completed in 1873, this building housed cutting-edge hydraulic technology to drain the dry docks and power the its cranes and other machinery. Part of it has been used for distilling spirits, including various types of gin, since 2016; you can take a 40-minute tour of the process at specific times on Thursdays to Sundays (check website for details). Also here is The Pumproom restaurant and bar (see opposite).

Military history enthusiasts will want to visit the **Royal Engineers Museum** (Prince Arthur Rd, Gillingham ⌀ 01634 822312 ⌆ re-museum. co.uk ⌚ 10.00–17.00 Tue–Sun), a one-mile walk east of the dockyards. Its collection of over a million items is incredibly diverse and ranges from Wellington's map of Waterloo to a Harrier Jump Jet and V2 rockets.

For panoramic views of Chatham, climb up to the ramparts and explore the trails around atmospheric **Fort Amherst** (Dock Rd ⌀ 01634 847747 ⌆ fortamherst.com ⌚ 08.00–19.00; free entry). Built during Napoleonic times to defend the Medway from a land-based attack, this is the most complete fortress of its type and part of the **Great Lines Heritage Park** that covers the high ground above Chatham and Gillingham. Tunnels dug into the cliff to provide secret access between the upper and lower areas of the fort were later used during World War II as an air raid precautions base. Guided **tours** of the tunnels take you through a labyrinth of passages to gun positions, ammunitions storage areas and an underground well for drinking water. There are also night-time ghost tours; find out more online and at the park's popular **Pantry Café** (◼ ⌚ 09.30–16.00 Mon–Sat, 10.00–16.00 Sun).

A final Chatham gem, hidden away off High Street, is the **Nucleus Arts Centre** (272 High St ⌀ 01634 812108 ⌆ nucleusarts.com) which includes the **Halpern Gallery** (⌚ 10.00–16.00 Mon–Sat) showcasing artworks by local creatives and a café.

FOOD & DRINK

Café Nucleus 272 High St ℰ 01634 406971 ⊘ nucleusarts.com ⊙ 09.30–17.00 daily.
Tucked away off Chatham's High Street is a branch of this Mediterranean-style garden café
serving quality coffees, all-day brunches and afternoon teas.

No 64 Coffee & Brunch 64 High St ℰ 01634 786080 ▊ ⊙ 08.00–15.00 Mon–Fri,
10.00–15.00 Sat. For good coffee, generously plump homemade sausage rolls and decadent
chocolate brownies, drop into this café in Chatham Intra.

The Pumproom ℰ 01634 931122 ⊘ crdpumproom.com ⊙ noon–17.00 Wed & Sun,
noon–22.00 Thu–Sat. This fine-dining restaurant and bar offers a tempting menu of
dishes using local seasonal ingredients. Their terrace provides wonderful views across
to Upnor Castle.

ISLE OF SHEPPEY

🏠 **Ferry House Inn** (page 307) 🏡 **Elmley Nature Reserve** (page 308), **Sandy Toes
Beach House** (page 308), **Mocketts Farm Cottages** (page 308)

Across the Swale channel, the Isle of Sheppey, named after the flocks of
sheep that have grazed here for centuries, is often overlooked by visitors to
Kent. That's a shame as within its 36 square miles are sublime countryside
and coastal landscapes, blue flag beaches (including one for naturists),

HOGARTH'S UNGRAND TOUR TO SHEPPEY

On 26 May 1732 the artist William Hogarth
(best known for *A Rake's Progress*) was
boozing in the Bedford Arms in Covent Garden
with his mates Ebenezer Forrest, Samuel
Scott, John Thornhill and William Tothall
when they decided on an impromptu visit,
the very next day, to the Isle of Sheppey. This
would be their version of a 'grand tour', all the
rage among their contemporaries. However,
Paris, Florence and Rome could go hang for
these ardent Londoners: the delights of the
north Kent coast would more than suffice!

The troupe's route to Sheppey ran through
Gravesend, Rochester and the Hoo Peninsula
to Grain where a boatman sailed them

across the choppy waters at the mouth of
the Medway to Sheerness. From here they
walked to Queenborough where they got
into a singing contest with lobster fishermen,
and then on to Minster where they visited
the remains of the abbey. Then it was back
on foot to Sheerness and home to London by
boat via Gravesend.

A jolly, inebriated time was had by all, the
adventure being immortalised in a book with
illustrations by Hogarth, published in 1782
under the appropriately garrulous title *The
Five Day's Peregrinations Around The Isle Of
Sheppey Of William Hogarth and His Fellow
Pilgrims, Scott, Tothall, Thornhill, and Forrest.*

amazing birdlife at two nature reserves, and a peaceful serenity in its most remote corners. It's not uncommon to find Eocene-era fossils along Sheppey's north coast between Minster on Sea and Warden Point. This is one of the UK's premier fossil-collecting sites, with the foreshore mud yielding anything from sharks' teeth to the remains of tropical plants that flourished here 50 million years ago.

"For an out-of-the-way location, Sheppey has a history packed with illustrious characters."

For what is, today, an out-of-the-way location, Sheppey has a history packed with illustrious characters and notable events. In the 7th century, Queen Sexburga (who later became a saint) founded an abbey at Minster. Henry VIII and Anne Boleyn visited Sheppey's Shurland Hall for three days in October 1532. The preserved body of Lord Nelson was brought to the Royal Navy dockyard at Sheerness in a barrel of brandy after the Battle of Trafalgar. And, in the early 20th century, the magnificent pioneers of British aviation tested out their flying machines in the remote east of the island. These, and many more fascinating facts and stories, can be discovered in Sheppey's charmingly quirky, community-run museums and cultural centres.

10 QUEENBOROUGH

The historic port of Queenborough lies on the island's southwest coast. When Hogarth and his travelling companions visited in 1732 (see box, page 115) they found the place pretty much deserted, with 'one street, clean and well-paved.' Little has changed since, and there's not a huge amount to detain you apart from some attractive heritage buildings, the most prominent of which is the 18th-century **Guildhall** (High St, ME11 5AA ✐ 01795 667295 ⌂ queenboroughguildhallmuseum.co.uk ⊙ 14.00–17.00 Sat, Apr–Oct) housing a rarely open history museum. If you're in search of a cuppa and slice of cake, **Bosuns** (9 High St ⌂ bosunsofqueenborough.co.uk ⊙ 10.00–16.00 Mon–Sat, 11.00–14.00 Sun) is an appealingly modern tea room and gift shop.

Both **X-Pilot** (✐ 01795 487568 ⌂ x-pilot.co.uk) and **Jetstream Cruises** (✐ 01634 525202 ⌂ jetstreamtours.com) use Queenborough's harbour for their boat tours, including ones to view the Maunsell sea forts (see box, page 72).

◀ **1** Elmley National Nature Reserve. **2** Faversham.

11 SHEERNESS
⚑ Barton's Point Coastal Park (page 308)

> To Sheerness where we walked up and down, laying out the ground to
> be taken in for a dockyard, a most proper place.
> Samuel Pepys, from his diary for 1665

When Pepys visited Sheerness in preparation for it to be transformed
into a Royal Naval dockyard, this northwestern point of Sheppey had
been a fort protecting the Thames Estuary for about 100 years. The area
next to the docks was nicknamed 'Blue Town' as the first homes built
here were covered them with grey-blue naval paint by the dockyard
construction workers. As the dockyard grew and more people settled
in Sheerness, another area sprang up known as a Mile Town – so called
because it was a mile east of the naval region. Mile Town is where central
Sheerness is today and the location of the train station.

The navy yard shut in 1960 and is now a busy commercial port,
closed to the general public. However, the site contains many historic
buildings, one of the most important of which is the **Dockyard
Church**. The Sheerness Dockyard Trust have been awarded £4.2
million to repair and repurpose the 1828 church which was badly
damaged by fire in 2001. The plans include creating a display space for
a highly detailed, 1,600 square ft wooden model of the dockyard as it
was in the early 19th century.

Shadowing the dock's tall brick wall (which is home to a colony of
two-inch-long, yellow-tailed scorpions!) Blue Town's High Street is
an evocative area to explore. Don't miss the **Criterion Blue Town**
(69 High St, Blue Town ✆ 01795 662981 ⌂ thecriterionbluetown.
co.uk ⏱ 10.00–15.00 Thu–Sat) where a Victorian music hall has been
resurrected and shares space with a fabulous heritage centre, history
research facility, community cinema and tea room. The passion project
of the building's owners and run by volunteers, the place is jam-packed
with memorabilia and displays relating to the dockyards and Sheerness
history and culture. **Bus tours** of the island's key sights are also offered
by the Criterion.

Before leaving Blue Town, wander through the display yards of
Whelans (Chapel St ⏱ 09.00–17.00 daily), a manufacturer of a mind-
bending range of concrete garden ornaments, from chubby little gnomes
to life-sized statues of Darth Vader and C3PO.

Mile Town is the modest, modern heart of Sheerness and it functions both as Sheppey's commercial heart and a nexus for visitors to the island. Stroll along the blue flag shingle **beach** here, with its views across the Thames Estuary to Southend in Essex.

Mile Town's central landmark is a brightly painted **iron clock tower** erected in 1902 to commemorate the coronation of Edward VII. Nearby is the charming weatherboarded **Rose Cottage of Curiosities** (10 Rose St ☏ 07775 712306 ⌂ rosestreetcottagc.co.uk ⊙ 11.00–15.00 Tue & Thu–Sat) a 'living arts centre' stuffed with artefacts, including a wonderful collection of photographic portraits by Lilian Mason from the early 20th century. Tea and cake are served in its courtyard garden.

¶ FOOD & DRINK

Boathouse Café Barton Point Coastal Park, ME12 2BE ⌂ bartonspointcoastalpark.co.uk ⊙ 10.00–17.00 Mon–Sat, 09.00–17.00 Sun. Enjoy a coffee or lunch at the rustic, lakeside café in this 40-acre nature park, which is a short walk from the beach and about a mile and a half east of Sheerness train station. From April to September you can also camp in the park.

Jacksonwood Vintage Tea Rooms 63 High St ⌂ jacksonwoodtea.myportfolio.com ⊙ 10.00–17.00 Mon–Sat, 11.00–17.00 Sun. Soak up the vintage nostalgia at this family-run tearoom, decorated with a mass of colourful curios and knick-knacks. All the bakes are homemade, using local, organic ingredients. They're vegan and dog-friendly, too.

12 MINSTER ON SEA

Three miles east of Sheerness is the quiet residential town of Minster on Sea where an abbey was founded by the Saxon Queen Sexburga around AD670, at the island's highest point. In the surviving part of **Minster Abbey** (Vicarage Rd), mainly dating from the 12th century, you can view the de Northwode brasses, dating from 1330 and notable for the rare detail they show of female dress from that period.

"Make every effort to schedule your visit to coincide with the twice-weekly opening of this Aladdin's cave of items."

Separate from the church is the abbey's 1,000-year-old gatehouse which now houses the **Minster Gatehouse Museum** (Union Rd, ME12 2HW ☏ 01795 872303 ⌂ minstergatehouse.co.uk ⊙ 14.00–16:30 Wed & Sat). Make every effort to schedule your visit to coincide with the twice-weekly opening of this Aladdin's cave of items ranging from ancient fossils to the passports issued to residents during the world wars so they could travel on and

SHEPPEY: CRADLE OF BRITISH AVIATION

The Sheppey villages of Leysdown-on-Sea and Eastchurch figure large in the history of powered flight in the UK. Just outside Leysdown, at the entrance to the Muswell Manor Holiday Park, stands a statue to three men: brothers Eustace, Horace and Oswald Short. In 1909 this trio of engineers set up an aeroplane workshop and flying ground here to which members of the Aero Club came to make pioneering test flights. John Theodore Cuthbert Moore-Brabazon became the first person in the UK to qualify as a pilot here, and to fly a circular mile.

The marshy, low-laying fields at Leysdown were found to be unsuitable for year-round flying so in 1910 the Short Brothers and the Aero Club moved their operations to higher ground, 4.5 miles to the west, at Stamford Hill near Eastchurch. Winston Churchill, then First Lord of the Admiralty, learnt to fly at Eastchurch in 1913 and the Shorts ran their plane factory here until 1934. This area now falls within one of the island's three HM prisons, beside which is the **Eastchurch Aviation Museum** (ME12 4AA ✆ 07450 621217 ⌖ eastchurchaviationmuseum. org.uk ⊙ 10.00–15.00 Tue & Thu–Sat), a couple of huts crammed with exhibits and information on these magnificent men and their early flying machines.

off the island. Of particular note are the vivid artworks of Sheppey by the untrained artist Harold Batzer, and the *Sheppey Timeline* mural by Julie Bradshaw and her daughter Anna Piles, decorating the twisting stone stairwell that leads up to the gatehouse roof. For drinks and light meals, the **Abbey Cake Shop** (1 Chapel St, ME12 3QF ⊙ 09.00–15.00 Mon–Sat), opposite the church, does the job nicely.

13 ISLE OF HARTY

At the eastern end of Sheppey is **Leysdown-on-Sea**, a textbook British seaside resort complete with holiday caravan villages, amusement arcades and ice-cream vendors. The blue flag shingle beach here offers shallow waters and so is popular with families. Further east, towards the hamlet of **Shellness**, there's a short stretch of beach that is clothing optional, near to which is the car park for the **Swale National Nature Reserve**.

You are now on the Isle of Harty, sliced from the rest of Sheppey by the Capel Fleet channel. There's a breezy seaside walk through the saltings and grazing marshlands with panoramic views across to Faversham and Whitstable on the way to **Harty**, the most remote spot on Sheppey. You can also spot wading birds and wildfowl and, in the summer months, flowers such as yellow horned poppies, sea lavender and sea purslane. Together with neighbouring **RSPB Capel Fleet** (ME12 4BG ℘ 01634 222480 ⟳ rspb.org.uk), which has a car park and viewing platform on Harty Ferry Road, this is one of the best vantage points in the UK for spotting birds of prey such as peregrine falcons, marsh harriers, kestrels and short-eared owls.

A vestige of the medieval hamlet of Harty is the remarkable **Church of St Thomas the Apostle** (Harty Ferry Rd, ME12 4BQ ⟳ stthomasharty. org ⊙ 9am–5pm daily) a place of worship much rebuilt over the centuries but possibly dating back to Saxon times. Notable features include decorative Victorian stained glass showing rural scenes and, in its south chapel, a fine 14th-century carved wooden chest. There is no electricity or running water, so lighting is provided by hanging paraffin lamps and by wall-mounted lamps.

Harty's other main building is the **Ferry House Inn** – for centuries, a ferry ran across the Swale from here but the service ceased in the 1950s. Walk out into the muddy estuary along the low-lying stone pier, which is caked in seaweed, for views across to the Oare Marshes Nature Reserve (page 130).

ᵀᵀ FOOD & DRINK

Ferry House Inn Harty Ferry Rd, ME124BQ ℘ 01795 510214 ⟳ theferryhouseinn.co.uk. This inn, which a superb place to overnight or for refreshments during a walk around Harty, has occupied this remote and beautiful spot overlooking the Swale since the 16th century. Their grounds include a superb kitchen garden providing many of the fresh ingredients used in their delicious food. Meat comes from the nearby farm which is owned by the same family as the inn.

14 ELMLEY NATIONAL NATURE RESERVE

Elmley, Isle of Sheppey ME12 3RW ℘ 01795 664896 ⟳ elmleynaturereserve.co.uk
⊙ Oct–Apr 09.00–16.00 Wed–Sun, May–Sep 09.00–17.00 Wed–Fri & Sun, but check in advance as opening days/times are subject to change

This 3,300-acre independently managed National Nature Reserve is the only one in England that it is possible to stay overnight in. Its epicentre is Kingshill Farm, accessed from the southwest corner of Sheppey, close by the bridge crossings over the Swale. Feel stresses melt away and a sense of calm descend as you drive slowly along the rutted track leading to the visitors' car park, taking in the beauty of this marshy haven for birdlife.

Breeding waders such as avocets and orange-billed oystercatchers are often sighted here. Lapwing, redshank and grebe breed and raise their young on Elmley's marshes in spring, while migrants such as the green sandpiper pass through for a handful of weeks each autumn. Raptors, including marsh harriers and peregrines, are common and you may also spot species such as little owls nestling in one of the ruined cottages on the reserve.

Grazing animals are essential to the healthy maintenance of the marshes so this working farm has around 800 beef cattle and, in the winter, a flock of Romney sheep. You can walk through this beguiling landscape of windswept grasses, bull rushes and big skies along a 3½-mile track to Spitend, the furthest of four hides at the eastern limit of the reserve. A short walk from visitors' car park is a sheltered beach at Sharfleet Creek – be careful to only enter the water here at high tide as the muddy Swale and marshes can be treacherous. Kingshill, where there's accommodation (page 308) and food and drink at the **Kingshill Barn**, gets its name from James II who, while fleeing the forces of William of Orange in December 1688, was taken hostage here.

15 FAVERSHAM

🏠 **Cave Hotel & Golf Resort** (page 307), **Read's Restaurant with Rooms** (page 307), **Shepherd House** (page 307), **Sun Inn** (page 307)

Home to one of the largest architectural conservation areas in the UK, Faversham owes its long prosperity to its sheltered position on a sea creek that winds inland from the Swale. Bricks, grain and gunpowder were all shipped from the port here and countless vessels were built in its shipyards. Meaning 'metalworkers' village', Faversham was a royal town during Anglo-Saxon times and its market – one of the oldest in England – is mentioned in the 1086 Domesday Book. In 1148 King Stephen founded an abbey here which rivalled those in Canterbury and Rochester. However, the abbey was destroyed during the Reformation, and with it the graves of King Stephen, Queen Matilda and their eldest son Eustace. Nevertheless, with over 400 listed buildings intact, Faversham remains a visual feast that is a joy to explore on foot. It also has a scrumptious food and drink scene, including England's oldest brewery, and will appeal to those who love to rummage around antique shops and street markets.

For a greater appreciation of Faversham's rich history and pointers on all things of interest in town, start your explorations at the **Fleur de Lis Museum** (10 Preston St ✆ 01795 534542 ⚘ favershamsociety. org ◷ 10.00–13.00 Thu, 10.00–16.00 Fri & Sat). Around a five-minute walk from the train station, the fascinating, artefact-stuffed displays are arranged inside a 15th-century building that was once a pub.

At the end of Preston Street, turn left to reach **Market Place**, at the head of which stands the mint-green **Guildhall**. The ground floor, with its timber arcades and octagonal columns, has been used by market traders for more than 500 years. The upper part of the building, including a clock tower and cupola, dates from 1814 when the hall was rebuilt after a fire.

Officially founded in 1698, but with roots dating back to the brewhouse at Faversham's medieval abbey, Shepherd Neame is a cornerstone of the town's economy, producing over 60 million pints of Kentish ales, lagers and ciders per year. The starting point for brewery tours is the **Shepherd Neame Visitor Centre** (10 Court St ✆ 01795 542016 ⚘ shepherdneame.co.uk ◷ shop 10.30–16.30 Mon–Sat), which occupies a beautifully restored medieval building with timber beams at the Court Street end of Market Place. The tours, which last around 80 minutes, take participants through all the processes in the brewery and culminate in an expert-led tasting of six ales. Most Fridays and on the second Wednesday of the month, an evening tour of brewery tour is combined with a two-course meal in the Visitor Centre bar. Come wearing covered, flat shoes as you'll be walking through a working brewery and across slippery cobbles and surfaces.

> "Shepherd Neame is a cornerstone of the town's economy, producing over 60 million pints of Kentish ales, lagers and ciders per year."

At the junction with Quay Lane, Court Street becomes Abbey Street, which – as its name implies – once led to Faversham's medieval abbey. Many fine heritage buildings line this street including, at number 80, **Arden's House**. What was once the abbey's outer gateway and guesthouse is named after Thomas Arden; a plaque notes how this one-time mayor of Faversham was murdered in the house in 1551, the victim of a plot instigated by his faithless wife and her lover. The events inspired the play *Arden of Faversham* which is rumoured to have been penned by Shakespeare.

The abbey's grounds once extended for eight acres, west out to Faversham Creek and south to **St Mary of Charity Parish Church** (🖰 stmaryofcharity.org). Even though it's off the main street, you can't miss this large church because of its late 18th-century corona spire, soaring above Faversham's roofline. Inside, a unique feature is the octagonal pillar in the nave's northeast corner that's been painted with an early 14th-century mural featuring ten scenes from the life of Christ.

Faversham two creeks walk

✿ OS Explorer map 149; start: Market Place, Faversham ♀ TR015613; 5 miles; easy

Partly following the courses of the Faversham and Oare creeks, this circular walk takes you from the historic town towards the saltmarshes, reed beds and intertidal mud flats of the Swale, with views of boats, sheep, cows and wildlife along the way. Faversham Railway Station is about a five-minute walk south of Market Place along Preston Street. If driving, there's paid parking at the Queen's Hall car park near the station and at the Central car park near Market Place. This walk involves no steep climbs, but it does have little shade and follows creeks side paths that can flood at high tide and marshy ground.

1 In Market Place, Kent's oldest market square, take a moment to admire the handsome Guildhall with its open gallery held up Tudor wooden pillars. If it's a market day (Tuesday, Friday and Saturday), you could pick up some snack supplies for the walk. Continue down Court Street, past the Shepherd Neame Brewery visitor centre, and turn left at Quay Lane.

2 Along Quay Lane is TS Hazard, a wonky beamed warehouse constructed in 1475 and named after a Faversham-built ship that fought against the Spanish Armada; it's now used by the town's sea cadets. Turn right into Bridge Road, cross the bridge and turn immediately right to follow the creek-side path. Continue past the Albion Taverna.

3 A narrow tributary creek splits off a slither of land known as Crab Island from the open grass area of the Upper Brents. There are plans for a walking path to follow the creek here beside the Faversham Reach and Waterside Close housing developments; this will be part of the English Coastal Path. For now, however, when you reach the housing, follow the signs inland for the Saxon Shore Way and skirt around the industrial estate to return eventually to the creek path. On the opposite bank is Standard Quay and the three-storey Oyster Bay House, originally built in the mid 19th century to store hops, but now converted into apartments.

4 Follow the raised path along the sea wall to the interpretation panel at Thorn Creek – a sluice was installed here in 1558 to stop the creek silting up and enable large cargo vessels to sail ▶

In the church's south chapel is an ornately carved but unnamed tomb, said by some to contain the bones of King Stephen.

Bordering the church yard is the organically managed **Abbey Physic Community Garden** (Abbey Pl ✆ 01795 539915 ⌖ abbeyphysic.org ⊙ 09.00–14.00 Mon & Wed–Fri, 11.00–15.00 Sat) which offers lessons in gardening and healthy eating. This walled garden is a serene spot in which to enjoy the flowers, plants and wildlife.

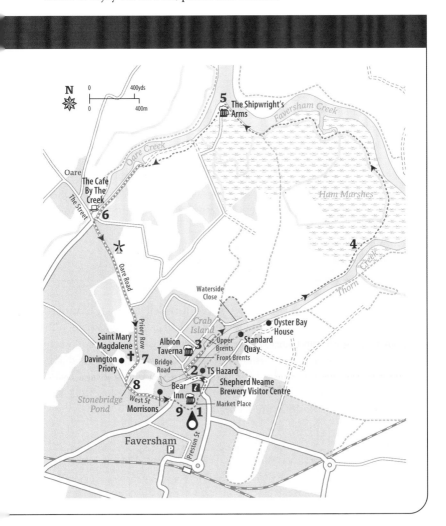

Faversham two creeks walk continued...

closer to the town centre. Keep to the Saxon Shore Way, shadowing the creek around to the northwest and keeping an eye out for oystercatchers feeding on the saltmarshes.

5 After about a mile, the route passes The Shipwright's Arms at Hollowshore (page 131), the ideal place to break for lunch or refreshments. This is the point where Oare Creek joins Faversham Creek to flow out into the Swale. After the pub, the footpath hugs the south bank of Oare Creek, passing a boatyard and boat moorings, eventually joining up with a creek-side road which leads to Oare village.

6 After passing the marina and The Cafe By The Creek, turn left on to The Street. Continue down this paved road, passing on the left an early 19th-century windmill that's missing its sweeps and fantail.

7 Keep straight ahead as The Street becomes Oare Road, then Priory Row, leading to St Mary Magdalene. With most of its constructing dating to the 12th century, this is the area's oldest building. Davington Priory, next to the church and once a Benedictine nunnery, is the home of pop singer Bob Geldof. Descend Davington Hill, turning left on to West Street at the junction.

8 You'll pass Stonebridge Pond on your left; this area was once the heart of Faversham's gunpowder industry. In 1781 three tons of powder blew up near the pond, killing three people and causing an explosion that was heard as far away as London. Keep following West Street, past Morrisons, and continue on to the pedestrianised section of the street that leads back to Market Place.

9 Slake your thirst with a pint in the Bear Inn, Faversham's oldest pub, dating back to the 16th century, or head to the café at Creek Creative (see opposite).

At the northeast end of Abbey Street, turn left to reach **Standard Quay** (✆ 01795 597616 🖥 standardquay.co.uk). The handsome 17th-century brick warehouses here now house antique, vintage and curio stores as well as food and drink businesses. This was once Faversham's main unloading quay and a busy wooden shipbuilding and repair yard. Historic craft, such as the sailing barges *Greta*, completed in 1892, and the 1925-vintage *Rusalka*, are moored here.

🍴 FOOD & DRINK

The Albion Taverna 29 Front Brents ✆ 01795 591411 🖥 albiontaverna.com ◷ noon–23.00 Mon–Sat, noon–22.30 Sun. Tuck into tacos, burrito wraps, sizzling fajitas and other tasty Mexican dishes at this lovely old pub in a weatherboarded building facing on to Faversham Creek.

The Bear Inn Market Pl 🕿 01795 532668 ⊘ bearinnfaversham.co.uk ⊕ 10.30–22.00 Mon–Sat, 11.30–22.00 Sun. Faversham is well served with atmospheric pubs, such as this one, opposite the Guildhall. The building dates back to medieval times and is said to be the town's oldest surviving inn – although much of what you'll see is the result of an early 20th-century rebuild. Still, it's a curio-packed and pleasingly traditional place with a public bar at the front, a snug in the middle and a lounge bar to the rear.

Macknade Selling Rd 🕿 01795 534497 ⊘ macknade.com ⊕ 09.00–18.00 Mon–Wed & Sat, 09.00–20.00 Thu & Fri, 10.00–16.00 Sun. Junk the supermarket and dive into the culinary heaven that is Macknade, a family business that has been trading for over 40 years from its original farm site. Here you'll find a wonderful café, outdoor food stalls, an amazing food hall, a butchers and a wine shop – all specialising in the best of Kentish produce.

Reads Macknade Manor, Canterbury Rd 🕿 01795 535344 ⊘ reads.com ⊕ noon–14.00 & 19.00–21.00 Tue–Sat. A Georgian manor house where you can stay overnight is the elegant location for the Michelin-starred cooking of chef David Pitchford. He combines local meats and fresh fish with ingredients grown in the walled kitchen garden to create dishes such as smoked haddock tart, slow-baked beetroot and roast Kentish lamb.

The Refinery 122 West St ⊘ refineryfaversham.co.uk ⊕ 09.00–16.00 Mon–Thu, 09.00–21.00 Fri & Sat, 10.00–16.00 Sun. A handy spot for a gourmet coffee and snack, such as a vegan sausage roll or a slice of homemade cake, close by Faversham's busy Market Place. There's pavement seating in good weather and the café-bar is also dog friendly.

SHOPPING

Apart from Faversham's three weekly **markets** there's also a food, arts and crafts market that spills over into Preston Street from Market Square on the first and third Saturday of each month and an antique and vintage market held on the first Sunday of the month; for full details see ⊘ favershammarket.org.

Apotheca 13 West St ⊘ apothecaclinic.co.uk ⊕ 10.00–17.00 Mon–Fri, 10.00–16.00 Sat. This marriage of a Victorian-style apothecary with a contemporary spa is the place to head for herbal remedies, teas, natural therapies and body care products, in a tranquil, vintage setting.

Creek Creative 1 Abbey St ⊘ creek-creative.org ⊕ 10.00-16.00 Tue–Sun. A gallery and artisan craft shop where 75% of the retail price goes to the creatives. Items on sale from local artists, some of whom rent studio space here, include jewellery, paintings, prints and pottery. There's also a very pleasant café with some outdoor tables.

Edible Culture The Horticultural Unit, The Abbey School, London Rd ⊘ edibleculture.co.uk ⊕ 09.00–17.00 Mon–Sat, 10.00–16.00 Sun. This self-described 'old-school nursery' is in fact very 'new school' in that everything it sells is peat, pesticide and plastic free – your choice of herbs, vegetable plants, fruit trees etc will be potted up in recycled, biodegradable cardboard containers.

Kentish Heritage Bookshop 13 Preston St ⌖ favershamsociety.org ⏱ 09.00–15.30 Mon–Sat. Among the wide range of subjects covered at the Faversham Society's second-hand bookshop is a superb collection of new books and pamphlets about Kent.

Tales on Market St 1& 2 Market St 🛈 ⏱ 10.00–16.00 Tue–Fri, 10.00–17.00 Sat. On the corner of Market Square, this indie bookshop carries a nicely curated range of titles as well as arty souvenirs and gifts from local creatives. Check their Facebook page for details of book readings and other literary events in town. The same team run The Hat Shop at 110 West Street.

AROUND FAVERSHAM

Some sights and attractions near Faversham, such as Brogdale National Fruit Collection and the Oare Gunpowder Works Country Park, you can easily walk or cycle to. Others, including a quartet of historic houses, are a bit further afield but are certainly worth searching out, particularly so if you're a garden lover.

16 BROGDALE NATIONAL FRUIT COLLECTION

Brogdale Rd, ME13 8XZ ☎ 01795 536250 ⌖ brogdalecollections.org ⏱ 10.00–16.00 daily; guided tours Apr–Oct 11.00, 13.00 & 14.30 Tue–Sun

The UK's National Fruit Collection has been curated and nurtured across the 150 acres at Brogdale Farm, a 25-minute walk south of Faversham railway station, since 1952. Year-round you can explore the orchards, which are planted with some 4,000 varieties of fruit and nut trees, from apples, cherries and pears to quinces, cobnuts and hazelnuts. On the guided tours you'll learn more about Brogdale's history, the incredible range of varieties they grow from around the world and be able to taste seasonal produce with experts. The late spring blossom season is one of the peak times to visit, with Brogdale staging its own twist on Japan's *hanami* (cherry blossom viewing) parties in a new area planted with over a hundred different varieties of ornamental cherry trees in 2021. It's not just about orchards, either: Brogdale has a wildlife garden and a music garden, featuring instruments from Africa, Asia and South – kids will love bashing away on the wooden glockenspiel and the tubular gongs.

1 Belmont House walled garden. **2 & 3** Brogdale National Fruit Collection. **3** Black-tailed godwits, Oare Marshes Nature Reserve. ▶

ORCHARD WALK

➔

PLEASE KEEP ON PATH

➔

➔

It's well worth looking into attending the many events and great short courses held at Brogdale during the year. These include foraging walks and classes in beekeeping, cider making and basket weaving. At the farm is also the **courtyard café** (⌂ thecourtyardatbrogdale.co.uk) for light meals and snacks, and other retail businesses including **Tiddly Pomme** (⌂ tiddlypommeshop.co.uk), selling fruit from the orchards and other fruit-related produce, including cider, and the artisan chocolate maker **Kakawa** (⌂ kakawaartisan.com).

17 OARE

The pretty little village of Oare, about one mile northwest of Faversham, has an explosive history. Like Faversham, its larger neighbour, Oare specialised in making gunpowder for over 400 years. You can learn all about the gunpowder process – and go for a nature walk – at **Oare Gunpowder Works Country Park** (off Bysing Wood Rd, ME13 7UD ⌂ www.gunpowderworks.co.uk ⊙ car park 09.00–17.00 Mon–Fri, 10.00–16.00 Sat & Sun; visitor centre Mar–Nov 10.00–16.00 Sat, Sun & public hols). Two Huguenot refugees – Peter Azire and Francis Grueber – ran separate gunpowder mills here from the late 17th century. The businesses were merged by the mid 19th century and the works here continued to produced gunpowder until 1934 when they closed. Woodlands were planted around the works as a blast screen and canals (known as 'leats') were dug to bring water to the mills and for the safe transport of gunpowder around the site. All of this, along with ruined remains of the works, makes for a fantastic wildlife sanctuary which can be explored on a series of short waymarked routes. In particular, look out for native bats and dragonflies.

From the village of Oare, follow Church Road to the banks of the Swale where a ferry once shuttled across to Harty (page 121) on the Isle of Sheppey: if the tide is low you'll be able to walk along the slippery stone gangway jutting into the mudflats. Church Road forms the western border of the 200-acre **Oare Marshes Nature Reserve** (Church Rd 🕿 01622 662012 ⌂ kentwildlifetrust.org.uk). This grazing marsh (one of a few remaining in Kent) with freshwater dykes, open-water scrapes, reed beds, saltmarsh and sea wall, is of international importance for migratory, overwintering and breeding wetland birds. Look out for spring migratory birds including the avocet, lapwing, black-tailed godwit and whimbrels.

🍴 FOOD & DRINK

The Shipwright's Arms Hollowshore ME13 7TU 🖉 01795 590088
🖮 theshipwrightsathollowshore.co.uk ⊙ noon–15.00 & 17.00–19.00 Tue–Fri, noon–21.00
Sat, noon–20.00 Sun. First licenced in 1738, but operating as an inn for centuries before that,
this atmospheric, low-ceilinged pub, once the haunt of smugglers, is now a welcome pitstop
on the footpaths beside Oare and Faversham creeks. There's a good selection of real ales on
tap and the food menu is solid and traditional, with Scotch eggs being a speciality.

Three Mariners 2 Church Rd, Oare ME13 0QA 🖉 01795 533633 🖮 thethreemarinersoare.
co.uk ⊙ noon–22.00 Wed–Sat, noon–19.00 Sun. The pick of Oare's two decent pubs,
the Three Mariners sparks interest with its ambitious menu that includes dishes such as
cauliflower panna cotta, crackling coated squid with chilli jam, and beetroot churros. The
interior of the 18th-century building is convivial and there's an extensive outdoor terrace
and beer garden including a heated tepee.

18 PROVENDER HOUSE

Provender Ln, Norton ME13 0ST 🖉 07773 790872 🖮 www.provenderhouse.co.uk
⊙ tours May–Oct 10.30 & 14.00 1st & last Sun of month & 1st Tue of month

This 13th-century country pile, 3½ miles west of Faversham, is named
after its founder Sir John de Provender, a favoured courtier of Henry
III. Through its long and colourful history, it has had associations with
Sir Joseph Banks, the naturalist, and the author Jane Austen. Today it is
the home of Princess Olga Romanoff, the daughter of Prince Andrew
Romanoff, the eldest nephew of Tsar Nicholas II. The prince was exiled
to the UK with his family after the Russian
Revolution, and Olga grew up in the house, *"The house has slowly been*
which was first rented by her maternal *coaxed back to life with*
great grandmother, and later bought by *repairs and restorations,*
her maternal grandmother. The princess, *revealing ancient*
who is quite a character (she's one of the *architectural features."*
stars of the TV show 'Keeping Up with the
Aristocrats'), took over its running after her mother's death in 2000 and
now gives occasional tours of the property to help fund its upkeep and
ongoing restoration.

The house, which was practically derelict when Olga inherited it, has
slowly been coaxed back to life with repairs and restorations under the
guidance of conservation architect Ptolemy Dean, revealing ancient
architectural features. Far from a prettified National Trust property,
this is very much a lived-in, endearingly messy home, plastered with a

SWALE STEAM RAILWAYS

Few 20th-century railways can claim – as the **Sittingbourne & Kemsley Light Railway** (Sittingbourne Retail Park, The Wall, Sittingbourne ME10 2XD ✆ 01795 424899 ⌂ sklr.net) does – to still be operating on their original line with two of its original steam engines and rolling stock. This 2ft 6in-gauge line is the preserved southern half of the former Bowater's Railway, built in the late 19th century to transport the raw materials for paper making and the finished products around the mill at Sittingbourne.

Trains depart from Sittingbourne Viaduct station, just off the B2006 and reached by a six-minute walk north from Sittingbourne mainline station. It's a 15-minute ride to Kemsley Down where you have 45 minutes before the return journey to explore the site and visit the café and shop. Kemsley Down, overlooking Milton Creek, the Swale Estuary and the Elmley Nature Reserve on the Isle of Sheppey, is a prime birdwatching location.

There are usually three round trips each Sunday with additional ones on bank holiday Mondays and Wednesdays in August.

At the nearby **Bredgar & Wormshill Light Railway** (The Warren, Bedgar, Sittingbourne ME9 8AT ✆ 01622 884254 ⌂ bwlr.co.uk), train enthusiasts restore and tinker with old locomotives and other industrial vehicles and bits of machinery. Among their collection are eight steam engines, most dating back to the early 20th century and with fascinating histories that saw them do duty in far-flung locations such as Mozambique and Cameroon in West Africa. There's also a G-scale model railway with a mountain section including a cable car and hot air balloon. One of the unique things you can do here is spend a day driving a steam engine (£200 including lunch). The site's tearoom is open 09.00 to 15.00 Wednesday to Sunday; check their website for other opening days and special events.

hodgepodge of good (and very bad) painted portraits and fascinating photos of a bewildering array of royal relations. The princess brings the handful of rooms open for public view alive with entertaining anecdotes and gossipy asides. A self-contained, two-bedroom wing of the house can also be rented via Airbnb.

19 DODDINGTON PLACE GARDENS

Church Ln, Sittingbourne ME9 0BB ✆ 01795 886101 ⌂ doddingtonplacegardens.co.uk
⊙ Apr–Sep 11.00–17.00 Wed, Sun & bank hols

Six miles southeast of Faversham, these gorgeous Edwardian-era gardens surround Doddington Place, a multi-gabled brick house designed by Charles Brown Trollope for Sir John Croft in 1870. Some impressive giant sequoia redwoods remain from the original Victorian gardens. There was a significant redesign of the gardens after the home was sold on to General Douglas Jeffreys and his wife in 1906. During this period the gardens gained their mile of box hedging, a rock garden and a series of descending waterways that empty into a large pool. In the 1960s, the discovery of three acres of acidic soil (a rarity on the chalky North Downs) enabled the planting of woodlands that burst with azaleas, magnolia and rhododendron in springtime. Other attractive features include mature, cloud-pruned yew hedges and a long lawn culminating in a brick and flint folly. Enjoy the lovely vistas a drink and slice of cake from the tea room.

20 BELMONT HOUSE

Belmont Park, Throwley ME13 0HH ℘ 01795 890202 ⊘ belmont-house.org
⊙ house 13.30–16.00 Tue & Thu, gardens 10.00–18.00 daily

This handsome, late 18th-century country house, 4½ miles south of Faversham and with commanding views over the North Downs, has been the home of the Harris family for over 220 years. The Harrises played key roles in British colonial expansion during the 19th century, which explains Belmont's globe-trotting collections of art and other decorative objects. The clock collection is the most significant, with some 340 pieces ranging from pocket watches to grandfather clocks. Timepieces were the passion of the 5th Lord Harris, who was the founding president of the Antiquarian Horological Society. On the last Saturday of the month, from June to September, an expert in horology conducts a tour of Belmont's clocks. There are also interesting collections of armoury and arms, and 34 delicate watercolours of the West Indies by the Trinidadian artist Michel Jean Cazabon (1813–1888) that were commissioned by the 3rd Lord Harris when he was Governor of Trinidad.

The 14 acres of gardens hold interest throughout the year. The highlight is a magnificent walled kitchen garden restored in 2001 by Lady Arabella Lennox-Boyd, and which includes a Victorian greenhouse and a sundial from 1790 when the house was first built. There's also a walled garden, its borders bursting with flowers, a pinetum that includes a Victorian shell grotto, and a parterre garden, planted with herbs and shaped like a mandala. Belmont's 3,000-acre estate also includes farmlands, woodlands, orchards, holiday cottages and a very well-used cricket pitch. Check the website for details of the cricket matches, other events, and various arts and crafts workshops.

21 MOUNT EPHRAIM GARDENS

Staplestreet Rd, Hernhill ME13 9TX ℰ 01227 751496 ℰ mountephraimgardens.co.uk
☉ Apr–Sep 11.00–17.00 Wed–Sun & bank hols

Mount Ephraim, 3½ miles east of Faversham, has been the home of the Dawes family since 1695, but its gardens were only laid out in the early 20th century. Having fallen into ruin during World War II, they were restored in the 1950s and have been added to and enhanced ever since, creating one of Kent's most enchanting horticultural ensembles. The recommended walking course will take you past a Japanese-style rock garden with a stream cascading into an ornamental lake, then on into shady woods and a small but impressively stocked arboretum. Next comes a 'miz maze', a labyrinth of swaying grasses and herbaceous perennials, before you climb back up the hill towards the house where there are terraced gardens, topiary and the Millennium rose garden, packed with spectacular blooms in June.

Check the garden's website for details of events that are held here during the summer season, including their cherry festival in early July. Also on Mount Ephraim's grounds is **Joe's Bows** (ℰ joesbows.co.uk), offering skills training in falconry, archery, axe throwing and other target practice.

⫙ FOOD & DRINK

Red Lion Crockham Ln, Hernhill ME13 9TU ℰ 01227 751207 ℰ theredlionhernhill.co.uk
☉ 11.30–22.00 Wed–Sat, 11.30–19.00 Sun. Mount Ephraim has a tea room but for a more substantial meal or a refreshing pint this characterful wood-beamed pub, dating back to 1364, is recommended. It is within easy walking distance of the gardens and overlooks Hernhill's village green, shaded by a mighty oak, next to which stands the 12th-century flint and stone church of St Michael's.

Mount Ephraim Gardens. ▶

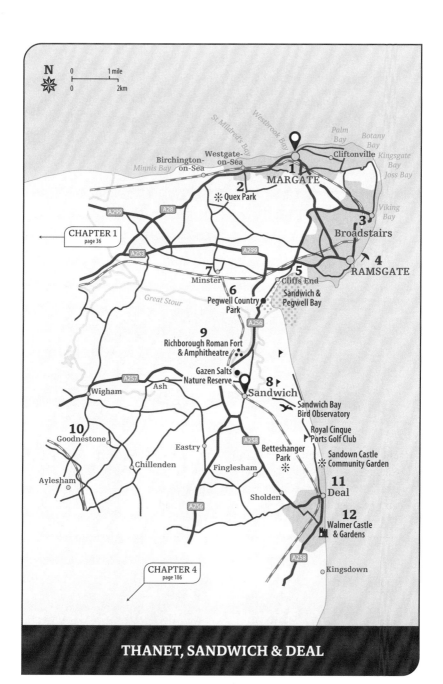

N

| 0 | 1 mile |
| 0 | 2km |

St Mildred's Bay
Westbrook Bay
Palm Bay
Botany Bay
Minnis Bay
Birchington-on-Sea
Westgate-on-Sea
Cliftonville
Kingsgate Bay
Joss Bay
1
MARGATE

2
☀ Quex Park

Viking Bay

3
Broadstairs

CHAPTER 1
page 36

A299
A28
A253
A299

7
Minster

5
Cliffs End

4
RAMSGATE

6
Pegwell Country Park

Great Stour

Sandwich & Pegwell Bay

A256

9
Richborough Roman Fort & Amphitheatre

Gazen Salts
Nature Reserve

A257
Wigham
Ash

8 ▶
Sandwich

Sandwich Bay
Bird Observatory

Royal Cinque
Ports Golf Club

10
Goodnestone

Chillenden

Eastry

A258

Betteshanger
Park
☀

Sandown Castle
Community Garden
☀

Finglesham

11
Deal

Aylesham

Sholden

A256

12
Walmer Castle
& Gardens

CHAPTER 4
page 186

Kingsdown

THANET, SANDWICH & DEAL

3
THANET, SANDWICH & DEAL

No spot in English history can be so sacred to Englishmen as that which first felt the tread of English feet.
John Richard Green, 1899

It's a lofty claim to fame, but Ebbsfleet on Kent's Isle of Thanet is the 'spot' recorded as the place where the Germanic brothers Hengist and Horsa launched their invasion of Britain in the 5th century. Back in AD43 the Romans established their first fort at nearby Richborough along the Wantsum Channel that once split Thanet from the mainland (which is why this most northeasterly point of Kent is still referred to as an isle). And it was to Pegwell Bay, also in the same vicinity, that St Augustine sailed in 597 in his mission to restore the Christian faith to pagan Britain.

The chance to stand at such historical locations is a pretty good reason to visit this area of northeast Kent, but it's far from the only one. Thanet's coastline of low chalk cliffs is fringed with some of Kent's most beautiful sandy beaches: walking or cycling along the Viking Coastal Trail is a wonderful way to discover them. The reviving sea water and fresh air here has been attracting vacationing Londoners since the late 18th century when towns such as Margate and Broadstairs began to develop into the popular resorts they are today. Margate was beloved by J M W Turner for the quality of its skies, and by the pop rock duo Chas & Dave, who rated it much better than the 'Costa Brava and all that palava'. It may not be as sunny as Spain but today, after spending the latter part of the 20th century in decline, Margate has regained its mojo by embracing contemporary art and supporting a thriving food and drinks scene.

Heading south along the coast will bring you to stately Ramsgate, the only Royal Harbour in the UK and another Thanet community on the up. Holding its own between its two larger neighbours is the charming seaside resort of Broadstairs, beloved by Charles Dickens.

Leaving Thanet, skirt around Pegwell Bay to Sandwich, an incredibly well-preserved medieval town that was one of the original Cinque Ports but which is now about two miles inland. Further south, the charming coastal towns of Deal and Walmer both sport seafront castles built during the reign of Henry VIII. Go a little inland from the coast and you'll discover other treasures including Quex Park's fascinating Powell-Cotton Museum and lovely gardens, and more gorgeous gardens at 18th century Goodnestone Park, a country estate frequently visited by the novelist Jane Austen.

GETTING THERE & AROUND

TRAINS

All the main resort towns of Thanet plus Sandwich and Deal are easily accessible by rail – it's by far the best way to reach and travel around this northeast corner of Kent. Direct trains from London St Pancras provide connections to Margate (1 hour 28 minutes), Broadstairs (1 hour 23 minutes) and Ramsgate (1 hour 17 minutes). For Sandwich (1 hour 45 minutes), Deal (1 hour 45 minutes) and Walmer (1 hour 40 minutes) the fastest routes involve a change of trains at Ashford. For schedules and fares see ⏀ southeasternrailway.co.uk.

BUSES

Stagecoach (⏀ stagecoachbus.com) run bus services around Thanet and the towns of Sandwich, Deal and Walmer; they also run the Loop, a frequent service connecting Margate, Broadstairs and Ramsgate.

CYCLING

You can circumnavigate the Isle of Thanet, from Reculver to Ramsgate across country, and then back again around the coast via Margate on the 32-mile **Viking Coastal Trail** (Regional Cycle Network 15). National Cycling Route 1 passes through Sandwich, Deal and Walmer.

The Miners' Way Trail is a 27-mile circular walking and cycling route which links Deal and Shepherdswell, taking you past some of the collieries that operated in this area in the early 20th century. The route starts at Sholden on one of the first cycle tracks in the country, alongside the A258, goes past Bettershanger Park and through the villages of Finglesham and Eastry to Shepherdswell (page 205).

ⓘ TOURIST INFORMATION

Broadstairs The Parade ⟨⟩ broadstairsinfokiosk.co.uk ☉ Apr–Oct 10.00–16.00 Sat & Sun.
Deal Town Hall, High St ✆ 01304 369576 ⟨⟩ whitecliffscountry.org.uk ☉ 09.30–12.30 Tue & Thu.
Margate Droit House, Stone Pier ✆ 01843 577577 ⟨⟩ visitthanet.co.uk ☉ 10.00–17.00 daily, 11.00–16.00 bank hols.
Ramsgate Custom House, The Harbour Pde ✆ 01843 598750 ⟨⟩ visitramsgate.co.uk ☉ 10.00–16.00 daily.
Sandwich Guildhall, Cattle Market ✆ 01304 613565 ⟨⟩ whitecliffscountry.org.uk ☉ 10.00–17.00 daily.

Col's Kent Bike Tours (✆ 07734 800812 ⟨⟩ colskentbiketours.co.uk) offers both group and private bike tours with itineraries radiating out from their Margate base towards Broadstairs, Ramsgate, Herne Bay, Whitstable and Canterbury.

BIKE HIRE

Albion House Albion Place, Ramsgate ✆ 01843 606 630 ⟨⟩ albionhouseramsgate.co.uk/bike-hire
The Bike Shed 71 Canterbury Rd, Margate ✆ 01843 228 866 ⟨⟩ thebikeshedkent.co.uk
Harbour Bikes Arch 20, The Royal Harbour, Ramsgate ✆ 07834 377 907 ⟨⟩ harbourbikes.co.uk
Hut 55 Marine Rd, Walmer ✆ 07745 527972 ⟨⟩ hut55.co.uk/bikehire
Ken's Bike Shop 26 Eaton Rd, Margate ✆ 01843 221422 ⟨⟩ kensbikes.co.uk

MARGATE & SURROUNDS

The artist J M W Turner, who spent many happy years in **Margate**, once told the critic John Ruskin: 'The skies over Thanet are the loveliest in all Europe.' Witness the sunlight filtering through the clouds and casting glitter across the sea and you will be hard pressed to disagree. Raffishly louche, artily bohemian and democratic in its many sensory pleasures, Margate epitomises the boom, bust and boom again cycle of Kent's seaside resorts.

West of Margate are a couple of smaller resort towns with fine beaches and invigorating seaside walks. **Westgate-on-Sea**, eulogised in a poem by John Betjeman, was conceived as an exclusive Victorian community, hence its nickname 'Mayfair by the sea'. **Birchington-on-Sea**, a village with 11th-century roots, was where the Pre-Raphaelite artist Dante Gabriel Rossetti had a studio. Nearby are the family-friendly sands of **Minnis Bay** and, heading into the countryside, **Quex Park**, with its quirky Powell-Cotton Museum and many other attractions.

1 MARGATE & SURROUNDS

🏠 **Albion Rooms** (page 308), **The Reading Rooms** (page 309), **No 42** (page 308) **Twentieth Century B&B** (page 309), **Walpole Bay Hotel** (page 309)

Back in the 12th century Meregate, as it was then known, and its sailors and ships supported Dover in the confederation of Cinque Ports (see box, page 167). In the 18th century the health benefits of sunshine, fresh air and sea bathing were pioneered at its Royal Sea Bathing Hospital and the town became a fashionable Georgian resort for the wealthy. The opening of the railway to Margate in 1846 saw mass tourism really take off here. As well as the marvellous soft sands and rippling waves, quirkier attractions such as the enigmatic Shell Grotto and the Margate Caves were hits with Victorian visitors. The game arcades and classic fairground rides of the amusement park Dreamland are the leitmotifs of Margate's early 20th-century heyday.

Like many of Kent's seaside towns, Margate languished as the new millennium approached and it's still tackling ingrained problems of poverty and deprivation. However, the resort's general revival since the opening of the Turner Contemporary gallery in 2011 has been remarkable, and cheap property prices have tempted many creative and entrepreneurial types to ditch London in favour of a relaxed seaside life. The Old Town and Northdown Road, which runs through the neighbouring suburb of Cliftonville, are both hives of activity, packed with appealing places to eat and drink, boutiques selling vintage jeans and retro light fittings, and small galleries exhibiting works by up-and-coming artists.

Directly opposite the train station and spanning a gently curved bay is Margate's main beach, which includes a tidal swimming pool. Take in the scene from the **Nayland Rock promenade shelter**, a Grade II-listed

1 Turner Contemporary, Margate. **2** Kingsgate Bay, Broadstairs. **3** Seals can often be spotted basking on sandbars in Pegwell Bay. **4** Broadstairs Folk Week. **5** Shell Grotto, Margate. ▶

RON ELLIS/S

TOURISM, THANET DISTRICT COUNCIL

VISIT KENT

TOURISM, THANET DISTRICT COUNCIL

TOURISM, THANET DISTRICT COUNCIL

Victorian structure where TS Eliot is believed to have drafted some lines of his poem *The Wasteland*. For Eliot, who was recovering from a nervous breakdown at the time, Margate Sands was a place where he could connect 'nothing with nothing'. Hopefully, your impressions will be nowhere as near as bleak.

Nearby, **Dreamland** (⌂ dreamland.co.uk ☉ 11.00–17.00 Sat, Sun & bank hols) has been entertaining with its classic fairground rides and amusement arcades for over a century. John Henry Iles spent the equivalent of £15 million in developing the original park, which has gone through several iterations during its lifetime. The star of the show remains the Scenic Railway, the UK's oldest rollercoaster, which opened along with the amusement park in 1920. There's also dodgems, waltzers,

MARGATE'S ART SCENE

Stroll through the Old Town, along the seafront and up Northdown Road to discover scores of small galleries and artists' studios such as **Resort** (50 Athelstand Rd ⌂ resortstudios.co.uk), **Kill Me Now** (33 Hawley St), **Pie Factory Margate** (5 Broad St ⌂ piefactorymargate.co.uk) and the **Community Pharmacy Gallery** (16 Market Pl ⌂ beepingbush.co.uk).

Tracey Emin, the boundary-pushing Young British Artist of the 1990s who has matured into a respected Royal Academician, was born in Margate. She's a champion of the town and, in 2017, bought the central, derelict Thanet Press building to transform it into her working studio and home. In the future it will house a museum of Emin's art, her legacy to Margate. Sharing floor space in this evolving project is **Carl Freedman** (28 Union Cres ☏ 020 7684 8890 ⌂ carlfreedman.com ☉ noon–18.00 Wed–Sun), Margate's largest commercial gallery with three big exhibition spaces. Three or four shows of works by emerging British and international talents are staged here each year and are well worth catching.

For a deeper dive into Margate's arts scene, schedule your visit to coincide with **First Friday Margate**, an after-hours event held on the first Friday of the month and organised by the Bus Café (⌂ thebuscafe.co.uk), the gift store Little Bit (⌂ littlebitmargate. com), the co-working space Marine Studios (⌂ marinestudios.co.uk), and the artist and writer Dan Thompson. Many of the town's usually off-limits artists' studios open to the public in the evening, and the Turner Contemporary opens from 19.00 to 21.00. Indie shops and café also stay open a little later, with some putting on special events of their own. Also keep an eye out for occasional events and future developments at **Cliftonville Cultural Space** (Albion Rd, Cliftonville ⌂ cliftonvilleculturalspace.com) a deconsecrated 1929 synagogue that is in the process of being transformed into a cross-cultural multi-arts venue.

a ghost train, roller disco and much more. Entry to the park is free with fees for each of the attractions.

Art lovers in search of creative stimulation need only cast their eye around the gently stepped sea defences and across the sands to the geometric form of the **Turner Contemporary** (Rendezvous ℰ 01843 233000 ⌃ turnercontemporary.org ☉ 10.00–17.00 Tue–Sun; free entry). Designed by David Chipperfield, this gallery is credited with kickstarting Margate's revival. It takes its name from the celebrated Victorian painter who used to stay at a guesthouse that once stood on the same site. Works by Turner – often ones he completed in and around Margate – are regularly on display in the gallery, sparking a lively artistic conversation with the regularly changing and expertly curated contemporary works also exhibited here.

The gallery's panoramic, sea-facing windows provide an ideal frame for Antony Gormley's *Another Time,* which stands on Fulsam Rock on the seashore. One in a series of 100 solid cast-iron sculptures by the artist, it has stoically endured Margate's rising and falling tides since 2017 and is scheduled to stay until at least 2030. If the tide is out, walk across the sand and seaweed slathered rocks for a close-up view of this barnacle encrusted figure.

Before heading inland, take a look at a couple of other public artworks. *I Never Stopped Loving You* is a neon sign by Tracey Emin who grew up in Margate and has returned to live and work in the town. It hangs over the entrance to Droit House, which now houses the tourist information centre but which was once the harbour customs building. At the end of the curving stone pier, known as the Harbour Arm, is a tall, brass sculpture of a lady made from seashells. *Mrs Booth*, by Ann Carrington, is a homage to Sophia Booth, the twice-widowed Margate landlady with whom Turner had a long love affair. The Harbour Arm is lined with bars, cafés and galleries and a walk along it to the lighthouse at the end provides wonderful views out to sea and back towards the town.

From the Turner Contemporary it's a very short walk into Margate's Old Town, an attractive quarter of tight-knit Georgian and Victorian buildings, most now turned into cafés, restaurants and shops. Here you'll find the town's oldest building, **Tudor House** (King St ℰ 01843 231213 ⌃ margatemuseum.org ☉ 11.30–14.30 Wed, Sat, Sun & bank hols), a half-timbered beauty dating back to 1525. The original owners were clearly wealthy as the house sports unusual features for its time, including glazed windows and two chimneys. The house is not often open, but the low surrounding walls permit views across into its Tudor knot garden and box hedge squares.

There's a chance to learn about Margate's history in the **Margate Museum** (Market Pl ✐ 01843 231213 ◈ margatemuseum.org ☉ 11.00–17.00 Wed, Sat & Sun) which is housed in the old Town Hall, a building that also served as a Victorian police station and magistrates' court. The exhibits cover a broad range of local topics from sea bathing machines and donkeys on the beach to artworks that trace the town's development from a humble fishing village to the holiday resort it is today.

The intriguing **Margate Caves** (1 Northdown Rd ◈ margatecaves. co.uk ☉ 10.00–17.00 daily) can be reached by walking up Northdown Road from the Old Town. 'The most surprising discovery of the age!' proclaimed posters promoting this attraction to Victorians as the Vortigen Caves in 1863. Said to date to AD454, these underground caverns were in reality an early 18th-century chalk mine that had been covered over and forgotten. Rediscovered in the early 19th century, their potential as a tourist attraction was given a boost by the addition of colourful paintings of soldiers, wild beasts and a hunting expedition across the towering chalk walls. Local art students added the Virgin Mary and a fluorescent Thanet Giant to these images in the 1950s. The caves closed in 2004 but, following a campaign to have them reopened, they have been made fit as a contemporary attraction – this time with accurate and fascinating historical interpretation in the award-winning visitor centre and café that sits above ground.

"There are far more questions than answers about the Shell Grotto which, so the story goes, was discovered by chance in 1835."

While the history of the Margate Caves is well documented, mystery swirls around Margate's second subterranean attraction which lies about a ten-minute walk away. There are far more questions than answers about the **Shell Grotto** (Grotto Hill ✐ 01843 220008 ◈ shellgrotto.co.uk ☉ 10.00–17.00 daily) which, so the story goes, was discovered by chance in 1835 under the garden of a residential cottage. Smaller and more compact than the Margate Caves, the chalk tunnels and underground rooms here are entirely plastered in decorative patterns and symbols created from seashells. Was it a rich 18th-century gentleman's secret hobby project or an even older pagan site of worship? No-one knows for sure. Nor can it be explained how some 4.6 million British shells were spirited here to create the elaborate wall designs. Dubbed 'one of the world's wonders' by popular Victorian novelist Marie Corelli, the grotto is perhaps best appreciated as an eye-boggling piece of installation art, rather than as an enigma to be solved.

The **Walpole Bay Hotel** (page 309) is a one-mile walk east from the Turner Contemporary along the Eastern Esplanade's clifftop promenade. Opened in 1914, this charmingly anachronistic hotel is the last remaining of several grand hotels that once marked out Cliftonville as Margate's most des-res address. Afternoon tea enjoyed on the flower-filled terrace of this retro gem is a must, as is exploring the hotel's public areas which constitute an eccentric museum of antique items, ranging from 80-million-year-old fossils found on nearby beaches to a collection of formal hats. Best of all is the 'Napery': a gallery of over 100 artworks created by guests on the hotel's white linen napkins. Framed pieces, including ones by celebrities such as Martin Parr and Tracey Emin, are displayed in the restaurant and along the upper floor corridors.

MARGATE'S BEACHES

Margate's **Main Sands** is exactly that: the resort's central beach, perfect for building sandcastles, paddling in shallow waters and with easy access to all the town's facilities. But if it's too busy for you, alternatives are just short walks away in either direction.

Heading west will bring you first to **Westbrook Bay**, a great family beach that's also patronised by windsurfers and waterskiers. The promenade is lined with bathing huts, a handful of drink and food stalls and an 18-hole minigolf course (⌖ margateminigolf.uk ⊘ 10.00–17.00 daily). At the west end of the bay is a grassy headland where you'll find the **Sunken Gardens**, landscaped in the early 1930s on the site of a former chalk quarry.

Next along are the golden sands at **St Mildred's Bay** and **West Bay**, both of which can easily be accessed from Westgate-on-Sea train station.

Head east from Margate's **Walpole Bay** with its Grade II-listed seawater lido (page 146) to access **Palm Bay**. The broad sandy beach here has at its west end, a café that is part of the local jet ski club (🅵 PalmBay. Kent). Keep on going east, though, to reach the best beach all: the Blue Flag awarded **Botany Bay**. Framed by towering chalk cliffs and stacks, the golden sands and rock pools here are prime fossil fossicking sites. Local lore has it that the beach got its name back in the 19th century when smugglers caught here were transported to Botany Bay in Australia.

Swimmers can enjoy a bracing dip in the **Walpole Bay tidal pool**, accessed by steps down the cliffside near the Walpole Bay Hotel, or via the sea-level promenade from Margate. Covering over four acres, this impressive structure was opened in 1937 and is the UK's largest seawater lido at 450 feet long.

ENTERTAINMENT

The performing arts have long been part of Margate's cultural DNA. The resort's Grade II-listed Theatre Royal, on the corner of swish Hawley Square and Addington Street, opened in 1787, is the second-oldest theatre in the UK. It's the last of Margate's upper-class Georgian-era entertainment venues, but at the time of research the theatre was closed awaiting refurbishment as part of the £22.2 million Margate Town Deal. The seafront Winter Gardens is also closed, its future hanging in the balance. Pop concerts and other events are frequently staged at Dreamland.

Carlton Cinema 29 St Mildred's Rd, Westgate-on-Sea ✆ 01843 832019
⌖ westgatecinema.co.uk. It's worth making the trip to Westgate-on-Sea just to peek at the delightfully quirky building that this privately-run, three-screen digital cinema is housed in. Built in 1910 as the town hall, it only served that function for two years before being converted into a cinema. The eccentric architecture combines Tudoresque brick chimney with Swiss-style decorative eaves, Moorish windows and a crenellated clock tower. It's a few minutes' walk from Westgate-on-Sea train station and the ticket prices make it a bargain.

Tom Thumb Theatre 2A Eastern Esplanade, Cliftonville ✆ 01843 221791
⌖ tomthumbtheatre.co.uk. This tiny jewel-box theatre, with some 50 seats, is housed in what was once a Victorian coaching house. It has hosted everything from spoken word performances and screenings of indie films to burlesque shows and experimental theatre.

🍴 FOOD & DRINK

Margate's restaurant, bar and café scene is booming. As well as great seafood, including exciting updates on that old seaside staple of fish and chips, there's a globe-trotting mix of cuisines available here, from Cambodian dumplings to South African curries.

Angela's 21 The Parade ✆ 01843 319978 ⌖ angelasofmargate.com ☉ lunch noon or 14.00 & dinner 18.00 or 20.15 Tue–Sat. Book well ahead for this pocket-sized restaurant with a view across to the Turner Contemporary. They offer a daily changing menu of ethically sourced seafood and organic vegetables, including ones from the kitchen garden at Quex Park's Powell-Cotton House.

Batchelors Patisserie 246 Northdown Rd, Cliftonville ⊙ 06.00–14.30 Tue–Sat. In business since 1967, this retro charmer of a patisserie and café is ideal for early birds and lovers of sweet treats, which are served in the most darling of interiors.

Beach Buoys 17 Marine Dr ⊘ beachbuoys.co.uk ⊙ noon–21.00 Wed–Sun. An inspired contemporary take on the fish 'n' chippie. Indulge your deep-fried cravings with a local skate wing or beer-battered banana blossom which is marinated overnight in miso and flakes just like fish. Three choices of chips (proper, skinny and sweet potato), toppings such as crab and yuzu, plus the option of gluten-free batter just add to the appeal.

Bottega Caruso 2–4 Broad St ⊘ 01843 297142 ⊘ bottegacaruso.com ⊙ noon–15.00 Wed & Thu, noon–15.00 & 18.00–19.00 Fri & Sat. Simona di Dio and her team serve the Italian comfort food of your dreams in the heart of the old town. The pasta is freshly made from ancient grain flour imported from Italy and paired with locally sourced ingredients including herbs and vegetables grown in Margate. Bookings are essential. Check their website to find out when they're running their pasta-making workshops and cookery lessons.

Dory's 24 High St ⊘ 01843 319978 ⊘ angelasofmargate.com ⊙ noon–23.00 Thu–Mon. If Angela's is booked up, do try their second nearby operation which serves equally delicious and fresh seafood in tapas-style plates that might include moreish smoked prawns and luscious slices of cured trout.

Fez 40 High St ⊙ 15.00–22.30 Mon–Thu, noon–23.30 Fri & Sat, noon–22.00 Sun. Every surface of this eye-catching bar is covered by vintage and retro bits and pieces including a barber's chair from Chicago, a pinball machine table and an old Waltzer ride carriage that's now booth seating. Get chummy with equally characterful locals sipping on pints of real ale, cider and a choice of 35 gins.

Fort Road 18 Fort Rd ⊘ 01843 661313 ⊘ fortroadhotel.com ⊙ 08.00–10.30, noon–14.15 daily, 18.00–21.30 Wed–Sat. A skip from the Turner Contemporary, a seafront hotel has been given a swish makeover that includes a wonderful ground-floor café-bar open to all comers. A leisurely breakfast here before exploring Margate is a treat and will have you sure to want to return for dinner for the best of British seasonal food such as smoked kipper paté, Braised Romney lamb shank and white pudding.

Forts Café 8 Cliff Terrace ⊙ 08.00–16.00 Mon–Fri, 09.00–16.00 Sat & Sun. Popular café that's long been a hit with local creatives for its reliable brunches and staples with a twist, such as their bacon sarnie served on focaccia with sliced apple and chipotle ketchup, or with chilli jam and pickled red onion.

Mala Kaffe Harbour Arm ⊘ 07375 534867 ▊ ⊙ 10.00–16.00 Mon–Fri, 09.00–16.00 Sat, 09.00–15.00 Sun. Among the several places to grab a drink and something to eat along the Harbour Arm, this Scandi-themed café is a standout for the quality of its coffee (roasted by East London's Allpress), baked goodies such as cinnamon buns, and Danish salami toasties oozing with melted cheese.

Northern Belle Mansion St ✆ 07552 338765 ⌂ thenorthernbelle.co.uk ⏱ 18.00–21.30 Wed–Fri, noon–21.30 Sat & Sun. There's been a pub on this spot since 1680, which makes this the oldest one in town. Serving Shepherd Neame beers on tap, the cosy bar is also the location of Khmer Kitchen where you can sample tasty and authentic Cambodian noodle, rice and dumpling dishes. The menu also has plenty of vegetarian and vegan options.

Sargasso Harbour Arm, Stone Pier ✆ 01843 229270 ⌂ sargasso.bar ⏱ noon–14.30 & 17.30–20.30 Mon, 17.30–20.30 Tue & Wed, noon–14.30 & 17.30–20.30 Thu, noon–14.30 & 17.30–21.30 Fri & Sat, noon–15.00 Sun. The website warns that the edge-of-the-sea location combined with weather can make keeping this restaurant open a 'challenge'. It's worth making that booking, though, for their superbly tasty small plates and larger meals which include salt fish beignets, mussels in cider and slip sole with sauce Café de Paris.

🛒 SHOPPING

Lovers of vintage and retro items can seek out hidden treasures among the Old Town's cobbled streets and along Northdown Road. On the last Sunday of the month, check out the Cliftonville Farmers Market (⌂ cliftonvillefm.co.uk) on the lawn opposite the Walpole Bay Hotel.

Aarven 34 King St ⌂ aarven.com ⏱ 11.00–17.00 daily. Browse a super colourful and inspiring collection of interior design, jewellery and other crafty products made by artisans from Africa, Indian and across the UK. Fair Trade principles are adhered to and there's an emphasis, too, on sustainability.

Cliffs 172 Northdown Rd ✆ 01843 297985 ⌂ cliffsmargate.com ⏱ 08.30–15.00 Mon–Sat, 10.00–15.00 Sun. Check out peak hipster Margate at this combo of a vinyl record shop, hair salon, café and recording studio, split over two levels with a grand central staircase.

Haeckles 18 Cliff Tce ✆ 01843 447234 ⌂ haeckels.co.uk, ⏱ 10.00–17.00 daily. Much of the raw materials for the natural, handmade skincare, bath and fragrance products of this Margate brand come for the local beaches and countryside. The brand is named after the 19th-century German botanist Ernst Haeckel and was founded by Dom Bridge, an evangelist for seaweed's healing powers and one of a handful of people in the UK with a licence to forage the marine plants from Thanet's beaches.

RG Scott Furniture Market The Old Iceworks, Bath Pl ✆ 01843 220653 ⌂ scottsmargate. co.uk ⏱ 09.30–13.00 & 14.00–17.00 Mon, Tue & Thu–Sat. You could easily spend hours browsing here. Based in Margate's rambling old iceworks building, Scott's is an attraction in its own right for its jumble of everything from architectural salvage to old postcards, books and ironmongery. Also check out the more curated retro goods of **Junk Deluxe** (⌂ junkdeluxe.co.uk) at the same location.

Sunny Vintage & Retro 262 Northdown Rd ⬨ bbears.co.uk ⊙ 10.00–noon Mon, 14.00–18.00 Wed & Thu, 10.00–noon & 14.00–18.00 Fri & Sat. If a much-loved family soft toy is needing some TLC, then bring it to Sunny's teddy bear hospital – it doesn't need to be an antique. At the other end of the retro scale, you can also find punk rock posters, lapel badges and the like here.

2 QUEX PARK

Birchington-on-Sea CT7 0BH ⬨ quexpark.co.uk

There's plenty to see and do at this historic country estate four miles west Margate and a 20-minute walk south of Birchington-on-Sea train station. By far the bulk of the estate's 1,800 acres are set aside for farming and nature conservation, but there's also many other leisure and tourism attractions, offering the likes of minigolf, paintballing, archery, and goat and alpaca walking – even, in summer, finding your way through a maze of maize. There's also a craft village where you can watch artisans and artists at work in their studios.

Anchoring it all is the **Powell-Cotton Museum** (⬨ 01843 842168, ⬨ powell-cottonmuseum.org ⊙ mid-Feb–Mar, Sep & Oct 11.00–15.00 Sat & Sun; Apr–Aug 11.00–16.00 Sat & Sun) which houses the natural history and anthropological collections of the hunter and explorer Percy Powell-Cotton (1866–1940), amassed from over 28 expeditions carried out in Africa and Asia. The star exhibits are the large-scale, remarkably detailed wildlife habitat dioramas, containing over 300 taxidermy animals, including aardvarks, cheetahs and an 11ft-tall African elephant. Since 2020, the museum has been engaged in reimaging the presentation of its collections to more appropriately reflect the colonial times in which the objects were gathered. Visitors to the museum can expect to see subtle changes in the interpretation while this work is ongoing.

The museum occupies part of 19th-century Quex House which is surrounded by lovely gardens. These include a Victorian walled kitchen garden, winter garden, woodland walk, fountain and croquet lawn. Peacocks and chickens pick their way along the paths and across the lawns. Look out for the collection of cannons at the front and back of the house, including 24-pounders salvaged from the *Royal George* which sank at Spithead, off Portsmouth in 1782. Cannons were one of the passions of former owner John Powell Powell, who also had a thing for bell ringing; he had built the 131ft **Waterloo Tower**

Margate to Broadstairs: countryside & coastline

❋ OS Explorer map 150; start: Margate train station, CT9 5AF ♥ TR347705; 10½ miles; easy

This full-day walk is perfect for combining some countryside with stunning coastal walking. Because it's nearly all along sealed roads and paths it's a good one to do in winter. But, if the weather is warm and sunny, do bring your bathing costume and a towel as you'll be passing some of Kent's best beaches and a huge tidal swimming pool. The route starts by following the cross-country Turner & Dickens Walk (⌀ visitthanet.co.uk/media/65154/td-website-leaflet.pdf) between Margate and Broadstairs and then joins up with the Viking Coastal Trail (⌀ explorekent.org/activities/viking-coastal-trail). It's also possible to cycle the route, although walking will give you easier access to the beachside promenades. As this is a circular walk you could start at any point on it, including Broadstairs train station (CT10 2AJ), and there is plenty of parking in both Margate and Broadstairs.

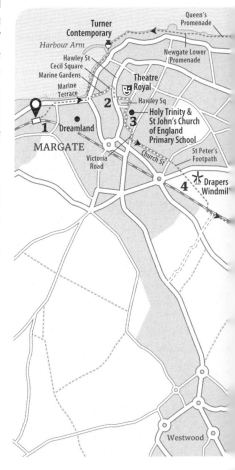

1 Turn right out of Margate train station and follow Marine Terrace past Dreamland and the strip of amusement arcades, keeping to the right when it becomes Marine Gardens. Continue on through Cecil Square, past the magistrates' court, to turn right on to Hawley Street.

2 Turn left on to Hawley Square, first laid out in the late 18th century as an enclosed pleasure ground for the occupants of the surrounding Georgian terraced buildings, who paid a subscription to enjoy its benefits. Continue to the junction with Addington Street, with the historic Theatre Royal Margate on the corner. Turn right here and walk uphill.

3 At the corner with St John's Road, note the mosaic panels inspired by J M W Turner's life and paintings in the brick wall of Holy Trinity and St John's Church of England Primary School. Continue along St John's Street, turning left at Charlotte Square. At the junction, turn right on to Victoria Road and then left at Church Street. By this point you will have started to notice the 'T&D' marker posts for the route. Continue along Church Street as it becomes St Peter's Footpath.

4 About one mile inland, opposite the Drapers Mills Primary School, is the black-painted Drapers Windmill (CT9 2SP ✆ 07985 147563 ⟳ draperswindmill.org.uk). This 1847 smock mill is usually open on Sunday afternoons from the start of June until late September. Shortly after, ▶

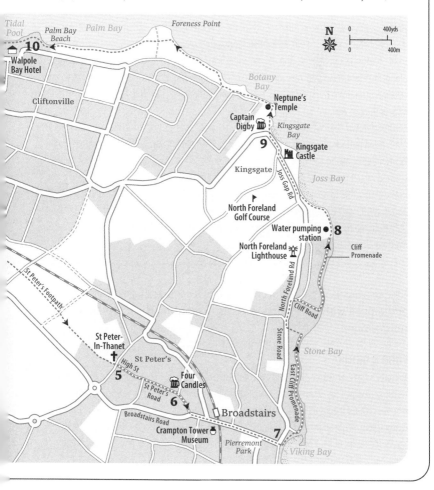

Margate to Broadstairs: countryside & coastline continued ...

where the path splits, veer right and take the footbridge over the railway line to continue on the foothpath through farm fields.

5 After about one mile you'll reach the long and picturesque graveyard of St Peter-in-Thanet (CT10 2TR ♂ stpeterinthanet.org.uk) which covers nine acres. The Norman-period church was extensively restored at the end of 19th century and its stained-glass windows and mosaics all date from this era. From the church, continue straight ahead along High Street, which becomes St Peter's Road.

6 At the junction with Upton Road, opposite the tiny brewpub Four Candles (1 Sowell St, CT10 2AT ♂ thefourcandles.co.uk), is a small landscaped area of mosaics inspired by characters from Charles Dickens' novels. The central panel is of Dickens face to face with Turner. Continue along St Peter's Road and veer left at the junction with Broadstairs Road; following this will take you straight to the seaside, passing the train station and Crampton Tower Museum (page 155) along the way.

7 Continue down High Street to Viking Bay (an ideal place to break for refreshments; page 156). Head to Harbour Street at the north end of the bay then stay on the beachside East Cliff Promenade, walking through the car park and on to Stone Bay, flanked by a row of brightly painted beach chalets. At the end of the bay, a footpath heads gently uphill between a gap in the chalk cliffs to Stone Road. Turn right and walk uphill along North Foreland Road. After about 200ft, turn right at North Foreland Avenue, heading into the private housing estate. Stay right along Cliff Road which soon swings left on to Cliff Promenade. Impressive houses overlook the sea to your left.

(♂ quexringers.org.uk), a secular bell tower containing a dozen clangers and topped with a white-painted cast-iron spire which can be seen for miles around.

¶¶ FOOD & DRINK

Felicity's Café at Quex ♂ felicityscafeatquex.co.uk ☉ 10.00–16.00 Tue–Sun. With tables nestling beneath the shade of the mature trees in front of Quex House, Felicity's offers a serene setting for a light lunch or afternoon tea.

Quex Barn ♂ quexbarn.com ☉ shop 09.00–17.00, restaurant 09.00–15.00 daily. Pick up a wide range of Kent produce at this well-stocked farm shop (including a butchers and fishmongers) at the entrance to the park. Also here is a café, restaurant and pizzeria (☉ noon–8pm Tue–Sun).

8 Continue along the coastal path to the water pumping station. To your left are farm fields and the North Foreland Lighthouse, to your right the sheer cliff edge. Ahead, beside Joss Gap Road, is the car park for Joss Bay, a lovely beach where there's also a surf school. Joss Gap Road is paralleled by a cycle track for a short stretch, but you'll soon emerge back on the main road to pass the 18th-century Kingsgate Castle. Built originally as a stables block and staff quarters, the 'castle' became a hotel in 1930s and was converted into flats in the 1990s. Just beyond here, drop down to the beach at Kingsgate Bay to inspect sea caves and view the chalk cliffs up close.

9 Returning to the clifftop path, continue past the car park of the **Captain Digby** pub to find the footpath to the right. Ahead, at the corner of one of the greens of the North Foreland Golf Course, are the flint walled remains of Neptune's Temple, an 18th-century folly. Continue for half a mile along the coastal path here to blissful Botany Bay, which has towering chalk stacks shooting up from the beach. Return from the beach to the clifftop path, which cuts through the chalk grasslands of Foreness Point which are sprinkled with wild flowers in summer.

10 About 500yds beyond Foreness Point, a gap in the chalk cliffs leads down to the concrete promenade which takes you past Palm Bay and then on to Walpole Bay and its immense tidal swimming pool. Stairs next to the pool take you back up to the clifftop path and the nearby Walpole Bay Hotel (page 145), where you can enjoy a traditional afternoon tea on its flower-filled front terrace. From here you can follow the clifftop Queens Promenade back to Margate. Alternatively, continue alongside the beachside Newgate Lower Promenade until you reach the Turner Contemporary and the Harbour Arm back in Margate.

3 BROADSTAIRS

> **You cannot think how delightful and fresh the place is and how good the walks.**
> Charles Dickens

The great Victorian novelist's enthusiasm for Broadstairs is as apt today as it was in 1851. Like the grand circle of a theatre, the town's Regency and Victorian buildings gaze down on the golden crescent sands of

DICKENS' BROADSTAIRS

Dickens was a frequent visitor to Broadstairs between 1837 and 1859. He eulogised the town in his essay *Our English Watering Place* and found inspiration in its buildings and local personalities for characters and locations in his novels. Fans should drop by the **Dickens House Museum** (2 Victoria Pde ✆ 01843 861232 ⌖ thanet.gov.uk/info-pages/dickens-house-museum) where the writer took tea and cakes with house owner Miss Mary Pearson Strong, who was the model for Miss Betsey Trotwood in his novel *David Copperfield*. In the house, which is set up as it would have been in its Victorian heyday, are letters that Dickens wrote about Broadstairs, early editions of his novels and many other items of Dickens memorabilia.

Part of *David Copperfield* was written during Dickens' residence at Fort House, the castellated building that's a prominent landmark on the hill overlooking Viking Bay. The property changed its name to **Bleak House** in the early 20th century to make plain its connection to Dickens (even though the writer rated it as a far from a bleak place given his affection for it as a holiday home). The author also holidayed in the building that now houses the Royal Albion Hotel (6–12 Albion St ⌖ albionbroadstairs.co.uk). Walks around these locations and other others connected with the writer form part of the **Dickens Festival** (⌖ broadstairsdickensfestival.co.uk) held each June.

Viking Bay. The coastal walks in either direction are glorious, leading to more beautiful beaches. Originally called Bradstow, meaning 'broad place', the history of this one-time fishing village and smugglers' haunt goes back to Roman times. From the late Georgian era it settled into its role as a gentile seaside resort. The town's intimate scale, pretty and well-maintained clifftop gardens and fine range of places to eat, drink and shop continue to make it a winner.

Viking Bay itself ticks all the boxes of the classic British beach, with neat rows of pastel-painted beach huts sheltering at the foot of chalk cliffs and fronting a broad sweep of soft sand. Hugging the northern end is the **Harbour Arm** and a stubby pier which dates back to Tudor times. The bay can get very busy, but if you're looking for a quieter beach there are excellent ones north at **Joss Bay** and south at **Louisa Bay**.

Returning to the harbour and walking back up the hill along Harbour Street you'll pass under the pointed arch that is all that remains of **York Gate,** built in 1540 to house a portcullis, with heavy wooden doors that could be shut if high storm tides threatened. Meander south along the sea-facing Parade or go one block inland to find Albion Street with its range of shops, pubs and cafés. Either way, turn right when you reach the High Street and continue uphill towards the shady gardens that surround **Pierremont Hall** (⌂ pierremonthall.co.uk) where a young Princess Victoria holidayed between 1826 and 1836.

If you keep going towards Broadstairs train station you will not fail to miss the 80ft water tower, designed by local engineer Thomas Crampton as part of his system to provide a guaranteed water supply to Broadstairs. You can learn more about this remarkable character, who also set up the first working telegraph cable under the English Channel, at the small **Crampton Tower Museum** (The Broadway ✆ 01843 601091 ⌂ cramptontower.co.uk ⊙ Apr–Oct 14.00–16.30 Sat & Sun).

ACTIVITIES

Joss Bay Surf School N Foreland Hill, CT10 3PG ✆ 07719 902025 ⌂ jossbay.co.uk. A 30-minute walk north of Broadstairs brings you to lovely Joss Bay where this operator runs surf and SUP lessons. You can also hire SUPs, surfboards and wetsuits from them.
Kent Surf School Viking Bay ✆ 01843 600330 ⌂ kentsurfschool.co.uk. Sheltered Viking Bay is a great spot to learn to surf or get the hang of SUPs. They also offer guided tours along the coast by SUP or kayak.
St Peter's Village Tours ✆ 01843 868646 ⌂ villagetour.co.uk. Reservations are essential for these entertaining guided walks around the historic village and extensive churchyard of St Peter's, about a mile east of Broadstairs. The walks, which last around 2½ hours and usually take place on Thursdays between July and September, involve local volunteers dressed in period costumes. There are also separate tours offered of St Peter's graveyard, which include the stories of those buried there who perished during service in both world wars.

ENTERTAINMENT

Broadstairs Folk Week ⌂ broadstairsfolkweek.org.uk. Running for over 55 years, this annual music festival takes place in August and involves many established and up-and-coming folk artists performing at an arena in the Memorial Recreation Ground near Broadstairs train station, and at other venues and pubs across the town.
The Chapel 44–46 Albion St ✆ 07837 024259 ⌂ chapelbroadstairs.com ⊙ 15.00–23.00 Mon–Thu, noon–24.00 Fri, noon–02.00 Sat, noon–23.00. Sunday DJs, live bands, open mic events and acoustic shows are among the entertainments staged at this cosy café-bar that's located in the Grade II-listed former St Mary's Chapel, a stone and flint building dating back to around 1070.
The Palace Cinema Harbour St ✆ 01843 865726 ⌂ thepalacecinema.co.uk. Something of a Tardis, this cosy 111-seat cinema with stalls and balcony seating occupies one-time

York Gate Hall, built in 1911 as a museum for the armoury collection of Sir Guy Laking. They specialise in screening films that are unlikely to be shown elsewhere in Thanet, as well as crowd-pleasing blockbusters. On Sundays they often screen silent films with live piano accompaniment.

¶¶ FOOD & DRINK

Flotsam & Jetsam 23 Harbour St ⌂ wyattandjones.co.uk ⊙ 11.30–17.00 Mon–Thu, 11.30–19.00 Fri–Sun. The lockdown pop-up from the team at Wyatt & Jones was so successful that it's become a permanent part of their business. This is a posh seafood and frites take-away with vegetarian, vegan and gluten-free options. Slather your cone of hand-cut chips or deep-fried seafood with 14 delicious sauces. All the wrapping is biodegradable.

Funicular The Parade, Viking Bay ⊙ 09.00–19.00 Mon–Sat, 09.00–17.00 Sun. This atmospheric café occupies the beach-level entrance to what was once the tunnel funicular that carried people up and down from the clifftop Parade to Viking Bay. They serve excellent coffee and cakes as well as light meals and local beers and wines.

Jetty Pier Head Kiosk, The Harbour ⌂ jettybroadstairs.co.uk ⊙ 08.00–22.30 daily. For the best sea views while dining at Broadstairs, head to this slickly designed and relaxed bistro and take-away at the end of the Harbour Arm. Options range from a sausage butty made with bangers sourced from St Peter's to homemade fishcakes or a vegan soya and avocado burger.

Morelli's Gelato 14 Victoria Pde ⌂ morellisgelato.com ⊙ 10.00–17.00 Mon–Thu, 09.00–17.00 Fri–Sun. Mario Morelli open this ice-cream parlour in 1932 and the family-run business has been doing a roaring trade ever since. Sink into pink leatherette booths, choose a song on the juke box and lick up the delicious, freshly made gelato.

Stark 15 Oscar Rd ⌂ starkfood.co.uk ⊙ 18.30–21.30 Wed–Sat. Ben and Sophie Crittenden have earned a Michelin star for their inventive, zero-waste cooking served in this intimate, rustically decorated restaurant. Expect quality meals with techniques such as the curing, pickling and smoking of ingredients.

The Tartar Frigate Harbour St ☎ 01843 862013 ⌂ tartarfrigate.co.uk ⊙ bar 11.00–23.00 daily; restaurant noon–14.00 & 18.30–20.45 Mon–Sat, 12.30 or 15.30 Sun. You can sense the ghosts of hard-drinking smugglers lingering at this 18th-century harbourside pub and restaurant that's made from flint and weatherboard. The bar menu includes doorstop sandwiches and smoked fish pie, while upstairs it's a bit more fancy, with good views from the window tables across Viking Bay.

Wyatt & Jones ⌂ wyattandjones.co.uk ⊙ 18.00–21.00 Thu, noon–15.00 & 18.00–21.30 Fri, noon–21.30 Sat, noon–17.00 Sun. Superior seafood such as tuna tartare, warm crab tart, lobster thermidor and slip sole with smoked seaweed butter are among the dishes that have earned this restaurant a devoted following. Switch between watching the cooks working in the open kitchen and the comings and goings of the beach through the big front windows.

SHOPPING

Albion Street is always worth a browse. There are also several good commercial art galleries to hunt down including **Broadstairs Gallery** (10 Charlotte St ⊘ broadstairsgallery.com ⊙ 10.00–17.00 Mon–Sat, 11.00–16.00 Sun), **The Little Art Gallery** (1–2 Eldon Pl ⊘ thelittleartgallerybroadstairs.com ⊙ 11.00–16.00 Sat & Sun) and **New Kent Art** (49 Albion St ⊘ newkentart.com ⊙ 11.00–16.00 daily).

RAMSGATE & SURROUNDS

Ramsgate's mix of handsome 19th- and early 20th-century architecture harks back to its heyday as a fashionable seaside resort. Two eminent Victorians – the architect Augustus Pugin and the philanthropist Sir Moses Montefiore – were great champions of the town and had homes here. It sports the only Royal Harbour in the UK and has a fascinating set of wartime tunnels beneath the ground. Nearby is the historic small town of Minster and the broad sweep of Pegwell Bay, protected as a nature reserve.

4 RAMSGATE

🏠 **Albion House** (page 308), **The Falstaff** (page 308), **Royal Harbour Hotel** (page 308)

Easily Kent's most attractive harbour is that of Ramsgate, built for naval and commercial purposes in the 18th century and today bobbing with yachts and other pleasure craft, conjuring the impression of a chic resort on the balmy Med rather than the North Sea. The harbour's full glory can be taken in from the elevated seafront perches of Nelson Crescent and Royal Parade, along with a fine swathe of beach beckoning beyond.

Like other Kent seaside resorts in the late 20th century, Ramsgate suffered from a downturn in local tourism and trades. But in 2017 it was designated a Heritage Action Zone by Historic England, kicking off a five-year project that has created new tourism trails and infrastructure improvements around town. The Royal Sands Ramsgate complex of luxury apartments is taking shape beside the beach, and up on the West Cliff side of town Addington Street is blooming with small galleries, boutiques and fun places to eat and drink.

Ramsgate's train station is just over a mile (20 minutes' walk) north of the harbour, but up until 1926 trains terminated right beside the main beach, having travelled down a tunnel cut through the chalk cliff. During World War II this repurposed tunnel formed part of a 3¼ mile network of 6ft-wide chalk-carved routes beneath Ramsgate for protection against enemy air raids. For an insight into this subterranean world, it's well worth joining the 90-minute walking tours of the **Ramsgate Tunnels** (Marine Esplanade ✆ 01843 588123 ⌂ ramsgatetunnels.org ⊙ exhibition & café Apr–Sep 10.00–16.00 daily, Oct–Mar 10.00–14.00 daily; tours every two hours, on the hour). Led by volunteer guides, the stories shared add a human dimension to the tunnels which sheltered 60,000 people and provided a home to around 1,000 people whose houses had been bombed.

The free exhibition at the entrance to the tunnels also provides good background information. Located near an RAF base at Manston, Ramsgate had suffered from bombing during World War I and as World War II approached local minds became focused on the need for air-raid shelters. The ambitious plan, masterminded by engineer Dick Brimmell and championed by Arthur Kempe, Ramsgate's 'top-hatted mayor', was initially mocked as an expensive folly. However, the tunnels' construction saved countless lives. During the worst air raid of 24 August 1940, over 500 bombs were dropped on Ramsgate, destroying or damaging over 1,200 buildings. Thanks to the tunnels only 31 people perished in that raid.

Emerging from the tunnels you are well placed beside Ramsgate's main sandy beach. On the way to the harbour, which is just a few minutes' walk away, you'll pass the Grade II-listed **Royal Victoria Pavilion**, a former assembly rooms and concert hall that has been sympathetically restored back to something of its former grandeur as a Wetherspoons pub. Construction of the harbour began in 1749 and lasted roughly 100 years. It is the only Royal Harbour in the country, an accolade granted in 1821 by George IV as a reward for the hospitality he had been shown by the people of Ramsgate during a visit there on his Royal Yacht.

Now an attractive **marina** (⌂ portoframsgate.co.uk), the harbour played a crucial role during the Napoleonic Wars and the Dunkirk evacuation of 1940. Some of this history and more is shared in the jumble of displays at the **Maritime Museum** (⌂ ramsgatemaritimemuseum. org ⊙ Mar–Sept 10.00–17.30 Wed–Sun), based in the handsome, early 19th-century Clock House. There's quite a bit to take in here, from

1 Ramsgate Harbour. **2** Montefiore Synagogue and Mausoleum. **3** Minster Abbey.
4 Pegwell Bay Country Park. ▶

CHRISTINE BIRD/S

LOIS GOBE/S

SS

CALLY ROBIN/S

model ships and a skeleton of a bottlenose dolphin to relics recovered from the numerous shipwrecks on the nearby Goodwin Sands. Moored outside in the former dry dock is the historic steam tug *Cervia*, also part of the museum's collection. The Clock House lies on the unique Ramsgate Meridian, from which the town's own particular Mean Time, 5 minutes, 41 seconds ahead of Greenwich, is calculated.

Walk around the Harbour to Military Road for a close-up view of the impressive red-brick arches and bays built into the cliffside, which are occupied by a variety of businesses, and which lead towards The Sailors' Church and Harbour Mission, dating back to 1878, and a Grade II-listed flight of stairs known as **Jacob's Ladder** built in 1826. Also here is the Smack Boys Home, a refuge for the young ships' apprentices ('smack boys') when they were ashore.

There are two equally attractive routes from the harbour up to the Eastcliff area. The **Kent Steps**, off Harbour Parade, is the most direct way. In 2020, the risers of the steps were covered in porcelain tiles in a kaleidoscope of colourful patterns. The 25 different designs were chosen

THE MONTEFIORE SYNAGOGUE & MAUSOLEUM

Ramsgate's Jewish population during the 19th century was never large, numbering maybe 100 people at most. However, because the town was home to the prominent Jewish financier and philanthropist Sir Moses Montefiore, the Jewish community's legacy here is a significant one. The neoclassical synagogue that Montefiore commissioned is rated by Jewish Heritage UK as one of the top ten synagogues in the UK.

The architect was another Jewish man, David Mocatta, a pupil of Sir John Soane, his design inspired by Montefiore's ancestral synagogue in Leghorn in Italy. An unusual feature is the chiming exterior clock inscribed with the motto 'Time Flies, Virtue Alone Remains'. The marble and granite clad interior, lit by numerous candelabra and an octagonal skylight, is beautifully maintained and used for worship during the Jewish high holidays. Next to the synagogue is the small, domed mausoleum in which Montefiore lies beside his beloved wife Judith, who passed away 23 years before him in 1862.

You can visit the synagogue, which lies off Hereson Road, are possible by appointment: contact ✉ ramsgate@montefioreendowment. org.uk to check on available dates and times. Surrounding the synagogue is the **Montefiore Woodland** (♂ montefiorewoodland.org.uk) a community-run nature sanctuary, where 'Bat Strolls' are held during the summer on the last Friday of the month. To discover more about Montefiore and other aspects of Jewish Ramsgate see ♂ jtrails.org.uk/trails/ramsgate.

from the 90 created by local school children in a project that took inspiration from Augustus Pugin. The other way is to follow **Madiera Walk** up to Albion Place, a sinuous road flanked by Pulhamite artificial rocks, modelled to create a rock garden, and overlooked by an attractive collection of Georgian, Victorian and Edwardian architecture.

Grassy promenades lead you past gently curving Wellington Crescent towards Victoria Parade where Edward Pugin's Grade II-listed **Granville Hotel** (1868) is now flats but continues to present a grand façade. Further on there's more Pulhamite rock gardens along with sea-facing sun shelters and a fountain pool at the 1920s **Winterstoke Gardens**, followed by the **King George VI Memorial Park**, occupying the grounds of an estate that was bought in 1831 by Sir Moses Montefiore and where he lived

"This is one of Kent's architectural treasures, something you'd barely guess from its austere knapped-flint exterior."

until his death in 1885, aged 101. The estate's house, East Cliff Lodge, was demolished in 1954 but its stable block, gatehouse remain, as does a splendid **Italianate Greenhouse** that is now the focus of a delightful **tea garden** (✆ 07868 722060 ☉ May–Aug 10.30–16.00 Sat & Sun); on sunny summer day, there's no finer location in Thanet to enjoy afternoon tea and homemade cakes.

While Montefiore was quietly colonising Eastcliff for the Jewish community, his contemporary Augustus Pugin was on a similar mission for Catholics on the Westcliff side of town. Famous for designing 'Big Ben' and the interiors of the Houses of Parliament, and for his passion for the Gothic Revival style, Pugin converted to Catholicism in 1835, just six years after Catholic churches were again permitted to be built in the UK after a break of almost 300 years. In 1844 he completed his family home, The Grange, before going on to build the neighbouring church, dedicated to St Augustine.

Eight years later, aged just 40, Pugin was dead and buried in the church that is his masterpiece. Now known as the **Shrine of St Augustine & National Pugin Centre** (St Augustine's Rd ✆ 01843 606756 ♂ augustine-pugin.org.uk ☉ 13.00–15.00 Mon–Thu & Sat; mass noon Mon–Sat, 08.30 & noon Sun), this is one of Kent's architectural treasures, something you'd barely guess from its austere knapped-flint exterior. In recent years the church has been expertly restored and its visitors' centre has a first-grade exhibition on Pugin's life and works. The approach to

VAN GOGH IN RAMSGATE

Vincent Van Gogh lived in Ramsgate for a couple of months in 1876 while working as a teacher at a boy's boarding school. To find out more about the Dutch painter's brief but happy time in Ramsgate, head to **Spencer Square**, which has tennis and pickleball courts and a small community park in which stands a bronze bust of Van Gogh sculpted by Anthony Padgett.

Van Gogh lived at 11 Spencer Square and worked nearby at 6 Royal Road; both buildings have blue plaques on them. Other Ramsgate locations that Van Gogh visited form part of a walking trail, one of several themed town walks for which there are free illustrated pamphlets from the tourist office, or which can be accessed freely through the Useeum app for smartphones.

the church is through an elaborately decorated cloister with side chapels, all completed after Pugin's demise. The showstopper here is the painted wood carving of the Stations of the Cross by the celebrated Flemish sculptors the De Beule brothers. Throughout the church are beautiful stained-glass windows and encaustic floor tiles. The Chantry Chapel in which Pugin is buried is the work of his eldest son Edward, also a talented architect. The church is now a shrine because it holds a small piece of the bone believed to be from the body of St Augustine. It is also the end point of the 70-mile **Augustine Camino** (⊘ augustinecamino.co.uk), which begins at Rochester Cathedral.

For an insight into how the Pugin family lived, join one of the weekly tours of **The Grange** (⊘ 01628 825925 ⊘ landmarktrust.org.uk ☉ tours 14.00 Wed by appointment only) – or you can even book the entire place (which sleeps eight) for self-catering accommodation. The Landmark Trust has excelled itself in restoring this property to its original, bold maximalist design, including jewel-coloured wallpapers, decorative tiles and glowingly varnished woodwork. The neighbouring **St Edward's Presbytery**, which is more compact and far simpler in design, is also available to rent through the Trust.

From The Grange you are well placed to stroll along **Westcliff Promenade,** a development from the 1920s which includes a bowling and croquet lawn (⊘ croquetramsgate.co.uk) and boating pool, flanked by a tearoom on one side and the **Ravensgate Arms** (page 164) on the other. At the eastern end of the promenade, near the Lookout Café, there are steps down to the sandy and usually quiet beaches of the **Western Undercliff,** next to the Port of Ramsgate.

ACTIVITIES

Boat trips out the harbour are offered by various operators including **Sea Searcher**
(⊘ seasearcher.co.uk) and **River Runner** (⊘ river-runner.co.uk).

Kite Pirates Kite School ⊘ 07739 369531 ⊘ kitepirateskiteschool.com. Ramsgate
is one of the UK's top kitesurfing destinations, hosting the British Freestyle Kitesurfing
championships in August. This locally based outfit can show you the ropes and provide you
with all the necessary kit. They also offer paddleboarding lessons.

ENTERTAINMENT

Mark your calendar for the **Ramsgate Festival of Sound** (⊘ ramsgatefestival.org), held
over nine days at the end of August and start of September and featuring everything from
sonic trails to cabaret, jazz, opera and community choirs.

Ramsgate Music Hall 13 Turner St ⊘ 01843 591815 ⊘ ramsgatemusichall.com. For lovers
of live music it hardly gets more intimate than this 130 people-capacity venue just off High
Street. Gigs range from local legends such as Robyn Hitchcock to up-and-coming bands like
Afflecks Palace who regularly sell out far larger venues.

⊘ FOOD & DRINK

Archive Home Store 17 Military Rd ⊘ archivehomestore.co.uk ⊘ 09.00–17.00 Mon &
Thu–Sun. Occupying one of the large red-brick arches beside the harbour, Archive offers
excellent coffee, cakes and light meals as well as a stylishly curated collection of books,
magazines, stationary, toys and homewares. On the menu are crowd pleasers such as
Swedish buns, grilled cheese sarnies and chocolate and raspberry tart.
Artillery Arms 36 West Cliff Rd ⊘ noon–11pm. Dating from the mid 19th century, this
charming little boozer with military-themed stained-glass windows is practically a museum
to a bygone age. There's a great selection of beers from independent brewers, including local
operation Gadds.
Belle Vue Tavern Pegwell Rd ⊘ 01843 593991 ⊘ thebellevuetavern.co.uk ⊘ noon–
21.00 Sun–Thu, noon–10.00 Fri & Sat. They're not joking about this being the 'balcony of
Kent'. The outdoor terrace and window seats of the pub's restaurant provide superb views
across Pegwell Bay which more than justify stopping by here for a pint of Shepherd Neame
or some pub grub, including tasty pizzas.
Eats 'n' Beats 2–3 The Broadway, Addington St ⊘ eatsnbeatscafe ⊘ 16.00–21.00 Fri.
noon–21.00 Sat, noon–16.00 Sun. This café-bar serves up great coffee, cocktails, coffee,
pastries and tapas. Keep an eye on their social media for live music and poetry events as well
as art exhibitions. It has a very cool courtyard decorated with a mosaic mural.

The Home Front Tea Room 13a King Street ☎ 01843 594383 ♦ 40stearoom.co.uk
🕐 10.00–16.00. Mon–Sat. Go back to the 1940s at this nostalgically themed tea parlour.
There are 17 types of tea to sample as well as oldie favourites such as Camp Coffee, Ovaltine
and Bovril. For the fully retro experiences, there's snacks such as pilchards on toast and fruit
cocktail with evaporated milk.

Little Ships 54–56 Harbour Prd ☎ 01843 585008 ♦ littleshipsramsgate.co.uk
🕐 07.00–22.00 daily. Named in honour of the flotilla of 'little ships' that left Ramsgate
to assist in the Dunkirk evacuations of 1940, this handsome harbourside restaurant is
like a small museum to that dramatic event. Most food is sourced from within 30 miles of
Ramsgate, which accounts for their good selection of northern French artisan beers and
cheeses, as well as barbecued courgettes from their own allotment.

Marc Pierre's Kitchen West Cliff Arcade ♦ marcpierreskitchen.com 🕐 17.00–21.30 Tue–
Thu, noon–21.30 Fri & Sat, noon–16.30 Sun. Chef Marc Campos offers something to suit
whatever your appetite, from Ramsgate cockle popcorn to Kentish fillet steak with red wine
reduction. There's also a wide range of Kent-produced wines and beers available and a great
view from their listed building overlooking the harbour.

Ravensgate Arms 56–58 King St ☎ 07943 628357 ♦ ravensgatearms.co.uk 🕐
16.00–22.00 Wed–Fri, noon–10.00 Sat, 14.00–22.00 Sun. This cosy, wood-panelled bar
specialises in the best of locally breed ales from independent breweries, as well as a fine
line in seasonal cocktails. On the first floor is **Arya** (book on ✉ aryaramsgate@gmail.com;
🕐 18.30–22.30 Wed–Fri, noon–15.00 & 18.30–22.30 Sat), which serves up inventive
tapas-style dishes such as grilled prawns, pak choi and pistachio, and beef shin, white
beans and parmesan.

Union Yoga + Café 25–27 Queen St ☎ 07563 903177 ♦ unionramsgate.com 🕐 09.00–
14.30 Tue–Sat. Combine a yoga lesson with some healthy food such as hazelnut, almond
and pumpkin granola or a lemony chickpea and tomato salad at this pleasantly designed
café. There's usually a choice of a farinata (chickpea flour pancake) or frittata for lunch.

🛍 SHOPPING

Margot McDaid 2a Addington St ♦ margomcdaid.com 🕐 11.00–16.00 Fri & Sat. McDaid's
simple graphic paintings and prints, often of young women in stripy clothes, would add a
splash of colour and style to any wall. Also check out her hand-painted vintage plates and
wooden art blocks. There are several other small galleries and vintage stores to mooch
around along Addington Street, too.

Petticoat Lane Emporium 47 Dumpton Park Rd ♦ petticoatemporium.com
🕐 10.00–17.00 Mon–Sat, 10.00–16.00 Sun. Vintage and retro fans could spend hours at
Kent's largest indoor marketplace, with some 200 stalls offering all kinds of collectables,
fashion and art. Refreshments are sold at the market's Baker Street Bistro & Bar.

Potters 23 Queen St ☍ pottersramsgate.com ☼ 10.00–16.00 Thu–Mon. In their Scandi-cool inspired gift and interior design store, friends Wednesday Lyle and Alison Murphy showcase the products of local artists including ceramicists and printers, alongside an on-trend selection of houseplants art books, scented candles and soaps.

Turner Rowe Art Centre & Gallery 19–21 Harbour St ☍ turnerroweartcentre.com ☼ 10.00–17.00 Tue–Sat, 10.00–16.00 Sun. This gallery and gift shop is run by artists Jo Turner, who specialises in glass, and Fran Ballard, who creates ceramics and amazingly detailed pencil drawings. It also stocks an appealing range of arts and crafts from other local creatives and runs craft classes. You'll be hard pressed to emerge without having purchased a little something.

5 CLIFFS END

The tranquil bay at Cliffs End, 2½ miles west of Ramsgate, has a long history as an international gateway to the British Isles. Legendary brothers Hengist and Horsa landed here CAD449 from Germany. The 1,500th anniversary of this event was commemorated by the sailing of a reconstructed Viking longship from Denmark to Thanet in 1949; *Hugin*, a replica of that ship, gifted from Denmark, now rests on the headland above the bay, just off Sandwich Road. St Augustine is also believed to have disembarked here in AD597, meeting King Ethelbert under a massive oak tree – a spot now marked by the intricately carved **St Augustine's Cross**, a 19th-century monument on nearby Cottington Road.

The world's first international hoverport opened in the bay in 1969, with hovercraft services running to Calais up until its closure in 1982. Since being demolished, nature has returned but the remaining concrete apron provides a wonderful vantage point across the bay and access to the base of the nearby chalk cliffs. It may not be the same bucolic scene as beautifully captured in oils by William Dyce in his painting *Pegwell Bay, Kent – a Recollection of October 5th 1858* but it's not far off.

6 PEGWELL BAY COUNTRY PARK

A coastal path leads from Cliffs End to Pegwell Bay Country Park (parking off Sandwich Rd ☼ 09.00–dusk daily), the main access point for the larger **Sandwich & Pegwell Bay National Nature Reserve** (☍ kentwildlifetrust.org.uk/nature-reserves/sandwich-and-pegwell-bay). The mudflats and salt marshes here are an internationally significant birding hotspot, attracting large numbers of ducks, geese, and birds including turnstones, terns, plovers and sanderlings. A circular path runs around the park taking you alongside the swaying bayside grasses for bird spotting. If you're lucky and have binoculars, you may also catch seals lounging at the mouth of River Stour. Inland, there's an enclosure for Exmoor ponies who happily munch away at the ground, naturally managing the park's grasslands. Next to the main car park are a couple of cafés in old shipping containers.

7 MINSTER

There's been a monastic settlement at Minster, five miles west of Ramsgate, since around AD670 when Ermenburga, great-granddaughter of King Ethelbert, was granted land to build a house of prayer. That first abbey was on the site of the quiet, attractive village's **St Mary the Virgin church**, while the location occupied by the current **Minster Abbey** (Church St ✆ 01843 821254 ⌂ minsterabbeynuns.org) dates back to 741. There were long periods when the abbey was either abandoned or used for non-religious purposes, but Ermenburga (also known as Domneva) would surely be delighted that since 1937 the estate has been home to a community of Benedictine nuns. The story of how these nuns escaped Bavaria after the Nazi authorities requestioned their monastery reads like a Kentish version of *The Sound of Music*. Free tours of the abbey grounds, which include lovely gardens and the romantic ruins of a medieval tower, can be arranged throughout much of the year. There's also a guesthouse available for retreats: see the website for full details. The abbey is the start (or finish) of a 36-mile walking route, the Royal Saxon Way (⌂ geopaethas.com/a-long-walk). Minster can also be easily accessed by train from either Canterbury or Ramsgate.

8 SANDWICH

🏠 **Bell Hotel** (page 308), **Molland Manor House** (page 309), **Number 37** (page 309)
Considered one of the most complete examples of a medieval town in the country, Sandwich's street plan has changed little since the 11th century when it was the leader among the five key ports in the Cinque Ports confederation. Meaning 'a village on the sand', the first mention of 'Sandwic' was in AD664 when it was recorded as a thriving Saxon settlement. Long before this there was sizeable Roman port at nearby Richborough. Around about the same time as its harbour began silting up in the 16th century, Sandwich was given something of a reprieve

CINQUE PORTS

From at least the 11th century English monarchs called on the confederation of the **Cinque Ports** to provide ships and sailors in times of war. Of the five original Cinque (pronounced 'sink') Ports, four – Sandwich, Dover, Hythe and New Romney – are in Kent; the fifth is Hastings in Sussex. In return for services to the Crown, the ports were granted freedom from many taxes, self-government, and other privileges. Neighbouring towns and villages were called upon to support the five main ports in their naval obligations, which led to Deal, Faversham, Folkestone, Margate, Ramsgate and Tenterden becoming 'limbs' of the Cinque Ports with similar obligations and special dispensations.

The ports were wealthy locations, as you can see from the quality of fine heritage buildings that exist in many of them. Sandwich is a particularly fine example,

with one of the longest blocks of medieval timber-framed houses in England. But as the River Stour silted up and its usefulness as a port began to wane in the 16th century, Sandwich's fortunes declined. It was a similar story for nearly all the other ports – changes in Kent's coastline wrought by weather and natural erosion eventually rendered them unusable by large vessels, if not several miles inland, cut off from the sea they were once beside. The nail in the confederation's coffin was Henry VIII's decision to create a purpose-built fleet of warships in the late 15th century that would evolve into the Royal Navy. Only Dover remains a working port today.

Nevertheless, the Cinque Ports are proud of their heritage and the Lord Warden of the Cinque Ports continues today as an honorary and prestigious position. The Warden's official residence is Walmer Castle (page 182).

economically by the arrival of Huguenot refugees who set up cloth-making businesses in the town.

Sandwich today is a quietly prosperous, handsomely appointed community that rewards aimless wandering. The abundance of half-timbered and other heritage buildings evoke the 13th-century golden era when this was a bustling port. The medieval earth ramparts cradling the town form pleasant, tree-shaded footpaths. Nearby are nature reserves and three internationally renowned golf courses.

The heart of the medieval town is the 16th-century **Guildhall**, about a ten-minute walk along New Street from Sandwich's train station. The building has been much altered in its 450-year history, with a brick exterior being added in 1812 and other extensions and renovations in the 20th century. There's a small **museum** (Cattle Market ✐ 01304 617197 ⬙ sandwichguildhallmuseum.co.uk ◷ 10.00–16.00 Wed–Sun) inside with artefacts that illustrate key moment's in Sandwich's history.

The most prized exhibit is a frail but original Magna Carta, dating from 1300, and its sister document, the Charter of the Forest, which sets out the rights of the common people.

Cattle may no longer be sold in the Cattle Market, but the cobbled square continues to host a produce **market** (◷ 08.00–13.00 Wed, Thu & Sat). Across the road from the Guildhall, the 900-year-old decommissioned **St Peter's Church** (Market St ⌀ visitchurches.org.uk ◷ 10.00–16.00 daily) has been put to good use as a craft and curios market and café. It's worth paying the charge to climb to the top of its tower for panoramic views over the town.

Next, make your way to the **Strand Street**, lined with more half-timbered houses than any other street in England. The historic **quay**, once the scene of much maritime activity, is nearby. Moored here are an assortment of yachts and small craft, some of which offer chartered tours that may go as far upstream as Fordwich or out to Sandwich Bay. Somewhat incongruous is the grey-painted metal gunboat **USN P22**, the last survivor of a fleet of 23 American-designed ships that patrolled the River Rhine in the 1950s and '60s during the Cold War. Further along, is *The Nicholas*, a work-in-progress replica of a Hanseatic medieval cog – a single-mast, round-bottom merchant vessel that could be converted into a fighting ship at times of war. It's one of the projects of **Sandwich Medieval Centre** (The Quay ✆ 07757 964113 ⌀ sandwichmedieval.org ◷ 10.00–16.00 Thu–Sat, 11.00–16.00 Sun Apr–Oct; free entry), where various other crafts and skills from centuries ago are demonstrated or taught in a variety of classes ranging from blacksmithing to illuminating manuscripts.

From The Quay, turn right on to the wonderfully named Knightrider Street, passing **The Salutation**, a grand house and garden designed in 1912 by the famed architect Sir Edwin Lutyens; the 3½-acre garden here is one of the most beautiful in Kent but, sadly, it was closed to the public at the time of research, pending the sale of the property. Continue along Knightrider Street to reach the graveyard of **St Clement's Church** (⌀ stclementschurchsandwich.org.uk) where Edward the Confessor attended mass in 1050. It's mainly a Norman-era building, but look

◀ **1** Goodnestone Park Gardens. **2** Richborough Roman Fort & Amphitheatre.
3 Short-eared owl, Sandwich Bay Bird Observatory. **4** Sandwich Medieval Centre.
5 The medieval town of Sandwich.

out for later decorative features including a very unusual 15th-century ceiling in the nave, decorated with gold winged angels.

On the northern edge of Sandwich, at the end of Strand Street, is the **Gazen Salts Nature Reserve** (St Mary's ⊘ gazensalts.co.uk). This 15-acre reserve has been nurtured by the community since 1973 to create a variety of wildlife habitats, including woodlands and wild flower meadows. Water voles, foxes and grey squirrels are among the wildlife that you may spot here. In May 2021 four hedgehogs – two male, two female – were

THE ROMANS IN KENT

In 2017, archaeologists from the University of Leicester working on a dig at **Ebbsfleet**, a hamlet near Pegwell Bay, uncovered evidence of Julius Caesar's short-lived invasion of Britain in 54BC. Here was a ditch that appeared to be part of a Roman fort as well as items such as pottery and the remains of iron weapons. Ebbsfleet is now about half a mile from the sea, but when Caesar led a force of about 800 ships, 20,000 soldiers and 2,000 cavalry to Britain, it was on the coast and the best sheltered location in east Kent for such a large invading army to land.

Nearly a century would pass before the legions of emperor Claudius reinvaded Britain – this time successfully. One of the initial landing spots is certain to have been the natural harbour of **Richborough** at the mouth of the Stour River. From this foothold the Romans marched towards the River Medway and onwards into London. **Canterbury** was the Roman regional base and there you can discover much about their occupation of Britain at the excellent **Roman Museum** (page 51), which includes significant in-situ archaeological remains and artefacts of the time. From Canterbury, which the Romans called Durovernum

Cantiacorum, a road system linked up with sea forts at Regulbium (Reculver; page 76), Dubris (Dover; page 189) and Lemanis (Port Lympne; page 228), as well as London.

Huge quantities of ragstone – the sandy limestone that is a feature of the Kent Weald – were quarried from deposits near Maidstone by the Romans to use as building material. Of the 100 or so Roman villas uncovered in Kent, the most notable is at **Lullingstone** (page 246) which was begun around AD100, then added to and amended for over two centuries before being consumed by fire in the early 5th century.

In Dover, a pair of 78ft-tall lighthouses (pharos) stood on either side of the harbour – the remains of one can be found within the grounds of **Dover Castle** (page 190). Dover also has the **Roman Painted House** (page 194), what's left of a AD200 mansion thought to have been built for senior officials visiting the port.

Roman rule in Britain ended around AD406 and it's thought the last of the colonists departed from Richborough, where they had first arrived so many centuries before.

released here in the hope that this endangered British mammal would start breeding. Among the resident birds are kingfishers, green and great spotted woodpeckers and chaffinches.

Another delight for bird watchers is **Sandwich Bay Bird Observatory & Field Centre** (Guilford Rd ✐ 01304 617341 ⊘ sbbot.org.uk ⊙ 10.00–13.00 daily), about 20 minutes' walk south of the town centre towards the Sandwich Bay Estate (note that if you drive here you may have to pay a toll to enter the road on this private estate). Regular visitors here include wood sandpipers, common snipes and little egrets. Courses, lectures and guided walks are among the centre's activities.

ACTIVITIES & TOURS

P22 The Quay ✐ 07836 754594. Call ahead to book a short cruise along the Stour River aboard this handsomely restored Cold War-era gunboat which once patrolled the Rhine in Germany. The P22 also featured in the 2017 film *Dunkirk*.

Royal St Georges Golf Course ✐ 01304 613090 ⊘ royalstgeorges.com. You need to have a golf handicap of 18 or below and there's a long list of other rules to follow before handing over the green fees to play at this storied course. Established in 1887, these links are among the best in the world and have been used 15 times for the Open Championship, more than any other course outside Scotland.

Sandwich Local History Society ✐ 07773 335612 ⊘ sandwichlocalhistorysociety.org.uk. Contact Mike Elmes, a representative of this local history group, to arrange a two-hour long guided walking tour of Sandwich.

🍴 FOOD & DRINK

No Name Shop 1 No Name St ✐ 01304 612626 🄵 nonameshopkent ⊙ 09.00–16.00 Mon–Sat, 09.00–15.00 Sun. At the time of research, their upstairs dine-in section Le Bistro was closed, but the deli is open for delicious French produce, including take-away sandwich baguettes, tartiflette and croque monsieurs. Or you could pull together a picnic from their selection of cheeses and charcuterie.

Number 37 37 The Street, Ash ✐ 07804 583513 ⊘ 37ash.co.uk ⊙ noon–22.00 Wed& Thu, 08.00–22.00 Fri & Sat, 08.00–19.00 Sun. The generous seafood, meat or vegetarian sharing boards are a great way to go at this cosy bistro and café in the charming village of Ash, 3½ miles west of Sandwich. Their breakfast choices are excellent and there are more substantial meals, including homemade burgers, chilli and a bouillabaisse packed with fish and seafood. It's also a nice place to stay (page 309).

The Old Pharmacy 39 King St ✐ 01304 274819 ⊘ oldpharmacybar.co.uk ⊙ 17.00–22.00 Thu & Fri, 16.00–22.00 Sat. There are plenty of classic but pedestrian pubs in Sandwich.

Sandwich: from medieval town to coast

✤ OS Explorer map 150 start; Sandwich train station, CT13 9RA ♀ TR332576; 5 miles; easy

This circular walk takes in some of the key sights of this most picturesque and historic town. It then heads out of Sandwich via the footpaths that run alongside the River Stour and then through the championship golf course of Royal St George to reach the shingle beach at Sandwich Bay. There's plenty of paid parking beside the Guildhall and The Quay in Sandwich. Sandwich is awash with places to eat and drink and the route is generally well signposted with no hills to climb.

1 From Sandwich train station, turn left at St George's Road, then right at New Street. A few yards later, turn on to the wide footpath on your left that runs along the top of steep grassy banks, shaded by lofty lime and plane trees. Built during the 13th century, these are the most complete example of defensive earth ramparts in England. The first section is known as the Rope Walk as reputedly it was used to lay the ropes for the rigging of sailing ships. The next, longer section of the ramparts' walk is called The Butts because it faces a field believed to have been used in medieval times for archery practice; imagine the archers in Henry V's army practising here before sailing for Agincourt in 1415.

2 Turn right when the footpath meets Strand Street. Opposite is Gallows Field, so-called because it was where public hangings took place until the 1790s. Proceed along Strand Street, admiring the many half-timbered houses as you go. At number 42, behind a high brick wall on the left, is King's Lodging, dating from 1400 and so called as both Henry VIII and Elizabeth I are said to have stayed here during visits to Sandwich.

3 Continue along Strand Street to the junction of roads next to the Barbican. This 16th-century bastion with chequered stonework guarded the toll bridge over the River Stour and was part of the town's defences. Proceed along The Quay, which takes you past Sandwich Medieval Centre (page 169) where you could pause to see how they are getting on with building *The Nicholas*, a replica of a medieval cog vessel.

4 From the Medieval Centre, follow the footpath that runs closest to the river. At each of the places the path forks, go left to stay on the route of the Stour Valley Walk, close by the meandering river. After about half a mile, cross the sluice gate to the road, turn left and rejoin the footpath immediately to the right. Stay on the well-defined path through rough pasture and then between the boundaries of the 27-hole Prince's Golf Course to the left and Royal St George's Golf Course to the right. Fourteen Open Championships have been played at St George's, more than any course outside of Scotland. ▶

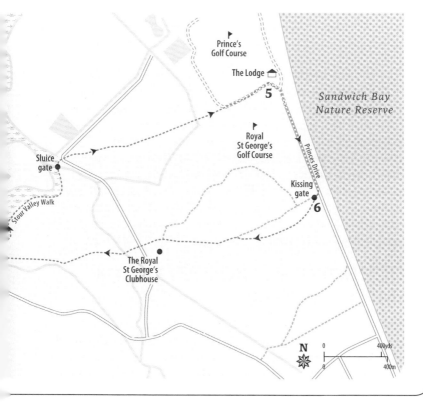

Sandwich: from medieval town to coast continued ...

5 At The Lodge, the accommodation for Prince's Golf Course, turn right and follow the shoreline path. After a few hundred yards, you'll see public toilets on the left.

6 When you reach a wooden kissing gate, take the footpath back towards Sandwich, across Royal St George's, keeping a careful look out for golfers and allowing them to play any shots before you cross a fairway. The route is well marked by yellow-topped stone markers. Ian Fleming was a member of this club and used the links as a setting in *Goldfinger* when James Bond and Auric Goldfinger play a round of golf. Passing the Royal St George's Clubhouse to your left, cross a road and pick up the footpath back to Sandwich and the Quay.

7 After about a mile on the left is the grassed-over moat and the Bulwark, another section of the medieval ramparts; over the wall you might be able to catch a glimpse of the Salutation Garden (closed at the time of research). Cross Sandown Road and continue along the Mill Wall footpath, so called because of the corn mills that were once located along it. When you reach New Street, you can either turn right and walk into the centre of Sandwich for refreshments and more sightseeing or go left and back towards your starting point at the train station.

For something more contemporary, head to this fun cocktail bar and lounge in a former chemist shop. There's courtyard for summer sipping and an open fire inside to keep it cosy in winter.

The Toll Bridge 7 Fisherman's Wharf ✆ 01304 613959 ⊘ thetollbridge.co.uk ⊙ noon–23.00 Mon–Sat, noon–22.00. Facing on to The Quay beside the old toll bridge, this contemporary restaurant specialises in home-smoked and roasted meat and fish, including smoked pork ribs, beef brisket and smoked salmon. There are good vegetarian options, such as the lentil and sweetcorn dahl burger and cauliflower hot wings.

The Sandwich Shop 17 Cattle Market ▮f▮ thesandwichshopinsandwich ⊙ 10.00–16.00 daily. It would be remiss not to eat a sandwich while in Sandwich. This place, with a prime view across the Cattle Market to the Guildhall, does very good ones that come with salad and homemade coleslaw. All profits from the enterprise go towards community events.

9 RICHBOROUGH ROMAN FORT & AMPHITHEATRE

Off Richborough Rd, CT13 9JW ✆ 01304 612013 ⊙ 10.00–17.00 daily; English Heritage

Two miles north of Sandwich, surrounded by green fields, are the atmospheric remains of what once was the official gateway to Roman Britannia. This was the beachhead for at least part of Claudius' invasion force of 40,000 men in AD43. The Romans called their garrison town

Rutupiae and ringed it with defensive ditches. Wandering around this peaceful and grassy archaeological site, you can get a fairly good idea of the port's evolution over Rome's nearly 400-year occupation of Britain. The centre piece was a 82ft monumental arch, clad in marble and built around AD85. It stood here for nearly two centuries but only a ghostly footprint remains now. The stone walls that encase three sides of the site date to the third century when the port was fortified against Saxon and Frankish raiders. However, the settlement itself was much larger, covering over 50 acres at its peak. It included an amphitheatre, a short walk away from the main site, that could have accommodated up to 5,000 people. At the main entrance to the site there is also a small museum displaying a few of the artefacts discovered during excavations in the 1920s and 1930s.

10 GOODNESTONE & SURROUNDS

Reached down minor country roads, Goodnestone (⌂ goodnestone.org. uk), six miles southwest of Sandwich, is the definition of 'off the beaten track'. The reason for heading here is **Goodnestone Park Gardens** (CT3 1PL ✆ 01304 840107 ⌂ goodnestoneparkgardens.co.uk ⌚ 10.00–16.00 daily), an elegant 18th-century house with Jane Austen connections, surrounded by 15 acres of garden and parkland. There are also some very pleasant places nearby to eat and drink.

Jane Austen's brother Edward was married to Elizabeth, a daughter of Brook Bridges, the owner of Goodnestone Park. The couple spent their early married life in Rowling House on the Goodnestone estate before inheriting Godmersham, near Chilham (page 86). The formal dinners and dances that Jane attended at Goodnestone are said to have inspired *Pride and Prejudice*, a novel she began after staying here in 1796.

Even though they have been substantially altered since Austen's visits, the grounds evoke Regency times. A highlight is the walled garden, with its rambling roses, clematis, jasmine and wisteria, beds packed with dahlias and pool reflecting the village's Holy Cross church. More recently introduced features include the box parterre at the front of the house, a peaceful grass and gravel garden, and an arboretum. You can pick up a leaflet to guide you along the estate's reinstated 18th-century Serpentine Walk from the garden's **Old Dairy Café** (⌚ 10.00–16.00 Thu–Sun). Also drop by the former stables to view exhibitions organised by the **Other Space Art Gallery** (⌂ other-art.network).

Two miles southeast across fields is the hamlet of Chillenden and the local landmark of the white-washed **Chillenden Mill** ($\hat{\partial}$ southbarn. plus.com $\odot$ May–Sept Sun). One of only three similar types of open trestle mills in England, this is a reconstruction of the original 1868 mill which collapsed after a gale in 2003.

¶❘ FOOD & DRINK

The Dog at Wingham Canterbury Rd, Wingham CT3 1BB $\mathcal{O}$ 01227 720339 $\hat{\partial}$ thedog. co.uk $\odot$ 08.00–10.00 & 11.00–23.00 Mon–Sat, 08.00–10.00 & 11.00–21.00 Sun. One of the region's best regarded gastropubs goes all out on the canine theme with its décor which includes dog-print wallpaper in the loos and free dog biscuits (of course, it's dog-friendly!). Thankfully, the cooking is several notches up from a dog's breakfast, including delicious seasonal ingredients such as heritage tomatoes and wild mushrooms. There are also eight individually styled rooms with en-suite showers.

Gibsons Farm Shop Crockshard Hill, Wingham CT3 1NY $\hat{\partial}$ gibsonsfarmshop.com $\odot$ shop 07.00–19.00 Mon–Sat, 09.00–18.00 Sun; café 09.00–18.00 Mon–Sat, 09.00–16.00 Sun. Gibsons is more of a farm supermarket, such is breadth and quality of its product range which not only covers the best edible goodies of Kent but also further afield. Their café also uses the food from the farm, such as their own sausages and bacon.

Griffins Head Griffin Hill, Chillenden CT3 1PS $\mathcal{O}$ 01304 840325 $\hat{\partial}$ griffinsheadchillenden. co.uk $\odot$ noon–23.00 Mon–Fri, 09.00–23.00 Sat & Sun. This atmospheric gastropub may be based in a 13th-century farmhouse but its menu is thoroughly contemporary and includes delights such as game terrine with prune and baby leek, pink potato dumplings, and a crab and lobster burger. In good weather there's a huge attached garden in which you can dine.

11 DEAL & SURROUNDS

🏠 **Bear's Well** (page 309), **The Rose** (page 308), **Royal Hotel** (page 308) 🏡 **Garden Cottage & Greenhouse Apartment** (page 309)

With its long shingle beach, modern pier, conservation area of handsome Georgian-era houses and High Street stacked with independent traders, Deal is, quite rightly, frequently tipped as one of the UK's best seaside towns. A large part of its appeal is that it is far from your average bucket and spade resort. This fiercely independent place has a strong community

1 Shingle beach, Deal. **2** Greenhouse in Walmer Castle's gardens. **3** Georgian-era houses, Deal. **4** Walmer Castle. ▶

and creative spirit, witnessed in many things, from its quirky retailers and art galleries to specialist museums and volunteer-created gardens.

Mentioned in the Domesday Book of 1086, Deal's big break came in the mid 16th century when Henry VIII, fearing invasion from the armies of Catholic Europe, ordered the construction of the Deal, Walmer and Sandown castles. Deal's proximity to the body of water known as the Downs – a safe anchorage between the town and the notorious Goodwin Sands – made it an important maritime and naval base. Deal's skilled boatmen also made a good living off smuggling. So notorious was it for the trade in contraband that troops, under the orders of Prime Minister William Pitt, destroyed all of Deal's boats in the winter of 1785. Undeterred, the smugglers were back in business after a few years and skirmishes with the authorities continued well into the 19th century.

"This coastal fortress surrounded by a dry moat saw its most action in 1648 when Royalist and Parliamentarian forces clashed here."

It's less than a ten-minute walk from Deal train station to the town's seafront, a straight, broad swathe of shingle running for around four miles from the site of the long-demolished Sandown Castle in the north to the village of Kingsdown in the south. Kick off your explorations at **Deal Castle** (Marine Rd ✆ 01304 372762 ⊙ mid-Feb–Mar 10.00–16.00 Wed–Sun; Apr–Oct 10.00–17.00 daily; Nov–mid-Feb 10.00–16.00 Sat & Sun; English Heritage). Built between 1539 and 1540 in the shape of a Tudor Rose, this coastal fortress surrounded by a dry moat saw its most action in 1648 when Royalist and Parliamentarian forces clashed here during the English Civil War. Known as a Henrician castle or 'device fort', the castle's distinctive circular design, with space for 140 guns, provides protection from all angles. It's also low lying so that attacking ships would not spot the fortress until it was too late. The castle has been restored as close as possible to its Tudor form, although the decorative crenelations date to the 18th century. Before moving on north up the beach, look across Victoria Road for the **Captain's Garden** (◉ CaptainsGardenDeal), a community project to revive the old garden that once belonged to the captain of the castle. The plan is to plant over a hundred fruit, nut and flowering trees here.

Walking north along the seafront, past small fishing vessels moored on the shingle, you'll pass the **Deal Timeball Tower** (⏀ dealtimeball.co.uk

☉ Apr–Sep 09.00–17.00 daily). The four-storey white-painted block is topped with a sliding ball on a tall post. Connected electrically to a similar structure at the Royal Greenwich Observatory, this device was installed in 1855. The raised ball would be dropped exactly at 13.00 every day so that passing ships could synchronise their clocks. The Timeball is still programmed to drop every day at 13.00, with additional ball drops on the hour between 09.00 and 17.00 from April to the end of September.

John Buck's 1998 bronze sculpture *Embracing the Sea* marks the entrance to **Deal Pier** (𝒶 dealpier.uk) This 1,026ft boardwalk, made from reinforced concrete and opened in 1957, is the third pier to have been built on this site. It's also the last remaining, fully intact structure of its type in Kent. At the end is a good café and sea-viewing decks that are popular with sport fishers.

Continue north around the Royal Hotel (where Lord Nelson met with his mistress Lady Emma Hamilton) and along the coast, passing some striking concrete sea shelters, with Art-Deco styling but dating from the 1950s. Eventually you'll end up at the southern edge of the **Royal Cinque Ports Golf Club** (𝒶 royalcinqueports.com) and the scant ruins of **Sandown Castle**. The remaining masonry is part of a sea wall and provides structure for the award-winning, community-managed **Sandown Castle Garden**.

Returning to the town centre, take a wander down **Middle Street**. Designated as Kent's first conservation area in 1968, this picturesque street is lined with 18th-century terrace houses and a few timber-framed cottages dating from the 17th century. The upper part of High Street is also part of the conservation area. On High Street is **Deal Town Hall** (𝒶 01304 361999), completed in 1803, with a colonnade at the front. Tours of the building can be arranged by appointment.

Around the corner from the Town Hall and housed in early 19th-century light industry buildings is the fascinating **Deal Museum** (22 St George's Rd 𝒶 01304 372098 𝒶 dealmuseum.co.uk ☉ Apr–Oct 13.00–16.00 Fri–Sun). The wide range of exhibits here cover all aspects of the town's history from its maritime and smuggling activities to the former Betteshanger Colliery (now transformed into a park) and the Royal Marines, who have long associations with Deal.

From the museum, turn left on to West Street and walk past the edge of St George's churchyard to find the excellent **Kent Museum of**

the Moving Image (Stanhope Rd ✆ 01304 239515 🖰 kentmomi.org ☉ May–Sep 11.00–18.00 Fri–Sun & bank hols, Oct–Apr 11.00–17.00 Fri–Sun & bank hols). Taking a broad-brush approach to the history of the moving image, this museum has displays ranging from shadow puppets and magic lanterns to posters, stills and production material from classic 20th-century British cinema such as *Kind Hearts and Coronets* and *Passport to Pimlico*. Set up by leading British film archivist David Francis and his wife Joss Marsh, daughter of the award-winning production designer Terence Marsh, there's much to admire here even if you're not a cinema enthusiast. The museum occupies a former retirement home so it's a quirky place that includes a well-stocked library, a licensed café, and a shop selling exclusive reproductions of Ealing Studio posters.

ACTIVITIES & TOURS

The Wild Kitchen ✆ 01304 369799 🖰 thewildkitchen.net. Join Lucia Stewart, a trained chef and member of the Association of Foragers, to hunt down wild plants and seaweed along the coasts near Deal. The two-hour tours usually run between July and October; check the website for exact dates.

ENTERTAINMENT

The Astor Community Theatre Stanhope Rd ✆ 01304 370220 🖰 theastor.co.uk. A varied range of events are staged at this multipurpose arts centre, including live music, theatre, talks and movie screenings. The Astor Palm Court Orchestra provide monthly concerts and there are also regular, fun cabaret-style shows from local historians The History Project (🖰 thehistoryproject.co.uk).

 ## FOOD & DRINK

Deal Hoy 16 Duke St ✆ 01304 363972 🖰 dealhoykent.co.uk ☉ noon–22.00 Mon–Fri, 11.30–22.00 Sat & Sun. This dog-friendly Shepherd Neame pub in Deal's conservation area has a cosy interior and a lovely beer garden. They also serve crisply baked, wood-fired pizzas from Monday to Saturday.

Deal Pier Kitchen Beach St ✆ 01304 368228 🖰 dealpierkitchen.com ☉ 10.00–16.00 Mon–Thu, 09.00–17.00 Fri–Sun. The sea views and chance to sample inventive brunch dishes such as cilbir (garlic roasted aubergine, lemon and cucumber yoghurt on toast) and miners benedict (poached eggs on black pudding with hollandaise sauce) make this end-of-the-pier restaurant a delight. Lunch mains, like vegan ramen and soy pork belly banh mi provide an Asian twist.

Frog & Scott 86 High St ✆ 01304 379444 ⌂ frogandscot.co.uk ◷ noon–13.30 &
17.30–21.00 daily. Run by French expat Benoit Dezecot and his Scottish wife Sarah, this
authentic bistro offers delicious food in classy surroundings. Dishes served here may include
such delights as rabbit terrine, breast of Stour Valley guinea fowl, and grilled lobster lightly
smoked over rosemary. A few doors down, at 102 High Street, they also run the temptingly
well-stocked wine shop and bar **Le Pinardier** (◷ noon–23.00 Wed–Fri, 11.00–23.00 Sat,
noon–17.00 Sun)

Hog & Bean 4 Victoria Rd ✆ 07403 023306 ⌂ thehogandbean.co.uk ◷ 08.30–17.00 daily.
Coffee beans are roasted in-house and ground to order to ensure the best quality drinks.
They also source local food for their menu that includes homemade quiche, Scotch eggs,
sugar-free cakes and, on Sunday, a very good-value roast.

Popup Café 16 High St ⌂ popupcafe.co.uk ◷ 09.00–15.00 daily. Vegetarians and vegans
are well catered for at this at this long-established café. Grilled sourdough cheese toasties
are justly popular and go well with their expertly made coffee.

The Rose 91 High St ⌂ therosedeal.com ◷ bar 08.00–22.00; food 08.00–10.00,
noon–2.30 & 18.00–11.00 Wed–Sat, 08.00–10.00 & noon–18.00 Sun. This old boozer
with a colourful history has probably never looked finer than in its current incarnation as
a slick restaurant, bar and boutique hotel. There's a fantastic cocktail menu and seasonally
changing food menu, designed in collaboration with top London-based chef Nuno Mendes.
Be sure to try the crab doughnut.

🛍 SHOPPING

Deal is heaven for lovers of antiques, vintage and retro goods. High Street is the main place
to look but also take a gander at the stalls along Sondes Road in the south of town where
you'll find the **The Village** (◷ 10.00–16.00 Sat), a market for local crafters and creators.

Don't Walk Walk Gallery 10 Victoria Rd ⌂ dontwalkwalkgallery.com ◷ 10.00–17.00
Wed–Mon. Artist Neil Horenz-Kelly is proud of the 'punk rock ethic' of his gallery and studio
space, practically guaranteeing that you'll find something eclectic and fun here. The entrance
hall sets the scene, with the walls and ceiling completely plastered with a constantly
evolving collage of images of old film posters, bands, book covers and the like.

Linden Hall Studio 32 St George's Rd ⌂ lindenhallstudio.co.uk ◷ 10.00–16.00 Tue–Sat.
Superb contemporary art gallery hosting a variety of exhibitions by solo and group artists.
Among those represented are former Keeper of the Royal Academy Eileen Cooper, Fred
Cumming, another RA, and the street photographer Harold Champman.

Mileage 156 High St ⌂ mileagevintage.co.uk ◷ 11.00–15.00 Thu & Fri, 10.00–16.00 Sat,
noon–15.00 Sun. Mileage stocks some of the best vintage and retro interior design pieces in
Deal, including ceramics, lamp shades, printed materials and lots of furniture.

Saturday Market Union Road Car Park, High St ⊘ deal.gov.uk/Markets_27245.aspx
⊙ Apr–Oct 08.00–14.00 Sat, Nov–Mar 09.00–14.00 Sat. There's been a Saturday market
in Deal since 1688. Traders today include those selling wines from small-scale producers,
artisan teas and Scandinavian cinnamon buns. A smaller market is held on Wednesdays
(⊙ 09.00–13.30) at the undercroft of the Town Hall.

Smugglers Records 9 King St ⊘ shop.smugglersrecords.com ⊙ 14.30–20.00 Mon–Wed,
14.30–22.00 Thu & Fri, 10.00–22.00 Sat, 11.00–17.00 Sun. This record shop also has a café,
to further encourage customers to hang out and browse the vintage and new vinyl platters
here (including artists released on Smugglers' own label).

Taylor Jones & Son 114 High St ⊘ taylorjonesandson.co.uk ⊙ 10.00–17.00 Wed–Sat,
11.00–15.00 Sun. BBC wildlife cameraman and fine-art photographer Richard Taylor-
Jones runs this gallery with his wife Sonja. It's based in listed Georgian building, with an
underground gallery that was once an entrance to one of the town's smuggling tunnels.

12 WALMER CASTLE & GARDENS

Kingsdown Rd, Walmer CT14 7LJ 🔗 ⊙ mid-Feb–Mar 10.00–16.00 Wed–Sun, Apr–Oct
10.00–17.00 daily, Nov–mid-Feb 10.00–16.00 Sat & Sun; English Heritage

The third and largest of the Henry VIII's coastal defences is at Walmer,
an easy and invigorating two-mile walk along the seashore from Deal.
By the 1750s, this military fortress had morphed into a comfortable
home, the official residence of the Lord Warden of the Cinque Ports.
Holders of this prestigious post have included William Pitt the Younger,
W H Smith and Elizabeth, the Queen Mother. But the castle is most
associated with Arthur Wellesley, the first Duke of Wellington. Walmer
is said to have been his favourite home and he died here, aged 83, in
1834. Memorabilia related to the duke that you can view during a tour
of the castle include his collapsible campaign bed and a pair of black
calfskin boots, his 'Wellingtons'.

In 1905 the castle, well past its days as an effective military fortress,
first opened to the public as a historic attraction. The surrounding eight
acres of elegant gardens and woodland have always been a highlight. The
kitchen garden was first established in the 18th century and successive
wardens added more sections. William Pitt, assisted by his niece Lady
Hester Stanhope, created the oval lawn planted with specimen trees,
the Paddock meadow (a blaze of yellow and white in early spring with
its displays of daffodils and snowdrops), and the Glen, an evergreen
shrubbery secluded in an old chalk pit. Lord Granville, who succeeded
Pitt as Lord Warden, made his mark with the yew-lined Broadwalk.

Over the years this has evolved into an undulating cloud hedge, a striking backdrop to relaxed drifts of colourful plants and flowers in the walk's double borders. In contrast are the formal lines and reflecting pool of the Queen Mother Garden, designed by renowned garden historian Penelope Hobhouse, a 1997 addition to Walmer's pleasure grounds. Look out for a sculpture of a corgi on one the benches.

¶¶ FOOD & DRINK

Walmer Castle also offers two very pleasant refreshment options: the Lord Warden's Tea Room in the castle and the Glasshouse Café in the gardens.

Goose on the Green 27 The Strand, Walmer ✐ 01304 271278 ⨍ GooseontheGreenCafe ⊙ 08.00–14.00 Mon, Tue & Thu–Sat, 08.30–14.00 Sun. It's worth getting up early to enjoy the hearty breakfasts served at this lovely little café. There are vegetarian and vegan options and the cappuccinos come with a dusting of chocolate in the shape of a goose. Book ahead for their Friday evening bistro menu (⊙ 17.30–20.30) when they also serve cocktails.
Hut 55 Marine Rd, Walmer ⊘ hut55.co.uk ⊙ 09.00–16.00 Thu–Sun. Right by the beach, this jaunty, off-the-grid coffee hut (solar panels on the roof power everything from the grinders to the till) serves coffee roasted by Garage in Canterbury. The teas also come from local Kent suppliers. There's plenty of classic seaside picnic grub and you can also rent a bike here.
The Lighthouse 50 The Strand, Walmer ✐ 01304 366031 ⊘ thelighthousedeal.co.uk ⊙ 17.00–23.00 Wed & Thu, 17.00–00.30 Fri, noon–00.30 Sat. As well as serving an interesting range of local beers, ciders and wines, this is an indie music and arts venue with most events being free entry. On the third Thursday of the month there's usually a quiz night.
Zetland Arms Wellington Parade, Kingsdown CT14 8AF ✐ 01304 370114 ⊘ zetlandarms. co.uk ⊙ 10.00–22.00 daily. Next to the shingle beach, this is one of the best-located pubs in Kent. Aim for here on a coastal walk from Deal or Walmer and you won't be disappointed. There's Shepherd Neame ales on tap and a food menu that showcases fresh, locally caught fish and seafood.

The award-winning Slow Travel series from Bradt Guides

Over 20 regional guides across Britain.
See the full list at bradtguides.com/slowtravel.

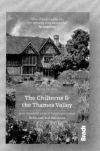

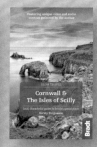

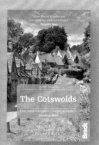

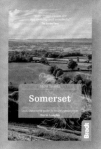

4
SOUTHEAST COASTAL KENT: DOVER TO DUNGENESS

A towering wall of craggy chalk cliffs rising from the sea, dazzling in the sunshine and topped with tufts of green grass: this has to be one of most visually famous stretches of coast in the world. The iconic White Cliffs run from Kingsdown in the east to Capel-le-Ferne and the Warren in the west, with the most famous section protected by the National Trust close to Dover. A coastal walk here is as close to hiking perfection as it can get.

Amid this natural splendour, Dover's Norman castle stands magisterial on a headland. The historic port also offers under-the-radar treasures such as the Maison Dieu and Western Heights, as well as a chance to stroll along its yacht and cruise marina, the departure point for the brave swimmers of the English Channel. Nine miles west, the old fishing village and former port of Folkestone is fast regaining its early 20th-century status as a fashionable getaway thanks to its courting of contemporary creatives and sponsorship of the arts. Both these towns, the largest in this part of Kent, are an easy day trip from London.

Dotted west along or near the coast are a series of smaller, but no less appealing, towns and villages, starting off with Sandgate where H G Wells had a home. Wells was not the only writer to have been attracted to and inspired by this part of Kent: Noel Coward and Ian Fleming both had holiday homes at St Margaret's Bay; Charles Dickens and Agatha Christie vacationed in Folkestone; and Russell Thorndike's *Dr Syn* series of smuggling novels used Dymchurch as backdrop.

The artists and film-maker Derek Jarman wrote passionately about his cottage and extraordinary garden, blooming out of the shingle in Dungeness. This elemental windswept landscape, the largest shingle foreland in Britain, with the ominous backdrop of a nuclear power station, is one of the highlights of moody, low-lying Romney Marsh. Known as the 'fifth continent', the marsh is also home to the Romney, Hythe and Dymchurch Railway, on which the largest collection of

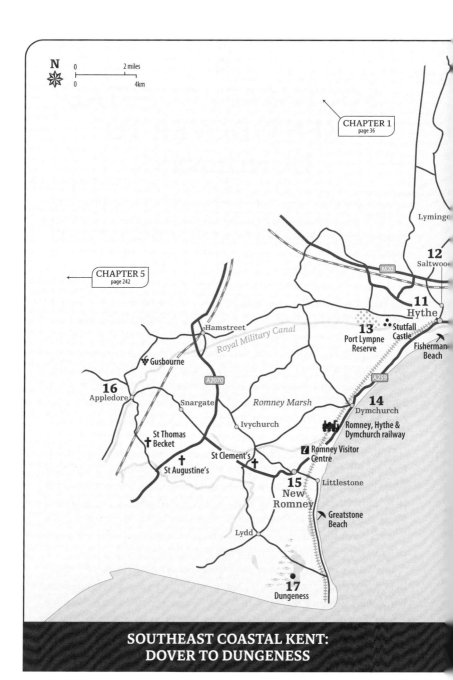

CHAPTER 1
page 36

CHAPTER 5
page 242

**SOUTHEAST COASTAL KENT:
DOVER TO DUNGENESS**

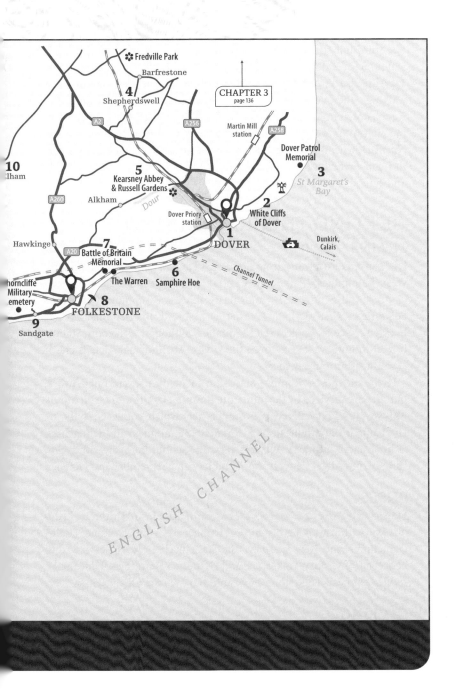

Fredville Park

Barfrestone

4 Shepherdswell

CHAPTER 3
page 136

Martin Mill
station

A256

A258

Dover Patrol
Memorial

10
lham

5
Kearsney Abbey
& Russell Gardens

3
St Margaret's
Bay

Alkham

A260

Dour

Dover Priory
station

2
White Cliffs
of Dover

Hawkinge

1
DOVER

Dunkirk,
Calais

A20

7 Battle of Britain
Memorial

Channel Tunnel

horncliffe
Military
emetery

6
The Warren

Samphire Hoe

8
FOLKESTONE

9
Sandgate

ENGLISH CHANNEL

one-third full-size steam locomotives in the world rattle along 15-inch-wide tracks. Riding this unique train service is one of the many Slow Travel pleasures of this seaside slice of Kent. If you prefer countryside walking, there couldn't be a simpler route than following the Napoleonic-era Royal Military Canal which zigzags its way west from the charming town of Hythe. Venturing a bit further inland into the North Downs, there's magnificent ancient trees to be viewed on hikes through Fredville Park near Nonnington, and gorgeous rolling fields and sinuous hedgerows along the Elham Valley.

GETTING THERE & AROUND

TRAINS

High-speed direct trains from London St Pancras connect to Folkestone West (52 minutes), Folkestone Central (55 minutes) and Dover Priory (1 hour and 5 minutes). Sandgate is about a 30-minute walk from Folkestone West station. Transfer at Ashford International for an hourly service to Appledore (13 minutes), although Appledore Station is a 30-minute walk away from the village. For timetable details check ⏁ southeasternrailway.co.uk.

Hythe and most of Romney Marsh are not on the national rail network, but they are serviced by the miniature **Romney, Hythe and Dymchurch Railway** (⏁ 01797 326353 ⏁ rhdr.org.uk) which connects Hythe to Dymchurch (20 minutes), New Romney (35 minutes) and Dungeness (1 hour and 4 minutes). Services vary throughout the year, with trains running most days between April and July and September and October.

BUSES

Stagecoach buses (⏁ stagecoachbus.com) run from Dover to Lydd-on-Sea (within walking distance of Dungeness) via Folkestone, Hythe, Dymchurch and New Romney. The Stagecoach Gold 16 service runs between Canterbury, Folkestone and Hythe, via Hawkinge, while the 17 service connects Folkestone and Canterbury via the Elham Valley.

CYCLING

The **Coast to Cathedral** trail is a marvellous 50-mile, circular ride on Regional Routes 16 and 17, linking Dover, Folkestone and Canterbury. The 27-mile **Miners' Way Trail** is a cycling and walking route connecting

i **TOURIST INFORMATION**

Dover Dover Museum, Market Sq ✆ 01304 201066 ⌂ whitecliffscountry.org.uk
🕐 09.30–17.00 Mon–Sat.
Folkestone Town Hall, 1–2 Guildhall St ✆ 01303 257946 ⌂ visitfolkestoneandhythe.co.uk
🕐 10.00–16.00 Mon–Sat.
New Romney Romney Warren Country Park ✆ 01797 367934 ⌂ rmcp.co.uk 🕐 Apr–Sep.
11.00–15.00 daily, Oct–Mar 11.00–15.00 Wed–Sun.

Shepherdswell and Deal over the North Downs and going past the remains of Kent's old coal mines. On ⌂ doverdistrictcycleforum.weebly. com you can find details of more cycling trails around Dover, includng the Skylark Trail which connect to Walmer (page 182). There is also a 13-mile cycle path from Seabrook to West Hythe that runs mainly alongside a stretch of the **Royal Military Canal** (page 224). Romney Marsh is also superb cycling country.

 BIKE HIRE

Channel Bike Hire ✆ 07583 401636 ⌂ channelbikehire.com. Free delivery of bikes to locations in Greatstone, Littlestone, Lydd, Romney Marsh, New Romney and Dungeness.
Click2cycle ⌂ click2cycle.com. An online bicycle hire company with docking stations in Folkestone, Sandgate and Hythe.
Renhams Cycles 17 Grace Hill, Folkestone ✆ 01303 241884 ⌂ renhamscycles.co.uk
🕐 09.00–17.30 Mon–Sat.
Romney Cycles (Kent) Ltd 77 High St, New Romney ✆ 01797 362155 ⌂ romneycycles.
co.uk 🕐 09.00–17.30 Mon–Fri, 09.00–17.00 Sat.
West Hythe Cycles Unit 17 Riverside Craft Centre, West Hythe Rd, Hythe ✆ 01303 479067
⌂ westhythecycles.co.uk 🕐 10.00–17.00 Mon–Wed & Fri, noon–17.00 Sat, 10.00–15.00 Sun.

1 DOVER & SURROUNDS

🏠 **Churchill Guesthouse** (page 310) 🏰 **Perevell's Tower & The Sergeant Major's House** (page 310) ⛺ **Greenhill Glamping** (page 310)

Few other places in Kent – or England – make as strong an initial visual impression as Dover. Your attention is immediately grabbed by the magnificent medieval castle topping the iconic White Cliffs, a pair of national symbols that pack a mighty punch. However, this is also Europe's busiest ferry port, with roads designed to shift large volumes of traffic in and out of Dover at speed; it's hardly the most enticing town in which to linger. Visitors tend not to explore much further than the two key sights, but there is much more to discover in this most historic of Kent locations, including remarkable Bronze Age and Roman remains and the awesome Napoleonic forts of the Western Heights, hiding in plain sight on the opposite headland to the castle. Hiking a section of the White Cliffs is a given, and for more gentle walks there are parks and gardens to be explored inland at Kearsney and on the coast at Samphire Hoe.

As a key military target, Dover endured heavy bombing during World War II. Post-war reconstruction was far from ideal, leaving the town centre brutally sliced up by roads, a situation that has not been improved by the new and unimaginative St James retail and leisure park beside the A2. However, the marina and associated new infrastructure that is part of the Western Docks Revival project have potential to inject life and activity into Dover's waterfront. There's also an ambitious plan to create the Dame Vera Lynn Memorial Park and amphitheatre on the Western Heights and talk about a cable car to connect the harbour with the castle. No question about it, things are looking up for Dover.

DOVER CASTLE
Castle Hill ✆ 0370 3331181 ⊙ mid-Feb–Mar 10.00–16.00 Wed–Sun, Apr–Jul & Sep 10.00–17.00 daily, Aug 09.30–18.00 daily, Nov–mid-Feb 10.00–16.00 Sat & Sun; English Heritage

Since the 11th century this impregnable castle, described as the 'key to England', has guarded Dover and served as the ceremonial gateway to the country. Built atop a pre-existing Iron Age hillfort, its 80 acres of grounds encompass a Roman lighthouse, a Saxon church, a recreation of the medieval court of Henry II inside the Great Tower, and a military museum. Burrowed into the chalk beneath the compound are some four miles of tunnels, the first created during the siege of 1216, then more extensive networks dug during the Napoleonic and world wars; troops were stationed here right up until 1958.

To fully explore this fascinating site takes at least half a day; the walk around its extensive battlements, offering panoramic views of the surroundings, is an hour on its own. Tickets are slightly cheaper if booked in advance online, and if you haven't brought a picnic (recommended), there are a couple of cafés within the grounds. For the ultimate experience, there are two fine self-catering properties within the castle grounds (page 310). If walking from the train station, be prepared for a stiff uphill hike that will take around 20 minutes. There's parking inside the castle grounds.

The logical place to start your explorations of the castle is its inner bailey, dominated by its central keep, the **Great Tower** so big as to be visible from far out in the Channel. Built under the order of Henry II between 1180 and 1189, this is one of England's best-preserved medieval buildings. The king wanted not only an unbreachable fortress that was a symbol of his authority, but also a magnificent residence fit to entertain visiting VIPs, many of whom were on pilgrimage to Canterbury. The vast rooms inside the stone tower have been lavishly and colourfully decorated, just as they would have been in Henry's time, with giant embroidered wall hangings, painted friezes, a royal four-poster bed and banqueting tables covered with silverware. There is a surprisingly intimate royal chapel illuminated by a stained-glass window depicting Henry's nemesis Thomas Becket (see box, page 46). Climb the stone stairs (all 150 of them) from the entrance to the roof for panoramic views across the port and Straits of Dover. So as not to disturb the illusion of time travel, there are no interpretation panels, but plenty of staff are around to explain things and on some days you may also encounter costumed interpreters.

Elsewhere inside the inner bailey, **Arthur's Hall** (one of the oldest sections of the castle, dating to the 1230s), is well used for an informative exhibition on the Angevins, Henry II's fractious and quarrelsome family. Next to hall is the **Princess of Wales' Royal Regiment and Queens's Regiment Museum**, covering over 400 years of history of this army regiment, right up to recent engagements in Afghanistan.

Tunnels were first dug beneath the castle during the prolonged sieges of 1216 and 1217 when the French prince Louis joined rebel barons battling King John. A section of these **medieval tunnels** are open for exploration, but it's the Casemates set of tunnels, first excavated 600 years later during the Napoleonic Wars, that are the most engaging subterranean section of the castle. Created to house some 2,000 troops drafted into Dover to strengthen the port against possible attack, the tunnels were largely abandoned after Napoleon failed to attack. Shortly before World War II they were pressed back into service as an air-raid shelter, a military command centre and, with extensions dug in the early 1940s, an underground hospital and for other operational uses.

It was from these tunnels that, in May 1940, Admiral Sir Bertram Ramsey directed Operation Dynamo, also known as the evacuation of Dunkirk, when 338,000 British and French troops were ferried back to England across the Channel under the most hazardous of circumstances. The guide-led **Operation Dynamo Tours**, lasting around one hour (and at the time of research requiring an additional ticket) plunge you into the thick of these dramatic events with films projected on to the tunnel walls and rooms dressed as they would have been during World War II. A separate 20-minute tour of the Annexe level of tunnels that housed the **underground hospital** is also available. Lighting and audio effects (the rumble of bombs exploding above, patients groaning, medical staff consulting each other) bring to vivid life the experience of what it was like to be a patient in this claustrophobic underworld.

From the early 1960s until 1984 a currently off-limits level of the tunnels was adapted to become a self-sufficient Regional Seat of Government in the event to nuclear attack. Learn more about this shadowy Cold War facility, and other historical aspects of the tunnels, from the Secret Wartime Tunnels exhibition set up at the entrance to the Dynamo Tours.

The first bomb to be dropped on England during World War I fell near Dover Castle on Christmas Eve 1914. To learn more about this period of the castle's history you don't have to go underground. With a panoramic view across the Channel, the fire command post spread over two levels recreates the time when the Straits of Dover were the most dangerous seaway in the world with British boats under attack from German U-boats and, later, aircraft. Mounted outside the command post is the only working British 3-inch gun in the world, built in 1915 to combat aerial attacks. On weekends between July and September, regular firing demonstrations are held, performed by costumed volunteers.

At the heart of the complex, and on its highest point, stand two of the castle's oldest structures. The **Roman pharos** was originally an octagonal lighthouse rising some 80ft and probably topped with a platform that held a form of brazier. In the early 15th century the much-diminished pharos was repurposed as a bell tower for the neighbouring

◀ **1** Maison Dieu, Dover. **2** St Margaret's Bay and the White Cliffs. **3** Dover Castle's war tunnels. **4** Leas Lift, Folkestone. **5** Battle of Britain Memorial. **6** Folkestone's colourful Creative Quarter.

church of **St Mary in Castro**. Believed to date from around AD1000, flint and tile from the ruined Roman building was used in the church's construction. It is one of the finest late Saxon buildings in Kent and has long been the garrison's church: Richard the Lionheart's knights scratched graffiti into the walls here – look for it near the pulpit. Major restorations were carried out by Sir George Gilbert Scott in 1862 and William Butterfield in 1888, the latter designing the decorative mosaic tiling that covers the interior wall. It's a working church with services held on Sundays at 10.00.

TOWN CENTRE

Dover's town centre is focused around pedestrianised Market Square, in a corner of which is the modern building housing the tourist office and **Dover Museum** (Market Sq ✆ 01304 201066 ⌂ dovermuseum.co.uk ⊙ Apr–Sep 09.30–17.00 Mon–Sat & 10.00–15.00 Sun; Oct–Mar 09.30–17.00 Mon–Sat). The highlight at this terrific free museum is the Bronze Age Boat Gallery which displays a remarkably well-preserved section of a boat constructed out of oak some 3,500 years ago and discovered in 1992 by construction workers building a section of the A20 road through Dover. Billed as the 'world's oldest seagoing boat' it is a remarkable find, surrounded by other archaeological relics and models of what the craft would have looked like when it was newly built. Other eras from Dover's history are well-covered in modest displays and there are also excellent online exhibitions about the history of cross-Channel swimming and coal mining in Kent.

A short walk west of Market Square, a utilitarian and uninviting building houses the best preserved of several Roman ruins discovered beneath Dover (all the others have been reburied after their initial excavations). Dating from around AD200, the **Roman Painted House** (New St ✆ 01304 203279 ⌂ karu.org.uk/roman_painted_house ⊙ Jun–Aug 10.00–17.00 daily) gets its name from the sections of painted plaster remarkably still intact on the ruin's walls. Once a fine residence for visiting Roman dignitaries, the building was destroyed when Dover's fort was enlarged in AD270. In the process, three of its main rooms were buried intact, the rubble protecting the delicate wall paintings and the building's hypocaust (underground central heating). The ruins are surrounded by many detailed information panels and other archaeological finds from the dig that uncovered the site in the early 1970s. Unfortunately, the lacklustre visual presentation is also stuck in the 1970s. Look out for a model of the Roman fort near the building entrance which shows how much Dover's geography has changed in the last 1,800 years.

Sitting at an angle to Cannon Street, Dover's central commercial thoroughfare, is **St Mary's Church** (Cannon St ⊘ stmarysdover.org.uk), likely one of the three churches in the town mentioned in the Domesday Book of 1086. The main tower mainly dates from Norman times but the rest of the church was largely rebuilt in Victorian Gothic Style. Cannon Street becomes Biggin Street which eventually leads to the **Maison Dieu**, one of Dover's most historic buildings with a stunning interior that is undergoing restoration until 2024. On the way back to Market Square, make a detour down narrow St Edmund's Walk to view **St Edmund's**

RESTORING THE MAISON DIEU

By the summer of 2024 Dover will have a splendid new attraction that is over 800 years old. Located on the corner of High Street and Ladywell, **Maison Dieu** (meaning 'House of God') was founded in 1203 by Hubert de Burgh, Constable of Dover Castle. Run by monks, it was a hospice providing temporary lodgings for pilgrims en route to Canterbury, and care for the poor and sick. Henry III consecrated its chapel (the oldest surviving part of the original building) in 1227 and was the first of many monarchs to visit.

Following the Reformation, Maison Dieu was used by the navy as a store depot for 300 years until it was bought by Dover Town Council in 1834 who wanted it for their town hall. To achieve this transformation, architect Ambrose Poynter was hired; he later brought on board the eminent architect and designer William Burges. Both died before their full vision for a reinterpretation of this medieval building was completed, leaving others to faithfully execute their plans. The most impressive section is the Stone Hall with its beautifully painted glass windows designed by Edward J Poynter (who became Director of the National Gallery and President of the Royal Academy), depicting six key scenes from Dover's history.

The 20th century was not kind to Maison Dieu, with much of Burges's elaborate wall art and decoration being overpainted. The current £9.1 million project aims to restore key elements of this Gothic Revivalist scheme. A new entrance to the building into Connaught Hall, a 19th-century addition to the complex, will lead to an atrium and café that will occupy part of the Victorian gaol cells that are beneath the ground floor. In a collaboration with the Landmark Trust, a holiday let will be created from the Mayor's suite of rooms which will be revived to their full William Bruges grandeur.

For details of current events at Maison Dieu see ⊘ maisondieudover.org.uk.

Chapel (Priory Rd ⟨⟩ stedmundschapel.co.uk), built in 1252 and said to be the smallest church in England.

THE HARBOUR

Dover's impressive harbour, with its piers and breakwaters, has evolved over many centuries. It is split into two regions: the Eastern Docks, from where all the cross-Channel ferries operate, and the Western Docks with its outstretched harbour arms providing moorings for enormous cruise liners and cargo ships.

To reach the Western Docks section on foot, keep following the pedestrianised street south from Market Square towards the A2 where an underpass leads across and out into a handsome set of Victorian terraces and the promenade running alongside the shingle beach and harbour. Look down to see the black granite start/finish line for the North Downs Way. To one side is a Sustans Portrait Bench with two-dimensional silhouettes of Olympic torchbearer Jamie Clark, the author Ian Fleming and singer Vera Lynn, cut from CorTen steel.

A pair of concrete plinths rise up dead ahead, each topped with the simplified image of a swimmer – one heading out to France, the other

DOVER ARTS DEVELOPMENT & CHALKUP21

Dover Arts Development (DAD; ⟨⟩ dadonline. uk) is a local artist-led non-profit company that highlights and supports a wide range of creative activities going on in and around Dover. One of its many projects is CHALKUP21 (⟨⟩ chalkup21.com), a 17-mile coastal trail between Capel-le-Ferne, two miles east of Folkestone, and Deal. Along the way nine pieces of contemporary architecture and public art built between 1999 and 2014 are highlighted, including The Wing building at the Battle of Britain Memorial (page 208), Samphire Hoe Education Shelter, White Cliffs Visitor Centre and the Deal Pier Café. It's an inspired alternative prism through which to consider an area where military history and the glories of the natural environment tend to predominate.

Also check DAD's website for details of a fascinating new public artwork commissioned from sound artist Emily Peasgood at **Fort Burgoyne** (Fort Burgoyne Rd, Guston CT15 5LP ⟨⟩ thelandtrust.org.uk/space/fort-burgoyne), built in the 1860s to protect the rear northern flank of Dover Castle. Entitled *I Would Rather Walk With You* (⟨⟩ emilypeasgood. com/iwouldratherwalkwithyou), the site-specific work is a contemporary choral piece comprising a choir, voice recordings and sound effects, many of which were recorded by Dover locals in their homes during the lockdown of 2021.

coming into Dover. If you walk east along Marine Parade, in the direction of the ferry terminal, you'll shortly come to a bust of Captain Matthew Webb – in 1875 he was the first man to swim the Channel unaided. In perhaps the ultimate approach to Slow Travel, it took Webb 21 hours and 45 minutes to swim from Admiralty Pier to Calais. In the century and half since, only just over 2,000 people have successfully matched Webb in tackling what is considered the Everest of sea swimming.

Attractive landscaping of the promenade by the architects Tonkin Liu in 2011, plus the ongoing regeneration works of the Western Docks Revival project to create a marina, boardwalks and, ultimately, waterside retail, is adding interest to Dover's Harbour. For a breezy walk out into the Channel, stride out down the half-mile long Prince of Wales Pier.

WESTERN HEIGHTS

Leave the Harbour by walking down Union Street towards the A20. Across the highway, behind a brick wall and large metal gate, is the entrance to the **Grand Shaft**, one of Dover's most remarkable, hidden architectural treasures. It's a triple helix staircase built into the cliffs between 1806 and 1809 to enable the troops stationed atop the Western Heights to quickly descend to the town. During Victorian times the three intertwined staircases, dropping 140ft, were separately used by different ranks: 'officers and their ladies', 'sergeants and their wives' and 'soldiers and their women'. The shaft is opened to the public by the Western Heights Preservation Society (♂ doverwesternheights.org) on the third Sunday of the month from March to November between 10.00 and 16.00.

The Grand Shaft is impressive, but the ingenious **Drop Reboubt** (Drop Redoubt Rd, CT17 9AP), nature-encroached remains of the Western Height's other Napoleonic fortresses, linked by towering brick-lined ditches, will blow your mind. The bomb-proof pentagonal fortress was made by cutting a deep, wide moat into the hillside. It is perfectly camouflaged against enemy attack and is awe-inspiring in its enormous scale, like an ancient and enigmatic ruin. Occupied by the army up until 1961 and now managed by English Heritage, the grounds are free to explore: the most direct access from town is via the steep set of steps that ascend from the side of atmospheric **Cowgate Cemetery** behind Albany Place. The Western Heights Preservation Society run tours inside the fort on the third Sunday of the month from April to September. This is the only way to access the grassy top, where you can see the scant remains of the second of Dover's Roman pharos (lighthouses).

Another ancient ruin to look for while up this way is the so-called **Knights Templar Church**, just off Citadel Road. All that remains of this compact medieval chapel is its stone foundations, with the circular-shaped nave indicating that it may have been built by the Templars, the 12th-century military and religious order that protected pilgrims travelling to the Holy Land.

"All that remains of this compact medieval chapel is its stone foundations, with the circular-shaped nave."

Immediately west of Dover Harbour, **Shakespeare Beach** is accessible from the west side of town via a foot tunnel under the A2 and a pedestrian bridge over the railway tracks. Head here to gain a close-up view of Shakespeare Cliff. This towering white chalk headland gets its name from the playwright, who visited Dover in 1597 with his theatrical company the Lord Chamberlain's Men. The cliff so inspired Shakespeare that he based a scene from King Lear at what could well be this location. Looking down, Edgar says:

How fearful and dizzy 'tis, to cast one's eyes so low! ... The fishermen, that walk upon the beach, appear like mice... almost too small for sight.

🍴 FOOD & DRINK

Breakwater Brewery St Martins Yard, Lorne Rd ✆ 01304 410144 🇫 ⊙ 17.00–23.00 Wed & Thu, 16.00–23.00 Fri, noon–23.00 Sat, noon–20.00 Sun. Beside the River Dour in a timber clad building, this micro-brewery gets the chalk-filtered spring water for its ales from a borehole that dates back to the 17th century. They serve pizzas to go with their dozen or so beers. Also look out at the seafront Marina Curve for their mobile bar.

Cullens Yard 11 Cambridge Rd ✆ 01304 211666 ⊘ cullinsyard.co.uk ⊙ 10.00–23.00 daily. Overlooking the marina, Cullens is a micro-brewery and restaurant based in an old converted shipyard. Nautical memorabilia decorates the place and there's a wide range of menu options including chunky sandwiches, burgers, seafood and steaks, as well as their ales Jimmy's Riddle and Pigs Ear on tap.

Dover Patrol The Esplanade ✆ 01304 207740 ⊘ thedoverpatrol.co.uk ⊙ 10.00–21.30 daily. The menu is heavy on seafood at this marina-located restaurant and bar. While the dishes are competently made and service is fine, it's really about the location here, with uninterrupted views across the harbour.

The White Horse St James St ✆ 01304 213066 🖉 thewhitehorsedover.co.uk 🕐 noon–
22.00 Mon–Thu, noon–23.00 Fri & Sat, noon–21.00 Sun. Occupying a building that dates to
1365, this is about as historic a pub as you can get in Dover. It has a leafy garden courtyard
and a decent menu, but the defining feature is its walls which are sport the signatures and
messages of those who have completed a cross-Channel swim.

2 WHITE CLIFFS OF DOVER

Reaching a commanding height of 350ft in places and pockmarked
by striations of dark flint, Dover's White Cliffs flank either side of
the port. The National Trust, custodians of around six miles of the
cliffs, describes them as 'a symbol of steadfastness, safety and home'.
A staunch repulse to invaders, a warm welcome to returning citizens
and a wonder of the natural world, they are as symbolic of England as
the Eiffel Tower is of France.

Created 66 million years ago when ocean floor deposits were raised
above sea level, the chalk cliffs appear monolithic. They were mentioned
by Julius Caesar as an impregnable piece of the coastline during his
attempts to invade Britain in 55BC. However, battered by the Channel's
stormy seas and exposed to the elements, the cliffs are fragile, slowly
but constantly eroding; occasionally, enormous chunks crash to the sea.
No matter how tempting it may be, venturing close to the cliff edges is
never advised.

The chalk grassland atop the cliffs is an important habitat for rare
wildlife, including some 30 species of butterflies and birds such as
the peregrine falcon, raven and skylark. Exmoor ponies act as benign
gardeners, naturally clearing invasive vegetation and creating space for
smaller, less robust native plants to thrive. Wild flowers are abundant
and include common plants such yellow rattle, ox-eye daisy and the
vividly blue and purple viper's bugloss which is at its best between June
and September; the rare spider orchid blooms in April and May. In June
2021, a wild flower meadow was named in honour of the late Dame Vera
Lynn, who immortalised the cliffs with her World War II hit *(There'll be
Bluebirds Over) The White Cliffs of Dover* and who lent her name to a
National Trust campaign to protect the grasslands for future generations.

Start exploring this treasured environment from the grass-roofed
National Trust visitor centre (Langdon Cliffs, Upper Rd, CT16 1HJ
✆ 01304 202756 🕐 car park 07.00–19.00, café Apr–Oct 10.00–17.00
daily; Nov–Mar 10.00–16.00 daily; National Trust) which blends

seamlessly with the greenery around it. The café here offers stupendous views across the Channel. One-and-a-half miles from the visitor centre is the entrance to the **Fan Bay Deep Shelter** (✆ 01304 207326 ⊙ Mar–Oct 11.00–15.00 Fri–Mon). Climb down 125 steep steps to explore this claustrophobic tunnel complex constructed in between 1940 and 1941 as accommodation for troops operating the gun battery that once existed above. Breath fresh air on the open-air ledge in the cliffs accessed from the tunnels, where there are a pair of concrete 'sound mirrors' (see box, page 207) from World War I. The five-mast German trade vessel the *Preußen* collided with the RMS *Brighton* just off the coast here in 1910.

3 ST MARGARET'S BAY

🏠 **The Lantern Inn** (page 310)

Half a mile east along the cliffs from Fan Bay. the whitewashed **South Foreland Lighthouse** (CT15 5NA ⊙ Mar–Oct 11.00–17.30 Fri–Mon) stands atop the headland above St Margaret's Bay. Some form of light beacon has illuminated this site since 14th century. The danger here is not so much the cliffs, but the treacherous Goodwin Sands, 'the ship-swallower' that lurks three miles offshore. The current lighthouse, dating to 1842, was powered by that novelty of the age, electricity, shining out nightly until it was decommissioned in 1988. An exhibition inside the lighthouse gives details of the world's first international wireless transmission sent from here in 1899, and of the Knott family, lighthouse keepers for five generations between 1730 and 1910. You can also climb to the balcony atop the light tower for elevated views of the surroundings. Tucked behind the lighthouse, the 1950s-themed **Mrs Knott's Tea Room** (page 201) is as good a reason as any for heading here as any.

On the way down to sea level from the lighthouse it's worth taking time to explore the organically managed **Pines Garden** (Beach Rd, CT15 6DZ ♦ baytrust.org.uk ⊙ Apr–Sep 10.00–17.00 daily; Oct–Mar 10.00–16.00 Mon–Fri, 10.00–15.30 Sat & Sun). A regenerative space, maintained with ecology and sustainability at its heart, this wildly beautiful six-acre garden includes a lake, poetry path, grass labyrinth and plots with over 40 different species of fruit and vegetables. Taking pride of place is a stern-looking, life-size bronze statue of Winston Churchill by Oscar Nemon. Also notable is its events venue the

Pines Calyx, an energy-efficient building with rammed chalk walls and dome roofs covered in grass. Across the road from the gardens is a pleasant tea room (page 204) and a small museum with exhibitions on local history, the environment and personalities associated with St Margaret's, including Ian Fleming and Noel Coward.

St Margaret's Bay is a compact, sheltered shingle beach nestling at the foot of towering white chalk cliffs; take care if you drive or cycle here as the access road from the larger village of St Margaret's at Cliffe on the hillside above is narrow, with several blind hairpin bends. At the foot of the cliffs on the northeastern side of the bay are an attractive set of Art Deco houses which were leased or owned by Noel Coward between 1945 and 1951. The actor, singer and playwright liked to take beach

"At the foot of the cliffs on the northeastern side of the bay are an attractive set of Art Deco houses which were leased or owned by Noel Coward."

breaks here with his relatives and famous friends, including Spencer Tracey, Katherine Hepburn and Ian Fleming. The last was so fond of St Margaret's that he took over one of the homes when Coward returned to his Romney Marsh property in 1951. Fleming continued to use the house as a weekend retreat until 1958 and set his James Bond novel *Moonraker* in the seaside village. His wife Anne was not as fond of the location, complaining of 'seaweed in the living room and boulders of chalk on the head.'

¶¶ FOOD & DRINK

The Coastguard The Bay, CT15 6DY ℘ 01304 853051 ⬡ thecoastguard.co.uk
◷ 10.00–21.00 daily. There's a jolly nautical theme at this pub and restaurant beside the beach at St Margaret's Bay. Kitchen specials include plenty of fresh seafood and beef bourguignon, a nod to France that, on clear days, can be viewed across this narrow stretch of the Channel.

Mrs Knott's Tea Room South Foreland Lighthouse, CT15 5NA ◷ Mar–Oct 11.00–17.00 Fri–Mon. This 1950s-themed tea room, part of the lighthouse complex, is a vintage gem. The counter is loaded down with a mouth-watering range of home bakes and the leaf tea is served in pots with mismatched patterned china cups and saucers.

The Lantern Inn The Street, Martin Mill CT15 5JL ℘ 01304 852276 ⬡ lanterninn.co.uk
◷ Jan–Mar 17.00–22.00 Wed & Thu, noon–22.30 Fri–Sun, Apr–Dec 17.00–22.00 Tue–Thu, noon–22.30 Fri–Sun. 'Gluttons welcome' says the sign hanging outside this convivial country pub, three miles inland from St Margaret's Bay and along the Skylark Cycling Trail

White Cliffs to St Margaret's Bay

❄ OS Explorer map 138; start: White Cliffs of Dover Visitor Centre ♥ TR336422; 7.2 miles; easy, but note there are some steepish climbs and descents from the clifftop paths

No bluebirds on this classic White Cliffs walk, I'm afraid – they are not actually native to the British Isles. Otherwise, this is the platonic ideal of a hike along the Kent coast. From mid-May to late June and then again from early August to the end of September you may be able to spot the rare Adonis blue butterflies as they flutter across the abundant wild flowers and grasses. Manmade attractions along the route include the South Foreland Lighthouse, the gorgeous Pines Garden at Margaret's Bay and the Dover Patrol Memorial.

If travelling by train, you can start and end at Dover Priory train station which adds around 1¾ miles (about 40 minutes) to the walk. Go through Dover town centre, use the underpass to cross the A20 and to reach the harbour beach. Turn left and follow Marine Parade across the A2 before walking up Athol Terrace to the hill footpath (renamed Dame Vera Lynn Way in 2021) that climbs the cliffs behind the ferry terminal. There is paid parking at the White Cliffs visitor centre. The route is well marked with the steepest sections being the paths down into and out of St Margaret's Bay.

1 Exit the visitor centre's grounds at its east end and follow the track past the coastguard station to the natural amphitheatre known as Langdon Hole. Look down to the base of the cliffs and you may just be able to make out the shattered hulk of the SS *Falcon*, a steamer which caught fire in 1926. When the tracks split, take the fork on the left, continuing along the track to Fan Hole.

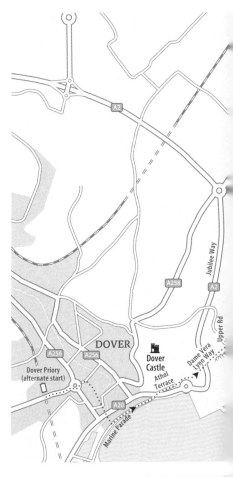

2 Pass the entrance to the Fan Bay Deep Shelter (page 200). If this World War II tunnels complex is open you might want to take the 45-minute underground tour. Continue along the path aiming for the South Foreland Lighthouse up ahead.

3 The path diverts inland past the lighthouse, behind which is former Wanstone Farm, an area of land the National Trust acquired in a £1 million campaign supported by Dame Vera Lynn. Restoring the landscape here to a wild flower meadow has provided habitat for ground-nesting birds such as meadow pipits, partridges and corn bunting; skylarks were ▶

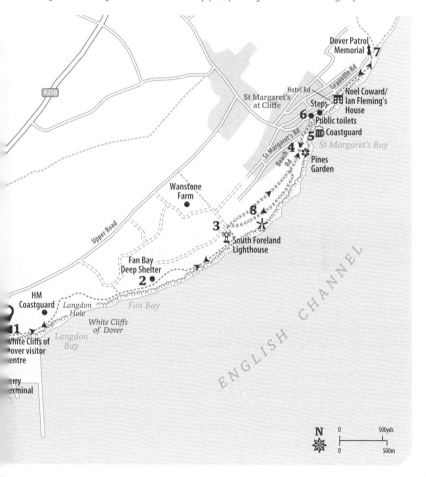

White Cliffs to St Margaret's Bay continued ...

also spotted at this site in 2021. Follow the narrow tarmac path to the first junction with the footpath; turn right here and then at the next junction go straight ahead along a clear track leading to the tarmacked Beach Road.

4 After about half a mile, you'll reach the Pines Garden (page 200); at the garden's entrance, on the right, is its tea room and the small St Margaret's Museum. Walk past the gardens and, at the junction with St Margaret's Road, turn right and keep heading downhill, following Bay Hill to the beach car park.

5 Facing the beach, on your right is The Coastguard (page 201) pub and restaurant. Walk in the direction of the far northeast end of the beach towards the cluster of Art Deco houses where Noel Coward and Ian Fleming once stayed.

6 Just past the public toilets at St Margaret's Bay, look to the left for the footpath with steps zigzagging back up the cliff. You'll eventually emerge to a level footpath, with the cliff edge to the right and the houses along Hotel Road to the left. Follow the path uphill to the right.

7 The footpath connects to Granville Road, at the head of which is the Dover Patrol Monument. This 75ft granite obelisk honours the 2,000 members of this naval flotilla who lost their lives while policing the southern part of the North Sea and the eastern end of the English Channel during World War I. From the Dover Patrol Monument, retrace your steps back to the Pines Garden. Where Beach Road ends and the footpaths begin, take the left path sharply uphill to reach the cliffside path back towards the lighthouse.

8 The route will take you past a windmill (built in 1929 to generate electricity for the attached house). Once you reach the lighthouse, return to the White Cliffs Visitor Centre following the same path by which you came.

between Walmer and Dover. There's every excuse for some over-indulging here with a good range of guest beers and ciders on tap as well as a superior food menu ranging from wood-fired pizzas and gut-busting Sunday roasts to interesting smaller plates such as a local crab, chip and samphire butty. The vibe is punk, old members' club. In their pleasant beer garden they host events such as cabaret nights and there's a cute wooden wendy house for kids. It's also a good place to stay.

The Pines Garden Tea Room Beach Rd, CT15 6DZ ✆ 01304 853173 ⌂ baytrust.org.uk/the-pines-garden-tea-room ⏲ 10.00–16.00 Wed–Sun. Some of the ingredients used to make the baguette sandwiches and quiches here are grown in The Pines Garden's organically managed gardens. The regular menu is supplemented on Sundays by a popular roast lunch; book ahead. From May to October you can also buy plants and veggies from a stall outside the café.

4 SHEPHERDSWELL & SURROUNDS

From the end of the 19th century to the 1980s, coal was mined across east Kent, including near the North Downs' village of Shepherdswell, a 24-minute train ride northwest of Dover Priory (the train station is spelled Shepherds Well). A minute's walk from the station is the **East Kent Railway** (EKR; Station Rd, CT15 7PD ♪ 01304 832042 ⌂ eastkentrailway.co.uk), which manages the former industrial rail link to Eythorne's defunct Tilmanstone colliery. On Sundays from Easter to mid-October, enthusiasts run train trips in vintage carriages on this two-mile stretch of track. Travelling at a sedate 15 miles per hour, the round trip takes about an hour, including a 20-minute pause at Eythorne where there is a platform café and a replica of a colliery winding tower. Extra trips are run during school holidays and there are also special events such as afternoon teas in their handsome buffet car – check their website for full details

The EKR's Shepherdswell base is heaven for railway enthusiasts and a fun place for family outings. Apart from the train trip, there are several model railways to inspect, including the four imaginative and different-scale layouts of the **Walmer Model Railway** club, based inside a set of restored carriages. There's also walking trails through the **Knees Woodland**, known for its snowdrops in February and bluebells in May and where the wildlife includes slow-worms, lizards, nightingales, turtledoves and green woodpeckers. The **Colonel's Café** (⊙ Mar–Dec 09.00–16.00 Tue–Sun) serves drinks, snacks and simple meals. Inside the café there's also information about the *Friendly Army*, six quirky World War I commemorative sculptures by Gabor Stark sited around Shepherdswell and Eythorne (⌂ artistsww1.uk/artists/gabor-stark).

"Travelling at a sedate 15 miles per hour, the round trip includes a pause at Eythorne where there is a platform café and a replica of a colliery winding tower."

A mile and a half north of Shepherdswell, in the tiny hamlet of Barfrestone, is the remarkable 11th-century church of **St Nicholas** (Eythorne Rd, CT15 7JQ ⌂ bewsboroughparish.org). Barely 50ft in length, the church is the canvas for some of the finest Norman stone carvings in Britain. The south door is particularly notable. At the centre of the tympanum is Christ, surrounded by angels, mermaids, a griffin and a sphinx. The outer circle of decoration has figures from medieval life including one believed to be St Thomas Becket, murdered at Canterbury Cathedral in 1170 (see box, page 46); Barfrestone was on the pilgrims' route to Becket's shrine from Dover. Inside the church, a triple arch frames a wheel window and there are narrow carved Caen stone friezes along the walls.

Just over half a mile northwest of Barfrestone, public footpaths and bridleways lead into and across the privately owned estate of **Fredville Park** (Nonnington CT15 4JG). Jane Austen might have visited the estate while staying with her brother in nearby Goodenestone Park (page 175). The grand house that once stood here suffered a catastrophic fire during World War II and was pulled down in 1945. What does remain is the many splendid centuries-old trees, including Spanish chestnuts and oaks. The most extraordinary oak, the so-called Pedunculate 'Majesty', is thought to be at least 900 years old – it stands in a private part of the park but you may catch sight of its magnificent crown and bulbous, mostly hollow truck as you walk along the main footpath from the hamlet of Frogham to Nonnington village.

5 KEARSNEY ABBEY & RUSSELL GARDENS

Alkham Rd, Temple Ewell CT16 3DZ ⊘ kearsneyparks.co.uk

Three miles inland along the Dour River valley from Dover's seafront, or a short walk from Kearsney train station, are this pretty pair of recreational parks. Both were once the sites of palatial mansions. Kearsney Abbey was mostly demolished in 1950; only the former billiard room of its west wing remains and is now attached to a modern café. The ten acres of informal gardens here have two adjoining ornamental lakes and a fine collection of trees, including an ancient cedar of Lebanon.

Across the road, Kearsney Court, still standing, was divided up into seven apartments in the 1950s. The originally owner, Edward P Barlow, Chairman of the Wiggins Teape Paper Mill in Dover, commissioned the eminent landscape architect Thomas Mawson to design the impressive gardens and parkland. These include a 557ft-long canal pond, Palladian-style pergola bridges and boathouse pavilion. The gardens were renamed after Hilton Russell, a Dover mayor who secured them for public use. The **Kearsney Loop** (⊘ kentramblers.org.uk/news/kearsney_loop/kearsney_loop.pdf) is a rewarding and easy-to-follow 2½-mile round walk that takes you past Bushy Ruff, a lake next to Russell Gardens, and atop the North Downs.

6 SAMPHIRE HOE

Off A20, CT17 9FL ⏣ samphirehoe.com ⊘ 07.00–dusk daily

If you're walking, the England Coast Path climbs over the top of Shakespeare Cliff (page 198) and along the headland towards the road-tunnel entrance to the nature park Samphire Hoe. Almost 176 million cubic feet of chalk marl were used to create this 74-acre park, jutting into the English Channel and threaded through with walking trails. Opened in July 1997, the park has evolved into a biodiversity hotspot, home to over 200 species of plants, 220 species of birds, and wildlife ranging from dragonflies to English Longhorn cattle and Romney sheep. Samphire Hoe takes its name from the rock samphire which was once collected from the cliffs here; a 'hoe' is a piece of land which sticks out into the sea. The **tea kiosk** (⊘ 11.00–17.00) beside the car park is open weekends throughout the year and most days from Easter to early September.

THE SOUND MIRRORS

Before there was radar, there were sound mirrors. Also known acoustic mirrors or listening ears, these concrete structures along the southeast Kent coast were an early warning detection system for enemy aircraft. Initially developed during World War I, sound mirrors used a large, curved surface to concentrate sound waves from as far away as 20 miles into a central point, which could then be heard through a stethoscope by a sound collector. As technology developed a microphone was used to pick up sounds instead of a human listener.

There are two mirrors at **Fan Bay** along the National Trust-managed stretch of the White Cliffs: one built in 1917 (and thought to be England's oldest surviving sound mirror) and one from the 1920s. Both mirrors were initially cut into the chalk and then lined with concrete. There's also a very impressive freestanding sound mirror along the England Coast Path at **Abbotscliff**, between Dover and Folkestone.

The most dramatic set of mirrors, however, are the trio (each one different in design) at Greatstone on the way to Dungeness (page 233). Known as the **Denge Sound Mirrors** they were built between 1928 and 1935 but became obsolete when radar was invented before the start of the World War II. The site has since become famous as an otherworldly backdrop for Vogue fashion shoots and pop videos by likes of The Prodigy and Nicki Minaj. Marooned on a manmade island in flooded gravel and sand pits, the mirrors are protected as part of a RSPB nature reserve. Check the RSPB events listings (⏣ events.rspb.org.uk/dungeness) for the handful of days a year that guided tours are run to the island, otherwise you'll have to observe them from afar.

7 BATTLE OF BRITAIN MEMORIAL

New Dover Rd, Capel-le-Fern ✆ 01303 249292 ⌨ battleofbritainmemorial.org ⏱ Mar–Sep
10.00–17.00, Oct–Feb 10.00–16.00 daily

On the England Coast Path, three miles west of Samphire Hoe and two
miles east of Folkestone, you'll find this evocative memorial dedicated
to those who fought in the aerial conflict that raged in the skies above
between 10 July and 31 October 1940. The memorial is composed of
various elements. Outside, surrounded by grassy mounds, is the central
larger-than-life statue of an airman, sitting on the ground, his knees
tucked up under his arms and his gaze fixed out to sea. The giant blades
of a propeller radiate in the ground around him. To one side is a wall
etched with the names of aircrew who flew sorties during the Battle of
Britain, while on another are replicas of a Hawker Hurricane Mk l and a
Supermarine Spitfire Mk 1.

During World War II, this part of Kent was known as 'Hellfire Corner'
because of the intensity of aerial warfare. The interactive exhibition in
the visitors' centre (called The Wing because it is designed in the shape
of a Spitfire wing) provides an insight into the experiences of fighter
pilots during that incredibly dangerous period. There's also the Cockpit
Café, with a grand view of the memorial and out to France on clear days
from its balcony.

8 FOLKESTONE

🏠 **Rocksalt Rooms** (page 310), **The View** (page 309) ⚔ **Little Switzerland Campsite**
(page 310)

Folkestone is blessed by its geography: the North Downs protect the
town's rear; an undulating strip of shingle and sand beaches is bisected
by a picturesque harbour at East Wear Bay; while to the west, a lush
park offers south-facing seaside and clifftop views across to France.
It's a location that has attracted human habitation for millennia –
there are Roman remains here as well as the possible bones of a 7th-
century AD saint. But it was the coming of the railway in 1843 that put
Folkestone on the modern tourist map; one of the town's most striking
landmarks is William Cubbitt's majestic railway viaduct bridging the
Foord Valley. In its early 20th-century heyday, Folkestone received the
royal seal of approval when Edward VII was a frequent visitor, trysting
with his mistress Alice Keppel at the Grand Hotel. Charles Dickens,

H G Wells and Agatha Christie were also fans. Cross-Channel ferries and hovercraft brought many European visitors and in 1961 the Paris-based dramatist Samuel Beckett hopped across to secretly marry his long-time lover Suzanne Dechevaux-Dumesnil here.

Forty years later, with the town's ferry port closed and the Channel Tunnel in full operation, Folkestone appeared to have hit rock bottom. Its revival can be traced to the launch of the first **Folkestone Triennial** in 2008. This visual arts festival, held every three years, has bequeathed the town with a free outdoor gallery of over 70 installations in quirky, site-specific locations – you can view some of my favourite pieces on the Folkestone Triennial Art Works walk (page 214). The Triennial is a key project of the arts charity Creative Folkestone (🖱 creativefolkestone.org.uk) and it has been the engine driving the town's regeneration. Also drawing metropolitan talent to Folkestone and providing more reasons to spend time here are the restored Harbour Arm and former Folkestone Harbour Station, centrepieces of the **Folkestone Harbour Seafront Development Co** (🖱 folkestoneseafront.com), an ambitious mixed-use residential and commercial development rising beside the sea.

THE BAYLE

Before hitting the beaches and harbour, head to The Bayle, one of the oldest parts of Folkestone. To reach, it head for the east end of Sandgate Road; the town's main commercial artery may be far from inspiring but along it are glimpses of Folkestone's illustrious past in buildings such as **Folca**, built in the 1930s as the department store Bobbies.

At the junction with Guildhall Street is the well-presented **Folkestone Museum** (☎ 01303 257946 🖱 folkestonemuseum.co.uk ⏲ 10.00–16.00 Tue–Sat), occupying part of the handsome town hall that dates from 1861. The eclectic collection, over two floors, ranges from prehistoric fossils to a Victorian painted silk parasol. A highlight is the 1915 canvas *Landing of the Belgian Refugees* by Fredo Franzoni, depicting Folkestonians opening their arms to World War I refugees. In 2019, some 300 locals gathered at the harbour to recreate the image as a large-scale photograph, also part of the museum's collection, as a demonstration of the town's continued welcome to those fleeing conflict and persecution.

About 100ft south of the museum is the atmospheric churchyard of **St Mary and St Eanswyth** (Church St 🖱 stmaryandsteanswythe.org ⏲ 11.00–13.00 Mon–Sat, 10.30–11.30 Sun). You are now in the Bayle, a charming village-like district of mainly 18th-century buildings. There was once a medieval wooden castle here and archaeological finds have pinpointed human habitation as far back as the Iron Age. This is also where, in the 7th century AD, Eanswyth, the daughter of Kent's King Eabald, established a nunnery, one of the first of its kind in England. Legend attributes several miracles to Eanswyth, hence her being proclaimed a saint on her deathbed at the likely age of 20, around 650. In 2020, a team of experts from Canterbury Christ Church University concluded that human remains discovered in the walls of the church in 1885 were those of a young female from the 7th century – a profile that makes it tantalisingly possible that these are the bones of Folkestone's patron saint herself. The church's interior is a gem. The underlying architecture is Gothic with 12th-century windows in the sanctuary, and the font and arcade of the chancel dating to the 13th century. The rest of this characterful stone structure hails to the 1850s when it was given a redesign by the Gothic Revivalist architect Richard Hussey. The church is the start (or finish) of a 36-mile walking route, the Royal Saxon Way (⌖ geopaethas.com/a-long-walk).

Immediately east of the churchyard is The Bayle, a road along which you'll find the **British Lion** (8–10 The Bayle), a cosy pub claiming to have served ale since 1460, and the landscaped pond where St Eanswyth is said to have performed one of her miracles. On walls around the district, information panels installed by the local residents' association (⌖ thebayle.org), provide insight into The Bayle's history.

CREATIVE QUARTER

A set of stone steps from the Bayle connects directly to the steeply raked and cobbled Old High Street – one side of a rough triangle bounded by Rendezvous Street and Tontine Street that constitutes the Creative Quarter. Ground zero for Folkestone's embrace of the creative industries over the last two decades, many of the zone's brightly painted buildings are rented out to artists, craftspeople and small businesses. Alongside artist studios such as the **Stables** (35–37 Tontine St), and small galleries such as **Fourth Wall Folkestone** (⌖ fourthwallfolkestone.co.uk), **The Brewery Tap UCA Project Space** and **Touchbase Gallery** are cafés, bars and independent shops. There's also plenty of public works of art, including Banksy's *Art Buff* along the Old High Street, on the wall next to the bar Folklore.

STRANGE CARGO

Working on community arts projects in Folkestone and around Kent since 1995 is **Strange Cargo** (The Factory, 43 Geraldine Rd, Cheriton CT19 4BD ⊘ strangecargo.org. uk). Their work tends to be overshadowed by that of Creative Folkestone but they have also made a significant impact with a broad variety of projects covering both permanent public artworks and one-off events. Look out around town, for their *Other People's Photos*, some 540 personal photos of family and friends erected on lampposts along the streets where they were taken. And as you leave or arrive at Folkestone Central train station take note of *Like the Back of My Hand*, bronze casts of the hands of 101 people, each born on a separate year from 1900 to 2000, embedded in a blue-tiled mosaic wall.

Strange Cargo's USP is working with schools and communities, and one of their most enduring and popular events is the street carnival Charivari, usually held in July, which includes a themed costumed parade along The Leas. They also publish a series of wonderfully unique guidebooks called *Everywhere Means Something to Someone*, shining a spotlight on what locals choose to be the most interesting destinations near to where they live, and stories connected with those locations. Titles cover Folkestone, the north Kent rail route from St Pancras to Margate and Romney Marsh. Check their website for details of their many other projects, including occasional exhibitions at their Cheriton base located a short walk from Folkestone West train station.

The quarter's development is largely down to the philanthropy of the Roger De Haan Charitable Trust and the commercial work of Creative Folkestone who, as well as organising the Triennial, also curate a packed schedule of events and happenings from their base at the **Quarterhouse** (page 218) on Tontine Street. Behind the Quarterhouse is **Payers Park**, an innovative social space designed by muf architecture in 2014 for that year's triennial. At the top of the park nearby, where it joins with the Old High Street, look for the **Pocket Gallery** (⊘ thepocketgallery.blogspot. com) atop a blue-painted post in the community garden; exhibitions in this tiny space change every three weeks.

On a much more monumental scale is **F51** (Tontine St ⊘ f51.co.uk ☉ 10.00–22.00 daily), the world's first multistorey skateboarding park with facilities also for BMX, climbing, bouldering and boxing, as well as a café. It's an extraordinary building, designed by Guy Hollaway Architects, wrapped in perforated aluminium panels and containing giant, suspended concrete skating bowls, as well as the largest lead climbing wall in southeast England.

FOLKESTONE HARBOUR

The harbour, bobbing with a small flotilla of fishing boats and pleasure craft, is split in two by the former railway viaduct bridge, now landscaped into a flower-planted walkway to the Harbour Arm. Henry VIII considered building a harbour at Folkestone in 1541 and for several centuries the town was also a limb of the Cinque Port of Dover. However, it was not until 1810 that the local fishermen swapped rudimentary jetties and small breakwaters for a proper stone harbour with an L-shaped quay and a solid western pier, designed by William Jessop and built by a team that included Thomas Telford. In 1842, the South Eastern Railway Company took over the harbour, subsequently constructing a branch line out to the pier, which had been completely rebuilt in concrete and granite by 1904.

This quarter-mile-long extension into the sea is the **Harbour Arm** (🖑 folkestoneharbourarm.co.uk) which in its contemporary iteration has become a place where Folkestonians come to eat, drink, fish, watch live music and films, attend events and promenade out to the lighthouse at its tip, also the venue for a champagne bar. The platforms of the old railway station have been restored as covered walkways, split by a dry garden, providing a sinuous connection from the harbour to the promenade and beach. The Harbour Arm has several triennial artworks, including Ian Hamilton Finlay's *Weather is a Third to Place and Time* painted across the lighthouse, and Antony Gormley's *Another Time XVIII*, a cast-iron statue lurking beneath the Arm which can only be viewed when the tide is low enough.

THE LEAS & LOWER LEAS COASTAL PARK

Snaking west along the shingle beach from the Harbour Arm, a pathway made of reclaimed wooden railway sleepers leads to the award-winning Lower Leas Coastal Park. Containing a green amphitheatre and a superb kids' play area including a wooden pirate ship, giant spider and zip lines, this lush park with meandering paths tumbles down the hillside to shingle beaches sheltered by granite groynes. The Lower Leas runs parallel with the upper Leas promenade, laid out in 1843 by Decimus Burton, the designer of Hyde Park and buildings at Kew Gardens. The two are linked by steps and footpaths, including the gently sloped Zig Zag Path that starts near Leas Bandstand, where concerts are held in the summer months. A listed structure, the path is a very believable replica of natural cliff faces and grottos, made from waste material coated in special a cement called Pulhamite, after its creator James Pulham.

At the far eastern end of The Leas is the **Step Short Commemorative Arch** (⟡ stepshort.co.uk), a 46ft-tall stainless steel span paying tribute to the troops who passed through Folkestone during World War I. 'Step Short' was the command given to the soldiers before they marched down Slope Road (renamed the Road of Remembrance) to the harbour. Near the Arch is the Leas Lift (⟡ leaslift.co.uk), a rare, water-powered funicular installed in 1885 to transport people between the seafront and the upper town promenade. Closed for repairs at the time of research, fundraising is ongoing to get the lift up and running again. Meanwhile, you can get a glimpse into the Victorian charm of the funicular by visiting the **Lift Café** (⟡ theliftcafe.co.uk ⊙ 09.00–16.00 Mon–Fri, 09.00–17.00 Sat & Sun) in the burgundy-painted station building at the seafront level.

Towards the western end of The Leas stand two stately late Victorian buildings: the red-brick and terracotta **Metropole**, opened 1897, and the **Grand Hotel**, which followed in 1903 and was a favourite seaside bolthole of Edward VII, who visited not only with the queen but also his mistress Alice Keppel. While part of the Grand still operates as a hotel, the Metropole has been private flats since the early 1960s. The original owners of the two properties engaged in a bitter rivalry, but it was the Grand, with its royal patronage and more sophisticated facilities, that eventually won out. Also at this end of The Leas, on the corner with Dixwell Road, is the handsome Arts and Crafts house that was retirement home of Lord Baden Powell, founder of the Boy Scouts movement.

EAST CLIFF

East of the Harbour Arm is the **Stade**, the remains of Folkestone's old fisherman's village. Nestled under the viaduct arches here is the **Folkestone Fishing & History Museum** (Ovenden Building, 2 Radnor St ⊙ 10.30–16.00 daily) where retired fishermen explain the various fishing-related exhibits and share stories of the industry that has been part of the town's work culture for centuries.

Beyond the East Head of the harbour is **Sunny Sands,** Folkestone's only truly sandy beach, overlooked by Cornelia Parker's *The Folkestone Mermaid*, a bronze sculpture lifecast from local resident Georgina Baker.

Steps up the hill at the beach's far eastern end lead to East Cliff, a grassy headland with superb views across the harbour. The squat round structure atop Copt Hill here is one of 16 remaining **Martello Towers** out of 27 built along the southern Kent coast in the early 19th century as defensive forts when fears of an invasion by Napoleon were at their height. Folkestone has three of these towers (four if you count the ruined one at the far western end of The Leas) with the first two, also in the East Cliff area, converted into private homes. A pitch-and-putt golf course surrounds the tower and there also public tennis courts. Nearby archaeological digs have uncovered remains going back as far as 10,000BC, with the most significant find being that of a large Roman villa built around AD100. The remains of the villa have been turfed over, but a selection of finds from the site are on exhibition in Folkestone Museum (page 209).

Folkestone Triennial artworks

✺ OS Explorer map 138; start: Folkestone Central train station, CT20 2QW ♀ TR220362; 3 miles; easy

The best way to experience Folkestone's incredible seaside location is to take a walk around its triennial artworks. The pieces I've highlighted on this walk are among my personal favourites. New works are added to the collection with each triennial. Some also might also be undergoing repairs – this is an outdoor art gallery, after all, subject to the elements. For a map detailing most of the current Folkestone artworks see ⊘ creativefolkestone.org.uk. The walk is mostly along flat surfaces with graduated climbs up and down between the upper and lower parts of The Leas.

1 At Folkestone Central Station, Bob and Roberta Smith's brightly coloured lettering *Folkestone is an Art School* is easy to spot across from the central platform, on the wall near the exit. Also, tucked beneath the bench outside the platform café is a tiny brass teddy bear by Tracey Emin, part of *Baby Things*, a series of highly realistic sculptures of childhood objects scattered around town.

2 Leaving the station, walk towards Cheriton Road and look up as you turn right and pass under the railway bridge. On four plinths are 3D-printed statues of local people, a quartet of lucky icons in the artwork *The Luckiest Place on Earth*. Embedded in the bridge wall on the right is the *Recycling Point for Luck and Wishes*, where you can leave a penny to make a wish or take a penny for good luck. ▶

THE WARREN

Accessed down a narrow hillside road veering off from Wear Bay Road, the Warren (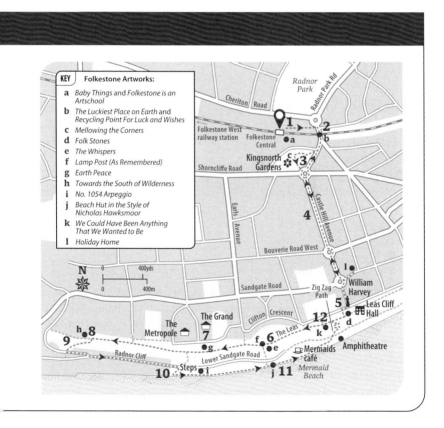 FolkestoneWarrenOfficial) is Folkestone's magnificently wild frontier. Just under two miles long and covering nearly 740 acres, this undulating undercliff, rich in plants and wildlife, tumbles down to a mostly sandy beach that is littered with fossils. It's a landscape formed by landslides, caused by powerful geological forces acting on the soft, erodible bedrock of Lower Greensand and Gault clay, which is overlaid with chalk. The most notable landslide of recent years was that of 1915, one so destructive it closed the railway line between Folkestone and Dover until 1919. Engineering works in order to mitigate further erosion were completed in the mid 1950s, creating a promenade, sea wall and broad concrete skirt along the Warren's coastline.

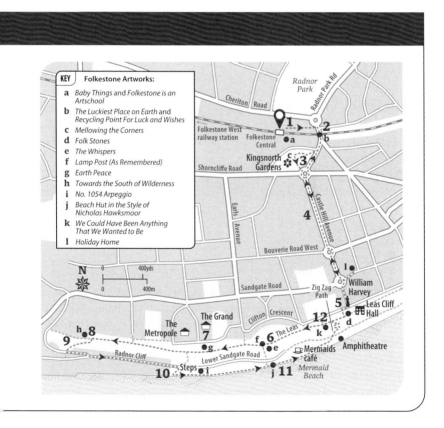

KEY | Folkestone Artworks:

a *Baby Things* and *Folkestone is an Artschool*
b *The Luckiest Place on Earth* and *Recycling Point For Luck and Wishes*
c *Mellowing the Corners*
d *Folk Stones*
e *The Whispers*
f *Lamp Post (As Remembered)*
g *Earth Peace*
h *Towards the South of Wilderness*
i *No. 1054 Arpeggio*
j *Beach Hut in the Style of Nicholas Hawksmoor*
k *We Could Have Been Anything That We Wanted to Be*
l *Holiday Home*

Folkestone Triennial artworks continued ...

3 Follow Cheriton Road round to the entrance to the lovely Kingsnorth Gardens, created in 1928 from a former clay pit. Amid the formal planting near the central pond is Mariko Hori's *Mellowing the Corners*. This sculpture of a topiary bush (one that was missing from the garden's design) is made out of Pulhamite. Into this 'time-capsule boulder' Hori has embedded objects donated from locals which will be revealed as the sculpture erodes over the years.

4 Exit the gardens on to Castle Hill Avenue following the footpath along the grass and tree-lined median strip. Cross the roundabouts at Bouverie Road West and Sandgate Road to emerge on The Leas, which is overlooked by a guano-splattered statue of Folkestone-born William Harvey, physician to Charles I and the discoverer of the circulation of blood around the body.

5 About 60yds southwest of Harvey's statue, embedded in the ground beside the raised beds of a sensory garden, is Mark Wallinger's *Folk Stones*: the 19,240 individually numbered pebbles each represent a soldier killed on 1 July 1916 during World War I, the first day of the Battle of the Somme. The Great War is also referenced in the next artwork, one you listen to; head west along The Leas past the ornate bandstand.

6 After about 800yds, you'll see a set of benches arranged around a balcony-like platform with a view across the Channel. Motion activated speakers beneath four of the benches trigger the audio of Christian Boltanski's *The Whispers*: actors reading letters to and from servicemen, written during World War I. Opposite the benches, hiding in plain sight, is *Lamp Post (As Remembered)*. David Shrigley invited another artist Camile Biddell to visit The Leas and spend 40 seconds memorising the lamp posts there. Biddell later created this 'replica' from her memories.

7 Continue ahead for another 200yds, towards the Grand Hotel. From the building's glass turret a flashing light beams out the message *Earth Peace* in morse code across the Channel. This plea for peace was created by Yoko Ono, and includes the same words carved in stone in a plaque in the grass. In 1966 Yoko Ono staged an event at the arts centre that used to be housed in the nearby Metropole building.

The rare plants and insects, such as the grayling butterfly and wild orchids, that are endemic here have led to the parkland being protected as a Site of Special Scientific Interest. You may also encounter Highland cattle, introduced to the Warren in 2015 as their grazing helps promote the area's biodiversity.

A multitude of footpaths make for glorious rambles through the Warren's mix of dense vegetation and more open grasslands, down to the generally quiet beach where locals and dog walkers love to come

8 Walk as far west as you can go along The Leas, to its highest point, and look for an entrance carved into a dense mass of vegetation. Enter to discover Cristina Iglesias' *Towards the Sound of Wilderness* – a platform surrounded by mirrors and bas-relief resin foliage that reveals the secreted remains of a Napoleonic-era Martello Tower.

9 From the ruined tower, backtrack along The Leas to find, on the right, a signed footpath down the slope in the direction of Sandgate. When the path emerges at Radnor Cliff, turn left and continue along it as it changes name to Lower Sandgate Road.

10 Lower Sandgate Road leads to the entrance of the Lower Leas Coastal Park; immediately on the right, take the steps down to seaside level, then turn left and follow the promenade past some 120 beach huts, each painted in a subtly graduated series of colours with contrasting arrow accents. This is Rana Begum's *No. 1054 Arpeggio*, an artwork providing a half a mile rainbow blaze of hues alongside the shingle beach.

11 As you approach the manmade cove called Mermaid Beach, note the odd beach hut out: it's Pablo Bronstein's *Beach Hut in the Style of Nicholas Hawksmoor*. The Mermaids Café (☉ 10.30–17.00 daily) overlooks the beach; the gently shelving shingle here makes it a popular spot for sea swimming. Just beyond the café a path leads up from the lower promenade towards the grassy-banked amphitheatre. Behind it is the Zig Zag Path which you should follow to return to the clifftop.

12 At the top of the Zig Zag Path is the curious ten-hour clock *We Could Have Been Anything That We Wanted to Be* by Ruth Ewan, a reference to 1783 when Republican France abandoned the 12-hour clock in favour of a decimal system of time (ten hour days, ten days a week, ten months a year). On clear days you'll get a superb view of France from the rooftop deck of the nearby Leas Cliff Hall. From here you can either continue along The Leas and down to the Harbour and Creative Quarter to find more artworks or return the way you came to the station. Look to the right at the junction of Sandgate Road and Castle Hill Avenue to see the red-painted *Holiday Home* by Richard Woods.

for exercise. If you're up for a challenge then search out the footpath that starts from beside the **Clifftop Café** (111A Old Dover Rd, Capel-le-Ferne CT18 7HT), taking you through a shaded hillside woodland with ground cover of prehistoric-looking hart's-tongue ferns to a footbridge over the railway line and on the beach.

Once beside the water, the ambitious walker can strike out for Samphire Hoe (page 207); with some rock clambering, this park on the edge of Dover can be reached in about an hour. Before tackling this, be sure to check on high tides and add on at least an extra hour to avoid becoming stranded along the way. Around the midpoint, just over a one-mile walk from the western end of the Warren, is an unofficial **nudist beach**, a swathe of fine shingle sheltering beneath the chalk-white Abbot's Cliff.

ENTERTAINMENT

Leas Cliff Hall The Leas ✆ 01303 228600 ⌂ atgtickets.com. This neoclassical concert hall is used for both musical and theatrical productions. It has a 1980s cantilevered terrace and outdoor seating on its roof, both with spectacular sea views.

Quarterhouse 49 Tontine St ✆ 01303 760750 ⌂ creativefolkestone.org.uk/folkestone-quarterhouse. With its fluted metal mesh cladding, illuminated at night from behind, this contemporary building has become the cultural hub of the town. Its flexible auditorium is used for a wide variety of events, from gigs and film screenings to presentations during Folkestone's annual book festival.

Silver Screen Folkestone Town Hall, 1–2 Guildhall St ✆ 01303 221230 ⌂ folkestonecinema.com. In 1886 one of the first moving picture screenings in Kent was held in Folkestone's Town Hall. Part of the building still serves as this wonderfully old-fashioned cinema with stalls and circle seating. There's also a more intimate second screen.

¶¶ FOOD & DRINK

Apart from the following there are some 20 other food and drink outlets spread along and around the Harbour Arm alone. The Old High Street also has plenty of good dining and drinking options.

Annapurna 15 Cheriton Place ✆ 07463 549194 ⌂ annapurnafolkestone.co.uk ⏲ 16.00–22.30 Thu–Mon & Tue. Since army regiment the Royal Gurkha Rifles moved to Folkestone in 2000 there has been a sizable Nepali community in Folkestone and surrounds. This translates to several excellent Nepali restaurants, of which Annupurna is one of the best. Come here for momo dumplings, steamed or fried, to be paired with tarkari curries and crispy pakoras.

Brewing Brothers Beachside Beachside, Harbour Arm ⌂ brewingbrothers.org ⏲ noon–20.00 Mon & Tue, noon–22.00 Wed & Thu, noon– 23.00 Fri & Sat, noon–22.00 Sun. Accessed directly from the old harbour station platform, this fine craft beer bar and wood-fired oven pizza restaurant taproom is housed in seven big shipping containers. It also has a massive outdoor deck which overlooks the beach and Putters! crazy golf course to the west – so it's brilliant for sunsets. From their pumps you can sample beers such as Grapefruit Gose and Reforestation Pale Ale.

Dr Legumes 10 Rendezvous Sq ✆ 07577 430235 ⌂ drlegumes.com ⊙ 10.00–16.00 Thu
& Sun, 10.00–16.00 & 18.00–20.00 Fri & Sat. 'Life Made Better' is the ethos behind this
superb plant-based-cuisine restaurant. Chefs Lee and Jim are passionate about blending
local and exotic flavours to create a unique dining experience. Tuck into delicious dishes
such as a pea meat ballotine or maple-smoked seitan sandwich made with sourdough
bread from local bakers and brewers **Dockers** (⌂ dockerbakery.com), who have a taproom
in nearby Sandgate.

Folkestone Wine Company 5 Church St ✆ 01303 249952 ⌂ folkestonewine.com
⊙ 12.30–14.30 & 18.00–21.00 Thu–Sat, 12.30–14.30 Sun. David Hart, an alumnus of Kent
gastropub The Sportsman (page 74), has set up this delightful, small-scale bistro in the
heart of town where the food is served on mismatched crockery. The short and sweet menu
– chalked up on a blackboard – features hyper-fresh Kentish produce and an expert selection
of wines.

Kipps' Alehouse 11–15 The Old High St ⌂ kippsalehouse.co.uk ⊙ 16.30–10.00 Wed &
Thu, noon–11.00 Fri & Sat, noon–10.00 Sun. Named after a character from a H G Wells novel,
Kipps is a convivial pub specialising in gravity poured, cask ales from local microbreweries.
They also serve very tasty and great value vegetarian food and occasionally host live music.

The Radnor Arms Christ Church Rd ✆ 01303 254435 ⌂ radnorarmsfolkestone.co.uk
⊙ noon–21.00 Wed & Thu, noon–21.30 Fri & Sat noon–18.00 Sun. This Victorian pub set
away a short walk away from The Leas has been given a wonderful renovation to make it an
appealing contemporary space with bags of arty character. There's a suntrap courtyard,
a great range of drinks including local beers and ciders and top-notch gastropub grub.

Rocksalt 4–5 Fishmarket ✆ 01303 212070 ⌂ rocksaltfolkestone.co.uk ⊙ noon–16.00
& 18.00–23.00 Fri & Sat, noon–17.00 Sun The showstopper of a seafood restaurant, a dark
timber and glass-walled jewel box, is cantilevered over the harbour, providing wonderful
views. Dig into premium dishes from a seasonally influence and locally sourced menu.
A great addition in 2021 to their stable of operations is **Little Rock** (⌂ littlerockfolkestone.
co.uk) which conjures up the atmosphere of a Greek seaside taverna next the shingle beach
beside the Harbour Arm.

Space Bar 7 Old High St ⌂ spaceseven.co.uk ⊙ 18.00–22.00 Thu, 13.00–midnight Fri
& Sat, 13.00–21.00 Sun. Far from your regular watering hole, this hip space is more like
somewhere you'd find in Hoxton or Peckham. They host DJ nights, pop-up supper clubs and
art exhibitions, and there's a nice courtyard garden at the back.

Steep St 18–24 Old High St ✆ 01303-247819 ⌂ steepstreet.co.uk ⊙ 08.00–18.00 Mon–
Fri, 09.00–18.00 Sat, 09.00–17.30 Sun. This Paris-inspired bibliophile café has been a huge
hit with locals ever since its Old High Street debut in 2015. No wonder, as genial owners Alice
and Stephen source, roast and grind their own coffee beans, bake their irresistible sponge
cakes on-site and always have vegan, vegetarian and gluten-free options.

🛍 SHOPPING

The Old High Street is a wonderful place to browse for works by local artists and designers such as **Folkestone Art Gallery** (⊘ folkestoneart.com), **Kitty McCall** (⊘ kittymccall.com), **Shane Record** (⊘ shanerecord.com) and Malcolm Allen, aka **Whelkboy** (⊘ whelkboy. co.uk). From late April through to just before Christmas, head to the Goods Yard of the Harbour Arm to find a variety of stalls at the Folkestone Marketplace selling local arts, crafts, vintage items, jewellery and more.

Country Fayre 3 Old High St 🇫 ⊙ 10.00–17.00 Mon–Fri, 10.00–17.30 Sat, 10.00–16.00 Sun. Stocks a broad selection of packaged food and drink hailing from Kent, including wines and beers. There's also some fresh food including, in season, locally grown strawberries.
R&R at Folkestone Rocks! 8 Old High St ⊘ richardson-and-richardson.co.uk ⊙ 10.30–17.00 Mon–Sat, 11.00–16.00 Sun. The laser-cut acrylic jewellery designed by mum and daughter team Wendy and Hannah Richardson is colourful and fun, inspired by everything from seagulls nicking chips to dinosaurs and space shuttles.
Rennies Seaside Modern 47 Old High St ⊘ rennart.co.uk ⊙ 10.00–17.00 Thu–Sun. One of the pioneers of the Old High St's revival, Rennies retro treasures range from limited-edition graphic posters to school badges, Hermes scarves and vintage toys. It's a treasure trove for retro and classic design lovers
Marrin's Bookshop 149 Sandgate Rd ⊘ 07982 731001 ⊘ marrinbook.co.uk ⊙ by appointment. A family-run business for over 50 years and stocked to the gills with an enviable collection of antiquarian books, maps and prints, including a library's worth of titles about Kent.

9 SANDGATE

The charming seaside village of Sandgate is easily accessed along the seaside promenade that continues from the western end of Folkestone's Lower Leas Coastal Park. One of Henry VIII's defensive castles was built here (completed in 1540) which Elizabeth I visited in 1573. What remains of the castle is a now a private residence that you can view over the low stone wall and wrought iron fence that separates it from the promenade.

In 1899, H G Wells commissioned the architect Charles Voysey to build Spade House on Radnor Cliff Crescent overlooking Sandgate (it's now a nursing home). A century later Saga, the holiday and finance company for the over 50s, constructed its headquarters on the grounds of the former estate of Enbrook. The sloping land around this contemporary glass and steel building and its nearby pavilion is a lovely, leafy public park with a community garden.

Continue west for about another mile from Sandgate alongside the broad shingle beach to reach Seabrook, the eastern end of the Napoleonic-era Royal Military Canal (page 224). Here, **Seapoint Canoe Centre** (Princes Pde, CT21 5ZY ✐ 07909 517812 ⌂ seapointcanoecentre.co.uk) provide canoeing, kayaking and SUP lessons.

"A walk of about a mile inland up into the hills overlooking Sandgate will bring you to Shorncliff Military Cemetery."

A walk of about a mile inland up into the hills overlooking Sandgate will bring you to **Shorncliff Military Cemetery** (off Sandy Ln ⌂ cwgc.org), devoted mainly to World War I burials, over 300 of which were of Canadian troops who were based at the adjacent Shorncliffe barracks. The beautifully designed burial ground covers a hollow in the hillside and provides panoramic coastal views.

You'll find plenty of places to eat and drink as well as shops selling antiques and vintage pieces, a Sandgate speciality. Try **Loaf** (61 Sandgate High St ☉ 08.00–17.00 Mon–Fri, 09.00–17.00 Sat & Sun) for coffee, cakes and snacks; **The Little Fish Shop** (6 Gough Rd ☉ 11.30–21.00 Mon–Sat, 11.30–20.00 Sun) for excellent take-away fish and chips; and the wine shop and tasting room **John Dory** (108 Sandgate High St ☉ 17.00–20.00 Mon–Wed, noon–22.00 Thu–Sat, noon–20.00 Sun).

10 ELHAM & SURROUNDS

With some 43 listed buildings, some many dating back to late medieval times, Elham is a peach of a village with quaint pubs and superb countryside hiking, eight miles inland from Folkestone. It's situated roughly at the midway point of the bucolic Elham Valley, which is traversed by a 22½ mile hiking route connecting Hythe with Canterbury. More walks, all taking a day or less, from the village are listed on the site of Elham Valley Walkers (⌂ elhamvalleywalkers.co.uk), with downloadable maps. This volunteer group organise the annual Elham Valley Walking Festival.

The focus of the village is The Square, also known as Market Square. On the southside is the ragstone and flint **St Mary's Church** (Vicarage Ln, CT4 6TT ⌂ elhamvalleygroupofchurches.co.uk), dating from the 12th century, while on the north is **The Kings Arms** (St Mary's Rd, CT4 6TJ ⌂ thekingsarmselham.com ☉ noon–23.00 Mon–Sat, noon–22.30 Sun), a tavern dating back to the 16th century. Around the corner on

High Street are a couple more historic inns, the **Abbots Fireside** (under renovation at the time of research), and the **Rose & Crown** (CT4 6TD ⏱ roseandcrownelham.co.uk ⊙ noon–23.00 Mon–Thu, noon–midnight Fri & Sat, noon–22.00 Sun) which also has accommodation.

Overlooking a small vineyard, about 2½ miles north of Elham is the lovely and worthy **Vineyard Garden Centre and Café** (Breach, Barham CT4 6LN ⏱ vineyardgardencentre.co.uk ⊙ café 09.00–16.00 Mon–Sat, garden centre 10.00–16.00, café 10.00–14.00 Sun), run by the Fifth Trust, which helps provide training and work opportunities for students with learning disabilities. On a sunny day, it's a delightful spot for a drink or light lunch surrounded by greenery.

Two miles further north, on the edge of the village of Barham, **Simpsons' Wine Estate** (CT4 6PB ⏱ simpsonswine.com ⊙ 09.00–17.00 Mon–Fri) offers a more sophisticated vinification experience. The estate planted their first vines in 2014 and now have 30 acres of Chardonnay, Pinot Meunier and Pinot Noir grapes across south-facing slopes that have their own sheltered microclimate. This holy trinity of grape varietals are used to make top-quality sparkling wine, which you can taste on wine-tasting experiences and vineyard tours at the estate.

HYTHE & SURROUNDS

🏠 **Hythe Imperial Hotel** (page 309), **The Old Post Office Boutique Guesthouse** (page 310), **Port Lympne Hotel** (page 309)

The characterful town of Hythe, a breezy 2½-mile seaside walk west from Sandgate, has a history stretching back to Roman times. The fort Portus Lemanis stood on the hills overlooking the old harbour, long since erased by the lowering sea levels and silting up that created Romney Marsh. The bare remains of that fort, known locally as Stutfall Castle, stand on private land around three miles northwest of the town centre. The new port of Hythe, created in the 11th century, was one of the original five Cinque Ports (see box, page 167) and a prosperous place. But the same steady forces of coastal erosion that did for the Roman harbour eventually robbed Hythe of its medieval port and the town fell into decline until the threat of invasion by the French in the early 19th century set it on a road to recovery. It was during this era

◄ **1** Sandgate. **2** Elham.

that the defensive chain of Martello Towers and the Royal Military Canal were built.

Inland on the higher ground above Hythe is Saltwood, a pleasant village with a medieval castle nearby. To the northwest are the extensive grounds of Port Lympne Reserve, a haven for endangered animals from around the world.

11 HYTHE

This placid and prosperous town's best features are a long shingle beach, an attractive High Street and many historic buildings. Most prominent is the Royal Military Canal, built between 1804 and 1809 during the Napoleonic Wars with France. After the Royal Navy in the Channel and the string of 74 cannon-mounted Martello Towers along the southern coast, this 28-mile canal, from Seabrook, just east of Hythe, to Cliff End near Hastings, was intended to be the third line of defence against enemy invasion. The channel was hand dug by civilian workmen called 'navigators' or 'navies' – there's a bronze **sculpture** of two of them on Prospect Road, near the Ladies Walk Footbridge. A kink was made at every 600yds along the canal's length to enable cannons to be fired down each stretch.

Today, the canal's tree-shaded banks in the centre of Hythe are part of a lovely walking and cycling route running for 4½ miles from Seabrook to West Hythe. There are interpretive panels along the way, including ones about the abundant wildlife, which includes dragonflies, marsh frogs and kingfishers. Next to the Ladies Walk Footbridge, **Electric Boat Hythe** (⌨ electricboathythe.co.uk ☉ Easter–Sep 10.00–17.00 daily) rents rowboats by the hour and runs the electric passenger boat service *La Tienne*, usually on the hour between noon and 16.00, for a short distance along the Hythe section of the canal. Every second year, on the third Wednesday in August, the **Hythe Venetian Fete** (⌨ hythevenetianfete. co.uk) along the canal includes a grand procession of floats and a fireworks display.

"Today, the canal's tree-shaded banks in the centre of Hythe are part of a lovely walking and cycling route running for 4½ miles."

Ladies Walk is a footpath, laid out in 1792, that leads south from the canal, past Hythe's cricket and sports grounds, to seaside Marine Parade. Walk west along the parade to reach **Fisherman's Beach** which, as it name suggests, is scattered with fishing boats and nets left out to dry.

ROMNEY, HYTHE & DYMCHURCH RAILWAY

The one-third-scale Romney, Hythe and Dymchurch Railway (Hythe station, A259, CT21 6LD ✐ 01797 326353 ⬦ rhdr.org. uk) covers 13½ miles between Hythe and Dungeness. Running at a leisurely 25 miles per hour, it is a hugely fun way of travelling across Romney Marsh and accessing some of the coastal beach resorts along the way. The miniature railway was the dream of Captain J E P Howey and fellow racing driver Count Louis Zborowski. It was Zborowski's racing car, named Chitty Bang Bang, that inspired Ian Fleming's children's book *Chitty Chitty Bang Bang*. When it first opened on 16 July 1927, the line connected Hythe and New Romney. A year later it was extended to Dungeness; the other stations along the line are Dymchurch, St Mary's Bay and Romney Sands. The fleet of 13 miniature steam and diesel locomotives pull up to nine coaches. Check the website for the exact timetable as the trains don't always run every day – the most frequent services are between April and September – and also to find out about special events. New Romney is the railway's headquarters where there is also a heritage centre with information on the line's history, a HO gauge model railway exhibition and a café.

Beyond are two Martello Towers, but be careful in straying any further along the beach here as it is a military firing range: there are signs indicating safe walking times, but if the red flags and/or lights are visible, regardless of the timings, do not walk through here.

A block inland from the Military Canal is Hythe's attractive and largely pedestrian High Street. Midway along is the **Town Hall**, completed in 1794. It has an undercroft where the town market was once held and an ornate clock protruding from its façade. Every Thursday at 10.30 from May until the end of September, members from **Hythe Civic Society** (⬦ hythecivicsociety.org) offer a guided walk around the town, starting from outside the old Town Hall. At the far west end of the High Street, the **Malthouse** (⬦ themalthousehythe.com ☉ 09.30–17.00 Fri & Sat) antiques and vintage market occupies the former bonded warehouse of Mackeson Brewery.

Walk up Malt House Hill and turn right on Bartholomew Street to find, at numbers 3–7, **Centuries**, a two-storey ragstone building dating at least to the 13th century. Hamo Hethe, who became Bishop of Rochester in 1319, is believed to have been born in this house. Follow the steps and footpath up the hill from here to reach the hillside graveyard surrounding venerable **St Leonard's Church** (⬦ slhk.org ☉ 08.30–17.30 daily). The building is a handsome mix of architecture, built on the site of the Saxon church of St Edmund but with a Norman nave and a 13th-century chancel. The 1870 pulpit is decorated with beautiful Venetian mosaics. However, it's what lies in St Leonard's crypt that makes this church remarkable.

An eerie **ossuary** (⊘ May–Sep 11.00-13.00 & 14.00–16.00 Mon–Sat, 14.00–16.00 Sun) contains the medieval and earlier bones of around 2,000 people, including 1,022 skulls neatly displayed on shelves in four arched bays, and a 25ft-long and 6ft-high stack of mainly thigh bones into which more skulls are embedded. The largest collection of its kind in Britain, the bones have fascinated people for centuries and have been displayed in their current form since at least the 19th century. They are believed to be the remains of people buried in St Leonard's and other neighbouring churchyards that were dug up and interred here from the 13th century onwards. More than simply a macabre pile of bones, the collection has provided researchers with clues as to the health and lifestyle of these ancient residents of Hythe. For example, the lack of cavities in the teeth are evidence of a sugar-free diet.

12 SALTWOOD

A mile north of Hythe, and within walking distance of Sandling train station, is the handsome village of Saltwood, named after 11th-century **Saltwood Castle** (CT21 4QU ⌂ saltwoodcastle.com). It was here that the four knights who murdered Thomas Becket in 1170 rested on the way to Canterbury and their lethal confrontation with the troublesome archbishop. It is now the property of Jane Clark, widow of the MP Alan Clark who had inherited the castle from his father, the art historian Sir Kenneth Clark. Jane Clark opens the castle grounds for special events a couple of times a year – check the website for details.

Similarly, the nearby **American Garden** (CT21 4EH ⬛) is only open on weekends in May when its spectacular glades of rhododendrons and azaleas are in full bloom. The gardens were created by Archdeacon Croft, rector of Saltwood from 1812 until his death in 1869. The deep, ancient peat soil here is favourable not only to the Asian flowering shrubs but also to the towering Californian redwoods that lend the garden its name. The adjacent **Garden House Orchards** has pick-your-

---

1 Romney, Hythe & Dymchurch Railway Station at New Romney. **2** Safari at Port Lympne Reserve. **3** St Leonard's Church ossuary. ▶

own fruit (including cherries, plums and apples) from June to October, and Christmas trees in December.

Open year-round is **Brockhill Country Park** (Sandling Rd, CT21 4HL ⌀ kent.gov.uk ☉ 09.00–dusk daily) which is centred around a small lake. There are two walking trails, the longest of which is 1.6 miles and provides views, from a lookout point, out to the Channel.

13 PORT LYMPNE RESERVE
Aldington Rd, Lympne CT21 4LR ✆ 01303 264647 ⌀ aspinallfoundation.org/port-lympne
☉ Apr–Oct 09.30–18.30 daily, Nov–Mar 09.30–17.30 daily

One of the most extraordinary experiences you can have in Kent is encountering hulking black rhinos, herds of antelope, a dazzle of zebras and a tower of giraffes freely roaming across an open grassy hillside with the English Channel in the background. This is the not untypical view across the African Experience section of Port Lympne Reserve, near the village of Lympne (pronounced 'lim'), five miles west of Hythe. Opened in 1976, the heart of this 600-acre estate is the majestic Edwardian mansion once owned by Sir Philip Sassoon, with gorgeous formal gardens designed by Sir Herbert Baker. The reserve is run by the Aspinall Foundation, the wildlife conservation charity which also manages Howletts Wild Animal Park near Canterbury (page 79) and which has had success in rewilding endangered species such as rhinos and gorillas.

Port Lympne is not a zoo, so there's no absolute guarantee that you will spot all of its 75 species of animal. That said, there are 900 animals on the reserve, so you won't come away disappointed. The basic day entry gains you access to a walking route around enclosures that include ones for lions, tigers, gorillas, tapirs, brown bears, black rhino and all kinds of apes and monkeys. To explore the full extent of the reserve and to see animals such as the cute pair of spectacled bears in the South American Experience section, you will need to pay an additional fee to go on a 45-minute safari in open-sided trucks that sit up to 48 people. Other longer-lasting ranger-led safari tours are also available, as are one-to-one encounters with specific animals such as their giraffes, lions and gorillas.

"Opened in 1976, the heart of this 600-acre estate is the majestic Edwardian mansion once owned by Sir Philip Sassoon, with gorgeous formal gardens."

There are several places to eat in the reserve; booking for Sunday lunch at the elegant Garden Room Restaurant is a good deal as it will also gain you access to the park. Otherwise, the best deal of all is to stay here overnight. There are levels of accommodation to suit most budgets, from self-catering glamping to the most luxuriously decorated of lodges that come with their own chefs to make you breakfast (page 309).

¶¶ FOOD & DRINK

The Bistro at Lympne Castle The Street, Lympne CT21 4LQ 🖉 01303 267644 🖱 thebistro-kent.co.uk 🕒 11.00–16.00 Thu & Fri, 09.00–16.00 Sat & Sun. Occupying part of a castle that has been around since the 12th century, this convivial bistro is a bit of a find, offering a good range of brunch and lunch dishes, from Welsh rarebit and poached egg to fancier mains like pan-fried bacon steak on sweet potato and chorizo mash. You can eat either inside or out and nearby there are panoramic views across Romney Marsh from the graveyard of St Stephen Lympne. Lympne Castle (🖱 lympnecastle.com) is an event's venue, but occasionally they are also open for afternoon teas, Sunday lunch and pop-up dinners.

Café on the Beach Marine Pde, Hythe 🖱 cafeonthebeach.co.uk 🕒 09.00–16.00 Tue–Sun. Quality coffee from Ozone, leaf teas from Hythe-based Debonair, tasty sandwiches and scrumptious cakes (including a luscious ginger cake) are served from this pint-sized café at the eastern end of Marine Parade.

Hide and Fox The Green, Saltwood 🖉 01303 260915 🖱 hideandfox.co.uk 🕒 noon–13.30 Wed–Sat, 18.15–20.00 Tue–Sat. Chef Alistair Barsby and front-of-house Alice Bussi are the experienced duo running this elegant little gourmet operation. Choose between five- or eight-course tasting menus (vegetarian options are available) made with top-quality seasonal, local produce.

The Lazy Food Company on Hythe Beach Fisherman's Landing Beach, Range Rd, Hythe 🖉 01303 266410 🖱 griggsofhytheuk.com 🕒 08.00–16.30 Mon–Sat, 09.00–15.30 Sun. Treat yourself to lobster and chips, grilled tuna or panko-coated calamari beside the beach at this wholesale fishmongers, greengrocers and café.

Noiy's Noodles at The Hope 82 Stade St, Hythe 🖉 01303 267370 🖱 noiys-noodles. business.site 🕒 noon–21.00 Tue–Sat. Authentically spicy Thai food is served at this take-away operation adjacent to the Hope Pub, near Hythe's seafront. You can eat your pad thai or red curry in the pub's beer garden, if you like.

Unit 1 Riverside Industrial Estate, West Hythe 🖉 01303 265000 🖱 unit1riverside.co.uk 🕒 10.00–21.00 Thu–Sat, 10.00–19.00 Sun–Wed. The reward for a 2½ mile-walk along the Royal Military Canal is the chance to pop into this rustic alehouse and kitchen. They serve locally brewed beers and pressed ciders, have homemade pizzas on Thursdays and a variety of street foods served by pop-up collaborators from Friday to Sunday.

ROMNEY MARSH

Pancake flat, low-laying and grazed by an indigenous breed of sheep, Romney Marsh was once mostly submerged beneath the English Channel. Land reclamation has been going on since at least the 13th century when the Rhee Wall, a 7½-mile-long raised watercourse between Appledore and New Romney, was built to help stop silt from the River Rother choking New Romney's harbour. A catastrophic storm in 1287 blocked up the harbour, leaving the town a mile from the sea and permanently reshaping the coastline. Subsequent embankments, ditches and dykes drained the adjacent Walland and Denge marshes, creating a 100 square mile area collectively named Romney Marsh. It's a singular location with a proud history and locals who jokingly refer to it as the 'fifth continent', after a famous quote by the 19th-century humourist Thomas Ingoldsby (the pen name of Revd Richard Harris Barham, rector at St Dunstan in Snargate): 'The World, according to the best geographers, is divided into Europe, Asia, Africa, America, and Romney Marsh'. The main towns are the seaside resort of Dymchurch, New Romney and Dungeness, the last an otherworldly seaside village buffeted by the elements on Europe's largest expanse of shingle beach, which is also the location for a foreboding nuclear power station.

14 DYMCHURCH

🏠 **CABU by the Sea** (page 310), ⛺ **Romney Marsh Shepherds Huts** (page 310)

For generations a seaside resort favoured by working-class Londoners, Dymchurch's pride and joy is its broad, sandy, three-mile-long **beach**, one of the best and cleanest in Kent. The sea is kept back from the town by a thick concrete defence wall which doubles as a promenade. Just off High Street and visible from the promenade **Martello Tower No. 24** (☉ Easter–Oct 14.00–16.00 Sat & Sun; English Heritage) is the only one of the Napoleonic military towers which is regularly open to the public. Enthusiasts have helped keep it much as it was when first built in 1806, with original design features such as the 24-pounder cannon atop the tower.

Compared to other Kent seaside towns there's nothing fashionable or arty about Dymchurch. Instead, it distinguishes itself by playing up to Romney Marshes' notoriety as a smuggling hotspot during the 17th and 18th centuries. Russell Thorndike's *Dr Syn* series of adventure yarns is set here. Reverend by day, a smuggler disguised as a scarecrow by night,

Dr Christopher Syn featured in seven books and several films. A stuffed model of this Robin Hood-style character sits on a chair in the cosy **Mortar & Pestle Vegan Tearoom** (37 High St ✎ 07858 279965 🅵 37 High St Dymchurch ☉ Apr–Nov 11.30–17.00 Thu–Sun) which has a totally vegan menu and a pleasant courtyard. Every two years, over the August bank holiday weekend, Dymchurch stages its **Day of Syn** festival with costumed parades, smuggler battles and mock trials, fireworks, sandcastle building contests and more.

Less than a mile inland from the seafront is **Alpaca Annie** (Haguelands Village, Burmarsh ✎ 01303 870527 ⬡ alpacaannie.com ☉ shop 09.00–17.00 Tue–Sat, 09.00–16.00 Sun; alpaca experiences 10.00 & 13.00 Tue–Sun), an alpaca wool farm, shop and café. The main draw is the chance to take these cute furry creatures for a meander across the marsh. Herdswoman Lara explains the difference between the soft, curly haired Huacaya and the shaggier coated Suri breeds, and then pairs participants up with one of the farm's over 100 alpacas for the roughly one-hour walk around a farm trail.

15 NEW ROMNEY & SURROUNDS

About 4½ miles southwest of Dymchurch is Romney Marsh's largest town, New Romney, one of the original set of Cinque Ports. Eight hundred years ago, ships once tied up in New Romney's harbour which lay beside the 12th-century church of **St Nicholas** (Church Ln ⬡ romneychurches.org). The sea now laps a mile away at Littlestone and this handsome Norman church is the sole survivor of New Romney's five medieval churches. Particularly striking is its five-tiered western tower with pinnacles at each corner; the rounded arch doorway is accessed by steps below ground level, an indication of how the ground level around New Romney rose after the Great Storm of 1287. Take in the church's antique architectural lines from the Old School Garden opposite. Dominated by a central copper beech, the garden's pathways have been zhuzhed up with a series of colourful mosaic roundels each with Romney Marsh-related themes – look out for the one of a spectral Dr Syn riding the RHDR train.

You can learn more about the evolution of the marshes at the **Romney Warren Country Park** (Rolfe Ln ✎ 01797 367934 ⬡ rmcp.co.uk ☉ Apr–Sept 11.00–15.00 daily; Oct–Mar 11.00–15.00 Wed–Sun), one mile east of the town centre. The visitor centre here has a wealth of background

ROMNEY MARSH'S MEDIEVAL CHURCHES

Characterful churches, dating from at least the 13th century, are scattered across Romney Marsh; 13 are in Kent and one (St Mary's in East Guldeford) is just across the border in Sussex. The **Romney Marsh Historic Churches Trust** (⊘ romneymarshchurches.org.uk) helps with the preservation of the churches and can arrange guided tours of them. Events such as **Art in Romney Marsh** (⊘ artinromneymarsh.org), a festival usually held in September and early October, make new use of these ancient sacred buildings as galleries for contemporary creative works. Check their website for details about the four downloadable Salt Audio Trails, around St Mary in the Marsh, Old Romney, Ivy Church and Dungeness.

In ten of the churches also look for the **Marsh Mosaics** created during 2021 as one of the several projects of the Fifth Continent Landscape Partnership Scheme (⊘ fifthcontinent.org.uk) across Romney Marsh. The mosaics, their design suggested by and created with the help of over 300 locals, include the medieval churches, heritage and wildlife of the marsh.

The poster child for the churches is **St Thomas Becket** (TN29 9RZ) in Fairfield – a hamlet that has long since disappeared, leaving the solitary church alone, surrounded by fields with grazing sheep and drainage ditches. This 13th-century timber and lath building, encased with brick walls and clay roof tiles in the 18th century, has a remarkable interior of white-painted box pews, a triple-decker pulpit and exposed roof beams. The church has often featured as a location for films and TV, including two adaptations of *Great Expectations*. Unlike most of the other Romney

information on Romney Marsh and its natural history. There are three short walking trails around the adjacent wild flower meadows and fields. Depending on the time of year, you may see sheep grazing or dragonflies buzzing over ponds that are also a habitat for frogs and great crested newts. Some services on the Romney, Hythe and Dymchurch Railway (see box, page 225) stop at the Romney Warren Halt next to the park.

It's easy to spot the 14 public artwork murals that are mainly along and just off New Romney's High Street, which feature local landmarks, personalities and images; there's also one at the main Romney, Hythe and Dymchurch Railway station off Littlestone Road and others on the walls of the local Sainsbury's. Around Sainsbury's you'll also find several quirky sculptures – I'm particularly fond of Robert Koenig's wooden column commemorating over a millennium of sheep farming across the Marsh. All these artworks are the result of projects undertaken by Briony Kapoor's private arts charity the **MOS Foundation** (⊘ imosfoundation.org). Since 2017, the foundation has taken care of the ruins of **Hope All** churches, it is kept locked but the key can usually be obtained from Becket Barn Farm, on the opposite side of the road a few hundred yards to the west of the pathway to the church.

On the way to or from Fairfield there are a couple of other churches worth making time to see. My personal favourite, sitting to the side of the A259 at Old Romney, is **St Clement's** (TN29 0HP). Derek Jarman is buried in the graveyard here; his dark grey slate headstone, topped with pebbles left by visitors, is easy to spot amid the older mottled gravestones. Inside the 12th-century church, the gallery and box pews were painted pale pink during filming here of the 1963 Walt Disney live action film *Dr Syn: The Scarecrow of Romney Marsh*, based on Russell Thorndike's novels.

In the village of Brooklands, 13th-century **St Augustine's** (TN29 9QR) is distinguished by a its detached octagonal wooden bell tower. Look inside its tall box pews (added by wealthy parishioners so that they would have a less draughty place to sit in church) to find old graffiti carved into the wood. High on the wall of the southeast chapel is a fragment of a medieval wall painting of the murder of Archbishop Thomas Becket, discovered beneath the plaster in 1964.

Romney Marsh Historic Churches Trust and Fifth Continent have collaborated on creating free, self-guided audio tours that highlight the history and folklore of all the medieval churches. Look for QR code signs within each of the churches, which prompt a download of the Izi Travel app (⊘ izi.travel/en/c61d-romney-marsh-medieval-churches-highlights-tour-all-churches/en) where you'll find the tours.

Saints (St Mary in the Marsh, TN29 0DE), a 1½-mile walk northwest of the town, creating a sculpture park and planting an orchard of fruit trees and willow around the 12th-century church.

Named after the pair of navigational markers that guided ships down a safe channel into New Romney's harbour, **Littlestone** and **Greatstone** are adjacent seaside communities connected by a glorious sandy beach. Undulating dunes, a habitat for rare plant species, separate the beach from the coastal road. As well as sunbathing and swimming, it's a popular spot for wind-based sports, including land yachting, windsurfing, kitesurfing and kiteboarding. Visible at low tide, the oblong-shaped platform off Littlestone Beach is one of the Phoenix breakwaters intended to create a floating harbour during World War II. These reinforced concrete caissons were constructed in advance of the D-Day landings, with several moored in the waters around New Romney and Dungeness. This one, now a listed monument, got stuck in the sand before it was due to be tugged over to Normandy and has been here ever since.

SS

KENTISH DWELLER/A

SIMON RICHMOND

♛ FOOD & DRINK

Deblyns 30 High St, New Romney ✆ 01797 369020 🖱 deblyns.co.uk ⏱ 09.30–16.00 Tue–Fri, 09.00–16.00 Sat. A 700-year-old building is the atmospheric setting for this charming tea shop. They serve their own blend of quality leaf tea in china pots, plus freshly baked treats like sweet and savoury scones and hot buttered crumpets.

16 APPLEDORE

🏠 **The Woolpack Inn** (page 309)

Eight and a half miles northwest of New Romney, the quintessential Kentish village of Appledore borders a stretch of the Royal Military Canal. Lovers of retro knick-knacks will have fun hunting around the local antique emporiums, including **Station Antiques** (The Old Goods Shed, Station Rd, TN26 2DF 🖱 stationantiques.co.uk ⏱ 10.00–17.00 daily), next to the train station, and the more central **Old Forge Antiques Centre** (16 The Street, TN26 2BX ⏱ 10.00–17.00 Mon, Tue & Thu–Sat, 11.00–16.00 Sun).

Appledore is also within walking distance of the classy wine estate **Gusbourne** (Kenardington Rd, TN26 2BE ✆ 01233 515238 🖱 gusbourne.com ⏱ 10.00–17.00 daily) which has gathered critical acclaim for its sparkling and still wines made from Chardonnay, Pinot Noir and Pinot Meunier varietals. The standard wine-tasting tours last two hours, or you could indulge in extended tours which tag on either seasonal sharing platters or a three-course lunch.

♛ FOOD & DRINK

Miss Mollett's High Class Tea Room 26 The Street, Appledore ✆ 01233 758555 🖱 missmollettstearoom.co.uk ⏱ 10.00–17.00 Wed–Sun. A suitably chintzy atmosphere in which to enjoy Kentish cream teas and chunky sandwiches with sides of homemade coleslaw and potato salad.

Red Lion Snargate TN29 9UQ ✆ 01797 344648 ⏱ noon–15.00 & 18.00–21.00 Tue–Sun. Time appears to have stood still for about a century at this pub three miles southeast of Appledore. With an old marble-topped bar and low-ceilinged interior crammed with retro decorations, it's a rare gem of a country boozer. Nurse a pint and imagine gatherings of 18th-century smugglers who were said to have stored their contraband in the medieval church of St Dunstan's across the road.

◀ **1** Romney Marsh. **2** Inside Martello Tower No 24, Dymchurch. **3** Prospect Cottage, Dungeness was home to film director Derek Jarman.

17 DUNGENESS

🏠 **Shingle House** (page 310), **Wi Wurri** (page 310)

Treeless, windswept and dotted with weathered wooden homes and shingle-stranded fishing boats, the private estate of Dungeness is mistakenly called a desert. There's far too much rain and general biodiversity in this national nature reserve for it to be a true desert but it is nevertheless an extraordinary and unique location. Sitting atop the largest expanse of shingle in Europe are a pair of lighthouses, a monumental nuclear power station, the cottage and garden of the late film-maker, artist and writer Derek Jarman, and an astonishing array of plants, invertebrates, and birdlife. Featuring as cover art on Pink Floyd's greatest hits album *A Collection of Great Dance Songs*, and a location in 1970s episodes of Dr Who, Dungeness is spellbinding in its oddness.

"There's too much rain and general biodiversity in here for it to be a true desert but it is an extraordinary and unique location."

It's a compelling place to linger, particularly for its sunsets which blaze across the panoramic sky in bands of burnt orange and purple.

The most fun way of arriving here is on the dinky Romney, Hythe and Dymchurch Railway (see box, page 225) which terminates next to the black-painted **Old Lighthouse** (Dungeness Rd, TN29 9NB ✆ 01797 321300 ⌂ dungenesslighthouse.com ⊙ Apr, May, Sep & Oct 10.00–16.00 Sat & Sun, Jun 10.00–16.00 Tue–Thu, Sat & Sun, Jul & Aug 10.00–16.00 Thu–Sun). Since 1615 eight lighthouses have been erected at Dungeness – five high and three low; this 150ft brick tower, completed in 1904 and in use until 1960, was the fourth of the high ones. From the balcony surrounding the light at the top, reached by 165 concrete steps, you'll get a good view of its successor, jutting up out of the shingle in black and white painted bands.

An access track off Dungeness Road leads to the **RSPB Dungeness Reserve** (Reedbed Rd, TN29 9PN ⌂ rspb.org.uk ⊙ visitor centre 10.00–16.00 daily) which covers nearly four square miles of the **Dungeness National Nature Reserve** (⌂ dungeness-nnr.co.uk). The two-mile long circular main trail starting at the visitor centre goes past six hides from which you may spot, among many other species, cormorants, marsh harriers and, in spring, bitterns. The RSPB also look after the former sand and gravel pits at Lade, just north of Dungeness, location of the three Denge Sound Mirrors (see box, page 207), monumental concrete listening devices from the 1930s. This area can be accessed on foot from Taylor Road, Leonard Road or Seaview Road in Greatstone. Avid birdwatchers may also want to reach out to **Dungeness Bird Observatory** (✆ 01797 321309 ⌖ www.dungenessbirdobs.org.uk) which keeps a detailed online blog on the region's wildlife (not just the birdlife) and offers dormitory-style accommodation.

Providing a brooding backdrop to the landscape is the monolithic nuclear power station, made up of two no-longer-functioning reactors which are in the decades-long process of being decommissioned. Scattered across the shingle are around a hundred homes, many now holiday lets. Some of the buildings are converted railway carriages from the 1920s and include the **Dungeness Gallery** (TN29 9ND ✆ 01797 320497 ⌖ dungenessgallery.co.uk) which occupies three vintage Edwardian carriages and showcases the works of photographer Chris Shore and watercolour artist Helen Taylor. The artist studios of **Helen Gillilan** (✆ 07970 148476 ⌖ ocean-view-studio.com ○ 10.00–17.00 Mon–Fri) is also open for visits, as is that of Paddy Hamilton, a talented painter and printmaker, whose **Dungeness Open Studios** (TN29 9ND ✆ 07815 047307 ⌖ paintings-for-sale.net ○ 10.30–dusk daily) comprises four quirky, small spaces standing in an attractive shingle garden.

The village's most famous creative resident was film director Derek Jarman, who owned **Prospect Cottage** (Dungeness Rd, TN29 9NE), around which he created a remarkable dry garden, as much an art installation as it is a collection of plants. The mingling of hardy grasses, red California poppies, yellow sedum and glaucus sea kale, with enigmatic sculptures crafted from rustic hunks of driftwood, rusting metal and large mottled pebbles is wonderful. The wooden cottage, weatherproofed with black tar, has a sunshine-yellow painted door and window frames. One wall is covered with raised relief lines, in the style of Jarman's handwriting, from the poem *The Sun Rising* by John Donne. It's a testament to Jarman's unique vision at Prospect Cottage, that in 2020, 26 years after his death, £3.6 million was raised to buy the cottage for the nation and keep it preserved much as he had left it. Visitors are free to explore the borderless garden which merges with the shingle. Creative Folkestone have been entrusted to take care of the property, and via ⌖ creativefolkestone.org.uk/prospect-cottage, you can book guided tours of the cottage.

FOOD & DRINK

Open at Easter and the May bank holidays as well as weekends in July and August, the **Ales by the Rails** (🅵) trackside bar next to the Romney, Hythe and Dymchurch Railway (see box, page 225) serves beers from the Romney Marsh Brewery.

Britannia Inn Dungeness Rd, TN29 9ND ✆ 01797 321959 ⌂ britanniadungeness.co.uk
🕙 11.00–22.00 daily. Created from two former air-raid shelters in the 1950s, this pub is part of the local Shepherd Neame chain. There's plenty of outdoor seating with views of both lighthouses, and an open fire to warm up beside inside after bracing winter walks.
Dungeness Snack Shack Dungeness Rd, TN29 9NE ⌂ dungenesssnackshack.net
🕙 11.00–15.30 Wed–Sun. My favourite place to eat in Dungeness, but come prepared to dine outdoors. A kitchen in a converted shipping container serves up deliciously cooked, sustainably caught fish and seafood meals. The family who run it use their own boat to catch the fish. Tuck into lobster and crab rolls, scrumptious homemade fishcakes and, in winter, smoked cod chowder. There is bench seating in front of the shack.
Pilot Inn Battery Rd, Lydd-on-Sea, TN29 9NJ ✆ 01797 320314 ⌂ thepilotdungeness.
co.uk 🕙 11.00–22.00 Mon–Sat, 11.00–21.00 Sun. On the northeastern seaside edge of Dungeness, this pub, famous for its fish and chips, is conveniently next to where the bus from Folkestone terminates. If you're looking for a sit-down meal indoors this is your best bet. Legend has it that the original inn incorporates the timbers of a Spanish ship the *Alfresia*, lured on the rocks by smugglers in the 17th century so that its cargo of alcohol could be looted.

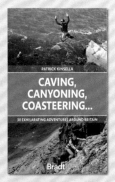

5
KENT WEALD & DOWNS

Kent's gently rolling, verdant countryside is the playground for an abundance of superb Slow Travel experiences. Much of the pleasure of travel here is that, for walkers, there are no great elevations or rocky traverses to conquer: 823ft Betsom's Hill near Westerham in west Kent is county's highest point. Still, the panoramic views from the crests of the North Downs are frequently splendid. The writer H E Bates, whose *The Darling Buds of May* is set in Kent, summed it up best when he described the Kent Downs as 'an unfailing compass-point with a magnetism that draws you towards them'.

The Downs are one of the county's two AONBs, which equal National Parks in terms of their legal protection and significance. Covering 339 square miles and stretching from the border with Sussex near Westerham to Dover, the Kent Downs (⊘ kentdowns.org.uk) include ancient woodlands, heathlands, farms and fruit and nut orchards. Chalk hills created millions of years ago are topped by grasslands blooming with wild flowers and rare orchids. Similarly beautiful is the undulating landscape of the High Weald (⊘ highweald.org), a

"The Kent Downs include ancient woodlands, heathlands, farms and orchards."

chunk of which is in Kent. With a foundation of sandstone and clay, this is countryside that has hardly changed in centuries – the region's scattered villages, forests, organically shaped fields and winding roads is a landscape medieval residents of Kent would still recognise.

The main towns of west Kent – Sevenoaks, Royal Tunbridge Wells and Tonbridge – are locations from which to access some of the county's most historic castles and stately homes, as well as gardens and natural landscapes. These include Knole, a former archbishop's palace that has been the estate of the Sackville family since 1605; Hever Castle, childhood home of Anne Boleyn; Chartwell, the family home of Winston

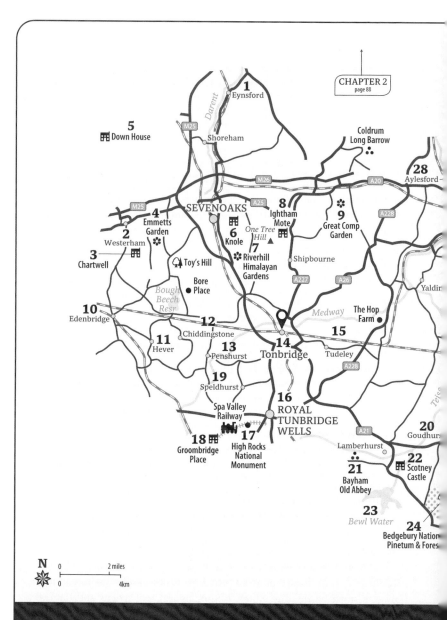

1 Eynsford

Darent

5
⊞ Down House

Coldrum
Long Barrow

Shoreham

M26

A20

28
Aylesford

M25

4 SEVENOAKS
Emmetts
Garden

A25

8
Ightham
Mote

9
Great Comp
Garden

A228

2
Westerham

6 *One Tree*
⊞ Knole *Hill*

7
❀ Riverhill
Himalayan
Gardens

Shipbourne

3
Chartwell

🌳 Toy's Hill

Bore
● Place

*Bough
Beech
Resr*

A227

A26

Yaldir

Medway

The Hop
Farm ●

10
Edenbridge

12

Chiddingstone

15

11
Hever

13
Penshurst

14
Tonbridge

Tudeley

A228

19
Speldhurst

16
ROYAL
TUNBRIDGE
WELLS

Spa Valley
Railway

20
Goudhur

18 ⊞
Groombridge
Place

17
High Rocks
National
Monument

Lamberhurst

22
⊞ Scotney
Castle

21
Bayham
Old Abbey

23
Bewl Water

24
Bedgebury Nation
Pinetum & Fores

N
0   2 miles
0   4km

KENT WEALD & DOWNS

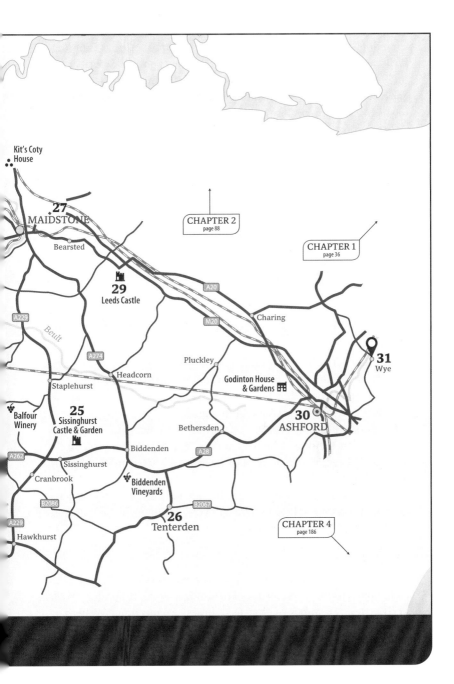

Kit's Coty House

27 MAIDSTONE

Bearsted

29 Leeds Castle

A229

Beult

A274

A20

M20

Charing

Pluckley

Headcorn

Staplehurst

Balfour Winery

25 Sissinghurst Castle & Garden

Bethersden

Godinton House & Gardens

30 ASHFORD

31 Wye

A262

Sissinghurst

Biddenden

A28

Cranbrook

Biddenden Vineyards

B2086

A229

Hawkhurst

26 Tenterden

B2067

CHAPTER 2
page 88

CHAPTER 1
page 36

CHAPTER 4
page 186

Churchill; the handsome Georgian architecture of Royal Tunbridge Wells, and the adjacent natural wonders of the High Rocks. East across the Weald are the spectacular gardens of Sissinghurst, created by Vita Sackville-West and her husband Harold Nicolson, and charming market towns like Tenterden, close to some of Kent's award-winning vineyards.

Picturesque villages abound and include Eynsford in the Darent Valley near the remains of a Roman villa and lavender farms; Aylesford near Maidstone with a Carmelite friary founded in the 13th century; and Wye, a historic settlement along the Kent Downs overlooked by a giant chalk crown. The region's largest towns are Maidstone and Ashford – travel a little outside of each to major attractions such as Leeds Castle, and under-the-radar gems like Godinton House.

GETTING THERE & AROUND

Winding country roads that climb up into the hills and down into valleys encourage slow driving or cycling around the Weald and Kent Downs.

TRAINS

There are direct trains from London Blackfriars to Eynsford (46 minutes), Shoreham (57 minutes) and Sevenoaks (69 minutes). From London Bridge, you can travel directly to Sevenoaks (24 minutes), Tonbridge (35 minutes) and Tunbridge Wells (44 minutes).

Maidstone has two stations: Maidstone East with direct services from London Victoria (1 hour 7 minutes) and Maidstone West on the Medway Valley Line, along which are stations for Aylesford to the north and Yalding to the south.

Ashford is on the high-speed line with services into London St Pancras (38 minutes); transfer here for trains to Wye. For timetables for all these services see ⊘ southeasternrailway.co.uk.

BUSES

Go Coach (⊘ go-coach.co.uk) provides bus services in west Kent, including around Sevenoaks, Edenbridge and Tunbridge Wells. **Arriva** (⊘ arrivabus.co.uk) has buses connecting Westerham, Sevenoaks, Tunbridge Wells, Tonbridge and Maidstone. **Stagecoach** (⊘ stagecoachbus.com) runs buses between Ashford and Tenterden, Ashford and Wye, and many other locations in east Kent.

TOURIST INFORMATION

Ashford & Tenterden 🖉 01233 330383 🖉 visitashfordandtenterden.co.uk.
Edenbridge Doggetts Barn, 72a High St 🖉 01732 865368 🖉 visitedenbridge.com.
Maidstone Maidstone Museum, St Faith's St 🖉 01622 602169 🖉 visitmaidstone.com
🕑 Jul–Aug 10.00–16.00 Mon–Sat; Sep–Jun 10.00–16.00 Wed–Sat.
Sevenoaks 🖉 01732 227000 🖉 visitsevenoaks.co.uk.
Tonbridge Tonbridge Castle, Castle St 🖉 01732 770929 🕑 08.00–17.00 Mon–Sat,
10.00–16.00 Sun.
Tunbridge Wells Corn Exchange, Pantiles 🖉 01892 515675 🖉 visittunbridgewells.com
🕑 10.00–15.00 Wed–Sat.

CYCLING

The hills and winding roads of the Kent Down and High Weald make cycling across the region something of a physical challenge. Regional Cycle Route 12 offers an excellent, almost entirely traffic-free ride from the heart of Tonbridge alongside the River Medway to Penshurst Place, some five miles to the west. More of a marathon is the 42-mile National Cycling Route 18 between Ashford and Tunbridge Wells, following the Weald's small country lanes.

There are also 18 miles of trails at Bedgebury Pinetum, while at Bewl Water the cycle paths around the lake are fairly flat, making it a great place for a family cycle ride. To find out more about cycling in this part of the county, contact the **West Kent CTC** (🖉 westkentctc.org.uk). The club has 15 groups providing rides of varying lengths, on different days of the week and to a wide range of destinations.

 BIKE HIRE

CountryBike 🖉 07858 595354 🖉 countrybike.co.uk. See ad, page 303. Delivers bikes around Tonbridge, or they can be hired via the Linka Go app at Penshurst Place and Groombrdige.
Cycle Ops Bank St, Tonbridge 🖉 01732 500534 🖉 cycle-ops.co.uk 🕑 09.00–17.30 Tue–Sat.
Homewood Cycles 119 Ellingham Industrial Centre, Ellingham Wy, Ashford 🖉 01233 621675, 🖉 homewoodcycles.co.uk.
Quench Cycles Bedgebury Visitor Centre, Bedgebury Rd, Goudhurst 🖉 01580 879694 🖉 quenchuk.co.uk 🕑 08.00–17.00 daily.
UK Electric Bike Centre Bloomsburys Biddenden, Sissinghurst Rd, Biddenden 🖉 07904 287485 🖉 ukelectricbike.co.uk 🕑 10.00–16.00 Mon–Sat. Bike hire plus self-guided tours of the area around Biddenden.

DARENT VALLEY

The Darent River runs about for about 25 miles through west Kent from its source in the springs of the Greensand Hills south of Westerham until it meets the Thames at Dartford. The river, which is believed to have been named after an early English word meaning 'river of oaks', flows through the Kent Downs Area of Outstanding Natural Beauty. The valley is particularly picturesque around the ancient village of Eynsford and nearby Shoreham, where the painter and writer Samuel Palmer, a key figure in the Romanticism movement of the 19th century, lived from 1826 and 1835. It's possible to walk most of the river valley by following the 19-mile, waymarked Darent Valley Path.

1 EYNSFORD & SURROUNDS

Stacked with timber-framed houses Eynsford epitomises an English country village. It can trace its roots back to the old Saxon settlement of Aegen's Ford, and it's still possible to drive across a shallow part of the Darent River as it flows through Eynsford. If you'd prefer not to risk that, a stone humpbacked bridge has provided a water-free traverse since at least the 17th century.

Nearby, just off High Street, are the ragstone ruins of **Eynsford Castle** (DA4 0AA ☉ Apr–Oct 10.00–18.00 daily; Nov–Mar 10.00–16.00 daily; English Heritage), likely built by William d'Eynsford in the 11th century. Abandoned in the 14th century, this is a rare example of a Norman fortified residence, also known as an 'enclosure castle', with no central keep or great tower. William d'Eynsford also built the church of **St Martin's** (4 Church Walk, DA4 0EH ⌖ efl-churches.org) on the site of an old Saxon church, a five-minute walk south of the castle; spot the rounded Norman arch inside the entrance porch.

Long before either the Saxons or the Normans had settled in the Darent Valley, the Romans were here. The remains of seven Roman villas have been unearthed along the river's course, with the most impressive of them located barely a mile outside of Eynsford. Follow the riverside path southwest out of the village, passing beneath the nine soaring brick arches of the 1862 railway viaduct, to reach **Lullingstone**

1 View towards Eynsford. **2** Down House. **3** Chartwell. **4** The World Garden at Lullingstone Castle. **5** Emmetts Garden. ▶

Roman Villa (Lullingston Ln, DA4 0JA ✆ 01322 863467 ☉ Apr & Oct 10.00–17.00 Wed–Sun; May–Sep 10.00–18.00 daily; Nov–Mar 10.00–16.00 Sat & Sun; English Heritage). The first house on this site could have been built as early as AD80. In the subsequent centuries it was enlarged, given grander decoration, including beautiful mosaics and wall paintings, and joined by two external buildings: a granary and a combined temple and mausoleum. Abandoned sometime in the fifth century, the villa was largely forgotten until full excavations of the site's ruins began in 1949. The discoveries were remarkable, and include a marble bust thought to be of Pertinax, raising the possibility that villa could have been used by the Governor of Britannia, who also reigned as Emperor for three months in AD193. Protected beneath a large modern building, the excavated ruins can be viewed from surrounding gantries, with coloured lights illuminating different sections of the villa. The highlight is the spectacular and virtually complete floor mosaics depicting two mythical scenes: the abduction of the princess Europa by the god Jupiter disguised as a bull; and Bellerophon astride his trusty winged steed Pegasus slaying the Chimera. The villa is also unique in having one of the earliest Christian chapels in the England, dating from the fourth century, built atop an earlier pagan shrine.

Five minutes' walk south of the roman villa stands **Lullingstone Castle & The World Garden** (DA4 0JA ✆ 01322 862114 ⟨⟩ lullingstonecastle. co.uk ☉ Apr–Oct noon–17.00 Fri–Sun & Bank Holiday Mon), the ancestral home of the Hart-Dykes who have lived here since 1497. Although called a castle, the three-storey red-brick manor house was never a fortress; its gatehouse, dating from the late 16th century, is the most castle-like part of the estate. Lullingstone's heir is the horticulturalist and rare plant hunter Tom Hart-Dyke, who hit the headlines when he was kidnapped during one his expeditions in the Panamanian jungle in 2000. During his nine months of captivity, Tom found solace in designing his dream garden, one that would have a place for all the plants he'd collected from around the globe. The two-acre World Garden, the realisation of Tom's dream, is not the most beautifully laid out or pristine garden in Kent (too much competition for that!) but is certainly to be admired for its ambition as a repository for broad range of species.

On display in the walled garden, accessed through a moon gate, are some 8,000 varieties of plants, including a Wollemi pine tree from Australia and the Penstemon 'Crac's Delight', discovered by Tom in

Mexico and named after his grandmother who inspired his love of plants. The plant beds are shaped into a very rough map of the world, with ornamental features, including a totem pole and giant wire baobab tree, providing clues to the geographical designation for non-horticulturists. Outside of the main walled garden there's a lot more to see including a 'Hot and Spikey' house packed with cacti, bromeliads and succulents, the Cloud Garden with venus fly traps and other carnivorous pitcher plants, an orchid house and a woodland walk. Check their website for events hosted on the estate throughout the year.

To really make a day of it, you can continue south for about a third of mile along this lovely stretch of the river to **Lullingstone Country Park** (Castle Rd, DA4 0JF ✆ 03000 411811), which has a collection of over 300 veteran trees, including oak, beech, hornbeam and sweet chestnut, some of which are believed to be up to 800 years old. In spring and summer the park's chalk grasslands bloom with orchids and wild flowers.

A five-minute walk south of the park entrance is **Castle Farm** (Redmans Ln, TN14 7UB ⌂ castlefarmkent.co.uk ◷ shop 09.00–17.00 Tue–Sat, 10.00–17.00 Sun; see ad, page 305). Late June to late July is the ideal time to visit here when you can enjoy pre-booked walks or picnics amid the farm's rippling fields of lavender. Covering 130 acres in varied shades of purple, this is UK's largest farm for this fragrant flower. Various lavender products are sold in their shop alongside other specialities of the farm, including hops, beef, apples and pumpkins.

⋔ FOOD & DRINK

Castle Hotel High St, Eynsford DA4 0AB ✆ 01322 633917 ⌂ castlehotelkent.com ◷ noon–23.00 Mon–Sat, noon–18.00 Sun. This convivial Georgian-era pub, part of Kent's Shepherd Neame chain, is a very pleasant place for a light meal, be it a superior version of a ploughman's lunch, an Eynsford sausage bap, or the Korean rice dish *bibimbap* topped with crispy marinated tofu or sticky pulled pork. There are also some nicely decorated rooms available.

Mount Vineyard The Mount, Church St, Shoreham TN14 7SD ✆ 01959 524008 ⌂ themountvineyard.co.uk ◷ noon–23.00 Wed–Sun. Tucked away in Shoreham, about three miles south of Eynsford, this ten-acre vineyard produces wines from eight different varietals, including chardonnay, pinot noir and Bacchus. Hour long tastings take place on Fridays, Saturdays and Sundays. There's also an airy, covered courtyard restaurant where you can dine on gourmet sharing boards of cheese or cold cuts, salads and their creatively topped pizzas.

The Plough Inn 24 Riverside, Eynsford, DA4 0AE 🖉 01322 862281
🖑 theploughinneynsford.co.uk com ⊙ 11.00–23.00 Mon–Thu, 11.00–23.30 Fri & Sat,
11.00–22.00 Sun. Signature dishes at this relaxed riverside gastropub include pork belly
with seared scallops, spit-roasted chicken with lemon and garlic confit, and homemade
beef burgers.
Riverside Tea Room 2a Riverside, Eynsford, DA4 0AE 🖉 01322 861551 🖑 riverside-
tearoom.co.uk ⊙ 09.00–16.30 Mon–Sat, 09.00–16.00 Sun. Next to Eynsford's humpbacked
bridge, this cute tea room has a delicious and filling range of breakfast and brunch options,
as well as sandwiches and cakes. Also on the menu are local products, including apple juice
from neighbouring Castle Farm and fine teas from Blends for Friends.

WESTERHAM & SURROUNDS

Three and half miles east of Oxted (the nearest train station) and six
miles west of Sevenoaks is the prosperous, pretty village of Westerham,
best known for its associations with Winston Churchill, who lived at
Chartwell, a jewel in the National Trust's crown of Kent properties.
There's a wonderful woodland walk from Chartwell via Toy's Hill to
Emmetts Garden, another Trust-managed property. Down House, home
of the great scientist Charles Darwin, can also be visited, six miles north
of Westerham.

2 WESTERHAM

Perched on a small hill near the source of the Darent River, Westerham
is one of Kent's oldest settlements, with archaeological finds nearby
including a 2000BC Celtic fort and the remains of Roman roads and
encampments. More recently, Winston Churchill resided at nearby
Chartwell (page 251); there's a statue of the politician, in a seated pose,
on Westerham's village green, alongside one of another war hero – the
sword-brandishing Major-General James Wolfe, who died aged just
32 during the battle to take Quebec. Wolfe, posthumously dubbed
the 'The Conqueror of Canada', was born and grew up in Westerham;
his childhood home was renamed **Quebec House** (Quebec Sq
🖉 01959567430 ⊙ Jun–Oct 11.00–16.00 Thu–Sun; National Trust) in
his honour. There's an exhibition about Wolfe in the coach house and
the house is set up as it would have been in the 1730s.

Four miles south of Westerham, the National Trust has guardianship
over the 200-acre woodland of **Toy's Hill**, where Octavia Hill sank a well

at the 771ft highpoint in 1898. Hill, a social reformer, philanthropist, artist and writer, co-founded the National Trust in 1895 and from the terrace that now surrounds the well there are spectacular views across the Kentish Weald as far as Ashdown Forest in East Sussex. Leafy walking trails extend from Toy's Hill (where there's a car park) east through the woods towards Emmetts Garden (page 252) and west in the direction of Chartwell and onwards to the village of Crockham Hill where Octavia Hill lived; she's buried in the churchyard of **Holy Trinity** (Oakdale Ln, Crockham Hill, TN8 6RL, ⌖ crockhamhillchurch.org).

3 CHARTWELL

Mapleton Rd, TN16 1PS ⌖ 01732 868381 ⊙ gardens 10.00–17.00 daily; house Mar–Oct 11.00–17.00 daily; studio Feb–Dec 11.00–16.00 daily; National Trust

> I have been searching for two years for a home in the country and the site is the most beautiful and charming I have ever seen.
> Winston Churchill

Located just under two miles south of Westerham, Chartwell has a history going back to at least Tudor times. When Churchill bought the property in 1922 for £5,000, it was an 82-acre lot with an undistinguished, dreary Victorian house in dire need of repairs. What it did have going for it were panoramic views across the Weald. Churchill had a vision for the place and, together with his wife Clementine, restored and refashioned the main house and redesigned the gardens, making it into a treasured home for their family for over 40 years. So ruinously expensive was the running and maintenance of Chartwell that Churchill eventually had to sell up. Fortunately, a scheme was devised by a group of their friends to raise the funds for the National Trust to buy the house in 1946 and to allow the Churchills to remain living there on a 50-year lease. After Winston's death in 1965, Clementine vacated the house and it was opened to the public exactly a year later. It has been a hugely popular draw ever since.

The extensive and beautifully designed grounds are Chartwell's highlight, but the house does offer an intimate insight into the private life of the Churchills. Clementine's refined sense of style comes through in the decoration of many of the rooms which have been preserved as they would have been in the 1930s; the exception is the secretaries' office which is set up as it would have been in the 1950s. Scattered throughout are the family's possessions, including a Monet painting (unfinished) of Charing Cross Bridge in the drawing room and a portrait of Lady Randolph Churchill, Churchill's mother, by John Singer Sargent, in his book-lined study. There are also more personal keepsakes like Churchill's emerald velvet 'siren suit' (a World War II-era onesie designed for wear in air-raid shelters) and the Golden Rose Book, containing 29 paintings of the blooms planted to celebrate the couple's golden wedding anniversary.

In summer, the avenue of gorgeous yellow roses, contrasting against clumps of purple flowering catmint, is one of the many horticultural pleasures of the 20 acres of gardens which also include an orchard of apple trees, a croquet lawn, the Butterfly Walk blooming with buddleia, a kitchen garden, and the splendid Terrace Lawn with its painted Marlborough Pavilion that leads into the fragrant walled Rose Garden designed by Clementine.

Churchill was an enthusiastic bricklayer: he laid most of the walls surrounding the kitchen garden and constructed the one-room 'Marycot' cottage for his daughters. He also took charge of major landscaping projects, such as adding an oval-shaped heated swimming pool and digging out the ponds he stocked with 1,000 golden orfes purchased from Harrods. Beyond the lake, in which black swans gifted from Australia glide, extend another 57 acres of parkland threaded through with walking trails that lead to World War II bomb craters, and a kids' playground with a two-storey treehouse.

When he wasn't writing in his study or laying bricks in the garden, Churchill liked nothing more than to take refuge in his painting studio. He's known to have painted over 530 canvases during his lifetime and Chartwell has the world's largest collection of his works, some of them unfinished. Most are hung on the walls of the studio which has been set up with paints, brushes and easels as it would have been when Churchill was alive. While far from masterpieces, the works – a mixture of landscapes, portraits and still lives – present yet another fascinating facet of a man of many talents.

4 EMMETTS GARDEN

Ide Hill, TN14 6BA ✆ 01732 868381 ⊘ 10.00–16.00 daily; National Trust

Four and a half miles southeast of Westerham is this charming hillside garden, laid out over six acres by the banker and passionate gardener Frederic Lubbock who bought the estate in 1890. Containing mainly trees and shrubs, including a soaring Giant Sequoia, the garden stands at one of the highest spots in Kent, providing panoramic views over the Weald. In spring there are great displays of daffodils, bluebells, camellias, magnolias and rhododendrons, while in summer it's the rose beds that take pride of place. In autumn, trees such as the katsura (which has a candyfloss aroma), the winged spindle and the acers look fantastic with their leaves the full spectrum of yellow, reds and russet browns.

5 DOWN HOUSE

Luxted Rd, Downe BR6 7JT ℘ 03703 331181 ☉ Mar–Oct 10.00–17.00 Wed–Sun, Nov–Feb 10.00–17.00 Sat & Sun; English Heritage

From 1842 until his death in 1882, Charles Darwin lived with his wife and their ten children at Down House, six miles north of Westerham. The Georgian-era house is not especially large for such a big family, and Darwin initially thought it 'ugly' and that the attached gardens were 'a detestable slip' of land. Three of their children died young at the house, but overall Down was a happy and very productive home for the family, and one that inside and outside became a living laboratory to test Darwin's scientific theories. It was here, following his round-the-world adventures and observations aboard the HMS *Beagle*, that the great naturalist developed his theories of evolution, leading to the publication in 1859 of *On the Origin of Species by Means of Natural Selection*. The well laid-out exhibition in the upstairs rooms of the house cover Darwin's life and work, clearly setting out the stages that led to his ground-breaking and, at the time, controversial book.

Several of the rooms have been set up as they would have been during Darwin's lifetime. The book- and specimen-cluttered study has many original pieces of furniture

"It was here, following his round-the-world adventures aboard the HMS Beagle, that Darwin developed his theories of evolution."

including the high-backed armchair and writing board Darwin preferred to work from. The dining room table is laid out with a full Wedgwood water lily pattern dinner service: Charles and his wife Emma (who was also his cousin) shared Josiah Wedgwood as a grandfather.

From their bedroom's three bay windows, Darwin had a commanding view across the gardens which he replanted to carry out a series of horticultural experiments. A dozen varieties of climbers, including Virginia creepers and Boston ivy, cover the back walls of the house, while beyond the main lawn and its experimental plant beds lies an elongated walled kitchen garden and a glasshouse in which Darwin collected orchids, climbing and carnivorous plants. The far end of the garden connects to the Sandwalk, a quarter-mile 'thinking path' along which Darwin took daily contemplative walks.

¶¶ FOOD & DRINK

Bottle Store Restaurant Squerryes Winery, Beggars Ln, Westerham TN16 1QP ℘ 01959 562345 ⌂ squerryes.co.uk ☉ noon–11pm Wed–Sun. The award-winning sparkling wines produced on the Squerryes estate are the stars of the show at this imaginatively decorated restaurant overlooking their 36 acres of vines. The menu features local produce such grass-fed beef from Ightham in their steak tartare and the cheeses in the twice-baked cheese soufflé. A tour of the vineyards and tutored tastings of three sparkling wines are offered on Fridays, Saturdays and Sundays from 22 April through to harvest in October and lasts around 90 minutes.

Flint & Oak Old Milking Parlour, Beggars Ln, Westerham TN16 1QP ⌂ flintandoak.shop ☉ shop 10.00–17.00 Mon–Sat, 10.00–16.00 Sun; café 08.30–16.00 Fri–Sun. Drop into this generously stocked deli and farm shop for choice Kent produce including wines, small-batch gin and rum, cheeses and meats. On weekends they also open an outdoor café with a view across Squerreys vineyards.

The Old Bank 8 Market Sq, Westerham TN16 1AW ℘ 01233 659890 ⌂ oldbank-westerham.co.uk ☉ noon–15.00 & 18.30–10.00 Thu–Sat, noon–20.00 Sun. See ad, page 305. Occupying a former NatWest bank, this fine-dining restaurant is helmed by Adam Turley, tipped by *Kent Life Magazine* as 2020's chef of the year. His culinary creations use the best seasonal and local ingredients. Complimentary canapes and fresh bread are a welcome touch of hospitality. The basement vault has been transformed into a wine cellar where tutored wine tastings are held.

Tudor Rose Tearooms 8 The Green, Westerham TN16 1AS ℘ 01959 562391 ⌂ tudor-rosewesterham.co.uk ☉ 09.00–16.00 Mon–Fri, 08.00–17.00 Sat, 09.00–17.00 Sun. A table laid with freshly baked cakes and other sweet treats greets customers at this convivial and long-standing tea room overlooking Westerham's central green. Also on the menu are the usual range of sandwiches and savoury light meals and snacks.

Westerham Brewery Tap Room Beggars Ln, Westerham TN16 1QP ℘ 01732 864427 ⌂ westerhambrewery.co.uk ☉ noon–22.00 Wed–Sat, noon–19.30 Sun. Beer brewing in Westerham dates to the 1600s. Carrying on that tradition since 2004 is this craft ale operation which draws on heritage recipes as well as heading off in delicious new directions – witness their triple-chocolate stout, Wally Winker's Death by Chocolate. Sample the beers at their tap house and order food from the various street food vendors that set up outside.

SEVENOAKS & SURROUNDS

The well-heeled commuter town of Sevenoaks, 28 miles southeast of London, has been a market town since at least the 13th century. It's best known for Knole, a 1,000-acre estate that's been the ancestral seat of the Sackville family since 1603 and which is accessed directly off the town's gently hilly High Street. Along here you find **Sevenoaks Bookshop** (147 High St ⌂ sevenoaksbookshop.co.uk ⊙ 09.30–17.30 Mon–Sat 10.30–16.30 Sun), an award-winning indie bookshop in business since 1948 that hosts events and also has a nice little café serving homemade cakes. Otherwise, there's little reason to linger in Sevenoaks itself, but there are several other gardens and historic estates that are a short drive or a manageable cycle ride away from the town.

Wildlife lovers will also want to visit the 180-acre **Sevenoaks Wildlife Reserve** (Bradbourne Vale Rd, TN13 3DH ✆ 01622 357879 ⌂ kentwildlifetrust.org.uk ⊙ 10.00–15.00 Wed–Sun) which is a one-mile walk north of the train station on a former gravel quarry leased to Kent Wildlife Trust. The five lakes surrounded by woodland here are excellent for spotting bird and animal life including bats, dragonflies, damselflies and glow-worms, as well as for enjoying diverse plants and fungi. The visitors' centre also hosts many workshops and guided walks.

6 KNOLE

TN15 0RP ✆ 01732 462100 ⊙ grounds dawn–dusk; car park 10.00–17.00; showrooms 11.00–16.00 daily; conservation studio 11.00–16.00 Wed–Sat; National Trust

'More like a medieval village than a private dwelling' is how Vita Sackville-West, who was born there, described Knole. This Jacobean showstopper, with around 400 rooms and a footprint of four acres, is one of the largest country houses in England. It is also the model for the setting of *Orlando*, a novel dedicated by its author Virginia Woolf to her lover Vita.

Taking its name from the rounded hill on which it stands, Knole was bought by Thomas Bourchier, Archbishop of Canterbury, in 1456. He began the remodelling of the core 13th-century house by adding the main courtyard Green Court and possibly the twin-towered gatehouse. However, it is Sackville-West's ancestor, Thomas Sackville, Lord Treasurer, first Earl of Dorset and favoured cousin of Elizabeth I, who left the most enduring architectural mark on Knole. Sackville

SVITLANAR/S

MARK BRIDGER/S

GEMMA STAPELEY/TWCC

CHRIS LAWRENCE TRAVEL/S

SS

SS

took possession of Knole in 1603 and proceeded to spend enormous sums, employing the finest craftsmen of the age to extensively upgrade the old archbishop's palace. These works, which included creating the showrooms and adding the stone leopards, his family emblem, atop the property's Dutch gables, were still in progress by his death in 1608. Some 400 years later, the leopards continue to gaze from on high across this 1000-acre estate that reaches to the edge of the Greensand Hills.

There are several pedestrian gates into the park from Sevenoaks, all clearly marked by signs in town; walking in the park is free. To drive in and park you will need to be a National Trust member or have pre-booked a ticket for a tour of the showrooms.

The showrooms

The house and 52 acres of the park were donated to the National Trust in 1947. Thirteen generations on, the Sackville-Wests continue to live at the property so only part of it is open to public. The completion of a £19.8 million building and conservation project in 2019 has resulted in these showrooms looking the best they have in four centuries.

The principal set of showrooms are accessed off Stone Court, so called because of its large paving stones, and kick off with the Great Hall which is hung with a series of large portraits of royalty and the members of the Sackville family. Next comes the aptly named Great Staircase, one of Thomas Sackville's most impressive modifications of the house, replete with stunning oil-painted wall murals and staircase newel posts topped with carved wooden leopards.

Upstairs highlights include a unique collection of Stuart furniture mostly acquired by Charles Sackville in the late 17th century. As a perk of his job as Lord Chamberlain to William and Mary, Charles helped himself to cast-off pieces from the royal palaces. This is how Knole comes to have such treasures as the original Knole settee, designed as a double throne chair for the king and queen. There are also three state beds: the Spangled Bed, named after the thousands of silver-gilt sequins sewn into its red satin curtains; the blue-green velvet James II Bed; and the gilded King's Bed.

◄ **1** Hever Castle Gardens. **2** Ightham Mote. **3** Happy Valley, Rusthall Common. **4** River Medway and Tonbridge. **5** Pantiles, Tunbridge Wells. **6** Knole.

Knole's art collection spans the centuries and includes portraits by Sir Anthony Van Dyck, Thomas Gainsborough and Joshua Reynolds. The Crimson Drawing Room is hung with works by Reynolds, the most striking of which is a delicately rendered portrait of Wang-y-Tong, a Chinese page boy who lived at Knole in the late 17th century. In the Cartoon Gallery are 17th-century copies of the Raphael Cartoons (the originals belong to London's V&A Museum), epic-scale designs for tapestries destined for the Vatican's Sistine Chapel.

Gatehouse Tower & Conservation Studio

Climb the spiral stone staircase of the Gatehouse Tower to gain a spectacular view over the house and estate. Beneath are a couple of more down-to-earth rooms set up as they were when occupied by Edward (Eddy) Sackville-West between 1926 and 1940. A novelist and music critic, the 5th Baron Sackville was gay and hung out with the Bloomsbury Group of artists and intellectuals, several of whose famous names are listed in the visitors' book on display. Graham Sutherland's masterful 1954 full length portrait of Eddy takes pride of place in the Music Room and captures, in Eddy's opinion 'a frightened man – almost a ghost'.

On the east side of the house, on the top floor of a converted 15th-century barn, is the Royal Oak Foundation Conservation Studio. Here you can watch the conservation team in action as they take care of objects from across all the National Trust's 200 or so properties, gaining a fascinating glimpse into their painstakingly detailed work.

The grounds

While many of the grand English country houses had their grounds landscaped in Georgian times, Knole's has remained pretty much unchanged since first being enclosed as a deer park in the 15th century; the main modern intrusion is **Knole Park Golf Club** (𝒜 knoleparkgolfclub.co.uk) created in 1924. Some 350 wild fallow and sika deer continue to roam freely through the park – look out for them shedding their winter coats and antlers in spring, calving and fawning in summer, and rutting in autumn. In 1967, the Beatles filmed videos for *Penny Lane* and *Strawberry Fields Forever* in the park, riding horses through an ornamental ruined arch that stands near the Gothic summerhouse known as the Bird House.

Knole's parklands are criss-crossed by a spider's web of walking routes. An almost straight and not particularly strenuous four-mile walking route connects Knole to Ightham Mote via **One Tree Hill** (Carter's Hill, TN15 0SN; National Trust). Rising 608ft above sea level and providing sweeping views over the Weald, the hill has been protected by the National Trust since 1911. The deciduous woodlands here are the habitat of the dormouse, one of the UK's most endangered species – but good luck in spotting one as they spend most of their lives living up in the trees.

A free guided walk around Knole's grounds departs at 14.00 on Thursday, Saturday and Sunday from the Visitor Centre in the Gatehouse Tower. On Tuesdays from April to September, and for an additional fee, it's usually possible to visit Knole's 26-acre walled gardens that are otherwise the private domain of the Sackville family.

7 RIVERHILL HIMALAYAN GARDEN

Riverhill TN15 0RR ✆ 01732 459777 ⌂ riverhillgardens.co.uk ⊙ Mar–Oct 09.00–17.00 daily

In the last decade, much work has gone into restoring and improving the gardens at Riverhill, two miles south of Sevenoaks. The 12-acre garden is now looking as good, if not better, than when John Rogers, a founding member of the Royal Horticultural Society and friend of Charles Darwin, first started laying out the site in the mid 19th century. What appealed to Rogers about Riverhill was its sheltered hillside location and the lime-free soil, perfect for the azaleas, camellias and rhododendrons that he wished to cultivate here. Over the years various elements were added including an Edwardian rock garden sprouting with a variety of ferns and a Himalayan hedge maze, close by the main viewpoint over the Weald. That maze, plus an adventure playground and various kid-friendly events throughout the year, make Riverhill an ideal family destination.

8 IGHTHAM MOTE

Mote Rd, Ivy Hatch TN15 0NT ✆ 01732 810378 ⊙ exhibition & garden Mar–Oct 10.00–17.00 daily; Nov–Feb 10.00–16.00 daily; house Mar–Oct 11.00–17.00 daily; Nov 11.00–14.00 daily; Dec–Feb 11.00–15.00 Sat & Sun; National Trust

Looking like an illustration ripped from a fairy-tale book, this 14th-century timber manor house, perched on an island and surrounded by a square-shaped moat, is secreted in a wooded valley, 6½ miles east of Sevenoaks. Dating from around 1350, the compact house's 700-year history is reflected in the 24 rooms open to the public and arranged around a picturesque central courtyard. These range from the Great Hall with its Tudor wood panelling and vaulted ceiling to the chintz in the lounge and library of Charles Henry Robinson, who was the last private owner of the house, from 1953 to 1985.

Robinson, who made his fortune by running a stationary company in Portland, Maine, was not the first US citizen to have lived at Ightham Mote: Mary Lincoln Mellen, aka 'Queen' Palmer, wife of General William Palmer, leased the property from 1887 to 1890. She had come to England to live because the high altitude of Colorado Springs was bad for her weak heart. Sadly, the British climate proved no better, with Palmer dying here in 1894. Before she passed away, Palmer entertained fellow expats, the writer Henry James and the painter John Singer Sargent at Ightham Mote. In 1890 Sargent painted Palmer's daughter Elsie at the property, creating the more-than-life-sized portrait that today hangs at the Colorado Springs Fine Arts Center.

The icing on Ightham Mote's historical architectural cake is the surrounding 14 acres of gardens which, like the rooms of the house, present a broad variety of styles. There's a walled cuttings garden, an apple orchard which in spring is carpeted with yellow and white daffodils, herbaceous borders sprouting roses in the summer and two lakes. The property also sits within a 546-acre estate through which you can follow waymarked trails to farmlands, bluebell woods and natural springs, and old brick cottages where seasonal hop pickers once bunked down.

9 GREAT COMP GARDEN

Comp Ln, St Mary's Platt TN15 8QS ℰ 01732 885094 ℰ greatcompgarden.co.uk
⊙ Mar–Oct 10.00–17.00; Nov–Feb 11.00–15.00 Thu–Sat

Even though it's a relative newcomer on Kent's illustrious garden scene, Great Comp, 8½ miles east of Sevenoaks, is a gem that offers plenty of interest to horticulturalists and lovers of beautifully designed landscapes. The estate was once owned by the Lambarde family, descendants of William Lambarde, author of *The Perambulation of Kent*, published in 1576 and the first ever guidebook to the country. But it was self-taught gardeners Roderick and Joy Cameron who bought Great Comp in 1957 that created and nurtured the superb gardens enveloping the

17th-century manor house for over 20 years. There's interest here throughout the year, from snowdrops in late winter, hellebores, magnolias, azaleas and rhododendrons that bloom in spring, and summer's superb array of salvias – Great Comp has one of the biggest collections of this species in Europe. Check out their website for the many events staged here through the year. There's also a pleasant tea room.

¶¶ FOOD & DRINK

There are cafés at Knole, Riverhill Himalayan Garden, Ightham Mote and Great Comp Garden.

Life on High 140 High St, Sevenoaks TN13 1XE ⌗ lifeonhigh.co.uk ⊙ 09.00–17.00 Mon, 07.30–17.00 Tue–Fri, 08.00–17.00 Sat, 09.00–16.00 Sun. Cutting a stylish and independent dash on Sevenoaks' chain-packed High Street, Life on High makes a great cup of coffee and has a tempting menu packed with tasty vegetarian and vegan options. Check their social media for details of occasional evening events such as tapas and cocktails.
White Rock Inn Underriver TN15 0SB ✆ 01732 833112 ⌗ thewhiterockinn.co.uk
⊙ noon–23.00 Fri & Sat, noon–22.00 Sun–Thu. Walkable from either Knole or Igtham Mote, this traditional country inn offers wood-beamed ceilings, a grassy beer garden and a classic pub food menu with dishes such as fish pie and Kentish gypsy tart (a local style of custard tart).

EDENBRIDGE & SURROUNDS

The historic little town of Edenbridge, 10 miles southwest of Sevenoaks, is useful as an access point by train for the nearby attractions of Hever Castle and Chiddingstone and for walking and cycling around the Eden Valley. For nearly a century, Edenbridge has also hosted one of Kent's biggest **Bonfire Night festivals** (⌗ edenbridgebonfire.co.uk), which includes a torchlight parade along High Street and the burning of two 30ft-tall effigies, one of Guy Fawkes, the other of a contemporary celebrity.

10 EDENBRIDGE

There's been a bridge crossing the Eden River at this attractive town since at least the Roman occupation of Britain, when a road ran through here from Lewes to London. Learn all about the town and surroundings at the **Eden Valley Museum** (Church House, 72 High St, TN8 5AR ✆ 01732 868102 ⌗ evmt.org.uk ⊙ 14.00–16.30 Wed, 10.00–16.30 Thu, 14.00–16.30 Fri, 10.00–16.30 Sat; Jun–Aug also 14.00–16.30 Sun) which occupies one of the oldest houses in Edenbridge, built around 1380. It's a wonderful time capsule of the valley with exhibitions on a fascinating range of subjects, from the leather tanning industry that thrived for centuries in Edenbridge to the cricket bats and balls that used to be made near Penshurst. A prize exhibit is the Chiddingstone Hoard – ten Gallo-Belgic E stater gold coins, dating to around 50BC and discovered by a metal detectorist near Chiddingstone in 2016.

If you have extra time, walk a minute or so east of the museum to the parish church of **St Peter & St Paul** (12 Church St, Edenbridge TN8 5BD ⌁ edenbridgeparishchurch.org), believed to have been built in Norman times on a Saxon site; it has some fine stained-glass windows, including one with designs by Edward Burne-Jones.

⨶ FOOD & DRINK

Ye Olde Crown 74–75 High St, TN8 5AR ⌁ 01732 926350 ⌁ yeoldecrown.co.uk ⌁ bar 11.00–22.30 Sun–Thu, 11.00–23.30 Fri & Sat, 11.00–22.00 Sun; restaurant 09.00–11.00, noon–15.00 & 18.00–21.00 Mon–Sat, noon–17.00 Sun. A pub at least since the late 16th century, Ye Old Crown has a pleasant restaurant and B&B rooms. It's famous for its unusual sign that spans the High Street. A tunnel running from the pub to the nearby church was used by smugglers in the 17th century.

11 HEVER

⌂ **Hever Castle B&B** & **Medley Court** (page 311)

This hamlet along the Eden River, three miles southeast of Edenbridge, is the location of **Hever Castle** (TN8 7NG ⌁ 01732 865224 ⌁ hevercastle. co.uk ⌁ castle Apr–Oct noon–16.30; Nov–Mar noon–15.30 daily; grounds Feb & Mar 10.30–16.30; Apr–Oct & Dec 10.30–18.00 daily; Nov 10.30–16.30 Wed–Sun). Appealing to lovers of history and gardens – and to families looking for an entertaining day out with the kids – Hever dates to the 13th century but it was during Tudor times that its compact manor house surrounded by a moat came into national focus. The diplomat and courtier Sir Thomas Bullen (also known as Boleyn) inherited the property in 1505 and brought up his daughter Anne here. Henry VIII was a frequent visitor, first wooing Anne's sister Mary and then Anne herself, who became the second of his six wives. Following Thomas Bullen's death, the castle became the property of the king, who later gave it to his fourth wife Anne of Cleves as part of their divorce settlement. She lived here for the last 17 years of her life.

When William Waldorf Astor bought Hever in 1903 the castle was in a perilous state. Astor spent £10 million on restoring the castle to an idealised version of its Tudor glory, with the discrete addition of Edwardian mod cons such as electric sockets and central heating. The American tycoon and British viscount hunted down Tudor works of art and artefacts with which to furnish the castle, including 16th-century furniture and tapestries and portraits of Henry VIII (one of them by Holbein), Anne and her older sister Mary.

On display are also two illuminated prayer books that belonged to Anne, one of which she is believed to have clasped as she went to her execution in 1536.

"When William Waldorf Astor bought Hever, the castle was in a perilous state. He spent £10 million on restoring it."

The reimagining of the castle extended to the addition of the Astor Wing, a mock Tudor village to provide guest accommodation; this is where Hever's B&B and self-catering rooms are now. Astor also supervised the creation of superb gardens which include a topiary chess set, a rose garden planted with over 4,000 rose bushes, and a gorgeous loggia and Japanese tea house, both overlooking the 38-acre hand-dug lake. The highlight is the Italian garden designed around Astor's collection of classical Italian statuary. Kids are well served with a playground and two mazes – one over a century old and made of yew, the other a series of concentric stepping-stone walkways sitting over water, with some of the stepping stones tilting when stood on to activate water jets. In summer, the grounds are the location for costumed jousting tournaments and the **Hever Festival** (⌂ heverfestival.co.uk) which includes outdoor music and theatre performances.

Directly opposite Hever's main entrance gate is **St Peter's Church** (⌂ threespires.wordpress.com/our-churches/st-peters-church-hever ⊙ 10.00–15.00 daily), inside of which is Sir Thomas Bullen's tomb, topped with a beautifully-engraved brass image of the grandfather of Elizabeth I.

⫪ FOOD & DRINK

King Henry VIII Hever Rd, TN8 7NH ✆ 01732 862457 ⌂ kinghenryviiihever.co.uk ⊙ noon–22.30 Wed–Sat, noon–21.00 Sun. The Boleyns' nemesis Henry VIII gets his name on this late 16th-century inn that looks the full Tudor part with its oak-beamed ceilings, wood panelling and open fires. The menu is traditionally English with fish and chips, homemade pies and Sunday roasts served alongside Shepherd Neame beers.

12 CHIDDINGSTONE

🏠 **Bore Place** (page 311), **Free Range Glamping** (page 312)

This immaculately preserved Tudor village, five miles east of Edenbridge and about a one-hour walk southwest of Penshurst train station, is a tiny, one-street community that looks like a period film set – which it has been on several occasions, most famously in the Merchant-Ivory version of *A Room with a View*. The National Trust has owned the village almost in its entirety (excluding the Victorian-built school and castle, and St Mary the Virgin church) since 1939.

The village said to take its name from a curiously bulbous sandstone outcrop that lies behind the single row of houses. This graffiti-carved 135-million-year-old rock is said by some to have been a druid's altar place as well as where nagging wives or wrongdoers were upbraided (or 'chided'). Perhaps – but it's much more likely that the settlement, which is mentioned in the Domesday Book, is named after Chidda (or Cidda), a local Saxon leader. Some of the village's half-timber sided and red-roof tiled buildings, including the village store, once belonged to Sir Thomas Bullen, Anne Boleyn's father. The village's oldest structure is the church which contains masonry from the 13th century, although most of the current building dates after a particularly destructive fire in 1624.

The village's key property is **Chiddingstone Castle** (Hill Hoat Rd, TN8 7AD ✆ 01892 870347 ♂ chiddingstonecastle.org.uk ◷ grounds 07.00–18.30 daily; museum 11.00–17.00 Sun–Tue), the grounds of which can be accessed directly off the end of Chiddingstone's High Street, through a gate next to the Castle Inn. Despite its name, this was never a real castle, but a house on to which decorative castellations were added in the early 19th century. The 35 acres of informal grounds, which include a fishing lake, orangery, woodlands and a grass maze, are pretty and worth exploring. It's best to coincide your visit here with the opening of the castle, which forms a museum displaying the wonderful antique and art collection of Denys Eyre Bower, who bought the property in 1955 and lived there until his death in 1977.

Bower was an eccentric but keen-eyed collector of beautiful decorative items such as samurai armour and lacquerware from Japan and ancient Egyptian pieces including a mummy casket. A practising Buddhist who was at one point in his life a banker, he also believed himself to be the reincarnation of Bonnie Prince Charlie, hence his collection of various Stuart and Jacobite artefacts. The most notorious aspect of the

BORE PLACE

Run to sustainable principles and certified as organic by the Soil Association since 2000, Bore Place (Bore Place Rd, TN8 7AR ✆ 07796 305324 🖰 boreplace.org) is a 550-acre dairy farm with flower and produce gardens, three miles north of Chiddingstone. It's the base for the Commonwork Trust, set up in the 1970s to promote living and working sustainably. As part of their mission, they host yoga retreats as well as many one-off educational events through the year, from learning how to make yoghurt or keep chickens to astronomy and beekeeping. There's also plenty of ways to volunteer at the estate.

Bore Place is open generally for visitors and there are three walking trails of between 1.2 and 2.8 miles around the farm. Download a trail map from their website, where there's also details of three longer circular walks connecting Bore Place to the Greensand Way, the village of Chiddingstone Causeway (home to Penshurst train station), and to Bough Beech Reservoir and a nature reserve managed by the Kent Wildlife Trust. Also at the farm you'll find Blackwoods Cheese Company (🖰 blackwoodscheesecompany.co.uk) which makes its award-winning soft cheese using milk from Bore Place's herd of cows.

twice-married Bower's life, however, was his lifetime conviction in 1957 for the attempted murder of his then girlfriend (Anna Lena White), and his own attempted suicide. Thanks to the tireless work of a lawyer Ruth Eldridge and her sister Mary, who believed this to be a miscarriage of justice, Bower was released from Wormwood Scrubs prison in 1963. The very survival of the house and its collection is in no small part down to the Eldridge sisters, who helped found the charitable trust that now owns the castle.

¶¶ FOOD & DRINK

Chiddingstone Castle has a tea room which is open when the castle is open.

The Castle Inn at Chiddingstone Chiddingstone Rd, TN8 7AH ✆ 01892 870371 🖰 castleinnchiddingstone.co.uk ◷ noon–18.00 daily. Light lunches are served at this atmospheric pub owned by the National Trust. Sample local Larkins Brewery (🖰 larkinsbrewery.co.uk) ales which include a bitter, pale ale and, from November to March, an award-winning porter.
The Tulip Tree The Village, Chiddingstone TN8 7AH 🖰 thetuliptree.biz ◷ 09.00–17.00 daily. Tucked behind the village store, this tea room specialises in home bakes, including quiches, sausage rolls and an array of cakes. Be prepared to wait, as it can get very busy here on weekends.

13 PENSHURST

The village of Penshurst, 5½ miles southwest of Tonbridge, is clustered around **Penshurst Place** (TN11 8DG ✆ 01892 870307 ⊘ penshurstplace. com ☉ house Apr–Oct 11.30–15.30 daily; gardens Apr–Oct 10.00–17.00 daily; parkland always open), a nearly 700-year-old house and garden that, since 1552, has been the ancestral home of the Sidney family. There are also two walking trails across the estate – the Parkland and the Riverside walks. Note that if you're travelling here by train, Penshurst station is in the village of Chiddingstone Causeway, two miles to the north of Penshurst.

This outstanding property was built in 1341 for the rich and powerful London merchant Sir John de Pulteney as his country residence. The Baron's Hall, the house's star attraction, dates from this period. Tall, arcaded windows illuminate the vast hall, revealing the fine detail of the chestnut-beamed roof, hanging 60ft above the stone-flagged floor. Ten life-sized wooden figures decorate the bases of the arched beams and there is more exquisite carving on the screen beneath the Minstrel's Gallery, a 16th-century addition to the hall.

Henry VIII stayed at Penshurst during his courtship of Anne Boleyn, who lived in nearby Hever Castle (page 262). Elizabeth I also visited – one of Penshurt's state rooms, luxuriously decorated with damask and silk furnishings and wall hangings, is named after her. In the State Dining Room, look for the rather risqué painting of Elizabeth dancing La Volta with her supposed lover Robert Dudley, Earl of Leicester. There's also an impressive collection of china in the Pages' Room, portraits of the Sidney family in the magnificent Long Gallery, and historic arms and armour in the Nether Gallery, including the funeral helm of Sir Philip Sidney who rhapsodised about his 'exceeding beautiful' home in his prose romance *Arcadia*.

The handsome state rooms of Penshurst are well matched by its glorious gardens and surrounding parkland. Yew hedges divide up the 11 acres of garden into smaller 'rooms' ranging from the 16th-century Italian Garden which explodes with 12,500 Jewel of Spring tulips in April, to the Jubilee Walk, a colour blocked, double herbaceous border that's a 21st-century addition to the grounds. Other highlights include the 330ft-long Peony Border, along which four varieties of the frothy pink flower bloom from late May to early June, and the Wilderness Garden of native trees, part of the Woodland Trail that is a joy to walk in autumn to admire all the changing colours.

After touring the house and gardens, take a moment to step inside the village's historic church **St John the Baptist** (High St, TN11 8BL ⊘ penshurstchurch.org). Dating from at least 1115, the church includes the Sidney Chapel, its highly decorative ceiling painted with the family's heraldic shields hanging from sinuous trees. The churchyard is accessed by passing through Leicester Square, a Tudor-era complex of wood-beamed houses beside the gatehouse to the Penshurst estate.

¶¶ FOOD & DRINK

Penshurst Place's **Porcupine Pantry** (⊙ 09.00–17.00 daily), next to the car park, is open year-round. On the first Saturday of the month, from 09.30 to noon, a farmers' market with some 25 stalls is held in the Penshurst Place car park.

Fir Tree House Tea Rooms Penshurst Rd, TN11 8DB ✆ 01892 870382 ⊙ 14.00–17.30 Wed–Sun. Freshly baked cakes, scones and tea breads are the accompaniment to quality loose-leaf teas and cafetiere coffee at this charming place. There's a lovely garden out the back in which to sit on good weather days. The tea room's tables are made from the 250-year-old Scots pine that one stood outside and gave the Fir Tree its name.
Kingdom Café Grove Rd, TN11 8DU ✆ 01892 577507 ⊘ thiskingdom.co.uk ⊙ 09.00–16.00 daily. About a mile and a half southwest of Penshurst, Kingdom is big timber structure, housing a café, events space, yoga studio and interior design shop. It's hidden up a hill, among 13 acres of woodland, with stunning views across the nearby valley. The roast chicken and vegetables for two (Saturday and Sunday only) is a bargain.
The Spotted Dog 6 Smarts Hill, TN11 8EP ✆ 01892 870253 ⊘ spotteddogpub.co.uk ⊙ 11.30–23.00 Mon–Sat, noon–10.30 Sun. The red spotted dog on the sign welcomes you to a convivial pub that makes for a good location to start, end or pause a walk around Penshurst. Its hillside location is beside a footpath through the estate and there's outdoor seating surrounded by greenery.

SHIPBOURNE MARKET

In 1285, Edward I granted the village of Shipbourne, four miles north of Tonbridge along the A227, permission to hold a weekly market. This tradition was revived in 2003 as a **farmers' market** (⊘ shipbournefm.co.uk/home ⊙ 09.00–11.00 Thu), held in and around St Giles' church beside the village green.

The market has won several awards for its range of quality local produce including fish, meats, baked goods and very quaffable sparkling wine from **Sanden Vineyard** (⊘ sanden-vineyard.business.site) in Groombridge. All of the profits are split between local and African agricultural charities.

TONBRIDGE & SURROUNDS

Pronounced 'Tunbridge' (as it was once spelled), this medieval market town sits on the River Medway, five miles north of its larger and more fashionable Wealden neighbour Tunbridge Wells. Its key sight is the remains of its Norman castle, while in the countryside close by is a kaleidoscopic jewel box of a church in the hamlet of Tudley and walking trails through the Tudely Woods RSPB Reserve.

14 TONBRIDGE

Overlooking the banks of the Medway River in the heart of town, **Tonbridge Castle** (℘ 01732 770929 ♦ tonbridgecastle.org ☉ castle 10.30–17.00 Mon–Thu, 10.30–16.30 Fri, 10.30–15.30 Sat & Sun; grounds 08.00–dusk) is one of England's best surviving examples of a motte and bailey fortress. The castle was founded in 1070 by Richard de Clare, a kinsman of William the Conqueror. Its motte (or mound) stands next to an impressive stone gatehouse that dates to around 1220. Four stout

OAST HOUSES

One of the most distinctive forms of Kent's vernacular architecture is the oast house. These kilns, topped with angled white vents (called cowls), were built to dry the hops grown across the county and used in beer brewing. The freshly picked hops were placed across the slatted ceiling of the kiln. Heat rising from furnaces below dried the hops, the moisture escaping as steam through the cowl which also worked as a wind vane helping to ventilate the building and keep the fire from going out.

Godwin House near Cranbrook, built around 1740 and reckoned to be Kent's oldest oast house, is a modified barn with the cowl on the roof ridge. By the 19th century the building design had evolved into the circular, funnel style of oast that are the most common ones you'll see. Made redundant by modern drying technologies, many oast houses have been converted into homes, some of which can be rented as holiday lets.

The largest collection of oast houses in one location – 20 in total – is at the **Hop Farm Village** (Maidstone Rd, Beltring TN12 6PY ℘ 01622 872068 ♦ thehopfarm.co.uk ☉ May–Dec 10.00–16.30 daily), seven miles east of Tonbridge. This was once the Whitbread brewery and hop farm which covered 300 acres and employed some 5,000 hop pickers during the harvest season. Today it's a family park with plenty of fun indoor and outdoor activities for kids including a hop-picking museum, an adventure playground and the chance to get up close to a variety of farmyard animals.

circular towers mark the corners and on a self-guided audio tour you can gain access and climb the spiral staircase for splendid views over the town from the roof. Inside, 13th-century castle life is recreated through a series of atmospheric tableaux that take you from the basement armoury and storeroom to the handsome main hall.

Tonbridge also promotes its connections to Jane Austen. There is no documentary evidence that the novelist ever visited the town, but her father George was born here and she had many other relations with family connections to Tonbridge, stretching back several generations. Between 1747 and 1757, George was a teacher at **Tonbridge School** (⌂ tonbridge-school.co.uk), the illustrious boys' boarding school whose handsome buildings front the High Street. The Austen family worshipped at the church of **St Peter and St Paul** (⌂ tonbridgeparishchurch.org.uk) which dates, like the castle, back to the 11th century. A pamphlet detailing a walk that connects these places and others in Tonbridge with an Austen family link is available at the castle's tourist information centre.

On the northside of the castle gatehouse, the old fire station has been transformed into the **Escape Art Centre** (Castle St ✆ 07712 789479 ⌂ escapeartcentre.co.uk ○ 10.00–17.00 daily) which has interesting local art exhibitions and doubles as a café-bar.

15 TUDLEY

This hamlet, 2½ miles east of Tonbridge, might not look much but there is one very good reason to visit. Tudley's **All Saints' Church** (TN11 0NZ ✆ 01892 833 241 ⌂ tudeley.org ○ 09.30–18.00 daily) is one of the oldest churches in the Weald, existing here, in one form or another, since the 7th century. What really sets it apart is its dozen windows featuring stunning stained-glass art by Marc Chagall of angels flying through a kaleidoscope of colours. The Russian artist was commissioned by Sir Henry and Lady D'Avigdor-Goldsmid to create a single window in memory of their daughter who had died, aged just 21, in a sailing accident in 1963. When this was installed in 1967, Chagall thought the church 'magnificent' and decided to continue the project, designing stained-glass images for the remaining 11 windows. The last one was installed just before Chagall's death in 1985.

Just off the A21 between Tonbridge and Tunbridge Wells, and about three miles south of All Saints', is **Tudely Woods RSPB Reserve** (Dislingbury Ln, TN11 0PT ✆ 01892 752430 ⌂ rspb.org.uk; free entry).

Tonbridge to Yalding: along the Medway

❋ OS Explorer maps 136 & 148; start: Tonbridge train station, Barden Rd, TN9 1TT
♥ TQ586460; 8.3 miles; easy

Kent's longest river, the Medway, rises at High Weald within Sussex and flows for some 70 miles via Tonbridge and Maidstone to emerge at the Thames Estuary near Chatham. This walk follows the first section of the Tonbridge to Rochester Medway Valley Walk, taking you past seven of the 11 locks that helped make the river navigable in the 18th century. The cargo barges that once sailed along this lovely section of the river have been replaced by paddleboarders, houseboats and the odd motor cruiser. This river-hugging route is simple to follow and clearly marked with level paths for its entire length. There are many spots to fish or jump into the river for a swim, and for a picnic along the way. If driving, park at or near Yalding train station (the finishing point) and take a train to Tonbridge to start the walk. You'll find loos and places for refreshments in both Tonbridge and Yalding.

1 Turn left out of Tonbridge Station and follow High Street towards Tonbridge Castle, turning right on to Medway Wharf Road before you reach the bridge over the river. Follow the riverside path past Tonbridge Moorings and the Town Lock.

2 At the junction with Vale Road, turn left, cross the bridge and take the riverside path on the right, heading into the countryside. After about two thirds of a mile you'll pass under a metal bridge. Continue along the riverside path past Eldridge's Lock and then Porter's Lock; the latter should take about an hour to reach from Tonbridge.

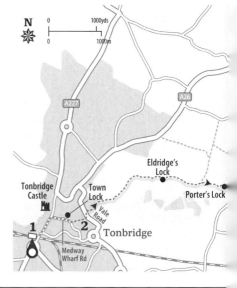

3 About 300yds from Porter's Lock, go under Hartlake Bridge. A short way later, in the trees to the left, are the remains of a 29mm spigot mortar, built to defend the bridge by the Home Guard during World War II. A little further on is a concrete pillbox from the same era. In the far distance to the left, keep an eye out for the Neo-Gothic, 175ft Hadlow Tower, dating from 1838. The octagonal castle-like folly, which was once part of a 18th century mansion, is taller than Nelson's Column.

4 At East Lock, cross the Medway and follow the path, with the river now to your left and grassy grazing fields to your right. Stay on this side of the river, passing the Fort Green footbridge and Oak Weir Lock. Veer right when the path forks and keep to the right when you reach the river again, continuing along the riverside path.

5 Walk past Sluice Weir Lock and on to Branbridges Leisure (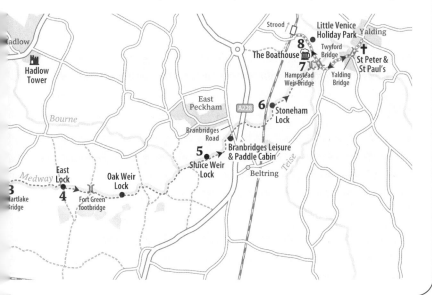), a pleasantly landscaped and shady compound that includes the Paddle Cabin (TN12 5HF; ⌀ paddlecabin.co.uk), where you can arrange paddleboard lessons. A few yards later, cross Branbridges Road and rejoin the path as it continues to shadow the Medway.

6 After about half a mile, pass the disused Stoneham Lock and continue walking alongside the river for about a mile towards Yalding and the prefab cottages adjacent to Twyford Bridge Marina. If you look at a map of this area, you'll see that Teapot Island sort of does look like a teapot; whether you see the resemblance or not, you won't be able to miss the more than 8,500 teapots on display in the kitschy museum here; the self-serve café (Hampstead Ln, ME18 6HG ⌀ teapotisland.co.uk ☉ Mar–Oct 10.00–16.00 Mon–Fri, 09.00–17.00 Sat & Sun; Nov–Feb 10.00–15.00 Mon–Fri, 09.00–16.00 Sat & Sun) is a welcome spot for a reviving cuppa and a slice of cake. If you fancy a beer or a freshly baked pizza, there's The Boathouse (ME18 6HG ⌀ boathouseyalding.co.uk ☉ noon–21.00 Mon–Thu, noon–22.00 Fri, 10.00–22.00 Sat, 10.00–20.00 Sun) ▶

Tonbridge to Yalding: along the Medway continued ...

on the opposite bank. Before moving on, admire the medieval stone Twyford Bridge from the adjacent Hampstead Weir Bridge.

7 From Hampstead Weir Bridge, turn right to cross the old stone bridge. Follow Hampstead Lane, then turn left at the junction with Lees Road, which will bring you into the village of Yalding. At the post office, turn left and cross Yalding's medieval stone bridge over the Beult River. There's a wonderful view of St Peter & St Paul's Church, which dates to the 13th century, from the bridge; in summer the water meadow here is a sea of golden yellow wild flowers. Retrace your steps back to Twyford Bridge and follow the Medway footpath north. It will soon join with Hampstead Lane.

8 Past a field with llamas, you'll reach Little Venice Holiday Park. Keep to Hampstead Lane as it veers left at Hampstead Lock shortly after and you'll soon arrive at Yalding train station, with connections at least once an hour back to Tonbridge (15 minutes) or to Strood (35 minutes).

There are couple of marked trails through these restored ancient wood- and heathlands which in spring are liberally sprinkled with bluebells, primroses and wood violets. One of the best times to visit is in autumn when you may be able to join a guided walk to help identify the many edible fungi that grow here: over a 1,000 different species of mushroom and toadstool have been found in Tudley Woods, including ceps, chantarelles, puffballs and blewits. The woods are also a haven for birds including the rare lesser spotted woodpecker, the nightjar and the marsh tit. Look out also for crossbills and mistle thrushes during winter walks.

¶¶ FOOD & DRINK

The Bakehouse at 124, 124 High St, Tonbridge ⬧ thebakehouse124.co.uk ◷ 08.00– 13.30 Wed–Sat. Pick up sandwiches made with their delicious sourdough bread and crème patissiere-filled 'cruffins' (a cross between a croissant and a muffin) at this award-winning bakery, steps away from the castle grounds.

The Chaser Inn Stumble Hill, Shipbourne ☏ 01732 810360 ⬧ thechaser.co.uk ◷ 09.30–22.30 Mon–Wed, 09.00–10.30 Thu, 09.00–23.00 Fri & Sat, 09.00–22.00 Sun. This multiroomed country pub with wooden floors and several log fires oozes atmosphere and is a good reason for making the trip out to Shipbourne from Tonbridge. The menu ranges from full English breakfasts to jackfruit cassoulet and vegan katsu curry.

Fuggles Beer Café 165 High St, Tonbridge ⬧ fugglesbeercafe.co.uk ◷ 16.00–23.00 Mon & Tue, noon–23.00 Wed, noon–midnight Thu–Sat, noon–22.30 Sun. Based in an old furniture maker's shop with a lovely tin-plate ceiling, at the top end of High Street, Fuggles offers over 20 different, and regularly changing, draught craft beers and real ciders, plus over 100 more in bottles. The food menu has eight different types of cheese toasties, including a vegan version.

Sixty Five MM Coffee Gilbert House, River Walk, Tonbridge ⊘ 65mmcoffee.co.uk
⊙ 08.30–15.30 Mon–Fri, 09.00–16.00 Sat & Sun. Just as 65mm film is considered superior to video for image quality, the coffee served at this riverside café is a cut above that served elsewhere in Tonbridge.

Verdigris 89 High St, Tonbridge ✆ 01732 366634 ⊘ verdigris-tonbridge.com
⊙ 08.00–14.00 Mon & Tue, 08.00–23.00 Wed–Sat, 08.00–21.00 Sun. Open for coffees and fresh pastries throughout the week and for lunch and dinner from Wednesday to Saturday, Verdigris is one of the most pleasant places to eat and drink in town. The menu changes seasonally and covers a classic range of dishes, including duck confit, gnocchi with wild mushrooms and a rib of beef for two to share. It's a classily decorated space with a vintage vibe and an outdoor terrace overlooking the Medway.

ROYAL TUNBRIDGE WELLS & SURROUNDS

🏠 **Hotel du Vin** (page 311), **The Mount Edgcumbe** (page 311), **One Warwick Park** (page 311), **Spa Hotel** (page 311) ⛺ **Feather Down Sunninglye Farm** (page 312)

> Tunbridge Wells is a place that to me appeared very singular. The country is all rock, and every part of it is either up or down hill ... the houses, too, are scattered about it in a strange, wild manner, as if they had been dropped by accident, for they form neither streets nor squares.
>
> Samuel Cripps, 1779

Granted its royal prefix in 1909 by Edward VII, this elegant spa resort owes its fortunes to the discovery of its iron-rich spring in the early 17th century. In the space of a handful of decades, royalty and fashionable society were flocking here to sip the restorative waters, said to cure everything from infertility to a 'moist brain', and to mix and mingle in a relaxing countryside setting. The spring may no longer be Tunbridge Wells' *raison d'être* but this comfortably off town continues to be a prime place to unwind with plenty of urban pleasures close at hand. Having had 400 years to hone its commercial acumen, it is one of the most attractive places to go shopping or have a meal in Kent.

The immediate proximity of natural landscapes to Tunbridge Wells is one of the town's most compelling attributes. Within a few minutes' walk of the town centre you can be surrounded by greenery and nature. There are plenty of great walking trails to follow and the nostalgic Spa Valley Railway is another way to connect to the extraordinary High Rocks and the gorgeous gardens of Groombridge Place. A little further afield, in Speldhurst, there's a church with superb stained-glass windows by the key Pre-Raphaelite artist Edward Burne-Jones.

16 ROYAL TUNBRIDGE WELLS

Local lore relates that in 1606 Lord Dudley North, while out riding from Eridge Castle, came across a spring bubbling with reddish brown waters. Recognising that this was a chalybeate (iron-rich) spring, the young nobleman began regularly drinking the waters to help restore his ailing health – the result of too much partying at court. Revived and back in London, Lord North shared his discovery, encouraging upper-class contemporaries to also search out this miraculous spring. The first royal visit to the spring was by Queen Henrietta Maria, wife of Charles I. She spent six weeks camped out here (there was no permanent accommodation at the site until much later in the century) in either 1629, having recently suffered the loss of her first-born child, or in 1630

THE COMMONS

Abutting The Pantiles are **The Commons** (twcommons.org) a nature-rich swathe of open grasslands and woods which has been largely protected from development since the early 18th century. An interlacing network of footpaths cuts across The Commons, leading further west of town to Rusthall Common and to fascinating sandstone outcrops known by descriptive names such as the Wellington Rocks and Toad Rock. These enigmatic rocks have been 65 million years in the making, dating to a time when southeast England was covered by the vast freshwater and brackish Wealden Lake. Sand and silt in this lake eventually compacted into the sandstone which, following the end of the Ice Age about 10,000 years ago, irregularly eroded to make the rocky outcrops seen today. Stone Age people built shelters under the rock overhangs, while during the Iron Age the outcrops were used to create defensive forts for the surrounding settlements. Noted as tourists attractions since the early 19th century, some of these giant knobbly boulders and cliffs are now popular with sports rock climbers – for more information on climbing and bouldering sites around Tunbridge Wells see southernsandstoneclimbs.co.uk.

after the successful birth of her son, the future Charles II. This led to the spring being briefly known as the Queen's Wells. The name that ended up sticking was Tunbridge Wells as Tonbridge (then spelled Tunbridge) was the nearest proper town. Fast-forward a century and Tunbridge Wells was well established, with Princess Victoria, later to be queen, another royal fan of the spa town.

"Work your way steadily uphill via High Street to its more modern suburbs to find the newly revamped museum The Amelia."

Much of what made Tunbridge Wells attractive to Regency and Victorian visitors endures today. The obvious place to begin is the pedestrianised Pantiles, the oldest part of town, after which you could work your way steadily uphill via High Street to its more modern suburbs to find the newly revamped museum The Amelia and the prestigious buildings and parks laid out by Decimus Burton. Alternatively, striking out northwest from The Pantiles, there are shaded strolls through the ancient woods of The Commons to the sandstone Wellington Rocks, and further afield to Toad Rock in Denny Bottom, about a mile west of central Tunbridge Wells.

Named after its paving of Wealden clay square tiles, **The Pantiles** has been Tunbridge Wells' epicentre of fashion and polite society for over 350 years. Distinguished by the colonnades added to the shopfronts in the 17th century, and its pedestrian upper and lower walks, it remains a place to indulge in eating, drinking, shopping and generally watching the world go by. At its northern most end is the chalybeate (pronounced 'ka-lee-bee-at') spring that made the town's fortunes. The rusty-coloured waters don't always flow but when they do (usually in the summer months) a 'dipper' in 18th-century costume is usually there to dispense them to anyone who wishes to find out what all the fuss was once about.

Opposite the north end of The Pantiles is the **Church of King Charles the Martyr** (3 Warwick Pk ⚲ kcmtw.org ☉ 11.00–13.00 Mon, Wed & Fri, plus Sun services). The London entrepreneur Thomas Neal, who recognised the commercial possibilities of the spring, commissioned the original 1684 chapel here. It was not only a place of worship but also somewhere for visitors to shelter when the weather turned nasty. The church has been much altered over the years, but has retained its original late 17th-century plasterwork ceiling with highly decorative domes made by John Wetherell and Henry Doogood, both of whom had gained their skills working with Sir Christopher Wren in London.

Chapel Place, behind the Church of King Charles the Martyr, leads on to High Street which climbs up towards the town's train station at the foot of Mount Pleasant Road. To the right and accessed off Mount Pleasant Avenue is **Claverley Grounds**. This park was laid out in 1825 as part of the private Calverley Estate, a project overseen by the eminent architect Decimus Burton to create a neighbourhood to rival the older Pantiles. Claverley is the location for the summer world music festival the **Tunbridge Wells Mela** (tunbridgewellsmela.com).

Burton also designed the nearby Trinity Church, a Gothic Revival-style building that today serves as the **Trinity Theatre** (Church Rd 01892 678678 trinitytheatre.net). Another grand historic building at this high end of town that has undergone a conversion of use is the old **Opera House** (88 Mount Pleasant Rd), now a Wetherspoons pub. Dating from 1902, the early Edwardian interior has largely been retained and on its walls you can read about some of the personalities with historical links to the town, including Richard 'Beau' Nash, Master of Ceremonies at Tunbridge Wells from 1735 until his death in 1765.

Opened in April 2022, **The Amelia** (Civic Way, off Mt Pleasant Rd theamelia.co.uk) is a new arts and culture centre that display the collections of Tunbridge Wells' old museum. Renamed after Amelia Scott, a local social reformer and women's suffrage campaigner, there are seven artworks integrated into the building's design, including gate panels that reference the history of ironmaking across the High Weald and a 'living-gallery' courtyard with plants and trees indigenous to the Kent countryside. The Amelia have also developed a free app, **Tales of Tunbridge Wells**, which you can download for an entertaining and informative audio-led walking trail through the town.

17 HIGH ROCKS NATIONAL MONUMENT

High Rocks Ln, TN3 9JJ 01892 515532 highrocks.co.uk 10.15–dusk Wed–Sun

Two miles west of Tunbridge Wells is a striking outcrop of sandstone rocks that has been astounding visitors for centuries. The site is believed to have been used by early Britons as a fortification against the Romans. James II is also said to have camped here when he visited Tunbridge Wells in 1670. The rocks, some split by deep gullies created by tension cracks, have an eerily mysterious atmosphere that has encouraged both diabolical legends and romantic notions. In the early 20th century, mountaineers training to climb Mt Everest used High Rocks.

Rock climbers continue to tackle the cliff faces with ropes and carabiners, but regular visitor access to the top of the rocks, about 30ft above the ground, is by a series of stone steps. The Aerial Way of wooden bridges provides an elevated path across the top of the rocks and vertigo-inducing views to the ground below. To access the eight-acre site, buy a ticket from the creeper-covered High Rocks pub and restaurant opposite the monument entrance. Weddings and other events are often held at this scenic venue, during which times the High Rocks themselves may be closed to the public – so it's best to call ahead before visiting. The Spa Valley Railway (see box, page 278) also stops here.

18 GROOMBRIDGE PLACE

Groombridge Hill, Groombridge TN3 9QG ⌀ 01892 861 444 ⌀ groombridgeplace.com
⊙ Apr–Oct 10.00–17.00 daily

The formal gardens of this 200-acre estate, 4½ miles west of Tunbridge Wells and a 15-minute walk from Groombridge station on the Spa Valley Railway, are a treat. It's also an enjoyable day out for families with young kids, who will most appreciate the playgrounds of its 'enchanted forest'.

There's been a moated manor house at Groombridge since the 13th century; the building that greets visitors today is from the mid 17th century when the property belonged to the barrister and architect Philip Packer who designed it along with Sir Christopher Wren. The gardens, also laid out by Packer, with help from eminent horticulturalist and diarist John Evelyn, are marvellous – fans of Peter Greenaway's *The Draughtsman's Contract* will recognise them from their appearance in that film. They include the weirdly shaped topiary of the 'Drunken Garden' (an inspiration to Conan Doyle who drew on Groombridge for the setting of his Sherlock Holmes novel *The Valley of Fear*), an Oriental Garden shaded by colourful acers, and the fragrant White Rose Garden, planted with 20 species of roses.

The Grom River, a tributary of the Medway, flows through the grounds – in the summer you can take a short canal boat ride along it to reach the Enchanted Forest section of the grounds. The woods here shade a fantastic range of kids' attractions such a cowboy fort and the shipwreck-themed Crusoe's World playground. There are also bird of prey displays by the UK Owl and Raptor Centre (⌀ owlandraptorcentre.co.uk) and chances to spot a menagerie of animals including deer, peacocks and a zedonk (a cross between a donkey and zebra).

19 SPELDHURST

A church has stood on the hill at this village, three miles west of Tunbridge Wells, for over 900 years. The current building, **St Mary's Church** (Southfields, TN3 0PD ⬧ speldhurstchurch.org), dates from 1871 and is particularly notable for its complete set of stained-glass windows made in the workshops of Morris & Co, ten of which feature designs by Edward Burne-Jones. The images of Christ, St Mary, the four evangelists and a host of angels playing musical instruments are remarkable, their colours rich and their design intricate.

Opposite the church is the **George & Dragon** (3 Speldhurst Hill, TN3 0NN ⬧ 01892 338549 ⬧ ganddspeldhurst.com ⬧ noon–23.00 Mon–Sat, noon–22.30 Sun), a 13th-century half-timbered inn, offering sandwiches and snacks as well as a more gourmet selection of dishes on its a la carte menu.

⟊ FOOD & DRINK

The Beacon Tea Garden Ln, TN3 9JH ⬧ 01892 524252 ⬧ illbemother.co.uk/thebeacon ⬧ bar 09.00–17.00 daily; restaurant noon–15.00 & 18.00–22.00 Thu–Sat, noon–16.00 Sun. One-and-a-half miles west of the town centre, this classy restaurant and bar occupies a stunning Arts and Crafts house amid 17 acres of gardens and woodlands. On a sunny day, a meal on their outdoor terraces is a delight. Dishes might include pigeon or venison,

SPA VALLEY RAILWAY

The **Spa Valley Railway** (⬧ 01892 300141 ⬧ spavalleyrailway.co.uk) is a volunteer-run, standard-gauge heritage line connecting Tunbridge Wells with Eridge, just across the border in Sussex. Originally part of the 19th-century East Grinstead, Groombridge and Tunbridge Wells Railway, the 5½-mile route starts from Tunbridge Wells West station, a few minutes' walk west of The Pantiles. The main intermediate station is at the village of Groombridge, from which you can walk to Groombridge Place (page 277). There's also a station at High Rocks (page 276), although services don't always stop there. Trains run mainly on weekends with additional weekday services during holiday seasons; there are no trains at all in November and January. A one-way journey takes 30 minutes.

Special trips include afternoon tea or a ploughman's lunch, or involve carriages being pulled by a steam locomotive. Also popular are their Easter and Christmas themed services and the Real Ale and Cider Festival, held over a weekend in October, when scores of local beers and ciders can be sampled at the Tunbridge Wells and Groombridge stations.

with the meat sourced from ethical meat and game suppliers. They also offer a creative vegetarian set menu.

The Black Dog 20 Camden Rd ✆ 01892 549543 ⌂ blackdogcafetw.co.uk ◷ 08.00–16.00 Wed–Sat, 09.00–15.00 Sun. A stalwart on the Camden Road dining and shopping strip in the upper part of Tunbridge Wells, the Black Dog belies its name by aiming for a sunny Aussie-café-style disposition. Drinks are made with beans from the London roasters Monmouth Coffee and dishes range from toasted banana bread to wild rice and barley grain bowls topped with falafel or battered haloumi.

Hattons 38 The Pantiles ✆ 01892 540555 ⌂ hattonsrtwstore.co.uk ◷ 09.00–16.00 Tue–Sat, 10.00–16.00 Sun. It's invidious to choose between the many appealing dining options along The Pantiles, but my default position is Hattons for its pleasant interior and always appealing menu, which includes plenty of vegetarian and vegan options such as a spiced pumpkin and lentil roll or their aubergine laksa. In the evenings, next door at number 40, they operate the slick wine and cocktail bar **The Wine Rooms** (⌂ thewineroomstw.com).

Juliets 54 High St ✆ 01892 522931 ⌂ julietsandmore.com ◷ 08.30–16.00 Tue–Fri, 08.30–17.00 Sat, 09.00–16.00 Sun. Going strong for over a decade, Juliets is the preferred High Street pitstop for its smoothies and homemade tonics, good coffee, big breakfasts and scrumptious slices of cake served on vintage china crockery.

The Mount Edgcumbe The Common ✆ 01892 618854 ⌂ themountedgcumbe.com ◷ noon–22.30 Mon–Sat, noon–22.00 Sun. On a sunny summer's day there's nothing better than sipping a local Kent beer or cider in the Edgcumbe's lush beer garden. Step inside the cosy bar to discover a lounge nook occupying a hand-chiselled sandstone cave that dates back at least 400 years.

The Plant Base 11 Camden Rd ✆ 01892 548870 ⌂ theplantbase.co.uk ◷ 10.00–15.00 & 18.00–23.00 Wed–Fri, 09.00–15.00 & 18.00–23.00 Sat, 09.00–15.00 Sun. Getting rave reviews for its wholly plant-based menu, this café is just the right side of hippy. In the evening they serve tapas-style plates that can include items like Korean fried cauliflower, king oyster mushroom scallops and blue corn tostada.

Sankey's The Old Fish Market The Pantiles ✆ 01892 511422 ⌂ sankeys.co.uk/the-old-fishmarket ◷ noon–midnight Wed–Sat. Whether its Dover sole from Brighton, crab and lobster from Cornwall or oysters from Essex, you can be sure that all the fish and seafood served at Sankey's is freshly caught and expertly prepared. The charming black and white pavilion the restaurant occupies is indeed the Pantile's original fish market. The same management run the **Seafood Kitchen & Bar** (39 Mount Ephraim) at the top end of town.

Thackeray's 85 London Rd ✆ 01892 511921 ⌂ thackerays-restaurant.co.uk ◷ noon–14.30 & 18.30–22.00 Wed–Sat, noon–14.30 Sun. The writer William Makepeace Thakeray stayed at this New England-style clapboard house during a visit to Tunbridge Wells in 1860. The restaurant that now occupies the house, and which is named in his honour, is an elegant space with affordable set lunch menu of French inspired cooking. Their meat-free menu includes imaginative options like avocado and pecorino tart and stuffed globe artichoke.

The Warren 5a High St ✆ 01892 328191 🖰 thewarren.restaurant ◷ noon–15.00 & 16.00–23.00 Mon–Sat, noon–16.00 Sun. Glittering chandeliers and huge arched orangery-style windows set the glamorous tone for this restaurant which showcases produce from the owner's Crowborough Estate. As well as goat, venison, wild boar and rabbit, the menu offers mussels fresh from Hastings or vegan options like a Hungarian goulash with dumplings and sauerkraut.

🛍 SHOPPING

The Pantiles hosts a broad range of retailers, from antique emporiums to camera and kitchenware shops – for a full list see 🖰 thepantiles.com. High Street is strong on fashion boutiques and art galleries. Major high-street chains cluster in the top end of town in and around the Royal Victoria Place (🖰 royalvictoriaplace.com) shopping mall.

Halls Bookshop 20–22 Chapel Pl 🖰 hallsbookshop.com ◷ 09.30–17.30 Mon–Sat. Halls has been in the business of buying and selling second-hand books in Tunbridge Wells since 1898. Their selection is brilliant and includes rare and collectable items from Adrian Harrington Rare Books (🖰 harringtonbooks.co.uk).

The Silver Sheep 10–12 Chapel Pl 🖰 thesilversheep.co.uk ◷ 10.00–17.30 Mon–Sat. Silversmith Caroline Smith and knitwear designer Sylvia Kus search out the products of fellow Kent craftspeople for their diverse stock which ranges from handmade soap and ceramics to colourful bedspreads and sustainable knitwear.

FURTHER INTO THE HIGH WEALD

🏠 **Bramley House** (page 311), **The Vineyard** (page 311)

East of Tunbridge Wells, deeper into the Kentish Weald, are a couple of attractive villages – Goudhurst and Lamberhurst – both suitable bases for surrounding attractions, including the romantic ruins of Bayham Old Abbey, the gardens of Scotney Castle and the nature parks of Bewl Water and Bedgebury National Pinetum.

20 GOUDHURST

Ten miles east of Tunbridge Wells, the A262 rises steeply to the hilltop village of Goudhurst, crowned by **St Mary's Church** (Church Rd, TN17 1BL 🖰 gkchurch.org.uk ◷ 09.00–18.00 daily). There's been a church here since the 12th century, and on Saturday and Sunday afternoons between Easter and mid-July it's possible to climb its tower and take in the panoramic views of the surrounding countryside. In 1747 the church's graveyard was the scene of a violent battle between the notorious Hawkhurst Gang of smugglers and the local militia. Subsequently, the body of the gang's leader Thomas Kingsmill was gibbeted in the village – he was already dead, having been executed in London after his capture. From the centre of Goudhurst, hikers can follow country footpaths through orchards and woods for about five miles east towards Cranbrook (page 285) or south to Bedgebury National Pinetum & Forest (page 282).

21 BAYHAM OLD ABBEY

Furnace Ln, Little Bayham TN3 8LJ ⊙ Apr–Sept 10am–17.00 Tue–Sun; Oct 10.00–16.00 Tue–Sun; English Heritage

On the border of Kent and Sussex, six miles east of Tunbridge Wells in the Tiese River valley, are the atmospheric ruins of this medieval abbey. Founded around 1208 for the Catholic religious order the Premonstratensians, the abbey grew to be a substantial complex by the time it was dissolved in 1525. In 1805, when the renowned landscape architect Humphrey Rempton was hired to redesign the grounds of the Bayham Estate, he insisted the abbey's romantic golden sandstone ruins remain a key feature. Today they are an evocative place to wander and imagine medieval monastic life. Look for the splendid 200-year-old beech tree growing atop a ruined wall at the east end of the site – it was on the Woodland Trust's shortlist for tree of the year in 2020.

22 SCOTNEY CASTLE

Lamberhurst TN3 8JN ✆ 01892 893820 ⊙ house Mar–Oct 11.00–17.00 daily; Nov–Feb 11.00–15.00 daily; gardens Mar–Oct 10.00–17.00 daily; Nov–Feb 0.00–16.00 daily; National Trust

A country retreat for Prime Minister Margaret Thatcher, who rented a flat in the grounds during her time in office, Scotney offers not one but two castles (neither of which were ever a fortress): the 'old castle', a 14th-century manor house set on an island in a small lake, and the Tudor Revival house designed by Anthony Salvin for the estate's owner Edward Hussey III in 1837. It was Hussey who had the vision for the spectacularly picturesque gardens that are Scotney's pride and joy. Reflected in the surrounding lake, the partially ruined old castle, adorned with clematis, roses or wisteria depending on the season, looks like an illustration from a fairy tale. The gardens are at their most romantic and colourful in autumn when mature maple trees blaze orange and red. In spring, rhododendrons, azaleas and kalmia add their frothy blooms across the Quarry Garden, created in the hollow left after sandstone was hacked from the ground to make the 19th-century castle. There's also an octagonal shaped walled garden for produce and cut flowers, and a Hobbit-like thatched icehouse. You can download a map outlining three walking trails around the surrounding 780-acre estate which includes woodlands and hop gardens from the National Trust website.

23 BEWL WATER

Bewlbridge Ln, Lamberhurst TN3 8JH ✎ 01892 890000 ◌ bewlwater.co.uk ⊙ car park 08.00–17.00 daily; café 10.00–15.00 Mon–Fri, 10.00–16.00 Sat & Sun

Created in 1975 when the Bewl River was dammed, this reservoir is the largest body of water in southeastern England. Covering 770 acres on the border of Kent and Sussex, the reservoir is incredibly scenic. Around its perimeter runs a 12½-mile route that takes about six hours to walk or 2½ to cycle. The visitor centre, which includes a café, is on the Kent side of the reservoir, ten miles southeast of Tunbridge Wells. Apart from walking and cycling, the reservoir is a popular destination for a variety of water sports, including sailing, canoeing and paddleboarding, plus laser-tagging in a woodland area and fishing (there are trout, pike and perch in the water), with boats available for hire from the visitors' centre.

24 BEDGEBURY NATIONAL PINETUM & FOREST

Bedgebury Rd, Goudhurst TN17 2SJ ✎ 01580 879820 ◌ bedgeburypinetum.org.uk ⊙ 08.00–dusk (20.00 in summer) daily

Bedgebury's world-beating and incredibly varied collection of conifers (cone-bearing trees) covers some 350 acres, 11 miles southeast of Tunbridge Wells. They account for around 70% of the 10,000 trees that grow in this lush forest nestled in the Dallimore Valley which is pitted with six lakes and ponds and laced with hiking trails. The collection includes many rare and endangered species as well magnificent examples of giant Californian redwoods, some topping 110ft, which have been growing here since 1935. The first exotic species were planted in 1836 by the Beresfords who owned the then private estate and wished

1 Bedgebury National Pinetum & Forest. 2 Oast houses at Lamberhurst.
3 Goudhurst village. ▶

to flaunt their wealth and show off to visitors. Kew Gardens and the Forestry Commission teamed up to manage the pinetum in 1925 and since 1965 it has been run solely by the commission. The forest also includes off-road cycling trails, a café with a beautiful lakeside view and the Go Ape treetop challenge adventure course (🖮 goape.co.uk). Highly recommended is an autumn hike out to Marshal's Lake at the northern edge of the forest, where the reflections of the deciduous swap cypress and dawn redwood in the water is stunning – it takes around an hour to complete this 1½-mile round-trip walk from the visitor centre.

🍴 FOOD & DRINK

The Poet at Matfield Maidstone Rd, Matfield TN12 7JH 🖉 01892 722416 🖮 thepoetatmatfield.co.uk 🕑 noon–18.00 Fri–Sun. Named in honour of the World War I poet Siegfried Sassoon who lived for a time in Matfield, six miles northwest of Goudhurst this rustic pub restaurant is helmed by South African chef Petrus Madutlela. He cooks up beautifully plated, gourmet grub that ranges from a traditional roast fillet of Scotch beef with all the trimmings to a UK brie-style cheese and Jerusalem artichoke pie.

The Small Holding Ranters Ln, Kilndown TN17 2SG 🖉 01892 890105 🖮 thesmallholding. restaurant 🕑 noon–15.00 & 17.30–20.30 Wed–Sat, noon–16.00 Sun. Award-winning chef Will Devlin and his team tend a one-acre fresh-produce plot beside this charming restaurant in an old village pub, 2½ miles southwest of Goudhurst. The menu changes on a daily basis and you can opt for either the full ten small courses or the smaller seven-course lunch.

The Vineyard The Down, Lamberhurst TN3 8EU 🖉 01892 890222 🖮 elitepubs.com/ the-vineyard 🕑 11.30–23.30 Mon–Fri, 09.00–23.30 Sat, 09.00–22.00 Sun. Close by Lamberhurst's vineyards, this smart modern pub with rooms occupies a 17th-century inn. The menu is wide ranging and fairly priced with options including fish and chips, steaks, artisan wood-fired pizzas and organic quinoa burgers.

SISSINGHURST & SURROUNDS

🏠 **The Milk House** (page 311), **Sissinghurst Castle Farmhouse** (page 311), **The West House** (page 311)

The village of Sissinghurst, 17 miles east of Tunbridge Wells and five miles south of the nearest train station at Staplehurst, is famous for the inspirational gardens laid out around the Tudor-era house Sissinghurst Castle. It's also close by the attractive village of **Biddenden** (🖮 biddendenkent.co.uk) with its row of half-timbered medieval houses down one side of the main street that were once used for weaving cloth by

WATER LANE

Deep in the Kentish Weald near the village of Hawkhurst is **Water Lane** (Walled Garden, Water Ln, Hawkhurst TN18 5DH ⌂ waterlane.net ☉ 08.00–17.00 Wed–Fri, 10.00–16.30 Sat & Sun), a restaurant, shop and organic kitchen and flower garden started in 2021 by entrepreneurs Nick Selby and Ian James, founders of upmarket North London grocers Melrose & Morgan. Their new project is to revive a gone-to-seed, one-acre Victorian walled garden on the grounds of the Tongswood Estate (now an independent school). Inside the garden are 13 Grade II-listed glasshouses, four of which have already been restored, and including ones designed to grow melons, cucumbers, pelargoniums and peaches. In the colder months, the restaurant tables are housed in the Carnation House, while in the summer you can sit outside within touching distance of the no-dig, organic beds from which head chef Jed Wrobel picks seasonal produce for the restaurant. From summer to autumn the flower beds are awash with cosmos, dahlias, sweet peas and zinnias, among other decorative and fragrant blooms, while architectural perennials such as acid green euphorbias add interest in spring. Selby and James reckon it will take a decade to bring this remarkable walled garden and all its greenhouses back to full glory by adding back features such as espaliered fruit trees. In the meantime, this is a delightful venue for a meal, or to attend one of their workshops on topics such as pottery, floral styling and calligraphy.

Flemish artisans who settled in the area during the reign of Edward III; and **Cranbrook** where the **Union Mill** (The Hill ⌂ unionmill.org.uk), a smock windmill built in 1814, stands atop a hill, its brilliant white sails and upper section a guiding beacon above the old market town's roofline. At the time of research the mill was closed for renovations.

25 SISSINGHURST CASTLE & GARDEN

Biddenden Rd, TN17 2AB ✆ 01580 710700 ⌂ nationaltrust.org.uk/visit/kent/sissinghurst-castle-garden ☉ castle Apr–early Nov 10.00–17.30 daily; early Nov–Mar 10.00–16.00; gardens Apr–early Nov 11.00–17.00 daily; early Nov–Mar 11.00–15.30 daily; National Trust

> I fell in love at first sight … It was Sleeping Beauty's Garden: but a garden crying out for rescue.
> Vita Sackville-West

Having taken no interest in gardening before her marriage in 1913 to the diplomat and diarist Harold Nicholson, the writer Vita Sackville-West proved to have remarkably green fingers. The couple had already

worked together on an experimental garden at Long Barn near Knole, Vita's ancestral home. When they bought Sissinghurst Castle in 1930 they were ready for an altogether more epic project. The estate, which had roots as a Saxon pig farm, was in Vita's words 'squalid to a degree' with 'a tangle of weeds everywhere.' It took three years of clearing before planting of the garden could begin, its overall design conceived by Harold. The result is one of the high-water marks of 20th-century British garden design, a magnet for garden lovers from around the world, and a pure pleasure for any visitor.

Sir John Baker, one of Vita's ancestors, built Sissinghurst's original castle around a pair of courtyards in the 1530s. It did service as a prison for 3,000 French sailors in the mid 18th century, an experience so traumatic for the property that two-thirds of it had to be demolished afterwards. This left mainly the long Elizabethan gatehouse, a moat and a separate brick tower which Vita would later make her private sanctum. Climb to the top of this tower to gain a bird's-eye view of the garden's five-acre layout – a series of mainly colourblocked and themed 'rooms' separated by neatly clipped hedges and old brick walls, punctuated by openings that allow tantalising glimpses of what lies beyond.

The renowned White Garden, as its name suggests, is planted with gladioli, irises, pompom dahlias and Japanese anemones, all in various shades of white. The Rose Garden has one of the world's finest collections of old garden roses and is a heady sensory delight when they bloom in late June. In the South Cottage Garden, look out for the early-summer-flowering rose Mme Alfred Carriere; it was planted at Sissinghurst by Vita and Harold, on the day their offer to buy the property was accepted. The South Cottage is where Harold had his study and library and where Vita arranged cut flowers – the rooms here have been respectfully preserved, as has the Long Library occupying part of the gatehouse. At every turn it is astounding what the self-taught couple achieved, but it's worth noting that, with the likes of Edwin Lutyens and Gertrude Jekyll as their friends, the Nicholsons did have the best horticultural and landscape expertise to call on.

Vita and Harold first opened the gardens to the public in 1938 and the entire 460-acre estate was handed over to the National Trust in 1967.

◀ **1** Sissinghurst Castle & Garden. **2** Union Mill, Cranbrook. **3** Biddenden.
4 Tenterden station.

Head gardeners since then have done an incredible job of balancing respect for Vita and Harold's masterplan, alongside contemporary innovations and the demands of maintaining a one of the UK's most popular gardens. In recent years, Delos, a half-acre garden of Mediterranean planting that evokes the thirsty, sun-drenched landscape of the Greek islands, has been added. It's been a controversial enhancement, but the inspiration was a failed 1930s project by Vita and Harold, and the modern interpretation is a triumph, with naturalistic layering of cypress, fig and cork oaks sprouting from the rocks and gravel and alongside grasses, thyme, field poppies and drought tolerant wild flowers.

Beyond the showpiece gardens, there's more than sufficient to occupy a full day here, from taking time to enjoy the public rooms and regularly changing exhibitions to meandering around the kitchen garden where

WINERIES NEAR SISSINGHURST

Established in 1969, **Biddenden Vineyards** (Gribble Bridge Ln, Biddenden TN27 8DF ✎ 01580 291726 ☼ biddendenvineyards. com ☉ shop Jan–Apr & Oct–early Nov 09.00–17.00 Mon–Fri, 11.00–16.00 Sat; May–Sep & early Nov–Dec 09.00–17.00 Mon–Fri, 10.00–17.00 Sat, 11.00–16.00 Sun), 1½ miles south of Biddenden. is Kent's oldest commercial vineyard. Twelve different varieties of grape are grown in its vineyards, the main varietal being Ortega, used for its white wines. Originally home to a 40-acre apple orchard, 23 acres have been given over to vines from which an award-winning range of white, red, rosé and sparkling wines are made. They also still harvest apples and pears to make still and sparkling ciders and farm-pressed juices. Self-guided tours of the estate run from April to early November and include a tasting flight of three of their wines; there are two routes to choose from which take either 40 or 20 minutes to complete.

Balfour Winery (Hush Heath Estate, Five Oak Ln, Staplehurst TN12 0HT ✎ 01622 832794 ☼ balfourwinery.com), five miles northwest of Sissinghurst, was set up in 2002. Five years later its Balfour Brut Rosé 2004 became the first English wine to win a gold medal and the trophy at the International Wine Challenge. Its state-of-the-art winery stands next to the spacious and modern cellar door with a shop, tasting rooms and a rooftop terrace, where you can match drinks with sharing platters of Kentish charcuterie, cheeses and locally grown vegetables. From the cellar door, you can walk one of two trails, both of which cross a wild flower meadow, ancient oak woodlands and apple orchards, to their vineyards planted with Pinot Noir, Pinot Meunier and Chardonnay varietals. See their website for details of monthly dining club events where you can enjoy Balfour wines paired with a seasonal four-course gourmet meal.

food is grown for Sissinghurst's café and following a three-mile walk around the wider estate. For cyclists, the National Trust website has a downloadable map of a 6½-mile route to Sissinghurst from Staplehurst train station.

🍴 FOOD & DRINK

Frankie's Farmshop Clapper Ln, Staplehurst TN12 0JT 🔗 01580 890713 🖥 frankiesfarmshop.co.uk 🕐 09.00–16.00 daily. The best reason to see a bit of Staplehurst on your way to or from Sissinghurst is the chance to drop by this superbly stocked farm shop, one of the best in Kent, that grew from the same team's plant nursery. There's lots of great take-away food for picnics, while booking is essential for the indoor dining at the attached café.

The Milk House The Street, Sissinghurst TN17 2JG 🔗 01580 720200 🖥 themilkhouse.co.uk 🕐 09.00–23.00 Mon–Sat, 09.00–22.00 Sun. The village's old coaching inn is the venue for this gastropub with rooms that has a snazzy contemporary vibe. Service is warm and friendly, and the menu offers a tempting range of affordable mains for vegetarians and vegans as well as meat lovers.

The Three Chimneys Hareplain Rd, Biddenden TN27 8LW 🔗 01580 291472 🖥 thethreechimneys.co.uk 🕐 11.30–23.00 Mon–Sat, noon–22.30 Sun. Midway between Biddenden and Sissinghurst, this award-winning country pub offers bags of convivial atmosphere, an excellent restaurant with five different dining areas, and comfortable overnight rooms. They source food and drinks from local suppliers where possible.

The West House 8 High St, Biddenden TN27 8AH 🔗 01580 291341 🖥 thewesthouserestaurant.co.uk. 🕐 noon–13.45 & 19.00–21.30 Thu & Fri, 19.00–21.30 Sat, noon–14.30 Sun. Graham Garrett switched his drumsticks and playing in stadium-filling rock and roll bands in the 1980s for heading up the kitchen at this multi-accoladed restaurant based in one of Biddenden's 16th-century weaver's cottages. You can choose between short and long multi-course menus (with one that is fully vegetarian) that showcase local, seasonal produce.

26 TENTERDEN & SURROUNDS

You may wonder why Tenterden, so inland from the coast, was once part of the historic confederation of Cinque Ports (see box, page 167). However, in medieval times ships could dock on an estuary of the Rother River in nearby Smallhythe. Back then, Tenterden was a prosperous town, its original fortunes built on the wool trade. Branded the 'Jewel of the Weald', it's still a choice place to live, notable for its handsome, tree-lined and unusually broad High Street, off which is located **St Mildred's Church** (⊕ tenterdencofe.co.uk ⊙ Apr–Oct 08.45–17.00 Mon–Sat; Nov–Mar 08.45–16.00 Mon–Sat) which dates back to at least the 12th century. Its 125ft tower, built in 1461 of Bethersden marble, a locally quarried limestone, can be seen for miles around and was once used a navigation beacon. Its nave is roofed with wooden shingles and there's much fine Victorian stained glass to admire.

Three minutes' walk north of High Street along Station Road is Tenterden Town Station, the starting point for the **Kent and East Sussex Railway** (✆ 01580 765155 ⊕ kesr.org.uk). Running regular passenger services from 1900 until the 1950s, the line was part of the light railway empire built and promoted by Colonel Holman Fred Stephens. Today, mostly between Easter and the end of October, 50-minute trips are run along the 10½-mile line through the Rother Valley to medieval Bodiam Castle in Sussex. The railway's vintage train sets include steam and diesel locos pulling carriages, some with old-fashioned family compartments. Book ahead for dinner in their plush Weadlen Pullman dining car, departing from Tenterden most Saturday evenings from April to December. Colonel Stephens Railway Museum is open on days the trains are running. The detailed exhibitions here record the career and achievements of one of the early 20th century's light railway visionaries.

Just under three miles south Tenterden, the hamlet of Smallhythe is home to the 25 acres of **Chapel Down Vineyard** (Small Hythe Rd, TN30 7NG ✆ 01580 766111 ⊕ chapeldown.com ⊙ 10.00–17.00 daily). It's one of Kent's longest-running and most sophisticated winemaking establishments with an extensive shop showcasing their own bottles and those of other wineries, two tasting rooms and a Michelin Guide-listed restaurant, The Swan Wine Kitchen (page 292), with terrace seating overlooking the estate. The varietal grown here is Bacchus, which is like a Sauvignon Blanc grape but more suited to the local terroir. They also have Chardonnay wines and a good range of crowd-pleasing bubbly, some of which you will get to sample on their various vineyard tour and tasting experiences.

A short walk south of the vineyard is **Smallhythe Place** (TN30 7NG ✆ 01580 762334; ⊙ 11.00–17.00 Wed–Sun; National Trust), a wonky-beamed, early 16th-century house that was owned by superstar Victorian actress Ellen Terry. She bought the property in 1899 and used it as her country retreat until her death in 1928. It's easy to see what appealed to Terry about this idyllic cottage, surrounded by pretty gardens that bloom with daffodils in early spring, and roses and wild flowers later in the summer. As dramatic in her private life as she was on stage, Terry was married three times and had two illegitimate children with her lover Edward Godwin, one of whom, Edith (Edy) Craig, lived next door to Smallhythe Place in the Priest House. Craig followed her mother into the theatre world as a costume designer, director and producer. She also was a suffragette and a lesbian who set up house with two lovers. It was Craig who preserved Terry's home as an intimate and revealing museum to her mother, and who converted the 17th-century thatched barn in the garden into a theatre. Performances are held here throughout the year, keeping alive Terry and Craig's artistic passion.

Four miles west of Tenterden, **Hole Park** (Benenden Rd, Rolvenden TN17 4JA ✆ 01580 241344 ⌖ holepark.com ☉ end Mar–early Jun 11.00–18.00 daily, mid-Jun–Sep 11.00–18.00 Wed & Thu, Oct 11.00–18.00 Wed, Thu & Sun) is open at certain times of the year for visitors to enjoy its 16 acres of gardens. These were originally laid out in the early 19th century and refashioned in 1911 after the 200-acre estate was bought by Colonel Arthur Barham, whose descendants continue live here. The two seasons in which Hole Park shines are spring and autumn. Head here between April and May to wander through woodland dells that are painted purple with bluebells and to enjoy frothy displays of wisteria, magnolias and rhododendrons. October brings on a blaze of reds, golds and browns as the garden's deciduous trees shed their leaves in the most spectacular fashion. The house itself is private but there are teas and light lunches available in the Coach House Tea Room.

🍴 FOOD & DRINK

ârtisserie 53 High St, TN30 6BD ⌖ artisserie.uk ☉ 09.00–16.00 Tue–Sat, 10.00–14.00 Sun. Master pastry chef Chris Underwood has worked patisserie magic at some of Britain's top restaurants. His luxurious mini cakes are delicious and gorgeous to look at, while his Old IPA loaf (a mixture of two French flours with fresh apple juice and local craft brewer Old Dairy's ale) is a chewy, crumby beauty.

The Nutmeg Delicatessen & Coffee Shop 3 Sayers Ln, Tenterden TN30 6BW 🛑 ☉ 08.30–17.00 Mon–Fri, 09.00–17.00 Sat, 10.00–16.00 Sun. Tucked off High Street, on the shopping arcade leading Waitrose, this is one of Tenterden's best cafés, great for coffee, cake or cheese toastie snack, as well as for picking up local artisan food treats from independent producers.

Old Dairy Brewery Tenterden Station Estate, Station Rd, Tenterden TN30 6HE
⌀ olddairybrewery.com ⊙ 10.00–18.00 Mon & Tue, 10.00–21.00 Wed & Thu, 10.00–22.00
Fri & Sat, 11.00–18.00 Sun. See ad, page 304. Nine different types of cask and keg ales are
sold in the taproom of this local brewery which also offer tours of their brewing set up. Street
food trucks set up outside on Friday and Saturday evenings.
The Swan Wine Kitchen Chapel Down Vineyard, Smallhythe TN30 7NG ✆ 01580
761616 ⌀ illbemother.co.uk ⊙ noon–15.00 Wed, noon–15.00 & 18.00–21.00 Thu–Sat,
noon–16.00 Sun. This relaxed, modern restaurant has inventive and tasty dishes on its menu
like orange-cured pigeon breast, glazed pak choi, and apple calvados sponge – all with
recommended wine pairings from Chapel Down's cellars.

MAIDSTONE & SURROUNDS

🏠 **Chilston Park Hotel** (page 310), **The Friars** (page 311), **Leeds Castle** (page 311)
While not an obvious destination like other large Kent towns such as
Canterbury and Tunbridge Wells, Maidstone is far from charmless.
Settled by the Romans and Normans, the town grew to prominence in
medieval times. Archbishops of Canterbury rested here on their journeys
to and from London, leading to the construction of the Archbishop's
Palace on the banks of the Medway in the 13th century. At the time of
research, the Palace served as a registry office for weddings, although
its use may change during 2022 when the building's lease comes up
for renewal. Today, the town's key draws are its superb museum and
riverside network of parks. A few miles northwest of the centre, along
the Medway, is the picturesque village of Aylesford, home to a tranquil
and historic Carmelite priory, while to the east of Maidstone are the
extensive grounds of storied Leeds Castle.

27 MAIDSTONE

Spread along the banks of the Medway as it flows through gaps in the
Greensand Hills to the south and the North Downs to the northwest,
Maidstone is Kent's county town. Its compact centre, served by two
train stations (Maidstone East and Maidstone Barracks, which are
on different branch lines), presents a hodgepodge of architecture and
historical eras, which while not unattractive can be jarring. Clusters
of handsome medieval buildings, such as those around the riverside

1 Devil's Kneading Trough. **2** Leeds Castle. **3** Aylesford. ▶

Archbishop's Palace, bang up against bland modern shopping arcades like the open-air Fremlin Walk and The Mall.

This collision of architectural styles is epitomised by the **Maidstone Museum** (St Faith's St ☏ 01622 602838 ⌖ museum.maidstone.gov.uk ☉ 10.00–16.00 Wed–Sat; school hols Mon–Sat), where the Tudor-period Chillington Manor forms the core of a complex that has matching Victorian gallery wings and a boxy contemporary extension clad in gold shingles. While architectural purists may be horrified, the museum's eclectic exterior design is a fitting introduction to the marvellously diverse collection of objects it houses. Thanks to generous donations by dedicated Victorian collectors, the displays range from fossilised dinosaur bones and a chair Henry VIII may have sat in, to a liquorice-allsorts-print dress from the 1960s and a 2,700-year-old mummy. That Egyptian preserved body, the only one of its kind in Kent, is called Ta-Kush and you can look her in her blackened and ancient shrivelled face as she lies, mostly unwrapped, in her decorated inner coffin. The museum's collection of Japanese arts and prints, the third largest in the UK, includes samurai armour, beautiful lacquerware and rustic everyday ceramics. There's also a brilliant assortment of ethnographic crafts and items gathered by Julius Brenchley, a Victorian gentleman explorer who, among many other things, brought a handsome 30ft canoe from the Solomon Islands back to Maidstone.

How much fun, you may wonder, would it be to take that canoe out for paddle on the nearby Medway. Instead, satisfy your slow-boat cravings with a trip down the river to Allington Lock on the **Kentish Lady** (☏ 01622 753740 ⌖ kentishlady.co.uk). Their cruises run between Easter and early October and on Tuesdays they usually offer an itinerary that include access to Allington Castle (⌖ allington-castle.com), a 13th-century property next to the river that is otherwise not open to the public.

There's lovely riverside walking and cycling routes along the Medway, including a 6½-mile towpath route between Barming to the south and Aylesford to the north: for full details see **Maidstone River Park** (⌖ maidstoneriverpark.co.uk).

ᵮᵮ FOOD & DRINK

Esquires Café 23 Gabriel's Hill ⌖ esquirescoffee.co.uk ☉ 08.30–17.00 Mon–Sat, 09.30–16.00 Sun. This is the Maidstone branch of a global café franchise that only sells organic and

Fairtrade coffee. It's one of the town's most attractively designed cafés, with tasty treats such as a hummus and falafel sandwich or luscious home-baked cakes to go with the generous beverage served.

The Old Boat Café Fairmeadow ⏦ theoldboatcafe.com ⊙ Apr–Oct 10.00–16.00 daily. You'll find this restored, former horse-drawn narrowboat serving as a seasonal floating café beside the Medway between the town's two main road bridges. Seating is all outdoors and the location can't be beaten. Tuck into a 'boatman's breakfast', a fry-up including traditional pork sausages from nearby Speldhurst, or a plate of vegan pancakes topped with banana, blueberries and maple syrup.

28 AYLESFORD

The rumble of traffic from the nearby M20 is the soundtrack to a riverside amble along the Medway to the ancient village of Aylesford, four miles north of Maidstone. The village's seven-arched Kentish

THE MEDWAY MEGALITHS

One of the earliest known examples of constructions using stones in Britain are Kent's Medway Megaliths. These are the remains of chambered long barrows (oblong earthen tumuli encasing a stone chamber) dating from the early Neolithic period, some 5,000 years ago. Thought to have been used as tombs, they are divided into two clusters, one west of the Medway River and the other to the east on Blue Bell Hill, about two miles northeast of Aylesford.

The largest and least damaged of the Megaliths is **Coldrum Long Barrow** (ME19 5EG; National Trust), set on a small hill, about a one-mile walk east of the North Downs village of Trottiscliffe (pronounced 'Trosley'). Excavations at the site have found the bones of over 22 people, more than likely all close family members. Annually, at dawn on 1 May, the Hartley Morris Men (⏦ hartleymorrismen.wixsite.com/home)

visit the stones to dance and welcome the sun rising over the North Downs.

Footpaths heading north from Aylesford, via the hamlet of Eccles, lead up Blue Bell Hill to **Kit's Coty House** (off Chatham Road, ME20 7EZ; English Heritage). Four large slabs of sarsen, a local fine-grained sandstone, form a crude shelter that was once the main chamber of this burial mound. The monument's name possibly derives from the old British word *kaitom* or *keiton*, meaning forest, with coty being a tomb – hence 'forest tomb'. It's surrounded by spiky metal railings erected in the late 19th century to prevent vandalism (there's plenty of old graffiti carved into the stones). While no Stonehenge, what Kit's Coty House lacks in scale it makes up for in its location: a bucolic surround of wild flower meadows and wheat fields with panoramic views across the Medway Valley.

ragstone bridge has straddled the river since the 14th century. With the High Street's 16th-century timber-framed buildings and the stone tower of St Peter & St Paul's Church in the background, it is a quintessential English country scene – one that J W M Turner sketched in 1798.

The Grade-I listed pedestrian bridge is about a half-mile walk from Aylesford train station, which is south of the Medway. From the bridge, it's another half-mile walk downstream along the north side of the river to **The Friars** (ME20 7BX ✐ 01622 717272 ⊘ thefriars.org.uk ⊙ chapels 09.00–17.00 daily; tea room 10.00–16.00 daily; restaurant 11.00–14.30 daily), a Carmelite priory and spiritual retreat set in 40 acres of grounds and woodlands. Carmelite links to Aylesford date to 1242 when Baron de Gray donated land here to the Christian hermits who had arrived in England from Mt Carmel in the Holy Land. Adjusting to life in Britain, the hermits became friars who lived a medicant (begging) lifestyle, helping the poorest and most needy in the community. Disbanded during the Dissolution of the Monasteries in 1538, the priory then became a private home known as The Friars. When the property came up for sale in 1949, the Carmelites jumped at the chance to buy back their English 'motherhouse'.

Today, this tranquil complex offers a spiritual retreat, a tea room in the 16th-century West Barn and a restaurant in the 13th-century Pilgrim's Hall, the oldest part of the friary. The open-air Shrine was designed by Adrian Gilbert Scott and completed in 1965. Here and in the side chapels and other parts of the priory you'll find striking artworks by the Polish ceramicist Adam Kossowski and the sculptor Phillip Lindsey Clark and his son Michael. Elsewhere there's a duck pond, a Peace Garden with lush flower borders, and **Aylesford Pottery** (✐ 01622 790796 ⊘ aylesfordpottery.co.uk ⊙ 10.00–17.00 daily) where you can buy ceramics made on-site and learn how to throw pots at the associated **Aylesford School of Ceramics** (⊘ school.aylesfordpottery.co.uk).

¶¶ FOOD & DRINK

There's both a restaurant (bookings required) and a self-serve café at The Friars.

The Chequers 63 High St ✐ 01622 717286 ⊘ thechequersaylesford.co.uk ⊙ 09.00–23.00 Mon–Thu, 09.00–23.30 Fri & Sat, 09.00–22.00 Sun. The village's oldest pub occupies a wool merchant's house dating from 1511 and offers a prime view of the medieval stone bridge from its rear beer garden.

The Hengist 7–9 High St ✆ 01622 885800 ⌖ hengistrestaurant.co.uk ⏲ 11.00–22.00 Wed & Thu, 11.00–23.30 Fri & Sat, 11.00–20.00 Sun. This riverside gastropub also occupies a 16th-century building by the river. It offers casual drinks and dining downstairs and a more formal restaurant upstairs with the fanciest menu offerings in Aylesford.

29 LEEDS CASTLE

Broomfield, near Leeds ✆ 01622 765400 ⌖ leeds-castle.com ⏲ grounds Apr–Sept 10.00–18.00 daily; Oct–Mar 10.00–17.00 daily; castle Apr–Sept 10.30–17.00 daily; Oct–Mar 10.30–15.00 daily

Like a fairy-tale illustration, Leeds Castle floats magically in a glassy lake formed by the damming of the Len River, 5½-miles east of Maidstone. The property has a history of over 900 years, during which time it has been the home of eight queens and, in the 20th century, a big-spending Anglo-American heiress. Surrounded by 500 acres of grounds that include, among other things, formal gardens, a golf course and a bird of prey centre, it offers a full day out – just as well, since the admission price is one of the steepest in Kent (that said, the ticket does cover unlimited revisits for a year).

If all you would like to do is admire the beautiful view of the castle and stretch your legs, then make use of the public footpaths that cut across the estate. The castle is also a good walk from Hollingbourne train station on the Maidstone to Ashford line, about two miles to the north. Consider bringing your own picnic as the food offerings at the castle are uninspiring, and often mobbed by visitors.

Named after the village of Leeds to the west, the castle has gone though as many makeovers as Madonna, starting as a wooden Saxon fort and ending as the luxurious domain of Olive, Lady Baillie, a fabulously wealthy society hostess whose mother was the American heiress Pauline Payne Witney. Its fascinating history is laid out in a good exhibition in the gatehouse before you enter the main set of buildings – a neo-Tudor castle completed in 1823 and the oft-rebuilt Gloriette, a keep on a second smaller island in the lake.

Lady Baillie bought the castle in 1925 and made it one of her three main residences for the next half century. Most of the rooms have been left exactly as they were during her lifetime and reflect her extravagant tastes. Her bedroom, in delicate shades of blue and cream, is one of the more restrained and successful designs. Elsewhere, you can access the castle's medieval period in the Queen's Room, furnished something as it would have been during the residency of Catherine de Valois, Henry V's widow, and the Tudor era in the Banqueting Hall, which is hung with narrative paintings relating to Henry VIII and Catherine of Aragon's trip to France in 1520 to meet with Francois I at the Field of Cloth of Gold.

The castle grounds may now lack the llamas and zebras that grazed here during Lady Baillie's tenure, but there's still plenty of interest. Lady Baillie's terraced Mediterranean garden facing the Great Water lake is the pick of the formally planted areas. Walk beyond here to find more modern additions to the estate, including a fiendish maze and subterranean grotto, and a fun kids' playground in the shape of a giant wooden castle. Free falconry displays, which are worth attending, are held daily from April to September and on weekends from October to March; there are also several other bird of prey experiences you can book ahead for. And don't miss the quirky, two-room Dog Collar Museum, displaying a collection of 138 pooch collars from the 15th to the 20th centuries.

30 ASHFORD & SURROUNDS

🏠 **Eastwell Manor** (page 311)

The old cattle market town of Ashford, dating back to Saxon times, has been a major transportation hub since the mid 19th century when its extensive Newtown locomotive works were built. From 2022, those historic buildings, which have been mostly empty since the works shut in the 1960s, are to be transformed into film studios, the most exciting development for Ashford since it became an international rail terminal as part of the Eurotunnel project in 1996.

There's nothing massively pressing to detain you in Ashford itself. The historic core of town, a short walk north of the train station, is around **St Mary's the Virgin Church** (Tufton St ⊘ stmaryschurchashford. wordpress.com). The church, which dates to at least the 13th century and has a handsome 120ft tower, doubles as **Revelation St Mary's** (⊘ revelationashford.co.uk), an atmospheric live music and performance venue. There's also a quirky museum in the churchyard.

On the southern side of the station, **Curious Brewery** (Victoria Rd ✆ 01233 528300 ⊘ curiousbrewery.com), opened its state-of-the-art brewery in 2019. Tours of the brewery's striking, contemporary-designed facility are available and there a big restaurant and taproom for tasting their award-winning beverages, including lager, cider and porter.

By far the area's best attraction is **Godinton House & Gardens** (Godinton Ln, TN23 3BP ☏ 01233 643854 ⌖ godintonhouse.co.uk ☉ house Apr–Oct 13.30–15.45 Fri & Sat; gardens Mar–Oct 13.00–18.00 Tue–Sun & bank hols), three miles northwest of Ashford and near the pretty village of Great Chart, Set amid a 900-acre working estate, the gardens of 14th-century Godinton House are a visual treat. You need to pre-book tickets to visit them or to take one of the guided tours of the house which has been preserved much as it was after the death of its last owner, Alan Wyndham Green, in 1995. Home to the Toke family for centuries, the house includes a medieval great hall with a hammerbeam roof, a carved Jacobean staircase and a 17th-century Great Chamber with ornate Georgian panelling and a frieze of soldiers drilling.

Godinton's glory is its gardens, a primarily Arts and Crafts layout designed by Sir Reginald Blomfield in 1895. Among the many features are topiary, an ornamental lily pond, a vast walled flower and produce garden with its original greenhouses, a rose garden and an Italianate garden with classical statuary. The wild garden is a mass of yellow daffodils in early spring and there are public footpaths through the surrounding parklands where you'll find ancient oaks and chestnut trees.

Approaching the village of Boughton Lees, 4½ miles north of Ashford, you won't fail to notice Eastwell Towers, made from knapped, squared and coursed flint and topped with four corner turrets. Built in 1848, this is the distinctive gatehouse to the Eastwell Park estate, within which is a huge lake dug out in the 19th century. On the lake's northern shore is the ruined 14th-century church of **St Mary's** (TN25 4JT ⌖ friendsoffriendlesschurches.org.uk). Legend has it that Richard Plantagenet, Richard III's illegitimate son, was buried in the churchyard here in 1550 – the spot is marked by a Victorian-era tomb.

The manor house that Plantagenet, a mason, may have had a hand in building is long gone, replaced by a handsome creeper-clad mock Tudor pile erected in the late 18th century and much altered since. Its most famous occupant was Queen Victoria's second son, Prince Alfred, who lived here for a period towards the end of the 19th century. Today it's the location of the luxurious **Eastwell Manor** (Eastwell Court, Boughton Lees TN25 4HR ☏ 0343 2241700 ⌖ champneys.com), a hotel and spa

Wye North Downs trail

✳ OS Explorer map 137; start: Wye train station, Bridge St, TN25 5EB ♀ TR048469;
5 miles; easy

This easy-to-follow circular walk from Wye up to the North Downs provides superb panoramic views of the surrounding countryside from the top of the Devil's Kneading Trough. This is Kent's largest dry valley, or 'coombe'. Of course, it wasn't Beelzebub but the steady attrition of geological forces that carved out the valley towards the end of the last ice age, between 9,000 and 8,000BC. In his cult science-fiction novel, *Riddley Walker*, set in a post-apocalyptic Kent, Russell Hoban renamed the valley 'Mr Clevvers Roaling Place' – on a sunny summer's day, you might well feel inclined to tumble down its steep grassy banks.

1 Exit Wye train station on to Bridge Street, turn left and cross the bridge (built in 1638) over the Great Stour River, passing The Tickled Trout riverside pub (page 302) on your left. Continue along Bridge Street until it becomes Upper Bridge Street, then turn right into Cherry Garden Lane and keep going, crossing over paved Jarman's Field and continuing along the footpath.

2 The footpath soon connects to a road, to the left of which you'll notice Withersdane Hall. Once part of the Wye Agricultural College, these buildings are now a rehabilitation and treatment centre for those suffering alcohol and drug dependency. Continue straight along the road and keep in the same direction as it becomes a footpath again across the flat agricultural fields ahead.

3 The footpath connects with a stile at Amage Road; turn right here and continue in the direction of Pickersdane Cottage, ahead on the right. Cross the road and take the signed footpath on the left and pass through a gate into the Wye Nature Reserve. Follow the path and pass through two more gates to reach the steep-sided dry valley that is the Devil's Kneading Trough. Note the ridges along the slopes – known as terracettes, they are thought to have been formed by centuries of sheep grazing and walking along the hillsides. Follow the path through the valley and up to top of the Downs.

4 Work your way around the natural amphitheatre to the right and take in the awe-inspiring vistas over the countryside from the Millstone panoramic viewpoint. From here, double back in the direction of the car park on Coldharbour Lane.

5 Running parallel to the road from the car park is the North Downs Way trail. With the car park to your right, head left along this footpath, through a more wooded area. The path joins Coldharbour Lane and restarts as a footpath along the edge of fields on the opposite side of the road. The footpath then runs along the high ground with the valley falling to your left.

6 After about half a mile, pause at the commemorative stone above the Wye Crown, a giant image of a crown carved in the chalk in 1902 to commemorate Edward VII's coronation.

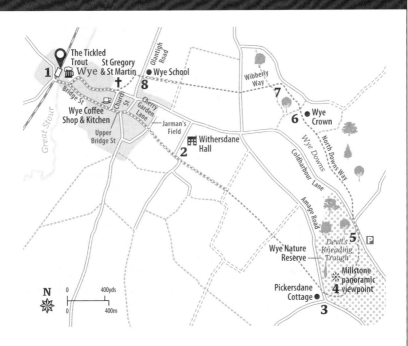

Above the crown, note several deep pits and hollows, evidence of Iron Age excavations for the ore buried in these hills. Continue along the North Downs Way, crossing a stile and entering another wooden area.

7 When you reach Wibberly Way, turn left to follow this chalky bridleway downhill back towards Wye. The chalk path joins a tarmac road and passes various light industry units on the left, leading to a junction with Olantigh Road.

8 Cross Olantigh Road and walk along the footpath that skirts around the back of Wye School, passing the village allotments on the right and eventually emerging in the graveyard around St Gregory and St Martin Church. On the left are the medieval buildings of Wye College. From the churchyard gate continue immediate ahead to Church Street, lined with a mix of handsome heritage buildings, some dating back to the 15th century. There's tea and cake at the Wye Coffee Shop & Kitchen (page 303) at the end of this road. Alternatively, turn right out of the churchyard and follow Churchfield Way around until it joins up with Bridge Road back at The Tickled Trout, for a pint by the river. From the pub it's a very short walk back to the start at Wye train station.

which offers lovely surrounding gardens and grounds including a croquet lawn, golf course and heated outdoor swimming pool. It's a romantic spot for a brasserie meal, posh afternoon tea or a relaxing spa break.

31 WYE

Four-and-a-half miles northeast of Ashford, this historic and picturesque village sits within the protected North Downs area. The Romans built on land near the village, which has been continually inhabited for at least a millennium. Next to the Wye's central 13th-century church, **St Gregory and St Martin** (38 Church St, TN25 5BL ⌂ wyebenefice.org.uk/wye), stands **Wye College**, a fine set of medieval buildings founded in 1447 by John Kempe, Archbishop of Canterbury, as a grammar school and training facility for priests. In 1890 the site became the South Eastern Agricultural College, part of the University of London's Imperial College, which operated here up until 2009 and had a worldwide reputation for excellence in its fields of study.

It was college staff and students that came up with the idea of celebrating King Edward VII's coronation in 1902 by carving the **Wye Crown** into the chalk hillside overlooking the village. The Crown is a beloved Wye landmark and is illuminated for royal and other special national occasions.

Having remained empty for over a decade, plans were approved in 2021 to convert Wye College into homes. Learn more about the history of the college and the village at the **Wye Heritage Centre** (High St ⌂ wyeheritage.org.uk) which is usually open from 10.00 to noon on the first and third Saturdays of the month, to coincide with the twice-monthly **Wye Farmers Market** (Village Green ⌂ wyefarmersmarket. co.uk), one of Kent's oldest such markets. The Heritage Centre is based in the college's old Latin School but will move to new premises within the complex following its residential conversion, due to happen in the next few years.

🍴 FOOD & DRINK

The Tickled Trout 2 Bridge St ✆ 01233 812227 ⌂ thetickledtrout.co.uk ⊘ 10.00–22.00 Mon–Sat, 10.00–21.00 Sun. There's been an inn on this prime riverside spot for over 400 years. They serve cask beers and ciders from local breweries including Canterbury Ales, Old Dairy Brewery and Kentish Pip Cider. Their wide-ranging menu offers up everything from pizza and toasted ciabatta sandwiches to Sunday roasts.

Wye Coffee Shop & Kitchen 1 Church St ✆ 01233 812452 ⬦ wyecoffee.co.uk
🕓 08.00–15.00 Mon, 08.00–16.00 Tue–Fri, 09.00–16.00 Sat, 09.00–15.00 Sun. Occupying part of an oak-framed hall house from 1450, this café is perfect for a hot drink and a slice of homemade cake, or a full afternoon tea after a walk on the North Downs. Their menu also has gluten-free, vegetarian, and vegan options and they are dog-friendly.

OLD DAIRY BREWERY

Craft beers from our award-winning brewery in Tenterden in 'The Garden of England'.

Moments from Tenterden High Street and open seven days a week, our Brewery, Shop and Taproom are housed in two WW2 Nissen huts; offering our range of traditional beers that have regular success in local and national competitions, and a long list of seasonal and occasional brews with the odd speciality beer thrown in for good measure.

With brewery tours and tastings available to book, a beer garden with glorious countryside views, food trucks at weekends and music on some Sundays, we are a great place to walk or cycle to and from.

Tenterden Station Estate
Station Road, Tenterden
Kent, TN30 6HE

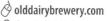

olddairybrewery.com
fineale@olddairybrewery.com
01580 763867

ACCOMMODATION

I have chosen the following places to stay for their unique character, location, hospitality and for generally standing out from the crowd. For longer reviews and more information, go to ⌔ bradtguides.com/kentsleeps.

Hotels and B&Bs are indicated by ♠ under the heading for the nearest town or village in which they are located. Self-catering is indicated by ⌂ and campsites, which cover everything from full-on glamping to no-frills pitches, are indicated with a ▲.

Good local accommodation booking sites offering superior self-catering rental properties across Kent include Bloom Stays (⌔ bloomstays.com), The Beach Studios (⌔ beachstudios.co.uk), Keepers Cottages (⌔ keeperscottages.co.uk) and Original Cottages (⌔ originalcottages.co.uk). Also check out the handful of historic properties managed in Kent by the Landmark Trust (⌔ landmarktrust. org.uk).

1 CANTERBURY & SURROUNDS

Hotels
Canterbury Cathedral Lodge The Precincts, Canterbury CT1 2EH ⌕ 01227 865350 ⌔ canterburycathedrallodge.org. Modern rooms at a prime location next to the cathedral.
The Falstaff 8–12 St Dunstans St, Canterbury CT2 8AF ⌕ 01227 462138 ⌔ thefalstaffincanterbury.com. A 15th-century coaching inn with boutique hotel rooms, just outside the city walls.
Hotel Continental 29 Beach Walk, Whitstable CT5 2BP ⌕ 01227 280280 ⌔ hotelcontinental. co.uk. Whitewashed rooms, some with sea

views. Also lets out 12 historic beachfront fisherman's huts.
House of Agnes 71 St Dunstans St, Canterbury CT2 8BN ⌕ 01227 472185 ⌔ houseofagnes. co.uk. Individually themed rooms with decorative features evoking global destinations such as a Marrakesh, Paris and Tokyo, some overlooking a tranquil walled garden, close to Canterbury West station.
The Pig – at Bridge Place Bourne Park Rd, Bridge CT4 5BH ⌕ 0345 2259494 ⌔ thepighotel.com/at-bridge-place. Pick between stylish rooms in the main 17th-century house, the coach house, the lodge or hop pickers' huts.

B&Bs

7 Longport 7 Longport, Canterbury CT1 1PE
℘ 01227 455367 🕭 7longport.co.uk. This
charming B&B occupies a cosy 15th-century
cottage hidden behind an 18th-century
townhouse. Also manages two neighbouring
self-catering properties on nearby Love Lane
that sleep up to five people each.

Beechborough Park Ln, Bishopsbourne CT4
5HY ℘ 01227 832283 🕭 beechborough.com.
Offers two boutique hotel-worthy bedrooms,
one of which is en-suite, both with king-sized
beds dressed in Egyptian cotton sheets. Enjoy
breakfast that includes house smoked bacon and
other local produce.

The Corner House Canterbury 1 Dover
St, Canterbury CT1 3HD ℘ 01227 780793
🕭 cornerhouserestaurants.co.uk. Rooms above
a restored medieval pub with an excellent
restaurant.

The Duke William The Street, Ickham CT3 1QP
℘ 01227 721308 🕭 thedukewilliamickham.
com. Four chic, contemporary rooms, each
named after celebrity British chefs. Six miles east
of Canterbury.

The Front Rooms 9 Tower Pde, Whitstable CT5
2BJ ℘ 01227 282132 🕭 thefrontrooms.co.uk.
Three light rooms decorated in shades of white
in a restored Victorian townhouse, a block from
the beach.

Camping & glamping

Glamping at Preston Court Court
Ln, Preston CT3 1DJ ℘ 07917 131058
🕭 glampingprestoncourt.co.uk. Comfortably
furnished bell tents in a meadow or a woodland
site from May to September. Ten miles east of
Canterbury.

Nethergong Camping Nethergong
Hill, Upstreet CT3 4DN ℘ 07901 368417
🕭 nethergongcamping.co.uk. Options include
Romany wagons, shepherds' huts and spacious
bell tents. From April to September. Six and a
half miles northeast of Canterbury.

2 NORTH KENT: GRAVESEND TO FAVERSHAM

Hotels

Cave Hotel & Golf Resort Brickfield Ln,
Boughton ME13 9AJ ℘ 01227 203417
🕭 cavehotels.com. Sleek, contemporary-styled
rooms and a good choice of restaurants at this
classy golf resort, 3½ miles east of Faversham.

B&Bs

Ferry House Inn Harty Ferry Rd,
Leysdown ME12 4BQ ℘ 01795 510214
🕭 theferryhouseinn.co.uk. A 16th-century
restaurant with rooms overlooking the Swale
Estuary in the peaceful hamlet of Harty on the
Isle of Sheppey. There are six more modern
rooms in the newly built coach house.

North Downs Barn Bush Rd, Cuxton ME2 1HF
℘ 01634 296829 🕭 northdownsbarn.co.uk.
Four miles west of Rochester, and within walking
distance of the Ranscombe Farm Nature Reserve,
this rustic B&B offers three spacious double
en-suite rooms.

Read's Restaurant with Rooms Macknade
Manor, Canterbury Rd, Faversham ME13 8XE
℘ 01795 535344 🕭 reads.com. Elegant,
traditional and spacious rooms in a Georgian
manor house surrounded by a leafy garden.

Shepherd House 56 Preston St, Faversham
ME13 8PG ℘ 01795 538835 🕭 shepherd-house-
bed-breakfast.hotelskent.com. Three bedrooms,
with freestanding baths and king-sized beds, in
a brightly painted former Georgian rectory with
many original features.

Ship & Trades Chatham Maritime,
Chatham ME4 3ER ℘ 01634 895200
🕭 shipandtradeschatham.co.uk. Go for the
Feature Doubles at this nautical-themed
gastropub with rooms – they have balconies
overlooking Chatham's marina.

Sun Inn 10 West St, Faversham ME13 7JE
℘ 01795 535098 🕭 sunfaversham.co.uk. Gaze
up at centuries-old wooden beams from your
bed above this cosy and centrally located pub.

Self-catering

Mocketts Farm Cottages Harty Ferry Rd, Isle of Sheppey, Sheerness ME12 4BG ⏚ mockettsfarm. co.uk. Run by the same management team as the nearby Ferry Inn, the 'cottages' are the former farm buildings, ranging from the cosy two-bed Harrier's Nest, which sleeps up to four people, to the renovated brick farmhouse with eight bedrooms and room for a party of 17 plus.
Sandy Toes Beach House Shellness Rd, Leysdown, Isle of Sheppey ME12 4BS ⏚ canopyandstars.co.uk. Take in the panoramic sea views from the deck of this rustic beach house that runs on solar energy.

Camping & glamping

Barton's Point Coastal Park Marine Pde, Sheerness ME12 2BE ⏚ 07909 994196 ⏚ bartonspointcoastalpark.co.uk. Pitches for tents, touring caravans and motorhomes at this tranquil lakeside park a short walk from Sheerness and Minster beaches.
Elmley Nature Reserve Elmley, Isle of Sheppey ME12 3RW ⏚ 01795 664 896 ⏚ elmleynaturereserve.co.uk. The only nature reserve in England that it's possible to overnight in. Choose between luxe glamping tents, self-contained shepherds' huts and cabins, or glamorously decorated rooms in the main farmhouse.
Eternal Lake Nature Reserve Buckland Lake Reserve, Salt Ln, Cliffe ME3 7RT ⏚ 01634 963718 ⏚ eternallake.org. Camp beside the reserve's spring-fed chalk lake or bed down in either a glamping cabin or a 'pod' with an en-suite shower and mini-kitchen.

3 THANET, SANDWICH & DEAL

Hotels

Albion House Albion Pl, Ramsgate CT11 8HQ ⏚ 01843 606630 ⏚ albionhouseramsgate. co.uk. Most of the comfortable rooms at this hotel, built in 1792, have sea views. Princess

Victoria stayed here shortly before she was crowned queen.
Albion Rooms 31 Eastern Esplanade, Cliftonville, Margate CT9 2HL ⏚ 01843 264041 ⏚ thealbionrooms.live. Inspiration for the glam rock rooms at this hotel owned by The Libertines came from the red, black and gold of the band members' jackets.
The Bay Tree Broadstairs 12 Eastern Esplanade, Broadstairs CT10 1DR ⏚ 01843 862502 ⏚ baytreebroadstairs.co.uk. Pleasantly decorated rooms, all named after British trees, in a sea-facing Victorian property. The library bar has Harry Potter-themed decorative touches.
Bell Hotel The Quay, Sandwich CT13 9EF ⏚ 01304 613388 ⏚ bellhotelsandwich.co.uk. Classically styled rooms decorated in neutral tones, some overlooking the Stour River.
The Falstaff 16–18 Addington St, Ramsgate CT11 9JJ ⏚ 01843 482600 ⏚ thefalstafframsgate.com. Along a street lined with eclectic shops, this gastropub offers boutique-style rooms and two self-catering apartments. The flower-filled back garden is a plus.
No 42 16 Marine Dr, Margate CT9 1DH ⏚ 01843 261200 ⏚ guesthousehotels.co.uk/no-42-margate. The biggest and best rooms at this stylish boutique hotel and restaurant offer views over Margate sands.
The Rose 91 High St, Deal CT14 6ED ⏚ 01304 389127 ⏚ therosedeal.com. Vivid colours, retro furniture and wonderfully comfortable beds make spending a night above this gastropub a delight.
Royal Harbour Hotel 10 Nelson Cr, Ramsgate CT11 9JF ⏚ 01843 591514 ⏚ royalharbourhotel. co.uk. Offering a good range of rooms, some with prime views over the harbour marina. The club-like Empire Room restaurant is excellent.
Royal Hotel Beach St, Deal CT14 6JD ⏚ 01303 375555 ⏚ theroyalhotel.com. Creaking and sloping floors add to the Georgian charm of this sea-facing hotel with contemporary décor in its rooms.

Walpole Bay Hotel Fifth Ave, Margate CT9 2JJ
✆ 01843 221703 ⌖ walpolebayhotel.co.uk. This
charming Edwardian seaside hotel is also part
museum and napkin art gallery.

B&Bs

Bear's Well 10 St George's Rd, Deal, CT14
6BA ✆ 01304 694 144 ⌖ bearswell.co.uk. A
beautiful double-fronted Georgian home with a
lush garden houses this superior family-run B&B.
Belvidere Place 43 Belvedere Rd, Broadstairs
CT10 1PF ✆ 01843 579850 ⌖ belvidereplace.
co.uk. Sophistically decorated rooms with
unique furniture, Egyptian cotton bed linen and
upmarket toiletries.
Copperfields Vegetarian Guest House 11
Queens Rd, Broadstairs CT10 1NU ✆ 01843
601247 ⌖ copperfieldsbb.co.uk/en-GB.
Edwardian house with three guest rooms. They
prioritise use of local and ethically sourced
products, and the breakfast is vegetarian.
Molland Manor House Molland Ln, Ash CT3
2JB ✆ 01304 814210 ⌖ mollandhouse.co.uk.
Offers large, classically furnished en-suite rooms
in a 13th-century manor house, 3½ miles west
of Sandwich.
Number 37 37 The Street, Ash CT3 2HH
✆ 07804 583513 ⌖ 37ash.co.uk. Cosy,
characterful rooms above a café in an old
Georgian building in a historic village, 3½ miles
west of Sandwich.
The Reading Rooms 31 Hawley Sq,
Margate CT9 1PH ✆ 01843 225166
⌖ thereadingroomsmargate.co.uk. The careful
restoration of this Georgian property with two
luxurious guestrooms has revived some original
architectural features and colours but also kept
the patina of time.
Twentieth Century B&B 102 Minnis Road,
Birchington-On-Sea CT7 9NX ✆ 01843 848632
⌖ twentiethcenturybandb.com. Gorgeously
restored Art Deco villa minutes from Minnis Bay
beach with four themed rooms, named after
people with Thanet connections.

Self-catering

Garden Cottage & Greenhouse Apartment
Walmer Castle, Walmer CT14 7LJ ✆ 0370
3331187 ⌖ english-heritage.org.uk. Stay within
the lovely grounds of Walmer Castle – both
properties sleep up to four people and are
pleasantly furnished in neutral tones.
**North Foreland Lighthouse Holiday
Cottages** 36 N Foreland Rd, Broadstairs CT10
3NN ✆ 01386 701177 ⌖ ruralretreats.co.uk.
Bookings for these two Trinity House-owned
lighthouse holiday cottages, sleeping up to
four people, are handled by Rural Retreats, who
also represent a handful of other self-catering
properties around Kent.

4 SOUTHEAST COASTAL KENT: DOVER TO DUNGENESS

Hotels

Hythe Imperial Hotel Princes Pde, Hythe CT21
6AE ✆ 01303 267 441 ⌖ hytheimperial.co.uk.
Originally built by the South Eastern Railway and
opened in 1880, the Hythe Imperial has both
sea- and garden-facing rooms, no two the same
but all pleasantly furnished.
Port Lympne Hotel Aldington Rd,
Lympne CT21 4LR ✆ 01303 264647
⌖ aspinallfoundation.org. Accommodation
options within the wildlife park range from
simple wooden cabins and glamping tents to
luxurious lodges. There are also suite rooms
in the hotel, occupying the glamourous 20th-
century house designed for Sir Philip Sassoon by
Herbert Baker.
The View 30–32 Clifton Rd, Folkestone CT20 2EF
✆ 01303 252102 ⌖ viewhotelfolkestone.co.uk.
Beside the Leas Coastal Park, this contemporary
design hotel offers three categories of rooms,
attentive staff and – yes – Channel views.

B&Bs

The Woolpack Inn Church Ln, Warehorne TN26
2LL ✆ 01233 732900 ⌖ woolpackwarehorne.

ACCOMMODATION

co.uk. Three miles north of Snargate, this inn has been welcoming guests since 1570. Narrow, steeply winding staircases lead to five en-suite rooms handsomely furnished with ornate antique beds, roll-top baths and small complimentary decanters of port. The marine-themed suite Frederick (named after the resident friendly ghost) also has a wood-burning stove.

Churchill Guesthouse 6 Castle Hill Rd, Dover CT16 1QN ✆ 01304 204622 🖰 churchillguesthouse.co.uk. Eight classically designed rooms with nice touches such as pretty bedspreads and quality rugs. There's also a self-catering apartment on the lower ground floor.

The Old Post Office Boutique Guesthouse 5 High St, Hythe CT21 5AB ✆ 01303 230828. Occupying a handsome building at the end of High Street, built in 1910. Three rooms in pastel seaside colours with cute artefacts referencing the building's original function.

Rocksalt Rooms 4–5 Fishmarket, Folkestone CT19 6AA ✆ 01303 212070 🖰 rocksaltfolkestone.co.uk. Four stylish, minimally furnished and compact rooms, two of which offer harbour and sea views.

Self-catering

CABU by the Sea Dymchurch Rd, St Mary's Bay TN29 0HF ✆ 01303 669033 🖰 holidays.cabu. co.uk. An old seaside camp for London kids has been transformed into this luxury village of sophisticated timber cabins built around the central brick Cabu House. Also has a heated outdoor swimming pool and guest bicycles.

The Lantern Inn The Street, Martin Mill CT15 5JL ✆ 01304 852276 🖰 lanterninn.co.uk. There's a dark and decadent vibe to this good-quality two-bed, self-catering apartment over the inn, while out in the beer garden you can bed-down in a plush yurt.

Perevell's Tower & The Sergeant Major's House Dover Castle, Dover CT16 1HU ✆ 0370 3331187 🖰 english-heritage.org.uk. A chance to stay within the precincts of Dover Castle. Perevell's Tower sleeps two and offers wonderful

views, while the four-storey Sergeant Major's House sleeps six and has its own grounds.

Shingle House Dungeness Rd, Dungeness TN29 9NE ✆ 020 3488 1584 🖰 living-architecture. co.uk. Designed by Scottish architectural practice NORD, this finely crafted house at the north end of Dungeness sleeps up to eight and is dog-friendly.

Wi Wurri Off Dungeness Rd, Dungeness TN29 9ND 🖰 wiwurri-dungeness.co.uk. An old fisherman's cottage has been upgraded to make this cosy holiday let, wood-lined throughout. There's a wood-burning stove and a suntrap deck to the rear.

Camping & glamping

Greenhill Glamping South Alkham, Dover CT15 7DG ✆ 01303 892056 🖰 greenhillglamping. co.uk. A shepherd's hut and a ploughman's wagon, both over a century old and beautifully restored, have been kitted out with comfortable beds and mod cons. Overlooking the peaceful Alkham Valley, midway between Dover and Folkestone.

Little Switzerland Campsite Wear Bay Rd, Folkestone CT19 6PS ✆ 01303 252168 ▮. This site has a fantastic location overlooking the Warren nature reserve and the Channel. Room for 16 caravans and 22 tents. Open March to the end of October.

Romney Marsh Shepherds Huts Gigger's Green Rd, Aldington TN25 7BT ✆ 01233 721800 🖰 romneymarshshepherdshuts.co.uk. Three bespoke, high-spec shepherds' huts, four miles northwest of Dymchurch, on a farm where 1,000 Kentish sheep graze on clover-rich pastures.

5 KENT WEALD & DOWNS

Hotels

Chilston Park Hotel Sandway, Maidstone ME17 2BE ✆ 01622 859803 🖰 handpickedhotels. co.uk/chilstonpark. Set in 22 acres of parkland, Chilston Park has 17th-century architectural features and antiques. Rooms range from the cosy Mews Classics in the converted coach house and stables, to the Tudor suite in the eaves of the manor house.

Eastwell Manor Eastwell Park, Boughton Lees TN25 4HR ✆ 0843 5612019 ♂ eastwellmanor. co.uk. Pamper yourself with a spa day and a stay in either the grand manor house or nearby mews cottages.

Hotel du Vin Crescent Rd, Tunbridge Wells TN1 2LY ✆ 01892 320749 ♂ hotelduvin.com. Classy hotel overlooking Claverely Park. Contemporary-styled rooms of various sizes, all with good quality linens and towels.

The Mount Edgcumbe The Common, Tunbridge Wells TN4 8BX ✆ 01892 618854 ♂ themountedgcumbe.com. Six boutique-style rooms with colourful bird and animal print cushions and other quirky decorative touches.

One Warwick Park 1 Warwick Pk, Tunbridge Wells TN2 5TA ✆ 01892 520587 ♂ onewarwickpark.co.uk. On the doorstep of The Pantiles, this appealing hotel with contemporary rooms occupies an old brewery and neighbouring schoolhouse.

Spa Hotel Langton Rd, Tunbridge Wells TN4 8XJ ✆ 01892 520331 ♂ spahotel.co.uk. Offers some of Tunbridge's most luxurious and elegantly decorated rooms. Tapping into the town's heritage, it also has a full spa with pool, steam room, saunas and gym.

B&Bs

Bramley House Rogers Rough Rd, Kilndown TN17 2RJ ✆ 01892 890855 ♂ bramley.house. Friendly couple Linda and Ray Carter offer two great en-suite rooms in their charming home that captures the rustic chic look of a glossy interior design magazine. It's an ideal stop over for those making a pilgrimage to the nearby gastro pub The Small Holding (page 284), or visiting other sights in this border region of Kent and East Sussex.

The Friars Aylesford ME20 7BX ✆ 01622 717272 ♂ thefriars.org.uk. Superb value rooms

at this Carmelite priory set within acres of tranquil grounds beside the Medway.

Hever Castle B&B and Medley Court Hever, Edenbridge TN8 7NG ✆ 01732 861800 ♂ hevercastle.co.uk. The B&B is in the Astor and Anne Boleyn wings of the castle, built in Edwardian times. Medley Court is a four-bedroom self-catering cottage with Tudor-inspired wood-panelled walls.

Leeds Castle Broomfield, ME17 1PL ✆ 01622 765400 ♂ leeds-castle.com. B&B accommodation is either in the Stables or Maiden's Tower. Also available are seven holiday cottages and Knight's Glamping – eight striped pavilion tents with four-poster beds and wood-burning stoves.

The Milk House The Street, Sissinghurst TN17 2JG ✆ 01580 720200 ♂ themilkhouse.co.uk. Four rooms decorated in appropriately creamy colours above a good pub and restaurant. The largest room, Byre, has a rolltop bathtub and overlooks the orchards to the rear.

Sissinghurst Castle Farmhouse Biddenden Rd, Sissinghurst TN17 2AB ✆ 01580 720992 ♂ sissinghurstcastlefarmhouse.co.uk. Luxurious nine-room B&B in a handsome Victorian farmhouse with lovely gardens, beside the entrance to Sissinghurst Castle.

The Vineyard The Down, Lamberhurst TN3 8EU ✆ 01892 890222 ♂ elitepubs.com/ the-vineyard. Spiral staircases lead up to the bedrooms in each of the four suites in the converted coach house of this stylish pub and restaurant.

The West House 8 High St, Biddenden TN27 8AH ✆ 01580 291341 ♂ thewesthouserestaurant.co.uk. Scandi, Art Deco, Serenity and Rock 'n' Roll are the themes of the plush rooms at this destination restaurant. Rock 'n' Roll has a black four-poster bed and hot tub in its private courtyard garden.

Self-catering

Bore Place Bore Place Rd, Chiddingstone TN8 7AR ✆ 07796 305324 ♂ boreplace.

org. There are five properties to rent on this 550-acre organic farm, from the 12-bedroom Bore Place House to the two-bedroom Small Barn. They also run **Free Range Glamping** (⊘ freerangeglamping.co.uk) with two yurts and two shepherds' huts.

Camping & glamping

Feather Down Sunninglye Farm Dundale Rd, Tunbridge Wells TN3 9AG ⊘ 01420 80804 ⊘ featherdown.co.uk. Each of the glamping tents on this farm, 3½ miles southeast of Tunbridge Wells, sleeps six and have wood-burning stoves . They're well designed and located in a woodland area near the Teise River.

INDEX

INDEX OF ADVERTISERS

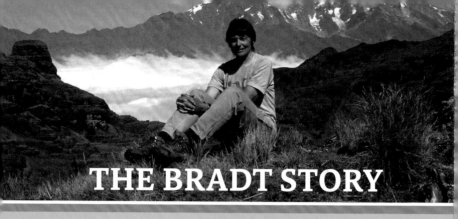

THE BRADT STORY

In the beginning
It all began in 1974 on an Amazon river barge. During an 18-month trip through South America, two adventurous young backpackers – Hilary Bradt and her then husband, George – decided to write about the hiking trails they had discovered through the Andes. *Backpacking Along Ancient Ways in Peru and Bolivia* included the very first descriptions of the Inca Trail. It was the start of a colourful journey to becoming one of the best-loved travel publishers in the world; you can read the full story on our website (www.bradtguides.com/ourstory).

Getting there first
Hilary quickly gained a reputation for being a true travel pioneer, and in the 1980s she started to focus on guides to places overlooked by other publishers. The Bradt Guides list became a roll call of guidebook 'firsts'. We published the first guide to Madagascar, followed by Mauritius, Czechoslovakia and Vietnam. The 1990s saw the beginning of our extensive coverage of Africa: Tanzania, Uganda, South Africa, and Eritrea. Later, post-conflict guides became a feature: Rwanda, Mozambique, Angola, Sierra Leone, Bosnia and Kosovo.

Comprehensive – and with a conscience
Today, we are the world's largest independently owned travel publisher, with more than 200 titles, from full-country and wildlife guides to Slow Travel guides like this one. However, our ethos remains unchanged. Hilary is still keenly involved, and we still get there first: two-thirds of Bradt guides have no direct competition.

But we don't just get there first. Our guides are also known for being more comprehensive than any other series. We avoid templates and tick-lists. Each guide is a one-of-a-kind expression of an expert author's interests, knowledge and enthusiasm for telling it how it really is.

And a commitment to wildlife, conservation and respect for local communities has always been at the heart of our books. Bradt Guides was championing sustainable travel before any other guidebook publisher.

Thank you!
We can only do what we do because of the support of readers like you – people who value less-obvious experiences, less-visited places and a more thoughtful approach to travel. Those who, like us, take travel seriously.

TRAVEL TAKEN SERIOUSLY